The contributors to this book believe that som...
life in American cities safer, to make growing up in the ci...
risky, and to reduce the violence that so often permeates urban childhoods.
They consider why there is so much violence, why some people become
violent and others do not, and why violence varies among areas. Biological
and psychological characteristics of individuals are considered, as well as
how the urban environment, especially the street culture, affects childhood
development. The authors review a variety of intervention strategies, considering when it would be appropriate to use them. Drawing upon ethnographic commentary, laboratory experiments, historical reviews, and program
descriptions, the authors present multiple opinions on the causes of urban
violence and the changes necessary to reduce it.

Violence and Childhood in the Inner City

Cambridge Criminology Series

Editors
Alfred Blumstein, *Carnegie Mellon University*
David Farrington, *University of Cambridge*

This series publishes high-quality research monographs of either theoretical or empirical emphasis in all areas of criminology, including measurement of offending, explanations of offending, police courts, incapacitation, corrections, sentencing, deterrence, rehabilitation, and other related topics. It is intended to be both interdisciplinary and international in scope.

Other titles in the series:

Violence and Childhood in the Inner City

Edited by

Joan McCord
Temple University

CAMBRIDGE
UNIVERSITY PRESS

PUBLISHED BY THE PRESS SYNDICATE OF THE UNIVERSITY OF CAMBRIDGE
The Pitt Building, Trumpington Street, Cambridge CB2 1RP, United Kingdom

CAMBRIDGE UNIVERSITY PRESS
The Edinburgh Building, Cambridge CB2 2RU, United Kingdom
40 West 20th Street, New York, NY 10011–4211, USA
10 Stamford Road, Oakleigh, Melbourne 3166, Australia

First published 1997

Printed in the United States of America

Typeset in ITC Baskerville

Library of Congress Cataloging-in-Publication Data
Violence and childhood in the inner city/edited by Joan McCord.
p.   cm. – (Cambridge criminology series)
ISBN 0-521-58326-8. – ISBN 0-521-58720-4 (pbk.)
1. Violence – United States.   2. Inner cities – United States.   3. Children and
violence –United States.   4. Violence in children – United States.   5. City children –
United States.   6. Urban youth – United States.   I. McCord, Joan.   II. Series.
HN90.V5V532   1997
303.6'0973 – dc21   96-40019
                                                                                                              CIP

*A catalog record for this book is available from
the British Library.*

ISBN 0-521-58326-8 hardback
ISBN 0-521-58720-4 paperback

Contents

Contributors

Elijah Anderson is the Charles and William L. Day Professor of the Social Sciences and Professor of Sociology at the University of Pennsylvania. He is the author of the highly regarded sociological work, *A Place on the Corner: A Study of Black Street Corner Men* (1978), and for his recently published ethnographic study, *Streetwise: Race, Class and Change in an Urban Community* (1990), he was honored with the Robert E. Park Award of the American Sociological Association. His newest book, *The Code of the Streets*, will be published by W. W. Norton. Professor Anderson was a member of the National Research Council's Panel on the Understanding and Control of Violent Behavior, which published its report in 1993.

Jacqueline Barnes has a Ph.D. in Developmental Psychology from the University of London, where she studied the influences of gender on parent-child interactions in the preschool years. She has since worked in London and at Harvard University. Her research interests include: identification and management of behavior problems of preschool children in group settings; methods for assessing parental behavior; the influence of coercive family interactions; and evaluation of child mental health and child abuse prevention programs.

Felton Earls is Professor of Human Behavior and Development at the Harvard School of Public Health and Professor of Child Psychiatry at the Harvard Medical School. He has conducted psychiatric epidemiological research on children and adolescents in many societies around the world, and is currently principal investigator of a landmark study, The Project on Human Development in Chicago Neighborhoods. This project is studying the multiple influences of neighborhood, school, and family contexts on the development of antisocial behavior in children and adolescents.

Nancy G. Guerra is Associate Professor of Psychology at the University of Illinois at Chicago. She has published widely in psychology journals on violence prevention and child development. She is a member of the President's Coordinating Council of Juvenile Justice, and is the principal investigator on a large-scale prevention research grant funded by the National Institute of Mental Health.

Joan McCord is Professor of Criminal Justice at Temple University. Past President of the American Society of Criminology, she has received the Prix Emile Durkheim from the International Society of Criminology (1993) and the Edwin H. Sutherland Award from the American Society of Criminology (1994) for her contributions to research. She has authored numerous articles on the causes of crime, intervention programs, and theory to professional books and journals.

Terrie E. Moffitt is Professor of Psychology at the University of Wisconsin-Madison, Professor of Social Behavior and Development at the Social, Genetic and Developmental Psychiatry Research Centre of the Institute of Psychiatry in London, England, and Associate Director of the Dunedin Multidisciplinary Health and Development Research Unit in New Zealand. She studies the natural history of antisocial behavior across the life course from early childhood to mid-life.

Robert J. Sampson is Professor of Sociology at the University of Chicago and Research Fellow at the American Bar Foundation. His most recent book, written with John Laub, *Crime in the Making: Pathways and Turning Points Through Life* (1993), received the outstanding book award from the American Society of Criminology, the Academy of Criminal Justice Sciences, and the Crime, Law and Deviance Section of the American Sociological Association.

Ronald G. Slaby is Lecturer on Education and Pediatrics at Harvard University and a Senior Scientist at Education Development Center. A developmental psychologist, Dr. Slaby has coauthored a national plan for preventing violence in America for the Centers for Disease Control and Prevention and a national report on violence and youth for the American Psychological Association. His books include: *Early Violence Prevention; Aggressors, Victims, and Bystanders; Viewpoints;* and *Social Development in Young Children.*

Preface

When Isaac Fulwood, Jr., resigned from the office of Chief of Police for the District of Columbia, he did so saying, "I want a sense that if my wife walks out into the yard, nobody's going to run into the yard and kill her. When she goes to the store, I don't want people to take her car. Fear is greater than the crime itself, because it changes everything" (quoted in the *New York Times*, Sept. 20, 1992, section 4, p. 7). Chief Fulwood was particularly troubled by the callousness represented in one young man's claim that he killed because his victim "deserved to die," and in another's because he felt like "busting somebody."

The Harry Frank Guggenheim Foundation brought together the authors of this book. We are people who believe that something can be done to make life in cities safer, to make growing up in cities less risky, and to reduce the violence that so often permeates urban childhood. Under the auspices of Karen Colvard and Joel Wallman, we met to present our ideas and defend or change them in the light of criticisms from our colleagues. As editor, I pushed to have the chapters present the strongest case possible for whatever points of view their authors chose to take. As a group, we committed ourselves to the task of trying to make a difference in the direction of reducing violence.

We present evidence suggesting why American cities have so much violence, why some people rather than others become violent, and why violence tends to occur in some places rather than in others. The authors, too, describe ways to reduce crime and violence. Chapters draw upon a variety of methods, including ethnographic commentary and laboratory experiments, historical reviews, and program descriptions. Although we do not completely agree about the causes of urban violence, we present a coherent image.

The shared image is one that sees violent crimes in urban ghettos as partly a response to policies and practices originating outside the ghettos. A reduction in violence, we believe, will occur only when public policies and practices match the rhetoric of a commitment to equal opportunities.

The first three chapters set urban violence into social and historical contexts. Elijah Anderson takes a microscope to urban ghetto cultures. Betrayed by and therefore distrustful of the judicial system and its representatives, he argues, many of those who live in inner cities create their own order, defend their own loved ones, and establish their own codes. In spelling out the code of the streets, Anderson shows how the willingness to use violence preserves an ordering in which respect supplies rewards.

Anderson explains why parents who want their children to have nothing to do with "street culture" nonetheless must instill in them one of its characteristics – the willingness to be violent. Tellingly, he suggests that respect, including self-respect, on the street requires showing nerve, and he states that nerve "is shown when someone takes a person's possessions (the more valuable, the better), messes with someone's woman, throws the first punch, gets in someone's face, or pulls a trigger." Anderson places responsibility for violence in the cities – at least in part – on those outside the cities whose policies of indifference (or contempt) have led blacks, particularly black males, to express contempt for mainstream society. Anderson urges mainstream Americans to give the disadvantaged poor a stake in the system.

In the next chapter, Robert J. Sampson picks up the theme established by Anderson. Sampson illustrates the ways in which a healthy social context provides a type of capital upon which children can depend. Social capital, Sampson argues, helps to establish norms that can be enforced. Sampson's "contextual perspective" solves the seeming paradox that fatherless families do not produce more criminals than their two-parent neighbors – although high crime rates are found in areas having many fatherless families. He provides a basis for understanding why violence is sometimes seen as a way of life in inner-city ghetto neighborhoods, even though a majority of residents may disapprove of the violence. Like Anderson, Sampson argues that ghetto life reflects distrust of mainstream values.

Sampson focuses on links that tie individuals to their communities through family socialization practices. He shows that healthful child development, which is related to neighborhood structure, has an important place in crime prevention.

Sampson points to many ways in which racial discrimination has had deleterious effects. He notes the "deliberate policy decisions to concentrate minorities and the poor in public housing," and he reminds readers that explanations for crime that focus on individuals' characteristics may be misspecifying the role of social contexts. In doing so, he exposes "the social basis of the race–crime connection."

In the third chapter, I show that American cities are more violent than cities in other developed nations and attempt to explain this phenomenon. The chapter considers and rejects the popular ideas that violence developed from requirements of a frontier culture and also that it has been exacerbated by immigrant populations before their acculturation.

The chapter presents evidence that social policies promoting industrial development and suburban growth have, perhaps unintentionally, contributed to violence. Federal policies that provided benefits to the advantaged served further to undermine and isolate poor black Americans in urban centers. In this chapter, I suggest that these macrolevel influences, coupled with values that assume that financial success represents individual worth, have created serious problems for our divided society. I argue that injustices "have undermined commitment to a social contract" so that "programs aimed simply at adjusting individuals to the present social system will not be sufficient."

Whereas the first three chapters focus on how the contemporary and historical milieus influence choices producing violence, the next three chapters focus on individual differences. They consider why particular individuals in urban settings are prone to violence. These chapters show how biological and psychological characteristics influence violence. They also describe deleterious neighborhood effects on children reared in poor urban environments.

Terrie E. Moffitt provides a comprehensive picture of connections between neuropsychological deficits and violence. She documents links between deficits in cognitive functioning and violence, and she suggests how urban poverty contributes both to neuropsychological deficits and to their exaggerated impact on subsequent development. Moffitt points out that poverty often leads to the absence of prenatal care, to poor nutrition, and to exposure to toxic chemical agents – conditions that increase the probability of verbal deficiencies and other neuropsychological problems that in turn increase risk for violent behavior.

Moffitt notes "that children whose hyperactivity and angry outbursts might be curbed by firm discipline will tend to have parents who are inconsistent disciplinarians; the parents are impatient and irritable too." In describing possible chains of interactions from verbal deficits to violence, Moffitt argues that those who suffer from neuropsychological difficulties may require special help in disadvantaged communities in order to reduce the probability that they will contribute to the production of violence.

Ronald G. Slaby presents an integrated view of conditions affecting children reared in contemporary inner-city communities in the United States. Victims and bystanders, as well as perpetrators of violence, are brought into his lens. Slaby also reminds readers that individuals differ in their responses to similar conditions. He identifies circumstances viewed by some as provocation, to which others respond differently. Slaby observes that bystanders contribute to violence by "instigating, encouraging, or passively accepting violence." Although they are clearly different roles, bystanders sometimes become victims and perpetrators, victims often become perpetrators, and "perpetrators of violence often feel as though they are primarily victims." These roles are learned from the media, from peer associations, and from the inner workings of family life. Parents, Slaby notes, "play a particularly influential role in the development of children's aggression." Slaby suggests that the use of physical punishment often contributes to an escalation of aggression.

Urban communities are likely to have an excessive dose of what Slaby calls "violence toxins." These include witnessing and experiencing violence, having unsupervised access to firearms, using and trafficking in alcohol or drugs, and facing racial and ethnic discrimination. Slaby urges two thrusts for violence prevention. One would reduce the toxicity of urban neighborhoods, and the other would "strengthen the child's antiviolence immune system" by teaching children to use nonviolent techniques for resolving social problems.

Felton Earls and Jacqueline Barnes grapple with the moral issue that comes into focus when family rights seem to interfere with social well-being. Child abuse presents such an issue. It typically occurs within the confines of families and yet has repercussions for the larger society, because child abuse often seems to cause violence. Earls and Barnes observe that poverty increases the risk of child abuse, that rates of abuse have been increasing since 1965, and "that black children are five times more likely to die as a consequence of abuse and neglect than are white children."

After reviewing the literature on risk factors for abuse, Earls and Barnes conclude that best guesses seem to indicate that family stress and isolation contribute to risk for abusing children, and parental alcoholism contributes to poor outcomes for child victims. The chapter provides both grounds for skepticism regarding official rates of abuse and grounds for concern over the varieties of damage that abuse and neglect seem to generate. Earls and Barnes report that the consequences of abuse or neglect include the lack of "normal" kindness, an inadequate ability to recognize the emotions of others, and labile relationships with adult caregivers. These are characteristics known to be related, in turn, to subsequent violent behavior.

Fortunately, Earls and Barnes report, a proactive prevention program for infants that used scientifically rigorous methods for evaluation produced favorable results, but they note that treatments for older children have seldom been mounted and are even less frequently well documented. The chapter concludes with a description of an attempt to change and monitor changes in a disadvantaged neighborhood at high risk for child abuse.

In the final chapter, Nancy G. Guerra considers a variety of intervention strategies, asking when these would be appropriate as well as what their targets should be. To approach these issues, Guerra reviews risk factors in children, families, peers, and schools. Before reviewing intervention programs, she reminds readers of the prevalence of stress, social disorganization, and violence in inner cities.

Guerra describes intervention strategies that include prenatal services, preschool enrichment, elementary school interventions, and programs for adolescents. She examines parent training programs and family therapy as well as a variety of strategies for working with peers, teachers, and school organizations. Some well-intentioned and carefully designed programs, she notes, have had harmful outcomes. Guerra rightly urges use of research trials to assess outcomes of prevention programs as developed in cultural contexts to see whether or not they have intended applications for preventing inner-city violence.

Every chapter points to the importance of addressing multiple problems in the inner cities. None of the contributors believes that change will come easily. We join together in suggesting that violence should be at least partly attributed to problems that can be ameliorated only by the concerted effort of citizens from many different environments.

Violence and the Inner-City Street Code*

ELIJAH ANDERSON

Of all the problems besetting the poor inner-city black community, none is more pressing than that of interpersonal violence and aggression. This phenomenon wreaks havoc daily on the lives of community residents and increasingly spills over into downtown and residential middle-class areas. Muggings, burglaries, carjackings, and drug-related shootings, all of which may leave their victims or innocent bystanders dead, are now common enough to concern all urban and many suburban residents. The inclination to violence springs from the circumstances of life among the ghetto poor – the lack of jobs that pay a living wage, the stigma of race, the fallout from rampant drug use and drug trafficking, and the resulting alienation and lack of hope for the future.

Simply living in such an environment places young people at special risk of falling victim to aggressive behavior. Although there are often forces in the community which can counteract the negative influences – by far the most powerful is a strong, loving, "decent" (as inner-city residents put it) family committed to middle-class values – the despair is pervasive enough to have spawned an oppositional culture, that of "the streets," whose norms are often consciously opposed to those of mainstream society. These two orientations – decent and street – socially organize the community, and their coexistence has important consequences for residents, particularly for children growing up in the inner city. Above all, this environment means that even youngsters whose home lives reflect mainstream values – and the majority of homes in the community do – must be able to handle themselves in a street-oriented environment.

This is because the street culture has evolved what may be called a "code of the streets," which amounts to a set of informal rules governing

*A version of this chapter appeared in *The Atlantic Montly*, Vol. 273, 5, 1994, pp. 80–94.

interpersonal public behavior, including violence.[1] The rules prescribe
both a proper comportment and the proper way to respond if challenged.
They regulate the use of violence and so supply a rationale which allows
those who are inclined to aggression to precipitate violent encounters in an
approved way. The rules have been established and are enforced mainly by
the street-oriented, but on the streets the distinction between street and
decent is often irrelevant; everybody knows that if the rules are violated,
there are penalties. Knowledge of the code is thus largely defensive, and it
is literally necessary for operating in public. Therefore, even though families with a decency orientation are usually opposed to the values of the
code, they often reluctantly encourage their children's familiarity with it to
enable them to negotiate the inner-city environment.

At the heart of the code is the issue of respect – loosely defined as being
treated "right" or granted the deference one deserves. However, in the
troublesome public environment of the inner city, as people increasingly
feel buffeted by forces beyond their control, what one deserves in the way
of respect becomes more and more problematic and uncertain. This situation in turn further opens the issue of respect to sometimes intense interpersonal negotiation. In the street culture, especially among young people,
respect is viewed as almost an external entity that is hard-won but easily lost,
and so it must constantly be guarded. The rules of the code in fact provide
a framework for negotiating respect. Individuals whose very appearance –
including their clothing, demeanor, and way of moving – deter transgressions feel that they possess, and may be considered by others to possess, a
measure of respect. With the right amount, for instance, such individuals
can avoid being bothered in public. If they are bothered, on the other
hand, not only may they be in physical danger, but they will have been
disgraced or "dissed" (disrespected). Many of the forms that dissing can
take might seem petty to middle-class people (maintaining eye contact for
too long, for example), but to those invested in the street code, these
actions become serious indications of the other person's intentions. Consequently, such people become very sensitive to advances and slights, which
could well serve as a warning of imminent physical confrontation.

---

[1] This phenomenon is to be distinguished from that described by Wolfgang and
Ferracuti (1967), who identified and delineated more explicitly a "subculture of
violence." Wolfgang and Ferracuti postulated norms which undergirded or even
defined the culture of the entire community, whereas the code of the streets
applies predominantly to situational public *behavior* and is normative for only a
segment of the community.

This hard reality can be traced to the profound sense of alienation from mainstream society and its institutions felt by many poor inner-city black people, particularly the young. The code of the streets is actually a cultural adaptation to a profound lack of faith in the police and the judicial system. The police are most often seen as representing the dominant white society and as not caring enough to protect inner-city residents. When called, they may not respond, which is one reason many residents feel they must be prepared to take extraordinary measures to defend themselves and their loved ones against those who are inclined to aggression. Lack of police accountability has in fact been incorporated into the status system: The person who is believed capable of "taking care of himself" is accorded a certain deference, which translates into a sense of physical and psychological control. Thus, the street code emerges where the influence of the police ends and where personal responsibility for one's safety is felt to begin. Exacerbated by the proliferation of drugs and easy access to guns, this volatile situation results in the ability of the street-oriented minority (or those who effectively "go for bad") to dominate the public spaces.

This study is an ethnographic representation of the workings of this street code in the context of the socioeconomic situation in which the community finds itself.[2] The material it presents was gathered through numerous visits to various inner-city families and neighborhood hangouts and through many in-depth interviews with a wide array of individuals and groups; these interviews included sessions with adolescent boys and young men (some incarcerated, some not), older men, teenage mothers, and grandmothers. The structure of the inner-city family, the socialization of its children, the social structure of the community, and that community's extreme poverty, which is in large part the result of structural economic change, will be seen to interact in a way that facilitates the involvement of so many maturing youths in the culture of the streets, in which violence and the way it is regulated are key elements.

[2] The ethnographic approach is to be distinguished from other, equally valid, approaches, most notably the social-psychological. A sensitive and compelling social-psychological analysis of the phenomenon of murder is to be found in Jack Katz's *Seductions of Crime: Moral and Sensual Attractions in Doing Evil* (New York: Basic Books, 1988). Katz's purpose is to make sense of the senseless, that is, to explain the psychic changes a person goes through to become, at a given moment, a murderer. In contrast, the analysis offered here focuses on conscious behavior, which, in the circumstances of the inner-city environment, is sensible (makes sense). Katz explores the moral dimension of violence, whereas I explore its practical aspect.

The Ethnographic Method

A clarifying note on the methodology is perhaps in order for those unfamiliar with the ethnographic method. Ethnography seeks to paint a conceptual picture of the setting under consideration, through the use of observation and in-depth interviews. The researcher's goal is to illuminate the social and cultural dynamics which characterize the setting by answering such questions as "How do the people in the setting perceive their situation?" "What assumptions do they bring to their decision making?" "What behavior patterns result from their choices?" and "What are the consequences of those behaviors?" An important aspect of the ethnographer's work is that it be as objective as possible. This is not easy since it requires researchers to set aside their own values and assumptions as to what is and is not morally acceptable – in other words, to jettison that prism through which they typically view a given situation. By definition, one's own assumptions are so basic to one's perceptions that it may be difficult to see their influence. Ethnographic researchers, however, have been trained to recognize underlying assumptions, their own and those of their subjects, and to override the former and uncover the latter (see Becker, 1970).

"Decent" Families: Values and Reality

Although almost everyone in the poor inner-city neighborhood is struggling financially and therefore feels a certain distance from the rest of America, the decent and the street family in a real sense represent two poles of value orientation, two contrasting conceptual categories.[3] The labels decent and street, which the residents themselves use, amount to evaluative judgments that confer status on local residents. The labeling is often the result of a social contest among individuals and families of the neighborhood, and individuals of the two orientations can and often do coexist in the same extended family. Decent residents judge themselves to be so while

---

[3] For comparisons in the ethnographic literature, see Drake and Cayton's discussion of the "shadies" and "respectables" in *Black Metropolis* (New York: Harper and Row, 1962, originally published 1945). Also, see the discussion of "regulars," "wineheads," and "hoodlums" in Anderson, *A Place on the Corner* (Chicago: University of Chicago Press, 1978). See also Anderson, "Neighborhood Effects on Teenage Pregnancy," in Jencks and Peterson, eds., *The Urban Underclass* (Washington, D.C.: Brookings, 1991).

judging others to be of the street, whereas street individuals may present themselves as decent, drawing distinctions between themselves and other even more street-oriented people. In any case, street is considered a highly perjorative epithet. In addition, there is quite a bit of circumstantial behavior among individuals – that is, one person may at different times exhibit both decent and street orientations, depending on the circumstances. Although these designations result from so much social jockeying, there do exist concrete features that define each conceptual category.

Generally, so-called decent families accept mainstream values more fully and attempt to instill them in their children. Whether a married couple with children or a single-parent (usually female) household, such families are generally working poor and so tend to be relatively better off financially than their street-oriented neighbors. The adults value hard work and self-reliance and are willing to sacrifice for their children. Because they have a certain amount of faith in mainstream society, they harbor hopes for a better future for their children, if not for themselves. Many of them go to church and take a strong interest in their children's schooling. Rather than dwell on the real hardships and inequities facing them, many such decent people, particularly the increasing number of grandmothers raising grandchildren, sometimes see their difficult situation as a test from God and derive great support from their faith and from the church community.

Intact families, although in the minority, provide powerful role models in the community. Typically, the husband and wife work at low-paying jobs; possibly, they are aided by the occasional financial contributions of a teenage child who works at a part-time job. At times, the man or woman may work multiple jobs. As the primary breadwinner, the man is usually considered the "head of household," with the woman as his partner and the children as their subjects. During bouts of unemployment, the man's dominance may be questioned, but the financially marginal black family with a decency orientation strongly values male authority. Typically, certain male decisions and behavior may be contested by the woman, but very rarely will they be challenged by the children. As they age, however, children, particularly males, may "try" (challenge) the authority of the father, which places some pressure on him to keep his children in line. In public, such a family makes a striking picture as the man appears to be in complete control, with the woman and the children often following his lead. This appearance is to some extent a practical matter, for the streets and other public places are considered dangerous and unpredictable, and it is the man who is most often placed in the public role of protector and defender against danger. In playing this role, the man may exhibit a certain exaggeration of concern, particularly when anonymous males are near; through his actions and words, and at times speaking loudly and assertively to get his small children in line, he lets strangers know unambiguously, "This is my family, and I am in charge."

Extremely aware of the problematic and often dangerous environment in which they reside, decent parents tend to be strict in their childrearing practices, encouraging children to respect authority and walk a straight moral line. They have an almost obsessive concern with trouble of any kind and remind their children to be on the lookout for people and situations which might lead to such difficulties. When disciplining their children, they tend to be liberal in the use of corporal punishment, but unlike street parents, who are often observed lashing out at their children, they tend to explain the reason for the spanking. Outsiders, however, may not always be able to distinguish between parents who are using corporal punishment as a means to uphold standards of decency and those whose goal is to teach toughness and intimidation or who have no goal. Such confusion of decent motives with behavior that mainstream society generally disapproves of is a source of frustration for many black parents who are attempting to lead mainstream lives. Here is the experience of a 48-year-old man with an intact family:

> My boy and this other boy broke into this church, aw right? Stole this ridin' lawnmower, just to ride on, nothin' else. And when I found out, I whupped his behind. Now two weeks after that, he got suspended for fightin', which wasn't his fault – but they suspended him and the other boy. Now he scared to come home and tell me. Now this is two weeks after I done already talked to him. He's cryin' and carryin' on in school. So the school sends a 24-year-old black girl, a 24-year-old white girl to my house. Now the first thing I asked them was did they have kids. None of 'em have kids. But I done raised seven kids. My oldest girl is 30 years old. I have nine grandkids. I'm 48. And I asked them how can they tell me how to raise my kids. And they don't have any of they own. I was so angry I had to leave. My wife made me get out of the house. But they did send me an apology letter, but the point is that I cannot chastise my child unless the government tells me it's OK. That's wrong. I'm not gon' kill my child, but I'm gonna make him know right and wrong. These kids today they know that whatever you do to 'em, first thing you know they call it child abuse. And they gon' lock us up. And it's wrong, it really is.

Consistent with this view, decent families also inspect their children's playmates for behavior problems, and they enforce curfews. For example, they may require their young children to come in by a certain time or simply to go no farther than the front stoop of their house, a vantage point from which the children attentively watch other children play unsupervised in the street; the obedient children may then endure the street kids' taunts of "stoop children." As the children become teenagers, these parents make a strong effort to know where they are at night, giving them an unmistakable message of their caring, concern, and love. At the same time, they are vigilant in guarding against the appearance of condoning any kind of delinquent or loose behavior, including violence, drug use, and staying out very late at night; they monitor not only their own children's behavior but also that of their children's peers, at times playfully embarrassing their own children by voicing value judgments in front of their children's friends.

A single mother with children may also form a decent family – indeed, the majority of decent families in the inner city are of this type – but she must work even harder at instilling decent values in her children. She may reside with her mother or other female or male relatives and friends, or she may simply receive help with child care from an extended family. She too may press for deference to her authority, but usually she is at some disadvantage with regard to young men who might "try" her ability to control her household, attempting to date her daughters or to draw her sons into the streets. The importance of having a man of the house to fill the role of protector of the household, a figure boys are prepared to respect, should not be underestimated. A mother on her own often feels that she must be constantly on guard and that she must exhibit a great deal of determination. A single mother of four boys, three of whom are grown, explains:

> It really is pretty bad around here. There's quite a few grandmothers taking care of kids. They mothers out here on crack. There's quite a few of 'em. The drugs are terrible.
>
> Now I got a 15-year-old boy, and I do everything I can to keep him straight. 'Cause they all on the corner. You can't say you not in it 'cause we in a bad area. They [drug dealers and users] be all on the corner. They be sittin' in front of apartments takin' the crack. And constantly, every day, I have to stay on 'em and make sure everything's O.K. Which is real bad, I never seen it this bad. And I been around here since '81, and I never seen it this bad.
>
> At nights they be roamin' up and down the streets, and they be droppin' the caps [used crack vials] all in front of your door. And when the kids out there playin', you gotta like sweep 'em up.
>
> It's harder for me now to try to keep my 15-year-old under control. Right now, he likes to do auto mechanics, hook up radios in people's cars. And long as I keep 'im interested in that, I'm O.K.

But it's not a day that goes by that I'm not in fear. 'Cause right now, he got friends that's sellin' it [drugs]. They, you know, got a whole lot of money and stuff.

And I get him to come and mop floors [she works as a part-time janitor] and I give him a few dollars. I say, "As long as you got a roof over yo' head, son, don't worry about nothin' else."

It's just a constant struggle tryin' to raise yo' kids in this time. It's very hard. They [boys on the street] say to him, "Man, why you got to go in the house?" And they keep sittin' right on the stoop. If he go somewhere, I got to know where he's at and who he's with. And they be tellin' him . . . He say, "No, man, I got to stay on these steps. I don't want no problem with my mama!"

Now I been a single parent for 15 years. So far, I don't have any problems. I have four sons. I got just the one that's not grown, the 15-year-old. Everyone else is grown. My oldest is 35. I'm tryin'. Not that easy. I got just one more, now. Then I'll be all right. If I need help, the older ones'll help me.

Most of the time, I keep track myself. I told him I'll kill him if I catch him out here sellin' [drugs]. And I know most of the drug dealers. He better not. I gon' hurt him. They better not give him nothin' [drugs or money]. He better not do nothin' for them. I tell him, "I know some of your friends are dealers. [You can] speak to 'em, but don't let me catch you hangin' on the corner. I done struggled too hard to try to take care of you. I'm not gon' let you throw your life away."

When me and my husband separated in '79, I figured I had to do it. He was out there drivin' trucks and never home. I had to teach my kids how to play ball and this and that. I said, "If I have to be a single parent, I'll do it."

It used to be the gangs, and you fought 'em, and it was over. But now if you fight somebody, they may come back and kill you. It's a whole lot different now. You got to be street-smart to get along. My boy doesn't like to fight. I took him out of school, put him in a home course. The staff does what it wants to. Just work for a pay check.

You tell the kid, now you can't pick their friends, so you do what you can. I try to tell mine, "You gon' be out there with the bad [street kids], you can't do what they do. You got to use your own mind." Every day, if I don't get up and say a prayer, I can't make it. I can't make it. I watch him closely. If he go somewhere, I have to know where he at. And when I leave him, or if he go to them girlfriends' houses, I tell the parents, "If you not responsible, he can't stay." I'm not gon' have no teenager making no baby.

There are so many kids that don't make 17. Look at that 16-year-old boy that got killed last week. Somebody was looking for his cousin. All this kinda stuff, it don't make sense. These kids can't even make 17. All over drugs. Drugs taken control. Even the parents in it. How a child gon' come home with a $100 sweatsuit on, $200 sneakers. Ain't got no job. A $1,000 in they

pocket. He ain't gon' come in my house and do that. Some parents use the
money. Some of the kids'll knock they own parents out. The parents afraid
of the kids. I've seen 'em knock the parents the hell down.

Probably the most meaningful expression for describing the mission of
decent families, as seen by themselves and outsiders, is instilling "back-
bone" in its younger members. In support of its efforts toward this goal, a
decent family tends to be much more willing and able than the street-
oriented family to ally itself with outside institutions such as school and
church. The parents in such families have usually had more years of schooling than their street-oriented counterparts, which tends to foster in them a
positive attitude toward their children's schooling. In addition, they place
a certain emphasis on spiritual values and principles, and church attendance tends to be a regular family ritual, as noted earlier, although females
are generally more so inclined than the males.

An important aspect of religious belief for the decent people is their
conception of death. The intertwined ideas of fate, a judgment day, and an
afterlife present a marked contrast to the general disorganization and sense
of immediacy that is known to characterize street-oriented families and
individuals. The situation of the street-oriented may then result in the
tendency to be indifferent or oblivious to the probable consequences or
future meaning of their behavior, including death. People imbued with a
street orientation tend not to think far beyond the immediate present; their
orientation toward the future is either very limited or nonexistent. One
must live for the moment, for they embrace the general belief that "tomorrow ain't promised to you." For religious people, the sometimes literal
belief in an afterlife and a day of reckoning inspires hope and makes life
extremely valuable, and this belief acts to check individuals in potentially
violent encounters. While accepting the use of violence in self-defense, they
are less likely to be initiators of hostilities. Religious beliefs thus can have
very practical implications. Furthermore, the moral feeling church-going
instills in many people strengthens their self-esteem and underscores the
sense that a positive future is possible, thus contributing to a certain emotional stability or "long fuse" in volatile circumstances.

In these decent families, then, there tends to be a real concern with and
a certain amount of hope for the future. Such attitudes are often expressed
in a drive to work to have something or to build a good life by working hard
and saving for material things; raising one's children – telling them to
"make something out of yourself" and "make do with what you have" – is an
important aspect of this attitude. But the concern with material things,

although accepted, often produces a certain strain on the young; often encouraged to covet material things as emblems testifying to social and cultural well-being, they lack the legitimate or legal means for obtaining such things. The presence of this dilemma often causes otherwise decent youths to invest their considerable mental resources in the street.

Involvement with institutions such as school and church has given decent parents a kind of *savoir faire* that helps them get along in the world. Thus, they often know how to get things done and use that knowledge to help advance themselves and their children. In the face of such overwhelming problems as persistent poverty, AIDS, or drug use, which can beset even the strongest and most promising families, these parents are trying hard to give their children as good a life – if not a better one – as they themselves had. At the same time, they are themselves polite and considerate of others, and they teach their children to be the same way. At home, at work, and in church, they work hard to maintain a positive mental attitude and a spirit of cooperation.

The Street

So-called street parents often show a lack of consideration for other people and have a rather superficial sense of family and community. Though they may love their children, many of them are unable to cope with the physical and emotional demands of parenthood, and they often find it difficult to reconcile their needs with those of their children. These families, who are more fully invested in the code of the streets than the decent people are, may aggressively socialize their children into it in a normative way. They believe in the code and judge themselves and others according to its values.

In fact, the overwhelming majority of families in the inner-city community try to approximate the decent-family model, but there are many others who clearly represent the worst fears of the decent family. Not only are the financial resources of these other families extremely limited, but what little they have may easily be misused. Often suffering the worst effects of social isolation, the lives of the street-oriented are often marked by disorganization. In the most desperate circumstances, people often have a limited understanding of priorities and consequences, and so frustrations mount over bills, food, and, at times, drink, cigarettes, and drugs. Some tend toward self-destructive behavior; many street-oriented women are crack-addicted ("on the pipe"), alcoholic, or repeatedly involved in complicated relationships with men who abuse them. In addition, the seeming intractability of their situation, caused in large part by the lack of well-paying jobs and the persistence of racial discrimination, has engendered deep-seated bitterness and anger in many of the most desperate and poorest blacks, especially young people. The need both to exercise a measure of control and to lash out at somebody is often played out in the adults' relations with their children. At the least, the frustrations of persistent poverty shorten the fuse in such people – contributing to a lack of patience with anyone, child or adult, who irritates them.

Many decent people simply view the street-oriented as lowlife or bad people. Even if they display a certain amount of responsibility, such "lowlife" people are generally seen as incapable of being anything but a bad influence on their neighbors. The following field note is germane:

On the fringe of the Village, there are houses of the inner-city black community. On one street is the home of Joe Dickens, a heavy-set, 32-year-old black man. He rents the house and lives there with his three children, who range in age from about $3\frac{1}{2}$ to 7. Dickens' wife is not around. It is rumored that the two of them were on crack together and his wife's habit got out of control. As has been happening more and more in this community, she gravitated to the streets and became a prostitute to support her habit. Dickens could not accept this behavior and so he had to let her go. He took over the running of the house and the care of the children as best he could. By doing what he can for his kids, he might be considered the responsible parent, but many of the neighbors do not see him as responsible. They observe him yelling and cursing at the children, as well as with his buddies, and allowing them to "rip and run" up and down the street at all hours. At the same time, Mr. Dickens lacks consideration of others, a lack which is a defining trait of street-oriented people. He often sits on his porch and plays loud music, either unaware of or insensitive to the fact that it disturbs the whole block. Sometimes the neighbors call the police, who do not respond to the complaint, leaving the neighbors frustrated and demoralized.

In general, however, the decent people on the street are afraid to confront Mr. Dickens because they fear getting in trouble with him and his buddies. They know that like all street people, he subscribes to the belief that might makes right, and so he is likely to try to harm anyone who annoys him. In addition, it is believed that Dickens is a crack dealer. His house is always busy, with people coming in and out at all hours, often driving up in their cars, running in, and quickly emerging and driving off. Dickens' children, of course, are witnesses to all this activity, and one can only imagine what they see inside the house. They are growing up in a family, but it is a street-oriented family, and it is obvious to the neighbors that these children are learning the values of toughness and self-absorption from their father and the social environment in which he is raising them.

The decent people firmly believe that it is this general set of cultural deficits – that is, a certain fundamental lack of social polish and commitment to norms of civility, which they refer to as "ignorance" – which makes the street-oriented quick to resort to violence to resolve almost any dispute. To those who hold this view, such street people seem to carry about them an aura of danger. Thus, during public interactions, the decent people may readily defer to the street-oriented, especially when they are strangers, out of fear of their ignorance. For instance, when street people are encountered at theaters or other public places talking loudly or making excessive noise, many decent people are reluctant to correct them for fear of verbal abuse that could lead to violence. Similarly, the decent people will often avoid a confrontation over a parking space or traffic error for fear of a verbal or physical confrontation. Under their breaths they may utter disapprovingly to a companion, "street niggers," thereby drawing a sharp cultural distinction between themselves and such persons. But there are also times when the decent people will try to approach the level of the "ignorant" ones by what they refer to as "getting ignorant" (see Anderson, 1990). In these circumstances, they may appear in battle dress, more than ready to face down the ignorant ones, indicating they have reached their limit, or threshold, for violent confrontation. And from this, an actual fight can erupt.

Thus, the fact that generally civilly disposed, socially conscious, and largely self-reliant men and women share the streets and other public institutions with the inconsiderate, the ignorant, and the extremely desperate puts them at special risk. In order to live and to function in the community, they must adapt to a street reality that is often dominated by the presence of those who at best are suffering severely in some way and who are likely to resort quickly to violence to settle disputes.

Coming Up in Street Families

In the street-oriented family, the development of an aggressive mentality can be seen from the beginning, even in the circumstances surrounding the birth of the child. In circumstances of persistent poverty, the mother is often little more than a child herself and without many resources or a consistent source of support; she is often getting by with public assistance or the help of kin. She may be ambivalent with respect to the child: On the one hand, she may look at the child as a heavenly gift; but on the other hand, as she begins to care for it, she is apt to realize that it is a burden, and sometimes a profound burden. These are the years she wants to be free to date and otherwise consort with men, to have a social life, and she discovers that the child slows her down (see Anderson, 1989). Thus, she sometimes leans on others, including family members, to enable her to satisfy her social needs for getting out nights and being with male and female friends.

In these circumstances, a woman – or a man, although men are less consistently present in children's lives – can be quite aggressive with children, yelling at and striking them for the least little infraction of the rules she has set down. Often little if any serious explanation follows the verbal and physical punishment. This response teaches children a particular lesson. They learn that to solve any kind of interpersonal problem, one must quickly resort to hitting or other violent behavior. Actual peace and quiet – and also the appearance of calm, respectful children that can be conveyed to her neighbors and friends – are often what the young mother most desires, but at times she will be very aggressive in trying to achieve these goals. Thus, she may be quick to beat her children, especially if they defy her law, not because she hates them but because this is the way she knows how to control them. In fact, many street-oriented women love their children dearly. Many mothers in the community subscribe to the notion that there is a "devil in the boy" that must be beaten out of him or that socially "fast girls need to be whupped." Thus, much of what borders on child abuse in the view of social authorities is acceptable parental punishment in the view of these mothers.

Many street-oriented women are weak and ineffective mothers whose children learn to fend for themselves when necessary, foraging for food and money and getting them any way they can. These children are sometimes employed by drug dealers or become addicted themselves. These children of the street, growing up with little supervision, are said to "come up hard." In the interest of survival, they often learn to fight at an early age, sometimes using short-tempered adults around them as role models. The street-oriented home may be fraught with anger, verbal disputes, physical aggression, and even mayhem. The children observe these goings-on, learning the lesson that might makes right. They quickly learn to hit those who cross them, and the dog-eat-dog mentality prevails. In order to survive, to protect oneself, it is necessary to marshal inner resources and be ready to deal with adversity in a hands-on way. In these circumstances, physical prowess takes on great significance.

In some of the most desperate cases, a street-oriented mother may simply leave her young children alone and unattended while she goes out. The most irresponsible women can be found at local bars and crack houses, getting high and socializing with other adults. Sometimes a troubled woman will leave very young children alone for days at a time. Reports of crack addicts abandoning their children have become common in drug-infested inner-city communities. Neighbors or relatives discover the abandoned children, often hungry and distraught over the absence of their mother. After repeated absences, a friend or relative, particularly a grandmother, will often step in to care for the young children, sometimes petitioning the authorities to send her, as guardian of the children, the mother's welfare check, if the mother gets one. By this time, however, the children may well have learned the first lesson of the streets: Survival itself, let alone respect, cannot be taken for granted; you have to fight for your place in the world.

The Shuffling Process

As indicated earlier, in order to carry on their everyday lives in poor inner-city neighborhoods, children from even the most decent homes must come to terms with the streets. This means that they must learn to deal with the various and sundry influences of the streets, including their more street-oriented peers. Indeed, as children grow up and their parents' control wanes, they go through a social shuffling process that can undermine, or at least test, much of the socialization they have received at home. In other words, the street serves as a mediating influence under which children may come to reconsider and rearrange their personal orientations. This is a time of status passage (see Glaser & Strauss, 1972), when social identity can become very uncertain as children sort out their ways of being. It is a tricky time because a child can go either way. For children from decent homes, for example, the immediate and present reality of the street situation can overcome the compunctions against tough behavior that their parents taught them, so that the lessons of the home are slowly forgotten and the child "goes for bad." Or a talented child from a street-oriented family may discover ways of gaining respect without unduly resorting to aggressive and violent responses – by becoming a rapper or athlete, for example, or, rarely, a good student. Thus, the kind of home a child comes from becomes influential but not determinative of the way he or she will ultimately turn out.

By the age of ten, all children from both decent and street-oriented families are mingling on the neighborhood streets and figuring out their identities. Here they try out certain roles and scripts – which are sometimes actively opposed to the wishes of parents – in a process that challenges both their talents and their socialization and may involve more than a little luck, good or bad. In this volatile environment, they learn to watch their backs and to anticipate and negotiate those situations that might lead to troubles with others. The successful outcomes of these cumulative interactions with the streets ultimately determine every child's life chances.

Herein lies the real meaning of so many fights and altercations, despite the ostensible, usually petty, precipitating causes, including the competitions over girlfriends and boyfriends and the "he say, she say" conflicts of personal attribution. Adolescents are insecure and are trying to establish their identities. Children from the middle- and upper-classes, however, usually have more ways to express themselves as worthwhile and so have more avenues to explore. The negotiations they engage in among themselves may also include aggression, but they tend to be more verbal in a way that includes a greater use of other options – options that require resources not available to those of more limited resources, such as showing off with things, connections, and so on. In poor inner-city neighborhoods, physicality is a fairly common way of asserting oneself. It is also unambiguous. If you punch someone out, if you succeed in keeping someone from walking down your block, "you did it." It is a *fait accompli*. And the evidence that you prevailed is there for all to see.

During this campaign for respect, through these various conflicts, those connections between actually being respected and the need for being in physical control of at least a portion of the environment become internalized, and the germ of the code of the streets emerges. As children mature, they obtain an increasingly more sophisticated understanding of the code, and it becomes part of their working conception of the world, so that by the time they reach adulthood, it comes to define the social order. In time, the rules of physical engagement and their personal implications become crystallized. Children learn the conditions under which violence is appropriate, and they also learn how the code defines the individual's relationship to his or her peers. They thus come to appreciate the give-and-take of public life, the process of negotiation.

The ethic of violence is in part a class phenomenon (see Wolfgang and Ferracuti, 1967). Children are more inclined to be physical than adults (because they have fewer alternatives for settling disputes), and lower-class adults tend to be more physical than middle- or upper-middle-class adults. Poor and lower-class adults more often find themselves in disputes that lead to violence. Because they are more often alienated from the agents and agencies of social control, such as the police and the courts, they are left alone more often to settle disputes on their own. And such parents, in turn, tend to socialize their kids into this reality.

But this reality of inner-city life is largely absorbed on the streets. At an early age, often even before they start school and without much in the way of adult supervision, children from such street-oriented families gravitate to the streets, where they must be ready "to hang," to socialize with peers. Children from these generally permissive homes have a great deal of latitude and are allowed to "rip and run" up and down the street. They often come home from school, put their books down, and go right back out the door. For the most severely compromised, on school nights, eight- and nine-year-olds remain out until nine or ten o'clock (and the teenagers come in whenever they want to). On the streets, they play in groups that often become the source of their primary social bonds. Children from decent homes tend to be more carefully supervised and are thus likely to have curfews and to be taught how to stay out of trouble.

In the street, through their play, children pour their individual life experiences into a common knowledge pool, affirming, confirming, and elaborating on what they have observed in the home and matching their skills against those of others. And they learn to fight. Even small children test one another, pushing and shoving others, and are ready to hit other children over circumstances not to their liking. In turn, they are readily hit by other children, and the child who is toughest prevails. Thus, the violent resolution of disputes – the hitting and cursing – gains social reinforcement. The child in effect is initiated into a system that is really a way of campaigning for self-respect.

There is a critical sense in which violent behavior is determined by situations, thus giving importance to the various ways in which individuals define and interpret such situations. In meeting the various exigencies of immediate situations, which become so many public trials, the individual builds patterns as outcomes are repeated over time. Behaviors, violent or civil, which work for a young person and are reinforced by peers whose reactions to such behavior come to shape the person's outlook, will likely be repeated.

In addition, younger children witness the disputes of older children, which are often resolved through cursing and abusive talk, and sometimes through aggression or outright violence. They see that one child succumbs to the greater physical and mental abilities of the other. They are also alert and attentive witnesses to the verbal and physical fights of adults, after which they compare notes and share their own interpretations of the event. In almost every case, the victor is the person who physically won the altercation, and this person often enjoys the esteem and respect of onlookers. These experiences reinforce the lessons the children have learned at home: Might makes right and toughness is a virtue; humility is not. In effect, they learn the social meaning of fighting. When it is left virtually unchallenged, this understanding becomes an ever more important part of a child's working conception of the world. Over time, the code of the streets becomes refined. Those street-oriented adults with whom children come in contact – including mothers, fathers, brothers, sisters, boyfriends, cousins, neighbors, and friends – help them along in forming this understanding by verbalizing the messages they are getting through experience: "Watch your back." "Protect yourself." "Don't punk out." "If somebody messes with you, you got to pay them back." "If someone disses you, you got to straighten them out." Many parents actually impose sanctions if a child is not sufficiently aggressive. For example, if a child loses a fight and comes home upset, the parent might respond, "Don't you come in here crying that somebody beat you up; you better get back out there and whup his ass. I didn't raise no punks! Get back out there and whup his ass. If you don't whup his ass, I'll whup yo' ass when you come home." Thus, the child obtains reinforcement for being tough and showing nerve.

While fighting, some children cry as though they are doing something they are ambivalent about. The fight may be against their wishes, yet they may feel constrained to fight or face the consequences – not just from peers but also from caretakers or their parents, who may administer another beating if they back down. Some adults recall receiving such lessons from their own parents and justify repeating them to their children as a way to toughen them up. Appearing capable of taking care of oneself as a form of self-defense is a dominant theme among both street-oriented and decent adults, who worry about the safety of their children. There is thus at times a convergence in their child-rearing practices, although the rationales behind them may differ.

The following field note graphically illustrates both the efficacy of these informal lessons and the early age at which they are learned:

Casey is four years old and attends a local nursery school. He lives with his mom and stepfather. Casey's family is considered to be a street family in the neighborhood. At home, his mother will curse at him and, at times, will beat him for misbehavior. At times, his stepfather will spank him as well. Casey has attracted the attention of the staff of the nursery school because of his behavior. Of particular concern is Casey's cursing and hitting of other children. When Casey wants something, he will curse and hit other children, causing many there to refer to him as bad. He now has that reputation of "bad" around the center. He regularly refers to members of the staff as "bitches" and "motherfuckers." For instance, he will say to his teacher,

"Cathy, you bitch" or "What that bitch want?" At times this seems funny coming from the mouth of a four-year-old, but it reflects on Casey's home situation. Around the center, he knows that such behavior is disapproved of because of the way the teachers and others react to it, though he may get reinforcement for it because of its humorous character. Once when his teacher upset him, Casey promptly slapped her and called her a "bitch."

Upon hearing of this incident, the bus driver refused to take Casey home, or even to let him on his bus. The next day, when Casey saw the bus driver again, he said, "Norman, you left me. Why'd you leave me? You a trip, man." When Casey desires a toy or some other item from a playmate, he will demand it and sometimes hit the child and try to take it. Members of the staff fear that Casey has a bad influence on other children at the center, for he curses at them "like a sailor," though "they don't know what he's talking about." In these ways, Casey acts somewhat grown up, or "mannish," in the words of the bus driver, who sometimes glares at him, wanting to treat him as another man, since he seems to act that way. Staff members at the center have found they can control Casey by threatening to report his behavior to his stepfather, to which he replies, "Oh, please don't tell him. I'll be good. Please don't tell him." It seems that Casey fears this man and that telling him might mean a beating for Casey. Other local decent blacks say his home life corresponds to that of the typical street family, which is rife with cursing, yelling, physical abuse of children, and limited financial resources.

Many of these parents do not want Casey to be a playmate for one of their own children. They think he would be a bad influence on their own children, particularly in encouraging them toward assuming a street identity. This is something most want to guard against, and children "like this one" worry them generally. They feel such children help to make their own children more unruly. They also feel that certain neighborhoods breed such children, and the decent children are at some risk when placed in an environment with the street kids.

In the minds of many decent parents, children from street families, because of their general ignorance and lack of opportunities, are considered at great risk of eventually getting into serious trouble.

Self-Image Based on Juice

By the time they are teenagers, most youths have either internalized the code of the streets or at least learned the need to comport themselves in accordance with its rules, which chiefly have to do with interpersonal communication. The code revolves around the presentation of self. Its basic requirement is the display of a certain predisposition to violence. Accordingly, one's bearing must send the unmistakable if sometimes subtle message to "the next person" in public that one is capable of violence and mayhem when the situation requires it – that one can take care of oneself. The nature of this communication is largely determined by the demands of the circumstances but can include facial expressions, gait, and verbal expressions – all of which are geared mainly to detering aggression. Physical appearance, including clothes, jewelry, and grooming, also plays an important part in how a person is viewed; to be respected, you have to have the right look.

Even so, there are no guarantees against challenges, because there are always people around looking for a fight to increase their share of respect – or "juice," as it is sometimes called on the street. Moreover, if a male is assaulted, it is important, not only in the eyes of his opponent but also in the eyes of his "running buddies," for him to avenge himself. Otherwise, he risks being "tried" or "rolled on" (physically assaulted) by any number of others. To maintain his honor, he must show he is not someone to be "messed with" or "dissed." In general, the person must "keep himself straight" by maintaining his position of respect among others; this involves in part his self-image, which is shaped by what he thinks others are thinking of him in relation to his peers.

Objects play an important and complicated role in establishing self-image. Jackets, sneakers, and gold jewelry reflect not just a person's taste, which tends to be tightly regulated among adolescents of all social classes, but also a willingness to possess things that may require defending. A boy wearing a fashionable, expensive jacket, for example, is vulnerable to attack by another who covets the jacket and either cannot afford to buy one or wants the added satisfaction of depriving someone else of his. However, if a boy forgoes the desirable jacket and wears one that isn't hip, he runs the risk of being teased and possibly even assaulted as an unworthy person. A youth with a decency orientation describes the situation:

> Here go another thing. If you outside, right, and your mom's on welfare and she on crack, the persons you tryin' to be with dress [in] like purple sweatpants and white sneaks, but it's all decent, right, and you got on some bummy jeans and a pair of dull sneaks, they won't – some of the people out there sellin' drugs won't let you hang with them unless you dress like [in] purple sweatpants and decent sneaks every day . . .
>
> They tease 'em. First they'll tease 'em and then they'll try to say they stink, like they smell like pig or something like that, and then they'll be like, "Get out of here. Get out. We don't want you near us. You stink. You dirty." All that stuff. And I don't think that's right. If he's young, it ain't his fault or her fault that she dressin' like that. It's her mother and her dad's fault.

To be allowed to hang with certain prestigious crowds, a boy must wear a different set of expensive clothes – sneakers and an athletic outfit – every day. Not to be able to do so might make him appear socially deficient. The youth may come to covet such items – especially when he sees easy prey wearing them. The youth continues:

> You can even get hurt off your own clothes: Like, say, I'm walkin' down the street and somebody try to take my hat from me and I won't let 'em take it and they got a gun. You can get killed over one little simple hat. Or if I got a gold ring and a gold necklace on and they see me one dark night on a dark street, and they stick me up and I won't let 'em, and they shoot me. I'm dead and they hide me. I'm dead and won't nobody ever know [who did it].

In acquiring valued things, therefore, a person shores up his or her identity – but since it is an identity based on having something, it is highly precarious. This very precariousness gives a heightened sense of urgency to staying even with peers, with whom the person is actually competing. Young men and women who are able to command respect through their presentation of self – by allowing their possessions and their body language to speak for them – may not have to campaign for regard but may, rather, gain it by the force of their manner. Those who are unable to command respect in this way must actively compaign for it. The following incident, which I witnessed, is a good example of the way one's things can be used to establish status in a given situation:

> It was a warm spring day, and my twelve-year-old son and I were in a local Foot Locker shoe store about a mile north of the community. We were being waited on when a brand-new purple BMW pulled up in front of the store, music blaring out of its stereo system. Leaving the engine running, two young black males of about 21 or 22 jumped out and swaggered into the store. They were dressed in stylish sweatsuits, had close-cropped hair, and sported shades and gold chains and rings. One of them had an earring. Ignoring the two white salesmen, who deferred to them, they went straight to the wall where the shoes were stacked in boxes. In an obviously demonstrative way, they snatched three or four boxes of shoes, swaggered over to the counter, and threw down a few hundred dollars. Then, without waiting for their change or carrying on any verbal exchange, they walked out with their shoes.
>
> The most striking aspect of this episode was the way in which these young men exhibited control over the resource of money. By their appearance, which was dominated by expensive clothing and jewelry; by the aplomb with which they moved; by the ease with which they threw large bills around; by not only leaving their keys in the car but even keeping the engine running

and the music playing enticingly, thus daring anyone to tamper with it – by all these means, they were demonstrating their total control over their possessions. And this display did make an impression. After the youths made their exit, they left a certain presence behind, a residue of their self-assurance. In their wake, the feeling in the store was, "What was that?" My son nodded knowingly, aware that these are the successful "homeboys." Indeed, these two unorthodox customers exuded success, albeit a deviant sort of success. Their gaudy car roared off, and things in the store slowly drifted back to normal.

One way of campaigning for status is by taking the possessions of others. In this context, seemingly ordinary objects can become trophies imbued with symbolic value that far exceeds their monetary worth. Possession of the trophy can symbolize the ability to violate somebody – to "get in his face," to take something of value from him, to diss him, and thus to enhance one's own worth by stealing that which belongs to someone else. Though it often is, the trophy does not have to be something material. It can be another person's sense of honor, snatched away with a derogatory remark or action. It can be the outcome of a fight. It can be the imposition of a certain standard, such as a girl getting herself recognized as the most beautiful. Material things, however, fit easily into the pattern. Sneakers or a pistol – even somebody else's boyfriend or girlfriend – can become a trophy. When individuals can take something from another and then flaunt it, they gain a certain regard by being the owner, or the controller, of that thing. But this display of ownership can then provoke other people to challenge him or her. This game of who controls what is thus constantly being played out on inner-city streets, and the trophy – extrinsic or intrinsic, tangible or intangible – identifies the current winner.

An important aspect of this often violent give-and-take is its zero-sum quality. That is, the extent to which one person can rise depends on his or her ability to put another person down. This situation underscores the alienation that permeates the inner-city ghetto community. There is a generalized sense that very little respect is to be had, and therefore every-one competes to get what little affirmation is actually available. The craving for respect that results often gives people thin skins. It is generally believed that true respect provides an aura of protection. Thus, shows of deference by others can be highly soothing, contributing to a sense of security, comfort, self-confidence, and self-respect. Transgressions by others that go unanswered diminish these feelings and are believed to encourage further transgressions. Hence, one must be ever vigilant against the transgressions of others; one cannot even allow the *appearance* of transgressions to be tolerated. Among young people, whose sense of self-esteem is particularly vulnerable, there is an especially heightened concern with being "disrespected." Many inner-city young men in particular crave respect to such a degree that they will risk their lives to attain and maintain it.

The issue of respect is thus closely tied to whether a person has an inclination to be violent, even as a victim. In the wider society, people may not feel the need to retaliate physically after an attack, even though they are aware that they have been degraded or taken advantage of. They may feel a great need to defend themselves *during* an attack or to behave in such a way as to deter aggression (middle-class people certainly can and do become victims of street-oriented youths), but they are much more likely than street-oriented people to feel they can walk away from a possible altercation with their self-esteem intact. Some people may even have the strength of character to flee, without any thought that their self-respect or esteem will be diminished.

In improverished inner-city black communities, however, particularly among young males and perhaps increasingly among females, such flight would be extremely difficult. To run away would likely leave one's self-esteem in tatters. Hence, people often feel constrained not only to stand up during and at least attempt to resist an assault but also to "pay back" – to seek revenge – after a successful assault on their person. This may include going to get a weapon. One young man described a typical scenario:

> So he'll [the victim] ask somebody do they got a gun for sale or somethin' like that. And they'll say yeah and they say they want a buck [a hundred dollars] for it or somethin' like that. So he'll go and get a hundred dollars and buy that gun off of him and then wait until he see the boy that he was fightin' or got into a argument [with] or somethin' like that. He'll sneak and shoot 'im or somethin' like that and then move away from his old neighborhood. . . .
>
> Or if they already have a gun, they gonna just go get their gun and buy a bullet. And then they gonna shoot the person, whoever they was fightin', or whoever did somethin' to 'im. Then they'll probably keep the gun and get into a couple more rumbles and shoot people. And the gun'll probably have like nine bodies on it. Then they decide to sell the gun, and the other person'll get caught with it.

Or one's relatives might get involved, willingly or not. The youth continues:

> For instance, me. I was livin' in the projects [public housing] on Grant Street, right, and I think my brother is fightin' one of the other person's brother or cousin. Me and my brother look just alike – they thought I was my

brother – and they try to throw me down the elevator shaft, but they threw me down three flights of steps. And I hit my face on a concrete rung, chipped my tooth, and got five stitches in my lip. And see, [later] my uncle killed one of them, and that's why he doin' time in jail now. Because they tried to kill me.

The very identity and self-respect – the honor – of many inner-city youths is often intricately tied up with the way they perform on the streets *during* and *after* such encounters. Moreover, this outlook reflects the circumscribed opportunities of the inner-city poor. Generally, people outside the ghetto have other ways of gaining status and regard, and thus, they do not feel so dependent on such physical displays.

By Trial of Manhood

Among males on the street, these concerns about things and identity have come to be expressed in the concept of "manhood." Manhood in the inner-city street means taking the prerogatives of men with respect to strangers, other men, and women – being distinguished as a man. It implies physicality and a certain ruthlessness. Regard and respect are associated with this concept in large part because of its practical application: If others have little or no regard for a person's manhood, his very life and that of his loved ones could be in jeopardy. But there is a chicken-and-egg aspect to this situation: One's physical safety is more likely to be jeopardized in public *because* manhood is associated with respect. The "man" becomes the target of others who want to prove their own manhood. In other words, an existential link has been created between the idea of manhood and one's self-esteem, so that it has become hard to say which is primary. For many inner-city youths, manhood and respect are flip sides of the same coin; physical and psychological well-being are inseparable, and both require a sense of control, of being in charge.

The operating assumption is that a man, especially a real man, knows what other men know – the code of the streets. And if one is not a real man, one is somehow diminished as a person, and there are certain valued things one simply does not deserve. There is thus believed to be a certain justice to the code, since it is presumed that everyone has the opportunity to know it. Implicit in this presumption is the belief that everybody is held responsible for being familiar with the code. If the victim of a mugging, for example, does not know the code and so responds "wrong," the perpetrator may feel justified even in killing him and may feel no remorse. He may think, "Too bad, but it's his fault. He should have known better." At the same time, it is assumed that, if attacked, a victim is entitled to retribution and may feel no compunction about retaliating even with deadly force. According to one youth who tries to avoid such encounters:

> They ain't got no conscience. They ain't got no kind of conscience. Like, say, what happens if you punch me, and I'm a devious person, and I'm mad and I see you again on the street and I got a gun. I'll shoot you and I won't have no kind of conscience because I shot you 'cause I'm payin' back for what you done did to me.

So when a boy or man ventures outside, he must adopt the code – a kind of shield, really – to prevent others from messing with him. In these circumstances, it is easy for people to think they are being tried or tested by others even when this is not the case. In such a climate, it is sensed that something extremely valuable is at stake in every interaction, and people are thus encouraged to rise to the occasion, particularly with strangers. For people who are unfamiliar with the code – generally people who live outside the inner city – the concern with respect in the most ordinary interactions can be frightening and incomprehensible. But for those who are invested in the code, the clear object of their demeanor is to discourage strangers from even thinking about challenging them or testing their manhood. And the sense of power that attends the ability to deter others can be alluring even to those who know the code without being heavily invested in it – the decent inner-city youths. Thus, a boy who has been leading a basically decent life can, in trying circumstances, suddenly resort to deadly force.

Central to the issue of manhood is the widespread belief that one of the most effective ways of gaining respect is to manifest "nerve." Nerve is shown when someone takes a person's possessions (the more valuable, the better), messes with someone's woman, throws the first punch, gets in someone's face, or pulls a trigger. Its proper display helps on the spot to check others who would violate one's person and also helps to build a reputation that works to prevent future challenges. But since such a show of nerve is a forceful expression of disrespect toward the person on the receiving end, the victim may be greatly offended and seek to retaliate with equal if not greater force. A display of nerve, therefore, can easily provoke a life-threatening response, and the background knowledge of that possibility has often been incorporated into the concept of nerve.

True nerve exposes a lack of fear of dying. Many feel that it is acceptable to risk dying over the principle of respect. In fact, among the hard-core street-oriented, the clear risk of violent death may be preferable to being dissed by another. The youths who have internalized this attitude and convincingly display it in their public bearing are among the most threatening people of all, for it is commonly assumed that they fear no man. As the people of the community say, "They are the baddest dudes on the street." They often lead an existential life that may acquire meaning only when faced with the possibility of imminent death. Not to be afraid to die is by implication to have few compunctions about taking somebody else's life. Not to be afraid to die is the quid pro quo of being able to take somebody else's life – for the right reasons, if the situation demands it. When others believe this is one's position, it gives one a real sense of power on the streets. Such credibility is what many inner-city youths strive to achieve, whether they are decent or street-oriented, both because of its practical defensive value and because of the positive way it makes them feel about themselves. The difference between the decent and the street-oriented youth is that the decent youth makes a conscious decision to appear tough and manly; in another setting – with teachers, say, or at his part-time job – he can be polite and deferential. The street-oriented youth, on the other hand, has made the concept of manhood a part of his very identity; he has difficulty manipulating it – it often controls him instead.

Girls and Boys

Increasingly, teenage girls are mimicking the males and trying to have their own version of "manhood." Their goal is the same – to get respect, to be recognized as capable of setting or maintaining a certain standard. They try to achieve this end in the ways that have been established by the males, including posturing, abusive language, and the use of violence to resolve disputes; but the issues for the girls are different. Although conflicts over turf and status exist among the girls, the majority of disputes seem rooted in assessments of beauty (which girl in a group is the cutest?), competition over boyfriends, and the attempts to regulate other people's knowledge of and opinions about a girl's behavior or that of someone close to her, especially her mother.

A major cause of conflicts among girls is "he say, she say." This practice begins in the early school years and continues through high school. It occurs when "people," particularly girls, talk about others, thus putting their "business in the streets." Usually, one girl will say something negative about another in the group, most often behind the person's back. The remarks will then get back to the person talked about. She may retaliate or her friends may feel required to "take up for" her. In essence, this is a form of group gossiping in which individuals are negatively assessed and evaluated. As with much gossip, the things said may or may not be true, but the point is that such imputations can cast aspersions on a person's good name. The accused is required to defend herself against the slander, which can result in arguments and fights, often over little of real substance. Here again is the problem of low self-esteem, which encourages youngsters to be highly sensitive to slights and to be vulnerable to feeling easily dissed. To avenge the dissing, a fight is usually necessary.

Because boys are believed to control violence, girls tend to defer to them in situations of conflict. Often, if a girl is attacked or feels slighted, she will get a brother, uncle, or cousin to do her fighting for her. Increasingly, however, girls are doing their own fighting and are even asking their male relatives to teach them how to fight. Some girls form groups that attack other girls or take things from them. A hard-core segment of inner-city girls inclined to violence seems to be developing. As one thirteen-year-old girl in a detention center for youths who have committed violent acts told me, "To get people to leave you alone, you gotta fight. Talking don't always get you out of stuff." One major difference between girls and boys is that girls rarely use guns. Their fights are therefore not life-or-death struggles. Girls are not often willing to put their lives on the line for their version of manhood. The ultimate form of respect on the male-dominated inner-city streets is thus reserved for men.

"Going for Bad"

In the most fearsome youths, such a cavalier attitude toward death grows out of a very limited view of life. Many are uncertain about how long they are going to live and believe they could die violently at any time. They accept this fate; they live on the edge. Their manner conveys the message that nothing intimidates them; whatever turn the encounter takes, they maintain their attack – rather like a pit bull, whose spirit many such boys admire. The demonstration of such tenacity shows "heart" and earns their respect.

This fearlessness has implications for law enforcement. Many street-oriented boys are much more concerned about the threat of "justice" at the hands of a peer than at the hands of the police. According to one young man trying to lead a decent life, "When they shoot somebody, they have so much confidence that they gonna get away from the cop, you see. If they don't, then they be all mad and sad and cryin' and all that 'cause they got time in jail." At the same time, however, many feel not only that they have little to lose by going to prison but that they have something to gain. The toughening-up one experiences in prison can actually enhance one's reputation on the streets. Hence, the system loses influence over the hard core who are without jobs and who have little perceptible stake in the system. If mainstream society has done nothing *for* them, they counter by making sure it can likewise do nothing *to* them.

At the same time, however, a competing view maintains that true nerve consists in backing down, walking away from a fight, and going on with one's business. One fights only in self-defense. This view emerges from the decent philosophy that life is precious, and it is an important part of the socialization process common in decent homes. A strategy strongly associated with hope, it discourages violence as the primary means of resolving disputes and encourages youngsters to accept nonviolence and talk as confrontational strategies. But if "the deal goes down," self-defense is greatly encouraged. When there is enough positive support for this orientation, either in the home or among one's peers, then nonviolence has a chance to prevail. But it prevails at the cost of relinquishing a claim to being bad and tough, and it therefore sets a young person up as at the very least alienated from street-oriented peers and quite possibly a target of derision or even violence.

Although the nonviolent orientation rarely overcomes the impulse to strike back in an encounter, it does introduce a certain confusion and so can prompt a measure of soul-searching – or even profound ambivalence. Did the person back down with his or her respect intact or did he or she back down only to be judged a "punk" – a person lacking manhood? Should he or she have acted? Should he or she have hit the other person in the mouth? These questions beset many young men and women during public confrontations. What is the right thing to do? In the quest for honor, respect, and local status – which few young people are uninterested in – common sense most often prevails, thus leading many to opt for the tough approach, in which they enact their own particular versions of the display of nerve. The presentation of oneself as rough and tough is very often quite acceptable until one is tested. And then that presentation may help individuals pass the test, because it will cause fewer questions to be asked about what they did and why. It is hard for people to explain why they lost the fight or why they backed down. Hence many will strive to appear to go for bad, while hoping they will never be tested. But when they are tested, the outcome of the situation may quickly be out of their hands, as they become wrapped up in the circumstances of the moment.

Conclusion

The attitudes of the wider society are deeply implicated in the code of the streets. Most people in inner-city communities are not totally invested in the code; but the significant minority of hard-core street youths who do embrace it have to maintain the code in order to establish reputations, because they have – or feel they have – few other ways to assert themselves. For these young people, the standards of the street code are the only game in town. The extent to which some children – particularly those who through upbringing have become most alienated and lack strong and conventional social support – experience, feel, and internalize racist rejection and contempt from mainstream society may strongly encourage them to express contempt for the more conventional society in turn. In dealing with this contempt and rejection, some youngsters will consciously invest themselves and their considerable mental resources in what amounts to an oppositional culture to preserve themselves and their self-respect. Once they do this, any respect they might be able to garner in the wider system pales in comparison with the respect available in the local system; thus, they often loss interest in even attempting to negotiate the mainstream system.

At the same time, many less-alienated young blacks have assumed a street-oriented demeanor as a way of expressing their blackness while really embracing a much more moderate way of life; they, too, want a nonviolent setting in which to live and raise a family. These decent people are trying hard to be a part of the mainstream culture, but the racism – both real and perceived – that they encounter helps to legitimate the oppositional culture; and so, on occasion, they adopt street behavior. In fact, depending on the demands of the situation, many people in the community slip back and forth between decent and street behavior.

A vicious cycle has thus been formed. The hopelessness and alienation that many young inner-city black men and women feel, largely because of endemic joblessness and persistent racism, fuel the violence they engage in. This violence serves to confirm the negative feelings many whites and some middle-class blacks harbor toward the ghetto poor, further legitimating the oppositional culture and the code of the streets in the eyes of many poor young blacks. Unless this cycle is broken, attitudes on both sides will become increasingly entrenched, and the violence – which claims victims black and white, poor and affluent – will only escalate.

R E F E R E N C E S

Anderson, E. (1978). *A place on the corner.* Chicago: University of Chicago Press.
    (1989). Sex codes and family life among poor inner-city youths. In *The ghetto underclass: Social science perspectives,* ed. William Julius Wilson. Special edition of *The Annals of the American Academy of Political and Social Science* 501, 59–78.
    (1990). *Streetwise: Race, class, and change in an urban community.* Chicago: University of Chicago Press.
    (1991). Neighborhood effects on teenage pregnancy. In C. Jencks & P.E. Peterson (Eds.), *The urban underclass.* Washington, D.C.: Brookings Institution, pp. 375–98.
Becker, H. (1970). *Sociological work.* Chicago: Aldine.
Drake, S. C., & Cayton, H. (1962). *Black metropolis.* New York: Harper & Row.
Glaser, B. G., & Strauss, A. L. (1972). *Status passage.* Chicago: Aldine.
Katz, J. (1988). *Seductions of crime: Moral and sensual attractions in doing evil.* New York: Basic Books.
Wolfgang, M. E., & Ferracuti, F. (1967). *The subculture of violence.* London: Tavistock.

A D D I T I O N A L   S O U R C E S

Block, F., et al. (1987). *The mean season: The attack on the welfare state.* New York: Pantheon.
Cloward, R. A., & Ohlin, L. (1960). *Delinquency and opportunity: A theory of delinquent gangs.* Glencoe, IL: Free Press.
Coleman, J. (1988). Social capital in the creation of human capital. *American Journal of Sociology* 94: S95–S120.
Katz, M. B. (1989). *The undeserving poor: From the war on poverty to the war on welfare.* New York: Pantheon.
Kirschenman, J., & Neckerman, K. (1991). "We'd love to hire them, but . . .": The Meaning of Race for Employers." In C. Jencks & P. E. Peterson (Eds.), *The urban underclass.* Washington, D.C.: Brookings Institution.
Merton, R. (1957). Social structure and anomie. In *Social theory and social structure.* Glencoe, IL: Free Press.
Short, J. F., Jr., & Strodtbeck, F. L. (1965). *Group processes and gang delinquency.* Chicago: University of Chicago Press.
Simmel, G. (1971). In D. N. Levine (Ed.), *George Simmel on individuality and social forms.* Chicago: University of Chicago Press.
Wacquant, L. J. D., & Wilson, W. J. (1989) The cost of racial and class exclusion in the inner city. In W. J. Wilson (Ed.), *The ghetto underclass.* Special edition of *The Annals of the American Academy of Political and Social Science* 501: 8–25.

Wilson, W. J. (1987). *The truly disadvantaged*. Chicago: University of Chicago.
    (1989). The underclass: Issues, perspectives, and public policy. In W. J.
    Wilson (Ed.), *The ghetto underclass*. Special edition of *The Annals of the
    American Academy of Political and Social Science* 501: 183–92.

The Embeddedness of Child and Adolescent Development:

A COMMUNITY-LEVEL PERSPECTIVE ON URBAN VIOLENCE*

ROBERT J. SAMPSON

I. Approaches to Understanding Violence

Two strategies dominate the study of crime and violence. The macrosocial or *community* level of explanation asks what it is about the nature of communities that yields differential rates of crime and its control (Short, 1985). Hence the goal of macrosocial research is not to explain individual involvement in criminal behavior but to identify characteristics of communities, cities, or even societies that lead to high rates of crime. Following the lead of Shaw and McKay's (1942) seminal research in Chicago earlier this century, a host of studies have examined the community-level relationship between crime rates and factors such as low economic status, ethnic heterogeneity, residential mobility, population density, and divorce rates (for detailed reviews, see Byrne & Sampson, 1986; Bursik & Grasmick, 1993; Sampson & Lauritsen, 1994). In this research tradition, the ecological fallacy of inferring individual-level relations based on aggregate data is not at issue because the unit of explanation and analysis is the community itself.

By contrast, the more common research strategy seeks to distinguish delinquents from nondelinquents. Influenced by the hegemony of survey research in the social sciences since the 1960s (especially the predominance of self-report surveys), researchers on delinquency and violence have focused primarily on the *individual* level of analysis. For example, a large body of research has examined how factors such as broken homes, parental supervision, erratic discipline, and school attachment are related to an

*Direct all correspondence to: Robert J. Sampson, Department of Sociology, The University of Chicago, 1126 E. 59th St., Chicago, IL 60637. I would like to thank Joan McCord, Joel Wallman, and the other contributors to *Violence and Childhood in the Inner City* for helpful comments on an earlier draft.

31

adolescent's involvement in delinquency (for overviews, see Rutter & Giller, 1983; Loeber & Stouthamer-Loeber, 1986; Gottfredson & Hirschi, 1990). This research tradition has generated an impressive array of consistent individual-level predictors of delinquent and violent behavior.

Recent years have witnessed a challenge to this bifurcated strategy in the form of calls for research that integrates the individual and community levels of analysis (see, e.g., Reiss, 1986a; Farrington, Sampson, & Wikström, 1993), calls that mirror the micro–macro debate in the discipline of sociology. This challenge stems from the recognition that the two levels of analysis are not incompatible – both individual and community factors loom large in the explanation of crime and violence (Reiss, 1986a; Sampson & Lauritsen, 1994). Of course, recognizing the need for multilevel research and implementing it are two different things. Methodological and theoretical disputes abound, and few studies have successfully demonstrated a unified approach to the individual and community-level dimensions of crime.

In this chapter, I attempt to fill this gap by advancing a contextual perspective on families, informal social control, and delinquency in the inner-city context. Drawing largely on social disorganization theory and linking it with the concept of social capital, I focus on the embeddedness of families and children in the social context of local communities. A major thesis of the paper is that community structure matters because of its role in facilitating or inhibiting the creation of social capital among families and children. In particular, I review evidence that family management practices – especially the monitoring and supervision of youth – are closely intertwined with networks of community social organization. This framework leads to a renewed focus on children and their early life-course – but without the "de-contextualization" common to much research on child and adolescent development. Indeed, the theme I pursue is the importance of bringing a structural or community-level perspective to bear on the lives of children.

This contextual approach is also used to extend a theoretical strategy to the subject, one that incorporates both structural and cultural arguments regarding race, violence, and inequality in American cities. In contrast to psychologically-based theories about frustration leading to aggression and subcultural theories that posit values prescribing violence, the current approach views the relationship between race and criminal violence through a contextual lens that highlights the very different ecological contexts within which black and white children are raised – and it does so regardless of individual and family characteristics. By expanding traditional arguments that focus on individuals and families to a more contextual framework on the social organization of inner-city neighborhoods, I attempt to forge a multilevel, integrative approach to understanding the social sources of urban violence in America.

These goals are accomplished in the following manner. Section II begins by explicating a social-disorganization approach to research and then using it to examine the structural factors underlying community-level variations in violent crime. This section includes a review not only of the demographic and structural correlates (e.g., poverty and mobility) emphasized in previous research but also the social organizational factors (e.g., informal social control and acquaintanceship networks). Section III examines the differential cultural contexts that characterize communities (e.g., social isolation), especially as they foster conduct norms conducive to violence. Section IV turns to research motivating an explicit focus on children – in particular on how community-level factors impinge on key aspects of child development (e.g., health care, maltreatment, and cognitive achievement). Section V then describes a theoretical strategy for linking the study of families, children, and community through the concept of social capital. In Section VI, I apply this strategy and address the connection between race and interpersonal violence from a contextual rather than an individualistic framework. I conclude in Section VII by summarizing the implications of using a community-level framework to explain crime in the inner city, including recent increases in urban violence.[1]

II. Community Social Disorganization: Structural Components

Steeped in the Chicago school tradition of urban sociology pioneered by Park, Burgess, and McKenzie (1925), Clifford Shaw and Henry McKay spearheaded the community-level approach to studies of ecology and crime. In their classic work, *Juvenile Delinquency and Urban Areas*, Shaw and McKay (1942; 1969) argued that three structural factors – low economic status, ethnic heterogeneity, and residential mobility – led to the disruption of community social organization, which in turn accounted for variations in crime and delinquency rates (for more details, see Short, 1963; Kornhauser, 1978). As recently extended by Kornhauser (1978), Bursik (1988), and Sampson and Groves (1989), the concept *social disorganization*

---

[1] My review of the literature and theoretical conceptualization borrows from previously published works, especially Sampson (1992; 1993), Sampson and Lauritsen (1994), and Sampson and Wilson (1995).

may be defined as the inability of a community structure to realize the common values of its residents and maintain effective social controls. The structural dimensions of community social organization include both the prevalence and interdependence of social networks in a community and the span of collective supervision that the community directs toward local problems. Social organization is a function of both informal networks (e.g., the density of local acquaintanceship, intergenerational ties, and mutual guardianship) and formal institutions (e.g., organizational density and social participation as well as institutional stability).

This social organizational approach is grounded in what Kasarda and Janowitz (1974: 329) call the *systemic* model, one in which the local community is viewed as a complex system of both friendship and kinship networks on the one hand and formal and informal associational ties rooted in family life and ongoing socialization processes on the other (for further elaboration, see Sampson, 1991). From this view, both social organization and social disorganization are inextricably tied to systemic networks that facilitate or inhibit social control.[2] When formulated in this way, social disorganization is analytically separable not only from the processes that may lead to it (e.g., poverty and residential mobility) but also from the degree of criminal behavior that may be a result (Bursik, 1988). This conceptualization also goes beyond the traditional account of community as a strictly geographical phenomenon by focusing on the social networks of local residents (Leighton, 1988).

Both Bursik (1988) and Sampson and Groves (1989) have explicated the structural dimensions of community social organization that bear on adolescence and the control of delinquency. Salient among these factors

---

[2] The systemic conceptualization of community addresses the early criticism that Shaw and McKay overemphasized disorganization and dysfunction. In *Street Corner Society*, W. F. Whyte (1943) argued that what looks like social disorganization from the outside is actually an intricate internal organization. Noting the relative nature of organization, he maintained that the real problem of "Cornerville" was simply that its social organization failed to mesh with the structure of the society around it. However, it is still possible for informal social controls with respect to delinquency to be weak even when certain forms of internal social organization seem to be present (e.g., political rackets, street-corner groups). The theory of social disorganization focuses primarily on what Bursik and Grasmick (1993) refer to as the public and parochial forms of social control. For example, a neighborhood may have *differential social organization* relative to the wider society (e.g., deviant peer networks) but still lack the capacity to exert informal social controls over youth in public spaces.

are local friendship ties, the density of acquaintanceship, organizational density, and local participation in formal and voluntary organizations. One of the most important constructs, however, is the ability of a community to supervise and control teenage peer groups – especially gangs. As discovered originally by Thrasher (1963: 25), the origins of many gangs can be traced to unsupervised, spontaneous play groups. Even nongang delinquency tends to be a group phenomenon (for a review, see Reiss, 1986b), suggesting that the capacity of the community to control group-level dynamics is a key theoretical mechanism linking community characteristics with crime. As Shaw and McKay (1969) argued, residents of cohesive communities are better able to control the teenage behaviors that are the setting for group-related crime (see also Short, 1963: xxiv). Examples of informal social controls include supervision of leisure-time youth activities, intervention in street-corner congregations (Maccoby, Johnson, & Church, 1958; Thrasher, 1963: 339; Shaw & McKay, 1969: 176–85), and challenging teenagers "who seem to be up to no good" (Taylor, Gottfredson, & Brower, 1984: 326; Skogan, 1986: 217).

Prior research largely supports the core hypothesis of Shaw and McKay (1942) that the structural factors of poverty and residential instability explain variations in crime and delinquency rates (for detailed reviews, see Bursik & Grasmick, 1993; Sampson & Lauritsen, 1994).[3] In addition, recent research has established that crime rates are positively linked to community-level variations in population and housing density, percent single-parent households, and rates of community change (for reviews, see Byrne & Sampson, 1986; Reiss, 1986a; Bursik, 1988). As hypothesized in

---

[3] Following the lead of Shaw and McKay's (1942) original research and using operational units of analysis at the *intra*-urban level, I focus in this chapter primarily on studies that make inferences about neighborhoods and other local community areas. Within most cities one can identify *local community areas* that have reasonable ecological integrity. Although containing fairly large populations (e.g., 10,000–75,000 people), these areas often have well-known names and borders such as freeways, parks, and major streets. For example, Chicago has 77 local community areas averaging about 37,000 persons that were designed to correspond to socially meaningful and natural geographic boundaries. *Census tracts* refer to smaller and more socially homogeneous areas of 3,000–5,000 people on average. Although administratively defined, census tract boundaries are usually drawn to take into account major streets, parks, and other geographical features. A third and even smaller area approximating the lay person's concept of neighborhood is the *block group* – a set of blocks averaging approximately 1,000 residents. Although local community areas, census tracts, and block groups are

Sampson and Groves (1989), family disruption, urbanization, and the anonymity accompanying rapid population change all undercut the capacity of a community to exercise informal social control, especially of teenage peer groups in public spaces (e.g., streets, parks, and play areas).

There is less support for Shaw and McKay's (1942) ethnic heterogeneity thesis. Although some research dating from the 1950s does seem to confirm the pattern of lower delinquency rates in ethnically homogeneous areas (see, e.g., Lander, 1954), more recent studies show that rates of violence in particular are positively related in a linear fashion to percent black in the population (for a review, see Sampson & Lauritsen, 1994). Times have changed with respect to patterns of immigration and racial segregation since Shaw and McKay were studying the city, a point to which I will return.

Although it is difficult to study the *intervening* mechanisms of social disorganization, a new generation of research has emerged in the last decade that attempts to measure directly the theory's structural dimensions. First, Taylor et al. (1984) examined variations in violent crime (e.g., mugging, assault, murder, and rape) across 63 street blocks in Baltimore in 1978. Based on interviews with 687 household respondents, Taylor et al. (1984: 316) constructed block-level measures of both the proportion of respondents who belonged to an organization to which co-residents also belonged and the proportion of respondents who felt responsible for what happened in the area surrounding their homes. Both dimensions of informal social control were significantly and negatively related to rates of violence, exclusive of other ecological factors (Taylor et al., 1984: 320). These results support the social-disorganization hypothesis that organizational participation by local residents and informal social control of public space are inversely related to rates of criminal violence in urban areas.

Second, Simcha-Fagan and Schwartz (1986) collected rich survey-based information on 553 residents of 12 different neighborhoods in New York City. Although the number of neighborhoods was small, they found a significant negative relationship between the rate of self-reported delinquency and rates of organizational participation by local residents. A

imperfect operational definitions of *neighborhood* or *local community* in empirical research, such areas generally possess more ecological integrity (e.g., natural boundaries and social homogeneity) than cities or metropolitan areas, and they are more closely linked to the mechanisms assumed by social disorganization theory to underlie the etiology of crime (Bursik & Grasmick, 1993).

limited multivariate analysis provided further support for this pattern – "level of organizational participation and residential stability have unique effects in predicting survey-reported delinquency" (Simcha-Fagan & Schwartz, 1986: 683).

Third, Sampson and Groves (1989) analyzed the British Crime Survey (BCS), a nationwide survey of England and Wales conducted in 1982 and 1984. Sampling procedures resulted in the proportionate selection of 60 addresses within each of over 200 local communities in Great Britain. After aggregating survey-based measures at the community level, Sampson and Groves (1989: 789) reported that the prevalence of unsupervised peer groups in a community had the largest overall relationship with rates of victimization by mugging/street robbery and stranger-violence in 1982. Local friendship networks (percent of friends in the neighborhood) had a significant negative effect on robbery, whereas rates of organizational participation had significant inverse effects on both robbery and stranger violence (1989: 789). Moreover, the largest overall effect on offender-based rates of personal violence was unsupervised peer groups (1989: 793). Unsupervised peer groups had similar positive effects on robbery and assault in the 1984 BCS, whereas local friendship networks again had significant inverse effects (1989: 798). Variations in these structural dimensions of community social disorganization were also shown to mediate in large part the effects of community socioeconomic status, residential mobility, ethnic heterogeneity, and family disruption in a manner consistent with social disorganization theory. Namely, mobility had significant inverse effects on friendship networks, family disruption was the largest predictor of the prevalence of unsupervised peer groups, and socioeconomic status had the largest (positive) effect on organizational participation.

Fourth, Elliott et al. (1996) examine survey data collected in 1990 from neighborhoods in Chicago and Denver. The Chicago site is based on data collected from approximately 500 black, predominantly poor families living in more than 50 Chicago census tracts in 1990, whereas the Denver site is based on data from over 1,500 youth living in over 30 block groups. A multilevel analysis revealed that a measure of informal control was significantly and negatively related to adolescent problem behavior in both sites. Control also mediated the prior effects of neighborhood structural disadvantage – declining poor neighborhoods displayed less ability to maintain social control, and in turn suffered higher delinquency rates.

Taken together, the research of Taylor et al. (1984), Simcha-Fagan and Schwartz (1986), Sampson and Groves (1989), and Elliott et al. (1996) supports the notion that communities characterized by (a) anonymity and sparse acquaintanceship networks among residents, (b) unsupervised teenage peer groups and attenuated control of public space, and (c) a weak organizational base and low social participation in local activities face an increased risk of crime and violence. Along with the results of research on gang delinquency that point to the salience of informal and formal community structures in controlling the formation of youth gangs (Thrasher, 1963; Short & Strodtbeck, 1965; Sullivan, 1989), the data suggest that the structural elements of social disorganization have relevance for explaining macrolevel variations in urban violence.

III. Social Disorganization and Community Culture

Although social disorganization theory is primarily structural in nature, it does address how the ecological segregation of communities gives rise to patterns of differential *cultural* organization. For example, an important assertion of Shaw and McKay (1942) was that disorganized communities spawned delinquent gangs with their own subcultures and norms perpetuated through cultural transmission. Extending and reshaping this idea, Kornhauser (1978: 75) argued that poverty, ethnic heterogeneity, mobility, and the accompanying structural features of social disorganization (e.g., anonymity and mutual distrust) impede communication and obstruct the quest for common values, thereby fostering cultural diversity with respect to nondelinquent values. From her viewpoint, the attenuation of societal values caused by structural disorganization leads to a state of cultural disorganization.

A rich tradition of ethnographic studies generally supports the notion that structurally disorganized communities are conducive to the emergence of age-graded subcultures that foster a sense of tolerance for crime and deviance. For example, Suttles' (1968) account of the social order of a Chicago neighborhood characterized by poverty and heterogeneity is consistent with Thrasher's (1963) emphasis on age, sex, ethnicity, and territory as markers for the ordered segmentation of slum culture. Suttles found that single-sex, age-graded primary groups of the same ethnicity and territory emerged in response to threats of conflict, communitywide disorder, and mistrust. Although the community subcultures Suttles (1968) discovered were provincial, tentative, and incomplete (Kornhauser, 1978: 18), they still tended to undermine mainstream societal values.

Anderson's (1978) ethnography of a bar in Chicago's Southside black ghetto shows how primary values coexisted alongside residual values associated with deviant subcultures (e.g., hoodlums) such as "toughness," "getting big money," "going for bad," and "having fun" (1978: 129–30, 152–8). According to Anderson, lower-class residents do not so much "stretch" mainstream values as "create their own particular standards of social conduct along variant lines open to them" (1978: 210). In this context, the use of violence is not valued as a primary goal, but it is expected and tolerated as a fact of life (1978: 134).

Anderson's recent research (1990; this volume) elaborates this idea further by suggesting that a "code of the streets" is more likely to emerge in the inner-city context. As he argues,

> [S]ince aggression at the hands of others, associates as well as strangers, is a central concern of public life [in the inner city], solutions for dealing with such situations have evolved into the tenets of a code of violence – a way of life replete with common and shared informal rules and understandings, a set of prescriptions and proscriptions of engagement for those who would effectively manage themselves in their everyday relations with others (personal communication).

Much like Rainwater (1970), Suttles (1968), and Horowitz (1987) before him, Anderson's research suggests that in certain community contexts, the wider cultural values are simply not relevant – they become "unviable."

Ethnographic evidence such as Anderson's notwithstanding, community subcultures have been criticized as reifications or mere "shadow cultures" (see especially Liebow, 1967). Moreover, a substantial body of survey research has failed to uncover the existence of cultural values that prescribe crime and violence (see Kornhauser, 1978: 214–16; Bursik, 1988). As Shaw and McKay (1942) argued, while the tradition of delinquency and crime is a powerful force in certain communities, it is only a part of the community's system of values. In fact, they write, "the dominant tradition in every community is conventional, even in those having the highest rate of delinquents" (Shaw & McKay, 1942: 180). Quantitative research – especially that which is survey-based – thus seems to contradict the idea of a differential system of deviant values.

What, then, do we make of ethnographies that point to the salience of age-graded subcultures and codes of violence in the inner city? One answer is that both streams of research evidence – ethnographic and survey-based – are compatible so long as we emphasize the *situational* and *contextual* basis of value attenuation rather than an autonomous culture that positively values violence at all times and places. That is, even though conventional norms may be pervasive in any community, it is still the case that tolerance of deviance, a cultural emphasis on toughness and bravado in the face of danger, and an overt readiness to use violence vary across structural and situational contexts. In this regard, community contexts shape "cognitive landscapes" (Sampson, 1992) or an ecologically structured "code of the streets" (Anderson, this volume) that produce appropriate standards and expectations of conduct. In socially disorganized communities, conventionality clashes with a street culture where crime, disorder, and drug use are expected and serve as a symbolic embodiment of the precariousness of everyday life (Anderson, this volume). These ecologically structured and situationally specific perceptions in turn appear to influence the probability of violent outcomes (e.g., fighting among adolescent males).

This interpretation may help to explain the lack of support shown for subcultural values in national surveys. The latter reflect standardized research designs that are often insensitive to contextual and situational variations (for a similar argument, see Sullivan, 1989). The limited evidence available suggests that when survey research designs are disaggregated and contextualized, systematic variations in subcultural orientation do emerge. In particular, the Simcha-Fagan and Schwartz (1986) study of 12 New York City neighborhoods described earlier showed that a survey-based indicator of community disorder/subculture was directly related to rates of both self-reported and official delinquency. Subcultures thus seem to vary not with broad social categories such as income and race/ethnicity but rather with highly contextualized and ecologically specific settings.

Social Isolation

A renewed appreciation for the contextual role of cultural adaptations is congruent with the notion of *social isolation* – defined as the lack of contact or of sustained interaction with individuals and institutions that represent mainstream society (Wilson, 1987: 60; 1991). According to this line of reasoning, the social isolation fostered by the ecological concentration of urban poverty not only deprives residents of resources and conventional role models, but it also prevents cultural learning by isolating them from mainstream social networks that facilitate social and economic advancement in modern industrial society (Sampson & Wilson, 1995). Social isolation is specifically distinguished from the culture of poverty by virtue of its focus on adaptations to constraints and opportunities rather than to the psychological internalization of norms.

As Hannerz (1969) noted in *Soulside*, it is thus possible to recognize the importance of macrostructural constraints – hence avoiding the extreme notions of the culture of poverty or the culture of violence – and yet see the "merits of a more subtle kind of cultural analysis" (1969: 182). Wilson hypothesizes a difference, for example,

> between a jobless family whose mobility is impeded by the macrostructural constraints in the economy and the larger society but nonetheless lives in an area with a relatively low rate of poverty, and on the other hand, a jobless family that lives in an inner-city ghetto neighborhood that is not only influenced by these same constraints but also by the behavior of other jobless families in the neighborhood (1991: 10).

The latter influence stems from culture – the extent to which individuals follow their inclinations as they have been developed by learning or by association with other members of the community (Hannerz, 1969: 184; Wilson, 1991: 10).

Practices such as an overt emphasis on sexuality and macho values, idleness, and public drinking are denounced by the majority of those who reside in inner-city ghetto neighborhoods. However, because such practices occur more frequently there than in middle-class society, due in major part to the social organizational forces delineated above, the transmission of these modes of behavior is more easily facilitated (Sampson & Wilson, 1995). In particular, youth are more likely to see violence as a way of life in inner-city ghetto neighborhoods – they are more likely to witness violent acts and have role models who do not adequately control their own violent impulses or restrain their own anger. Given the availability of and easy access to firearms, knives, and other weapons, adolescents can experiment with violent behavior – often with deadly consequences (Prothrow-Stith, 1991; Sampson & Wilson, 1995). The concept of social isolation captures this process by implying that contact between groups of different class and racial backgrounds is either lacking or has become increasingly intermittent – and that the nature of this contact enhances effects of living in concentrated poverty.

Social isolation and the attenuation of mainstream cultural values also combine to heighten the collective "anomie" (Merton, 1938; 1964) in ghetto areas of our major cities. *Anomie* refers to the presence of contradictory norms and the collective sense that moral order is too weak to warrant trusting other people (see also Kapsis, 1978: 1140). Anomie is a macrolevel concept that has a parallel at the individual level in the form of estrangement and alienation. Still, the cohesion of the community's social order is not merely the aggregation of individual properties. For example, the individual-level experience of alienation and isolation is conceptually distinct from community-level variations in moral or social integration. As Merton has argued, "the degree of anomie in a social system is indicated by the extent to which there is a lack of consensus on norms judged to be legitimate, with its attendant uncertainty and insecurity in social relations" (1964: 227). This uncertainty and mistrust erects a barrier between fellow residents and hence renders the collective body less able to organize itself against predatory crime.

In short, cultural influences in social disorganization theory stem from processes by which cognitive landscapes rooted in the dynamics of urban social ecology influence behavioral expectations. Community and situational contexts characterized by social disorganization and cultural isolation attenuate the existential relevance of mainstream values, and this process in turn facilitates diversity of values and a collective state of anomie and mistrust. These conditions provide fertile soil for the emergence of deviant patterns of behavior that the community cannot effectively resist and that in time become rationalized. For these reasons, the evidence suggests a renewed appreciation among researchers for the ecology of culture of the *cultural structure* of a community, one that is opposed to the seemingly noncontextual culture implied by the subculture of violence.[4]

IV. Bringing Children Back In

As reviewed to this point, extant research on the ecology of crime has focused largely on structural and cultural factors thought to influence adolescents and young adults. This is not surprising – a voluminous body of research shows that age-specific rates of property and violent crime peak in the late teenage and early adult years (see Sampson & Laub, 1992).

Nevertheless, two empirical facts suggest that we need to bring children back into explanations of communities and crime. The first fact, discovered by Shaw and McKay in the 1920s, is that communities characterized by high rates of crime and delinquency are also plagued by high rates of

---

[4] The basic tenet of the subculture of violence theory is that the overt use of violence "is generally viewed as a reflection of basic values that stand apart from the dominant, central, or parent culture" (Wolfgang & Ferracuti, 1967: 385). However, neither the theory of lower-class culture nor that of the subculture of violence refers explicitly to community-level processes of the sort explicated herein. In point of fact, Wolfgang and Ferracuti (1967) are rather silent on the origins of subcultures.

infant mortality, low birth weight, tuberculosis, physical abuse, and other factors detrimental to child development. Shaw and McKay thus argued that delinquency "is not an isolated phenomenon" (1969: 106) and went on to document the close association of delinquency rates with a host of social problems that directly influence children. The relationship between delinquency and social problems documented by this general empirical finding has remained remarkably stable over time. For example, Wallace and Wallace (1990) present evidence that rates of violent death across communities in New York City covary with rates of low birth weight and infant mortality. Clearly, there is a connection between the healthful development of young children and community structure.

The second motivation for linking communities, families, and early child development comes from research showing the early onset of delinquency and its relative stability over the life-course (Robins, 1966; Glueck & Glueck, 1968; Olweus, 1979; Loeber, 1982; Huesmann, Eron, & Lefkowitz, 1984). For example, Olweus's (1979) review of over 16 studies on aggressive behavior revealed "substantial" stability – the correlation between early aggressive behavior and later criminality averaged .68 for the studies reviewed (1979: 854–5). Loeber (1982: 1433) completed a similar review of the delinquency literature and concluded that the data favor the stability hypothesis. The linkage between childhood misbehavior and adult outcomes is also found across life domains that go well beyond the legal concept of crime. For instance, a specific behavior in childhood might not predict exactly the same behavior in later adulthood but may still be associated with outcomes that are conceptually consistent with that earlier behavior. Although not always criminal *per se,* adult behaviors falling into this category include excessive drinking, traffic violations, marital conflict, and the harsh disciplining of children (Huesmann et al., 1984; Robins, 1966). Findings of moderate-to-strong continuity are thus supported by a rich body of empirical research that spans several decades.

These two sets of facts underscore the need to bring children back into the criminological picture. Not only does much delinquency emerge early in the life-course and remain relatively stable over time; there is also an empirical connection between the health- and development-related problems of children and rates of adult crime. Although not fully appreciated in the social science literature, these facts about early childhood are no accident from the viewpoint of social disorganization theory. Rather, community structure and the mediating processes of community social organization appear to influence variations in prenatal care, child health services, and general child development. This section therefore builds upon and extends a recent social-disorganization theory explicating the contextual influences of community structure on these and other developmental pathways – and their repercussions for later crime and violence (see Sampson, 1992).

Child Development, Health Care, and Community

One of the most visible indicators of child health problems is the dramatic variation among communities in rates of infant mortality and low birth-weight babies. Within New York City, rates of infant mortality range from a low of 6.6 per 1,000 live births in some health districts to as high as 43.5 in others (Lash, Signal, & Dudzinski, 1980: 176, 200). Wallace and Wallace (1990) and Coulton and Pandey (1992) document similar variations in other communities. Although the causes of this variation are obviously complex, one pattern does stand out in the research – controlling for individual-level correlates of health care utilization (e.g., education), we find that infant mortality and low birth weight vary with the availability and quality of prenatal care. For example, Lash et al. (1980) indicated that a substantial part of the variance in infant mortality and child health care is explained by the availability of services (see also Bronfenbrenner, Moen, & Garbarino, 1984: 296). Physician rates and the quality of health care also vary significantly by community (Lash et al., 1980: 179, 210), with the poorest services found in lower-income, minority, and residentially un-stable areas (Bronfenbrenner et al., 1984: 299).

Also consistent with social disorganization theory, Coulton and Pandey's (1992) recent study of community change in Cleveland showed that the increasing ecological concentration of ghetto poverty was a major risk factor for young children in the form of low birth weight and infant death rates. The influence of concentrated poverty extended to adolescent risk factors as well, including the teen birth rate, delinquency, school reading performance, and the high school dropout rate. Interestingly, however, most of the effect of concentrated poverty and all of the effect of percent black (in the community) were indirect and mediated by family disruption, public housing, and substandard housing. These findings suggest that conditions of economic and racial disadvantage influence children's health and development through community-level patterns of family and housing disadvantage.

Additional evidence on child health is found in a series of studies by Wallace and colleagues of community-level variations in low birth-weight babies and infant mortality (Struening, Wallace, & Moore, 1990; Wallace, 1990; Wallace & Wallace, 1990). These authors document the strong upsurge in infant mortality and low birth weight in the late 1970s in New York City, especially in devastated areas of the Bronx. In particular, they found that poverty, overcrowded housing, and rapid population change were the main predictors of increased rates of low birth weight (Struening et al., 1990; Wallace, 1990). Community instability was especially salient – population loss was strongly associated with increases in infant mortality, above and beyond what was expected based on migration patterns alone (Wallace, 1990; Wallace & Wallace, 1990). Even in the most extreme poverty areas where minorities were concentrated, rates of low birth weight were directly proportional to the loss of housing and to the community devastation associated with the forced migration out of and the demographic collapse of the South Bronx in the mid- to late-1970s (e.g., from the reduction in municipal services, the increase in arson, and the instability triggered by relocation of public housing). Struening et al. thus argue that understanding rates of low birth weight "cannot be divorced from an understanding of the processes affecting the communities in which women of childbearing age are embedded" (1990: 476–7).

These studies suggest that rapid population loss, when coupled with inadequate health care services, is detrimental to the health of children in low income communities. Failure to provide municipal services in terms of public health also appears to be implicated in the social disintegration of poor communities. As Wallace and Wallace (1990) concluded after an analysis of the "planned shrinkage" of New York City services in recent decades,

> The consequences of withdrawing municipal services from poor neighborhoods, [and] the resulting outbreaks of contagious urban decay and forced migration which shred essential social networks and cause social disintegration, have become a highly significant contributor to [the] decline in public health among the poor (1990: 427).

They went on to argue that the loss of social integration and networks from planned shrinkage increases behavioral patterns of violence which themselves further disrupt social networks and cause further social disintegration (1990: 427). This pattern of destabilizing feedback underscores the role of governmental policies toward local communities in fostering the downward spiral of high crime areas (see also Skogan, 1986).

Wallace and Wallace (1990: 417–18) further argued that community-level interventions to increase the accessibility and quality of health services helped to reduce the infant mortality rate in New York from 1966 to 1973 (see also Olds, 1980). Child health, it seems, is undermined by the failure of institutional structures to link pregnant mothers with support systems. A related dimension of community support pertains to the *informal* protective factors that stable communities and intact social networks provide to mothers coping with young children. Wallace (1990) identified at least three:

1. knowledge of or linkage to prenatal clinics, and encouragement to follow the clinic's recommendations
2. social support known to be positively related to personal health
3. social support to limit such high risk maternal behavior as smoking, drinking, or other substance use during pregnancy

This last point is related to the literature noted earlier on variations in community tolerance of deviance. Although quantitative evidence is sparse, it is reasonable to argue that community value systems are salient influences on mothers' drug use during pregnancy. Community culture may thus play a role in either promoting or inhibiting behavioral tendencies crucial to healthful and successful childbearing. This may be one of the most important but overlooked aspects of recent increases in drug use among pregnant inner-city young women.

In a similar vein, Osofsky (1990) reports that informal social supports play a crucial role in understanding early childbearing among lower-income girls. Comparing pregnant and nonpregnant girls matched on key individual-level factors, she found "striking differences" in the degree of stability and support in their lives. The pregnant teenagers – in contrast to the nonpregnant teens – experienced considerable residential instability, whereas the nonpregnant teenagers reported a greater network of support in the areas of providing advice, positive feedback, physical assistance and social participation (Osofsky, 1990: 2). This finding is congruent with the idea stemming from social disorganization theory that the impact of communities is found primarily in the factors that facilitate or inhibit networks of social support. As Bronfenbrenner et al. argued, on the basis of their review of the literature on community effects, "A key factor determining [health care] accessibility is the existence of social networks that connect families and individuals with the main sources of material and social assistance" (1984: 320).

Cognitive Development and School Achievement

Although scarce, empirical evidence links community structure to cognitive development and school achievement in childhood. Brooks-Gunn, Duncan, Kato, and Sealand (1993) examined IQ differences in the Infant Health and Development Program (IHDP), an eight-site randomized clinical trial testing the efficacy of educational, family, and health support systems in the first three years of life.[5] They found that neighborhood socioeconomic status (proportion of families in the subject's census tract with incomes greater than $30,000) had a significant positive relationship with IQ at age three as measured by the Stanford-Binet, even after adjusting for family-level socioeconomic status, race, and single-parent households. Although it was not possible to determine a direct link, the findings of Brooks-Gunn et al. (1993) suggest that a higher proportion of affluent neighbors enhances the learning environment of the home, which, in turn, enhances the cognitive development of children. Interestingly, the effect of neighborhood wealth on IQ was greater for whites than blacks.

Analyzing adolescent outcomes from the Panel Study of Income Dynamics (PSID), Brooks-Gunn et al. (1993) also found that the proportion of affluent neighbors had a significant negative relationship with teenage childbearing and school dropout rates. The PSID is a national longitudinal sample that was started in 1968. The analyses were based on a sample of 1,132 black and 1,214 white women who were between the ages of 14 and 19 when observed in the PSID. Mirroring the findings for cognitive development, this study found that the neighborhood effect of affluence (percent families with incomes greater than $30,000) persisted after controls were introduced for family-level socioeconomic status and other background characteristics (e.g., race, mother's education, and female head-of-household).

In perhaps the most interesting pattern of results, Brooks-Gunn et al. (1993) reported that for all outcomes, the *absence* of affluent neighbors was more important for child development than the *presence* of low-income neighbors. In particular, high economic status proved to be more impor-

---

[5] The research design resulted in a sample of 985 infants who weighed less than 2,500 grams at birth and who were born in one of eight medical institutions: in Little Rock, the Bronx, Boston, Miami, Philadelphia, Dallas, Seattle, and New Haven.

tant than the poverty status, racial composition, or family structure of the neighborhood. They argued that this finding supports neighborhood theories focusing on *collective socialization*, where neighborhood adult role models and monitoring are seen as important ingredients to a child's socialization, rather than on *contagion*, wherein the power of peer influences is thought to spread problem behavior (1993: 383). Brooks-Gunn et al. (1993) concluded that neighborhood affluence contributes to child development through collective socialization as reflected in enhanced home learning and neighborhood monitoring, regardless of background differences in social class and family structure.

A related set of studies has expanded the scope of inquiry to include academic achievement, successful transitions from elementary to junior to senior high school, and factors that inhibit dropping out of school. For example, Aber (1992) examined neighborhood influences on adolescent school outcomes among more than 1,000 elementary and junior high school youth living in over 250 census tracts in New York, Baltimore, and Washington. Neighborhood poverty and the prevalence of single-parent families were negatively related to achievement test scores, net of the individual's race, gender, family structure, and economic resources. Aber (1992) also found that neighborhood poverty and joblessness interacted to predict individual outcomes – it was under conditions of high joblessness that the absence of affluent neighbors served to depress scores on academic achievement tests (compare Brooks-Gunn et al., 1993). Similarly, Connell, Clifford, and Crichlow (1992) found that neighborhood disadvantage contributed to problematic adjustments to school, especially among African Americans. Steinberg and colleagues (Darling & Steinberg, 1993; Steinberg & Darling, 1994) found that in addition to family factors, forces in the broader community (e.g., socioeconomic advantage) significantly influenced adolescent school performance. And Entwisle (1993) found that neighborhood affluence increased math scores of boys during the first two years of school.

Extending the analysis of Brooks-Gunn et al. (1993), Duncan (1993) used the nationally representative data from the Panel Study of Income Dynamics to explore in more depth the effects of neighborhood affluence on completed schooling among adolescents. Consistent with theories of collective socialization, Duncan (1993: 1) reported that the presence of affluent neighbors appears to confer benefits on white males and both white and black females that facilitate high school graduation and college attendance. These findings remained despite controls for family-level factors and economic status.

Overall, then, recent empirical research points to the main and interactive effects of neighborhood context – especially socioeconomic (dis)-advantage – on cognitive development (IQ), academic achievement scores (including improved scores in mathematics), school adjustment, out-of-wedlock birth, and educational attainment.

Physical Abuse

A final link between community structure and child development comes in the form of physical abuse and maltreatment. Probably the best known work in this area stems from a body of research conducted by Garbarino and colleagues on the connections between community ecology and parent–child interactions involving maltreatment. In an early study, Garbarino (1976) reported strong correlations at the county level relating socioeconomic and demographic sources of maternal stress to rates of child abuse. In a second study of 20 subareas and 93 census tracts within a city, Garbarino and Crouter (1978) found that poverty, residential mobility, and single-parent households accounted for over 50 percent of the variation in rates of child abuse.

Drawing on these insights, Garbarino and Sherman (1980) conducted a more detailed study of two neighborhoods that were matched on socioeconomic level and demographic composition but that varied dramatically in rates of child maltreatment. Going beyond census data, they conducted interviews with key informants (e.g., school teachers and mail carriers) and then constructed detailed neighborhood profiles. Samples of families were then drawn from each area, and interviews were conducted to examine sources of stress, informal social networks, family support, and neighborhood support systems. Their findings suggest the idea of neighborhood risk factors for abuse, regardless of socioeconomic position and other compositional factors. Even though high-risk families may drift toward high-risk neighborhoods (a compositional effect), neighborhood characteristics directly influence family functioning (Garbarino & Sherman, 1980: 196). In terms of child abuse, families in high-risk areas were exposed to what was termed *social impoverishment* and weak systems of social support (1980: 180). One can infer, then, that above and beyond their predispositions, mothers in high-risk areas characterized by social isolation, sparse networks, and weak social supports are more apt to abuse their children than mothers in low-risk areas.

This possibility is given added support in recent studies by Coulton and colleagues of community structure and child maltreatment in Cleveland.

Coulton, Korbin, Su, and Chow's (1995) analysis specifically showed that
children who live in neighborhoods that are characterized by poverty, high
population turnover, and the concentration of female-headed families are
at highest risk of abuse (see also Coulton & Pandey, 1992). Like Shaw and
McKay (1942), they suggest that child maltreatment is but one manifesta-
tion of community social disorganization and that its occurrence is related
to the same underlying social conditions that foster other urban problems
(Coulton et al., 1995).

Implications for Delinquency

From before the time of Shaw and McKay (1942), a long tradition of
research has demonstrated a substantial connection between community
structure and childhood development. As Bronfenbrenner, Moen, and
Garbarino argued, "Health care is the sine qua non of adult and child
development, and yet access to the health care system, even health itself, is
contingent on the community in which one lives" (1984: 299). And as
Brooks-Gunn et al. (1993) found, even "individual-difference" constructs
such as IQ and cognitive development appear to be shaped by the social
environment of the neighborhood (see also Connell et al., 1992; Entwisle,
1993; Steinberg & Darling, 1994). The adoption of a contextual perspective
on child development thus allows us to move beyond the implicit assumption in many criminological theories that the causes of juvenile delinquency – whether cognitive impairment, poor scholastic achievement,
social disability, or low self-control – are *exogenous* factors. Rather, the
evidence supports the hypothesis that structural disadvantage and social
disorganization combine to generate a community-level concentration of
child abuse, infant mortality, low birth weight, cognitive impairment, and
other adjustment problems (see also Earls and Barnes, this volume), which
in turn constitute major risk factors for later delinquency and violence. The
relevance of this possibility is further suggested by preliminary indications
that child neglect and abuse are risk factors for long-term patterns of
violence among adults (see Widom, 1989).

V. Bridging the Micro and Macro Levels: Families, Social Capital, and Community

Having explicated the general domain of social disorganization theory and
the relevance of community structure for child health and cognitive development, I now turn to a more specific focus on the family mechanisms

through which communities influence children. Drawing on a body of recent research, I argue that *family management* and *social capital* play key roles in mediating the effect of communities on adolescent delinquency.

The importance of the family in understanding crime and delinquency has been well established. Based on a recent meta-analysis of existing research, Loeber and Stouthamer-Loeber (1986: 29) found that socialization variables, such as lack of parental supervision, parental rejection, and parent–child involvement, were among the most powerful predictors of delinquency. Similarly, Hirschi (1983) and Patterson (1982) describe a set of parenting skills that revolve around the monitoring and supervision of youth behavior, consistent punishment, and the formation of close social bonds between parents and children. These three dimensions of socialization in the family – discipline, supervision/monitoring, and attachment – are consistently related to delinquency according to existing research (see Laub & Sampson, 1988; McCord, 1991).

When considering the role of families and crime, however, criminologists and developmental theorists alike tend to view childrearing as a dyadic or mostly interpersonal activity that takes place within individual families or "under the roof." Although this viewpoint is not incorrect, it is incomplete and neglects the fact that parenting styles are an adaptation to considerations outside the household, especially the social organization of the community (Furstenberg, 1993: 233). Exactly how parents perceive and manage their children's involvement in the world outside the household is a topic that has not received much research attention. This is unfortunate, for as Furstenberg (1993: 233) notes, family management strategies tied to the community may be no less consequential for children's development than the more direct, proximate controls observed inside the home. Therefore, in this section, I extend a community-level approach to what is often treated as a purely *familial* or within-household fact – childrearing.[6]

Central to an integration of families and community is the concept of *social capital.* As Coleman (1990: 302) argued, the distinguishing feature of social capital lies in the structure of interpersonal relations. Social capital is

---

[6] Although there is a rich tradition of research on social networks in the fields of urban sociology and family sociology (see, e.g., Bott, 1957; Fischer, 1982), there have been few explicit connections of this work to the study of crime (for a theoretical review, see Krohn, 1986). Moreover, there are even fewer empirical analyses of community social networks, family management styles, and delinquency data. This section draws on the integration in Sampson (1992) of concepts from social disorganization, family management, and social capital theory.

created when relations among persons facilitate action, "making possible the achievements of certain ends that in its absence would not be possible" (Coleman, 1988: 98). By contrast, *physical capital* is embodied in observable material form, and *human capital* is embodied in the skills and knowledge acquired by an individual. Social capital is even less tangible, for it is a social good embodied in the relations among persons (Coleman, 1990: 304). A core idea, then, is that social capital facilitates effective family management, independent of the physical and human capital available to families (e.g., education and job skills).

Coleman's notion of social capital can be linked with social disorganization theory in a straightforward manner – lack of social capital is one of the primary features of socially disorganized communities as defined earlier (see also Coleman, 1990: 307). The theoretical task is to identify the characteristics of communities that facilitate making social capital available to families and children. One of the most important factors according to Coleman (1990: 318–20) is the closure or connectedness of social networks among families and children in a community. In a system involving parents and children, communities characterized by an extensive set of obligations, expectations, and social networks connecting the adults are better able to facilitate the control and supervision of children. This notion highlights parent–child relations that are not just household-based. For example, when closure is present through the relationship of a child to two adults whose own relationships transcend the household (e.g., in friendships, work-related acquaintanceships, and so on), the adults have the potential to "observe the child's actions in different circumstances, talk to each other about the child, compare notes, and establish norms" (Coleman, 1990: 593). This form of relation can also provide reinforcement for disciplining the child, such as when parents in communities with dense social networks and high stability assume responsibility for the supervision of youths who are not their own (Coleman, 1990: 320; Sampson & Groves, 1989). Closure of local networks can thus provide the child with norms and sanctions that could not be brought about by a single adult alone – or even by married-couple families in isolation.

Since the mere presence of a relationship among adults is not sufficient to produce social capital, the idea of social capital goes beyond the notion of density of acquaintanceship (Sampson, 1991) – that is, cross-generational networks that tie parents and children to the parents or guardians of their child's friends in a community prove most effective in transmitting norms and supervising children. A simple example is the situation in which the parents' friends or acquaintances are the parents of their children's friends. By contrast, a parent who has many friends or acquaintances – even within the community – is constrained in social capital if the friends do not include parents or relatives of his/her own children's friends. One can extend this model to closure among networks involving parents and teachers, religious and recreational leaders, businesses that serve youth, and even agents of criminal justice (Sampson, 1992).

Community-Level Ethnographic Evidence

A recent ethnographic study by Furstenberg (1993) of family management practices in two inner-city neighborhoods of Philadelphia lends some support to the hypothesis that the lack of social capital among adults and children is an important component of ineffective childrearing and problematic child development. Whether highly skilled as a parent or not, residents he studied in a poor, unstable, and socially disorganized neighborhood in North Philadelphia tended to adopt an individualistic style of parental management – that is, families usually isolated themselves and their children from the surrounding community and were not part of neighborhood institutions. They distrusted local schools, regarded local services suspiciously, and, to the extent they used supportive services at all, took their business outside the community (Furstenberg, 1993: 237–43). The family system was thus largely disconnected from the community, and parents were left to "manage on their own" (1993: 243). The result was not only that children suffered greater risks associated with decreased supervision and monitoring, but they also missed out on positive opportunities to be connected to the wider society through job, school, and friendship ties. This concept of individualistic strategies is similar to Wilson's (1987) notion of the *social isolation* prevalent in areas of concentrated urban poverty.

In contrast was a poor but nonetheless socially cohesive neighborhood in South Philadelphia labeled Garrison Heights. Although Furstenberg found the same range of parenting skills as in North Philadelphia, what differed was the form of social networks among families – even among those with poor parenting skills. Thus, despite similar backgrounds (e.g., poverty and family structure), the youth in South Philadelphia and North Philadelphia faced quite different structural constraints. For example, parents in Garrison Heights shared parental responsibility and participated in the informal social control of youths in public space, and they were bound together by kinship and friendship bonds that connected local institutions with the family. Youths could not easily escape the scrutiny of the neighborhood, and the task of parents inside the home was reinforced by the mutual support of other neighborhood parents.

In short, parenting was viewed as a *collective activity* that "contrasts to the individualistic mode of family management forced upon parents in more anomic neighborhoods" (Furstenberg, 1993: 249). The density and intergenerational closure of social networks in Garrison Heights made it possible for children in the community to be socialized not just by parents but also by friends, relatives, and neighbors. This form of social cohesion was especially useful to families with problems in the daily management and supervision of their children. Furstenberg's (1993) research (see especially his description of "Meg," pp. 243–9) suggests that even marginal families without the benefit of human capital (e.g., skilled and knowledgeable parents) or physical capital (e.g., material resources) may have counterbalancing sources of support in communities of dense social networks and social capital.

Quantitative Evidence

Unfortunately, there is limited quantitative evidence on the contextual effects of community structure on family management and delinquency. There are some excellent studies that have examined quantitative dimensions of informal social control (see, e.g., Maccoby et al., 1958; Simcha-Fagan & Schwartz, 1986), but they have been limited to relatively few communities, precluding comprehensive analysis.[7] A focus on inner-city neighborhoods and minority groups is especially rare in prior research.

Two current studies have attempted to counteract these past trends and shed new light on the multilevel sources of crime and delinquency in urban environments. One set of studies has been supported by the Research Network on Successful Adolescent Development of the MacArthur Foundation, involving multimethod, multilevel data collection efforts in Philadelphia, Chicago, and Denver (see especially Elliott et al., 1996). A second project now underway is the Project on Human Development in Chicago

---

[7] Simcha-Fagan and Schwartz's (1986) study of 553 youth in 12 New York City neighborhoods showed that community-level rates of organizational participation were positively related to school attachment, which in turn inhibited adolescent delinquency. However, this study did not examine the mediating roles that family management and informal social control play in explaining the contextual effects of community social organization.

Neighborhoods (PHDCN). The PHDCN is a large-scale, interdisciplinary study that aims to increase our understanding of how community-, family-, and individual-level factors interact in the development of both prosocial and antisocial (including criminal) behavior.[8] The major component of the PHDCN is a longitudinal design incorporating seven age cohorts (from birth to age 18) and some 7,000 subjects, half male and half female. Individuals will be followed and developmental change will be examined for eight years, approximating what would be learned from tracking a single birth cohort for some 25 years. To study neighborhood effects, age-eligible subjects are drawn from a multistage probability sample that represents the ethnic and socioeconomic diversity of Chicago. Data collection at the neighborhood level is designed to tap dimensions of social organization using survey and observational techniques.

Overall, these ongoing studies will permit examination of variations in community social organization – especially informal social control – and of how they are related to variations in family management and adolescent delinquency. Results to date from the Denver and Chicago sites seem to support the hypothesis that dimensions of social organization mediate the effect of structural disadvantage on delinquency rates in the direction specified by social disorganization theory (Elliott et al., 1996; Sampson, 1996). The Denver and Chicago studies are exploring new ground in another respect: They were designed to allow a detailed investigation of African-American and Hispanic neighborhoods – disadvantaged as well as middle-class.

Family Disruption and Social Capital

A theoretical framework combining social disorganization theory with the idea of social capital also helps us to make sense of the effects of community family structure on crime. It is fairly well established in individual-level research that broken homes do not have much direct influence on delinquency (Loeber & Stouthamer-Loeber, 1986). However, the *structure* of family relationships in a community may have important contextual or threshold influences (Sampson, 1992). For example, high levels of family disruption (such as divorce rates and single-parent families with children) may facilitate crime by decreasing local networks of informal social control

[8] The PHDCN is jointly funded by the John D. and Catherine T. MacArthur Foundation and the National Institute of Justice. The project is administered at the Harvard School of Public Health, Felton Earls, Principal Investigator.

(such as taking note of or questioning strangers, watching over others' property, and assuming responsibility for supervision of youth activities).

This interpretation is consistent with Coleman's idea of social capital (e.g., facilitation of action such as supervision) and does not assume that it is the children of divorced or separated parents who are engaging in crime. Rather, I suggest that youth in stable family areas, regardless of their own family situation, have more controls placed on their leisure-time activities, particularly with peer groups, than those in nonstable areas (see also Sullivan, 1989: 178; Anderson, 1990: 91). Because of the common occurrence of group delinquency, neighborhood family disruption is likely to influence the extent to which neighborhood youth are provided the opportunities to form a peer-controlled system free of the supervision or knowledge of adults (Reiss, 1986a).

The empirical support for this notion is indirect but nonetheless fairly consistent. As reviewed in Sampson and Lauritsen (1994), several recent studies report a large positive relationship between neighborhood family disruption (usually percent female-headed families or divorce rate) and rates of crime. For example, Sampson's (1985) analysis of a representative sample of U.S. residents in the National Crime Survey showed that rates of victimization were 2–3 times higher among residents living in neighborhoods with high levels of family disruption compared to those living in stable family areas – regardless of alternative predictors of victimization such as percent black and poverty. The percentage of female-headed families also helped to explain the relationship between percent black and crime. As in many other studies, Sampson (1985) found that percent black and percent female-headed families were positively and significantly related. But when the factor of percent female-headed families was controlled, the relationship between percent black and violent victimization was eliminated (1985: 27). Similarly, Smith and Jarjoura (1988) reported that family structure, especially percent single-parent families, helps account for the association between race and violent crime at the community level: Racial composition was not significantly related to violent crime in multivariate models once percent single-parent families was included.

Integrative Hypotheses

The forgoing conceptualization leads to a theoretical distinction between social capital at the individual and community levels. At the individual level, social capital inheres in informal social controls (e.g., monitoring and supervision as well as intergenerational ties) provided by families. The analog at the community level is aggregate patterns of informal social control and cohesion (e.g., collective supervision and neighborhood monitoring) found in areas with high levels of social organization. Integrating social disorganization theory with the literature on delinquency, social capital, and family management, I thus derive two general sets of hypotheses (see also Sampson, 1993):

1. At the macro (community) level, the effect of structural disadvantage and concentrated urban poverty on delinquency rates is accounted for by intervening dimensions of social disorganization.
2. At the micro (individual) level, both neighborhood social organization and family social capital inhibit delinquent outcomes independent of individual-, family-, and group-level background characteristics (e.g., IQ, income, broken homes, and race/ethnicity).

From Furstenberg's (1993) work, a more specific hypothesis is also suggested: Community social cohesion has indirect contextual effects on the control of delinquency by facilitating social capital available to families – especially the establishment of effective monitoring through parent–child and adult–peer social networks.

VI. The Race–Crime Puzzle

The ideas and empirical evidence presented to this point provide the groundwork for a fresh exploration of one of the most crucial issues facing urban America – the connection between race and violent crime. This connection is revealed on several fronts: The leading cause of death among young black males is homicide (Fingerhut & Kleinman, 1990: 3,292), and the lifetime risk of being murdered is as high as 1 in 21 for black males compared to only 1 in 131 for white males (U.S. Department of Justice, 1985). Although rates of violence have been higher for blacks than whites at least since the 1950s (Jencks, 1991), record increases in *juvenile* homicide rates since the mid-1980s in cities such as New York, Chicago, and Philadelphia (Hinds, 1990; Recktenwald & Morrison, 1990) also appeared to be racially selective. For example, whereas white rates remained stable, the firearms death rate among young black males more than doubled from 1984 to 1988 alone (Fingerhut et al., 1991). Moreover, the drug war and the resulting surge in prison populations in the last decade have taken their toll disproportionately on the minority community (Mauer, 1990). Overall, the evidence is clear that African Americans face dismal and apparently worsening odds when it comes to crime in the streets and the risk of incarceration (see also McCord & Freeman, 1990; Sampson & Lauritsen, 1996).

Despite or perhaps because of these facts, the discussion of race and crime is mired in an unproductive mix of controversy and silence.[9] Although articles on age, social class, and gender abound, criminologists have for too long seemed reluctant to speak openly about the explanatory mechanisms that might account for the race and crime connection. To be sure, numerous empirical analyses in criminology have included race/ ethnicity as a variable (usually as a control). It is the theoretical foundations that, until recently, have been neglected. And when the subject is broached, social scientists have tended to reduce the race–crime debate to *cultural* versus *social structural* arguments. On the one side, structural theorists argue for the primacy of relative inequality and economic strain in trying to understand high rates of black crime (see, e.g., Blau & Blau, 1982). On the other side, cultural theorists focus on a subculture of violence that flourishes in black ghettos (see, e.g., Curtis, 1975).

As Sampson and Wilson (1995) argue, one key to solving the race–crime conundrum is traceable to Shaw and McKay (1942). Arguably the most significant aspect of Shaw and McKay's research was their demonstration that high rates of delinquency persisted in certain areas over many years, regardless of population turnover. More than any other, this finding led them to reject individual-level explanations of delinquency and to focus instead on the processes by which delinquent patterns of behavior were transmitted across generations in areas of social disorganization and weak social controls (1942; 1969: 320). This community-level orientation led Shaw and McKay to an explicit contextual interpretation of correlations between race/ethnicity and rates of delinquency. Their logic was set forth in a rejoinder to a critique by Jonassen (1949), who had argued that ethnicity had direct effects on delinquency. Shaw and McKay wrote:

> The important fact about rates of delinquents for Negro boys is that they too, vary by type of area. They are higher than the rates for white boys, but it cannot be said that they are higher than rates for white boys in comparable areas, since it is impossible to reproduce in white communities the circumstances under which Negro children live. Even if it were possible to parallel the low economic status and the inadequacy of institutions in the white

---

[9] For further discussion of this issue, see the theoretical position originally explicated in Sampson and Wilson (1995).

community, it would not be possible to reproduce the effects of segregation and the barriers to upward mobility (1949: 614).

Shaw and McKay's insight almost half a century ago raises two interesting questions still relevant today. First, to what extent do rates of black crime vary by type of ecological area? Second, is it possible to reproduce in white communities the structural circumstances under which many blacks live? The first question is crucial, for it signals that blacks are not a homogeneous group any more than are whites. Indeed, it is racial stereotyping that assigns to blacks a distinct or homogeneous character, thus allowing simplistic comparisons of black–white group differences in crime. As Shaw and McKay recognized, the key point is that there is *heterogeneity* among black neighborhoods (see also Warren, 1975; Kapsis, 1978) that corresponds to variations in crime rates. To the extent that the structural sources of variation in black crime are not unique, rates of crime by blacks should thus vary with specific ecological conditions in a manner similar to whites.

Structural Variations in Black Juvenile Violence

To disentangle the contextual basis for race and crime requires racial disaggregation of both the crime rate and the explanatory variables of theoretical interest. This approach was used in recent research that examined racially disaggregated rates of homicide and robbery by juveniles and adults in over 150 U.S. cities in 1980 (Sampson, 1987). Substantively, this study focused on the effects of joblessness among black males on violent crime through the mediating influence of black family disruption. The results supported the main hypothesis and showed that the scarcity of employed black men relative to black women was directly related to the prevalence of families headed by females in black communities (Wilson, 1987). In turn, black family disruption was substantially related to rates of black murder and robbery, especially by juveniles (see also Messner & Sampson, 1991). These effects were independent of income, region, density, city size, and welfare benefits.

The finding that family disruption had stronger effects on juvenile violence than on adult violence, in conjunction with the inconsistent findings of previous research on individual-level delinquency and broken homes, supports the idea that the effects of family structure are related to macrolevel patterns of social control and guardianship, especially regarding youth and their peers (Sampson & Groves, 1989). Moreover, the results suggest why unemployment and economic deprivation have had weak or inconsistent direct effects on violence rates in past research – joblessness and poverty appear to exert much of their influence indirectly through family disruption.

Despite a large difference in mean levels of family disruption between black and white communities, the percentage of white families headed by a female also had a significant positive effect on white juvenile and white adult violence. In fact, the relationships for white robbery were shown to be in large part identical in sign and magnitude to those for blacks. As a result, the cause-and-effect connection linking black family disruption and black crime was independent of factors proposed by common alternative explanations for black crimes (e.g., region, income, density, and age composition), and this effect could not be attributed to unique cultural factors within the black community because of the similar effect of white family disruption on white crime. Black communities are thus homogeneous neither in their crime levels nor their social organization (compare Warren, 1975; Kapsis, 1978). That these considerable variations are patterned by generic features of urban social structure goes some way toward dispelling the idea of a unique black subculture.[10]

As argued by Sampson and Wilson (1995), however, a structural perspective need not dismiss the relevance of culture. Rather, cultural influences may be seen as varying systematically according to structural features of the urban environment. How else can we make sense of the systematic variations *within* race – for example, if a uniform subculture of violence explains black crime, are we to assume that this subculture is three times as potent in, say, New York as in Chicago (where black homicide differed by a factor of three in 1980)? or in San Francisco as in Baltimore (3:1 ratio)? These distinct variations exist even at the state level. For example, rates of black homicide in California were triple those in Maryland in 1980 (see Hawkins, 1986; Wilbanks, 1986). As Sampson and Wilson (1995) ask, must whites then be part of the black subculture of violence in California, given that white homicide rates were also more than triple the homicide rates for

[10] There is recent evidence that black crime rates and white crime rates are related to different structural features (see Harer & Steffensmeier, 1992; LaFree, Day, & O'Day, 1992). However, these studies have been based on different units of analysis – national time series and large metropolitan areas. In particular, variations in arrest rates over time for the nation as a whole do not necessarily bear on race-specific patterns of criminal offending at the neighborhood level. Besides, the question is whether the general patterns of offending are similar across race, not whether each and every variable predicts crime in a race-invariant fashion.

whites in Maryland? It does not seem likely. The sources of violent crime appear to be remarkably similar across race and are rooted instead in the structural differences among communities, cities, and regions in economic and family organization.

The Ecological Concentration of Race and Social Dislocations

Bearing in mind the similarity of black–white variations by ecological context, consider the next logical question. To what extent are blacks as a group differentially exposed to criminogenic structural conditions (Sampson & Wilson, 1995)? More than 50 years after Shaw and McKay's assessment of race and urban ecology, we still cannot say that blacks and whites share a similar environment – especially with regard to concentrated urban poverty. Although approximately 70% of all poor non-Hispanic whites lived in nonpoverty areas in the ten largest U.S. central cities (as determined by the 1970 census) in 1980, only 16% of poor blacks did. Moreover, whereas less than 7% of poor whites lived in extreme poverty or ghetto areas, 38% of poor blacks lived in such areas (Wilson et al., 1988: 130). In the nation's largest city, New York, 70% of poor blacks live in poverty neighborhoods; by contrast, 70% of poor whites live in nonpoverty neighborhoods (Sullivan, 1989: 230). Potentially even more important, the majority of poor blacks live in communities characterized by high rates of family disruption. Poor whites, even those from broken homes, live in areas of relative family stability (Sampson, 1987; Sullivan, 1989).

The combination of urban poverty and family disruption concentrated by race is particularly severe. As an example, consider Sampson and Wilson's (1995) examination of race-specific census data on the 171 largest cities in the United States as of 1980. To get some idea of concentrated social dislocations by race, they searched for cities where the proportion of blacks living in poverty was equal to or less than that of whites *and* where the proportion of black families with children headed by a single parent was equal to or less than that of white families. Even though it is known that poverty and family disruption among blacks are generally higher than among whites, the number of distinct ecological contexts in which blacks achieve equality to whites is striking. Namely, in not one city over 100,000 in the United States do blacks live in ecological equality to whites when it comes to these basic features of economic and family organization. Accordingly, racial differences in poverty and family disruption are so strong that the worst urban contexts in which whites reside are considerably better off than the average context of black communities (Sampson, 1987: 354; Sampson & Wilson, 1995).

Taken as a whole, these patterns underscore what Wilson (1987) has labeled "concentration effects" – the effects of living in a neighborhood that is overwhelmingly impoverished. These concentration effects, reflected in a range of outcomes from degree of labor-force attachment to social dispositions, are created by the constraints and opportunities that the residents of inner-city neighborhoods face in terms of access to jobs and job networks, involvement in quality schools, availability of marriageable partners, and exposure to conventional role models.

Moreover, the social transformation of the inner city in recent decades has resulted in an increased concentration of the most disadvantaged segments of the urban black population – especially poor, female-headed families with children. Whereas one of every five poor blacks resided in ghetto or extreme poverty areas in 1970, by 1980 nearly two out of every five did so (Wilson et al., 1988: 131). This process of social transformation has been fueled by macrostructural economic changes related to the deindustrialization of central cities, where disadvantaged minorities are concentrated (e.g., shift from goods-producing to service-producing industries; increasing polarization of the labor market into low wage and high wage sectors; and relocation of manufacturing out of the inner city). The exodus of middle- and upper-income black families from the inner city has also removed an important social buffer that could potentially deflect the full impact of prolonged joblessness and industrial transformation. Wilson's thesis is based on the assumption that the basic institutions of a neighborhood (churches, schools, stores, recreational facilities, and so on) are more likely to remain viable if the core of their support comes from more economically stable families (1987: 56). The social milieu of increasing stratification among blacks differs significantly from the environment that existed in inner-city neighborhoods in previous decades (see also Hagedorn, 1988).

Recent research by Land, McCall, and Cohen (1990) has shown the relevance of Wilson's (1987) theoretical framework even at the macrolevel of cities, metropolitan areas, and states. Specifically, Land et al. (1990) analyzed the relationships among the following structural covariates represented in 21 macrolevel studies of homicide: population size, population density, percent of the population that is black, percent youth (ages 15–29), percent divorced males, percent of children not living with both parents, median family income, percent families living in poverty, the Gini index of income inequality, the unemployment rate, and a dichotomous variable indicating those cities or metropolitan areas located in the South. A factor labeled *resource deprivation/affluence* was consistently found over time (i.e., 1960, 1970, and 1980) and space (i.e., cities, metropolitan areas, and states).[11] This factor included three income variables – median income, percent of families below the poverty line, and the Gini index of income inequality – in addition to percent black and percent of children not living with both parents. Although these variables tap different conceptual domains, they could not be separated empirically.

Land et al. (1990) then examined how resource deprivation/affluence, along with other variables, explained homicide rates across time and space. Their results suggested that, all else equal, cities with a large poor population, in conjunction with a high percentage of black residents and single-parent families with children, have disproportionately high homicide rates. Similarly, homicide rates are higher in cities/states/regions with a large population and a high male divorce rate. In terms of magnitude, resource deprivation had the largest effect, generally followed by the divorce rate and population structure.

Wilson's (1987) concept of social isolation in areas of concentrated poverty is consistent with the Land et al. (1990) findings and also with those of Taylor and Covington (1988), who found that increasing entrenchment of urban poverty was associated with large increases in violence. Land et al.'s (1990) results also go beyond Wilson by suggesting that the clustering of economic and social indicators appears not only in 1980 and in neighborhoods of large cities but also for the two previous decennial periods and at the level of macrosocial units as a whole. Moreover, Land et al. present evidence in support of Wilson's argument that concentration effects grew more severe from 1970 to 1980 in large cities – "the numerical values of the component loadings of percent poverty, percent black, and percent of children under 18 not living with both parents are larger in 1980 than 1970" (1990: 945). Therefore, various indicators of urban disadvantaged populations are not only highly related, but they are also increasing in concentration (see also Massey & Eggers, 1990).

At the same time, inner-city neighborhoods have suffered disproportionately from the sort of severe population and housing loss which was identified by Shaw and McKay (1942) as disruptive of the social and institutional order. Skogan (1986: 206) has noted how urban renewal and forced

---

[11] The other factors were divorce rate and urbanization, both of which were positively related to homicide rates.

migration contributed to the wholesale uprooting of many urban black communities, especially the extent to which freeway networks driven through the hearts of many cities in the 1950s destroyed viable, low-income communities. For example, in Atlanta one in six residents was dislocated through urban renewal, the great majority of whom were poor blacks (Logan & Molotch, 1987: 114). Nationwide, fully 20% of all central city housing units occupied by blacks were lost in the period 1960–70 alone. As Logan and Molotch (1987: 114) observed, this displacement does not even include that brought about by more routine market forces (evictions, rent increases, or commercial development).

An understanding of concentration effects is not complete without recognizing the negative consequence of deliberate policy decisions to concentrate minorities and the poor in public housing. Opposition from organized community groups to the building of public housing in "their" neighborhoods, de facto federal policy to tolerate extensive segregation against blacks in urban housing markets, and the decision by local governments to neglect the rehabilitation of existing residential units (many of them single-family homes) have led to massive, segregated housing projects which have become ghettos for the minorities and disadvantaged. The cumulative result is that even given the same objective socioeconomic status, blacks and whites face vastly different environments in which to live, work, and raise their children. As Bickford and Massey (1991: 1,035) have argued, public housing represents a federally funded, physically permanent institution for the isolation of black families by class, and it must therefore be considered an important structural constraint on the ecological area of residence. When segregation and concentrated poverty represent structural constraints embodied in public policy and historical patterns of racial subjugation, concerns that individual difference (or self-selection) explain community-level effects on violence are considerably diminished (see Tienda, 1991; Sampson & Lauritsen, 1994).

Race and Explanatory Fallacies

These differential ecological distributions by race lead to the systematic confounding of correlations between community contexts and crime with correlations between race and crime. Analogous to research on urban poverty, simple comparisons between poor whites and poor blacks ignore the fact that poor whites reside in areas which are ecologically and economically very different from those of poor blacks. This means that observed relationships involving race are likely to reflect unmeasured advantages in the ecological niches that poor whites occupy with respect to jobs, marriage opportunities, and exposure to conventional role models (see Wilson, 1987: 58–60). For example, regardless of whether or not a black juvenile is raised in an intact or single-parent family – or in a rich or poor home – he or she is not likely to grow up in a community context similar to whites with regard to family structure and concentration of poverty. Put differently, the returns of a black family from its educational and economic resources (in terms of neighborhood environment) are usually much less than the returns of a white family from similar resources (Sampson, 1987). Developmental and psychological models tend to over-look these race differences in the structural context of childrearing.

More to the point, community-level inquiry exposes what Sampson and Wilson (1995) call the *individualistic fallacy* – the often-invoked assumption that individual-level causal relations necessarily generate individual-level correlations. In particular, research conducted using samples of individuals – especially national probability samples – rarely questions whether obtained results might be spurious and confounded with com-munity-level processes. For example, some of the most common strategies in criminology involve searching for individual-level (e.g., constitutional), social–psychological (e.g., attachment and relative deprivation), or group-level (e.g., social class) explanations for crime. That these efforts have largely failed to explain the race–violence linkage is, I believe, a direct result of the de-contextualization that attends individual-level explanations.

To appreciate this claim fully also requires addressing the *materialist fallacy* (Sampson & Wilson, 1995) – that economic (or materialist) causes necessarily produce economic motivations. Owing largely to Merton's (1938) famous dictum about social structure and anomie, it is normally assumed that if economic structural factors (e.g., poverty) are causally relevant, it must be through the motivation to commit acquisitive crimes. Indeed, *strain theory* was so named to capture the hypothesized pressure on members of the lower classes to commit crime in their pursuit of the American dream. But as is well known, strain or materialist theories have not fared well empirically (Kornhauser, 1978). Katz is perhaps the most explicit in dismissing poverty-based explanations of crime as "twentieth-century sentimentality about crime" (1988: 314).

However, the assumption that those who posit the relevance of eco-nomic structure for crime rely on motivational pressure as an explanatory concept is itself a fallacy. Although the theory of social disorganization does see relevance in the ecological concentration of poverty, it is not for the

materialist reasons Katz (1988: 313–17) alleges. Rather, the concept explicated here and in Sampson and Wilson (1995) rests on properties of
structural and cultural organization that are inhibited by the concentration
of poverty and joblessness.

In short, linking social disorganization theory with research on political
economy and urban poverty suggests that both historic and contemporary
macrosocial forces (e.g., segregation, migration, housing discrimination,
and structural transformation of the economy) interact with local
community-level factors (e.g., residential turnover, concentrated poverty,
and family disruption) to impede the social organization of inner cities.
This viewpoint focuses attention on the proximate structural characteristics
and mediating processes of community social organization that help explain crime and its connection to race in contemporary American cities; at
the same time, it recognizes the larger historical, social, and political forces
shaping local communities.

VII. Discussion

As Kotlowitz (1991) provocatively argued, no explanation of violence in the
inner city is complete that does not account for child socialization in its
community context. Unfortunately, such integration is all too rare in sociological and community-level theories of crime – the dominant perspectives
on community emphasize structural characteristics thought to influence
the motivation in later adolescent and adult crime (e.g., economic deprivation and inequality). Aspects of child development such as prenatal care,
cognitive development, abuse/neglect, and the daily supervision of children are usually not considered. On the other hand, those who study
child development often neglect community context and focus instead on
individual families "under the roof."

In this paper, I have attempted to overcome these limitations of disciplinary isolation by bringing together a theory of social disorganization
and social capital with theoretical concerns of family management and
child development. A key motivation was the close inverse relation between indicators of healthy child development and rates of crime. This
connection turned out to be predictable from the vantage point of social
disorganization theory. As implied by Shaw and McKay's discovery many
years ago, the essence of social disorganization theory is its recognition
that a disorganized community cannot realize the common values of its
residents and maintain effective social controls (Bursik 1988; Sampson &
Groves, 1989).

The extension of social disorganization theory outlined in this paper helps to explain how mediating constructs – such as institutional-family connectedness; the observability, monitoring, and supervision of youth; intergenerational closure among adult–child networks; control of street-corner peer groups; mutual social support and extensiveness of social networks; perceived normative consensus on parenting; and social trust – directly and indirectly influence the care of children, and ultimately the rates of delinquency and crime. In this integrated theory, childrearing is treated as a complex phenomenon that has not only individual components but contextual ones as well. A major component I have highlighted is the social capital generated in areas of social organization. Here not only the health-related aspects of early child development become relevant (e.g., low birth weight, child abuse, quality of prenatal care, and adequate day care); the viability and effectiveness of family management practices in general – above and beyond personal character-istics – are important considerations too. Hence the embeddedness of families and children in the community context is a central feature of the theory.

In contrast to the individualistic and materialist approaches, this paper has also attempted to delineate a theoretical perspective that incorporates both structural and cultural arguments about race and violence in Ameri-can cities. Drawing on insights linking social disorganization theory and research on urban poverty, this strategy provides new ways of thinking about race and crime.

First, the connection between race and crime is interpreted from a contextual perspective that highlights the very different ecological contexts that blacks and whites reside in – regardless of individual and family char-acteristics. Second, I emphasized that despite their disadvantaged position compared to white areas, black neighborhoods – even so-called underclass ones – are not monolithic. To the contrary, they vary considerably among themselves in structural and cultural conditions. Third, I reviewed recent evidence suggesting that crime rates among blacks vary systematically by these same community-level characteristics. In particular, I argued that variations in crime among urban black neighborhoods are explained by the attenuation of informal social organization, which is itself explained prim-arily by variations in the ecological concentration of poverty and family disruption. Other community-level sources of social disorganization that are concentrated in urban black communities include residential mobility and population turnover, housing density, and inadequate health-care re-sources (Sampson & Lauritsen, 1994).

This paper suggests a powerful role for community context in explaining the link between race and crime. Specifically, I posit that the most important explanation of the relationship between race and crime is the differential distribution of blacks in communities characterized by the (a) *structural social disorganization,* (b) *cultural attenuation,* and (c) *social isolation* that stem from the concentration of poverty, family disruption, and residential instability. When linked to the evidence that community social organization has contextual effects on family management and social capital (Furstenberg, 1993) and that family disruption is pronounced in black poverty areas, the social basis of the race–crime connection is unveiled (see also Sampson & Wilson, 1995).

This community-level explanation departs from conventional wisdom regarding poverty, race, and crime. Rather than attributing to acts of crime a purely economic motive springing from relative deprivation – a social–psychological concept – I have focused instead on the mediating dimensions of community social organization in an attempt to understand variations in crime across areas. Moreover, I acknowledge and try to specify the macrosocial forces that contribute to the social organization of local communities. Implicit in this attempt is the incorporation of the political economy of place and the role of urban inequality in generating racial differences in community structure. As Wacquant observed, American urban poverty is "preeminently a *racial poverty*... rooted in the *ghetto* as a historically specific social form and mechanism of racial domination" (1991: 36). This intersection of race, place, and poverty goes to the heart of this paper's theoretical concern with societal and community organization.

Furthermore, I incorporate culture in the form of social isolation and cognitive landscapes that shape perceptions and situational patterns of learning. This *cultural structure* is not seen as inevitably tied to race; rather it is more tied to the varying structural contexts produced by residential and macroeconomic change, concentrated poverty, family instability, and intervening patterns of social disorganization. I thus differ from the recent wave of structuralist research on the culture of violence (for a review see Sampson & Lauritsen, 1994). In a methodological sleight of hand, scholars have completely rejected the relevance of culture, and they have done so based on their analysis of census data that provide no measures of the culture (see, e.g., Blau & Blau, 1982). Structural criminologists have thus too quickly dismissed the role of values and normative diversity as they interact with concentrated poverty and social isolation. In my view, macrosocial patterns of residential inequality give rise to the social isolation and concentration of the truly disadvantaged, thus engendering cultural adaptations that undermine social organization and the collective moral order.

Implications for Recent Changes in Urban Violence

Finally, and perhaps most important, the logic of this theoretical model suggests that the profound changes in the structure of urban minority communities in the 1970s may hold the key to understanding recent increases in violence (see Sampson & Wilson, 1995). As noted earlier, research has consistently demonstrated the early onset of delinquency and its long-term stability (Glueck & Glueck, 1950; Robins, 1966; Sampson & Laub, 1992). These differences among individuals that are stable over time imply that to understand the present high crime rates among youth, we must come to grips with their experiences in early adolescence. Longitudinal research shows that delinquent tendencies are fairly well established at early ages – at eight or so, and certainly by the early teens (Glueck & Glueck, 1950). Socialization and learning begin even earlier, prompting us to consider the social context of childhood as well.

Seen from this perspective, the roots of urban violence among today's 15–21-year-old cohorts may in part be attributable to childhood socialization that took place in the late 1970s. Indeed, recent large increases in crime among youth – but not adults – may be a harbinger of things to come as the massive secular changes that transformed the context of childhood socialization in the 1970s and 1980s are now beginning to exert their influence on those entering the peak years of offending. Cohorts born in the 1970–6 period spent their childhoods in the context of a rapidly changing urban environment unlike that of previous points in U.S. history. As documented in more detail by Wilson (1987), the concentration of urban poverty and other social dislocations began increasing sharply just about 1970 and continued throughout the decade and into the early 1980s. For example, the proportion of black families headed by women increased over 50% from 1970 to 1984 alone (Wilson, 1987: 26). Large increases were also seen for the ecological concentration of ghetto poverty, racial segregation, population turnover, and joblessness. By comparison, these social dislocations were relatively stable in earlier decades.

In sum, by recasting traditional race and poverty arguments in a dynamic contextual framework that incorporates both structural and cultural concepts, I conclude that community-level social disorganization may go a long way toward explaining how current patterns of crime have been shaped by rapid social change within the macrostructural context of inner-city ghetto poverty and childhood socialization (Sampson & Wilson, 1995). The unique value of this community-level perspective is that it leads away from a simple "kinds of people" interpretation of crime to a focus on how changing social characteristics of communities bear on the lives of children and families.

Of course, none of the above suggests that assessing a community-level framework is easy; nor does it imply that extant research is in any way definitive. Elsewhere I have laid out in detail the limitations and pitfalls associated with community-level research, such as the selective aggregation of individuals into communities, cross-level misspecification, multicollinearity, a static conceptualization of community structure, and the crude measurement of community characteristics (see Sampson, 1993; Sampson & Lauritsen, 1994). Nonetheless, I hope that as a result of this effort to synthesize recent research on inner-city violence and community social organization, new research and policy efforts to solve some of these issues might be stimulated.

R E F E R E N C E S

Aber, L. (1992). Adolescent pathways project. Paper prepared for the conference of the Committee for Research on the Urban Underclass, Social Science Research Council. New York: Russell Sage Foundation.

Anderson, E. (1978). *A Place on the Corner.* Chicago: University of Chicago Press.
    (1990). *Streetwise: Race, Class, and Change in an Urban Community.* Chicago: University of Chicago Press.
    (This volume). Violence and the inner-city street code. In ed., Joan McCord, *Violence and Childhood in the Inner City.* New York: Cambridge University Press, pp. 1–30.

Bickford, A., & Massey, D. (1991). Segregation in the second ghetto: Racial and ethnic segregation in American public housing, 1977. *Social Forces* 69: 1011–36.

Blau, J., & Blau, P. M. (1982). The cost of inequality: Metropolitan structure and violent crime. *American Sociological Review* 47: 114–29.

Bott, E. (1957). *Family and Social Network: Roles, Norms, and External Relationships in Ordinary Urban Families.* New York: Free Press.

Bronfenbrenner, U., Moen, P., & Garbarino, J. (1984). Child, family, and community. In ed., R. Parke, *Review of Child Development Research, Volume 7: The Family.* Chicago: University of Chicago Press, pp. 283–328.

Brooks-Gunn, J., Duncan, G., Kato, P., & Sealand, N. (1993). Do neighborhoods influence child and adolescent behavior? *American Journal of Sociology* 99: 353–95.

Bursik, R. J., Jr. (1988). Social disorganization and theories of crime and delinquency: Problems and prospects. *Criminology* 26: 519–52.

Bursik, R., Jr., & Grasmick, H. (1993). *Neighborhoods and Crime: The Dimensions of Effective Community Control.* New York: Lexington.

Byrne, J., & Sampson, R. J. (1986). Key issues in the social ecology of crime. In eds., J. Byrne & R. J. Sampson, *The Social Ecology of Crime.* New York: Springer-Verlag, pp. 1–22.

Coleman, J. (1988). Social capital in the creation of human capital. *American Journal of Sociology* 94: S95–S120.

(1990). *Foundations of Social Theory.* Cambridge, MA: Harvard University Press.

Connell, J., Clifford, E., & Crichlow, W. (1992). Why do urban students leave school?: Neighborhood, family, and motivational influences. Paper prepared for the conference of the Committee for Research on the Urban Underclass, Social Science Research Council. New York: Russell Sage Foundation.

Coulton, C., Korbin, J., Su, M., & Chow, J. (1995). Community level factors and child maltreatment rates. *Child Development* 66: 1262–76.

Coulton, C., & Pandey, S. (1992). Geographic concentration of poverty and risk to children in urban neighborhoods. *American Behavioral Scientist* 35: 238–57.

Curtis, L. (1975). *Violence, Race, and Culture.* Lexington, MA: Heath.

Darling, N., & Steinberg, L. (1993). Community integration and value consensus as forces for adolescent socialization: A test of the Coleman and Hoffer hypothesis. Paper presented at the 60th meeting of the Society for Research in Child Development. New Orleans, LA.

Duncan, G. (1993). Families and neighbors as sources of disadvantage in the schooling decisions of white and black adolescents. Paper presented at the 60th meeting of the Society for Research in Child Development. New Orleans, LA.

Earls, F., & Barnes, J. (This volume). Understanding and preventing child abuse in urban settings. In ed., J. McCord, *Violence and Childhood in the Inner City.* New York: Cambridge University Press, pp. 207–55.

Elliott, D., Wilson, W. J., Huizinga, D., Sampson, R. J., Elliott, A., & Rankin, B. (1996). Effects of neighborhood disadvantage on adolescent development. *Journal of Research in Crime and Delinquency* 33: 389–426.

Entwisle, D. (1993). The gender gap in math: Its possible origins. Paper presented at the 60th meeting of the Society for Research in Child Development. New Orleans, LA.

Farrington, D. P., Sampson, R. J., & Wikström, P.-O. H., eds. (1993). *Integrating Individual and Ecological Aspects on Crime.* Stockholm, Sweden: National Council for Crime Prevention.

Fingerhut, L. A., & Kleinman, J. C. (1990). International and interstate comparisons of homicide among young males. *Journal of the American Medical Association* 263: 3292–95.

Fingerhut, L. A., Kleinman, J. C., Godfrey, E., & Rosenberg, H. (1991). Firearms mortality among children, youth, and young adults 1–34 years of age, trends and current status: United States, 1979–88. *Monthly Vital Statistics Report* 39 (11): 1–16.

Fischer, C. S. (1982). *To Dwell Among Friends: Personal Networks in Town and City.* Chicago: University of Chicago Press.

Furstenberg, F. (1993). How families manage risk and opportunity in dangerous neighborhoods. In ed., W. J. Wilson, *Sociology and the Public Agenda.* Newbury Park, CA: Sage, pp. 231–58.

Garbarino, J. (1976). A preliminary study of some ecological correlates of child abuse: The impact of socioeconomic stress on mothers. *Child Development* 47: 178–85.

Garbarino, J., & Crouter, A. (1978). Defining the community context for parent–child relations: The correlates of child maltreatment. *Child Development* 49: 604–16.

Garbarino, J., & Sherman, D. (1980). High-risk neighborhoods and high-risk families: The human ecology of child maltreatment. *Child Development* 51: 188–98.

Glueck, S., & Glueck, E. (1950). *Unraveling Juvenile Delinquency.* New York: The Commonwealth Fund.

  (1968). *Delinquents and Nondelinquents in Perspective.* Cambridge: Harvard University Press.

Gottfredson, M., & Hirschi, T. (1990). *A General Theory of Crime.* Stanford, CT: Stanford University Press.

Hagedorn, J. (1988). *Gangs, Crime and the Underclass in a Rustbelt City.* Chicago: Lake View Press.

Hannerz, U. (1969). *Soulside: Inquiries into Ghetto Culture and Community.* New York: Columbia University Press.

Harer, M., & Steffensmeier, D. (1992). The differing effects of economic inequality on black and white rates of violence. *Social Forces* 70: 1035–54.

Hawkins, D. F., ed. (1986). *Homicide Among Black Americans.* Lanham, MD: University Press of America.

Hinds, M. (1990). Number of killings soars in big cities across U.S. *New York Times,* July 18, p. 1.

Hirschi, T. (1983). Crime and the family. In ed., J. Q. Wilson, *Crime and Public Policy.* San Francisco: Institute for Contemporary Studies, pp. 53–68.

Horowitz, R. (1987). Community tolerance of gang violence. *Social Problems* 34: 437–50.

Huesmann, L. R., Eron, L. D., & Lefkowitz, M. M. (1984). Stability of aggression over time and generations. *Developmental Psychology* 20: 1120–34.

Jencks, C. (1991). Is violent crime increasing? *The American Prospect* (Winter): 98–109.

Jonassen, C. (1949). A reevaluation and critique of the logic and some methods of Shaw and McKay. *American Sociological Review* 14: 608–14.

Kapsis, R. (1978). Black ghetto diversity and anomie: A sociopolitical view. *American Journal of Sociology* 83: 1132–53.

Kasarda, J. D., & Janowitz, M. (1974). Community attachment in mass society. *American Sociological Review* 39: 328–39.

Katz, J. (1988). *Seductions of Crime: The Sensual and Moral Attractions of Doing Evil.* New York: Basic.

Kornhauser, R. (1978). *Social Sources of Delinquency.* Chicago: University of Chicago Press.

Kotlowitz, A. (1991). *There are No Children Here: The Story of Two Boys Growing up in the Other America.* New York: Doubleday.

Krohn, M. (1986). The web of conformity: A network approach to the explanation of delinquent behavior. *Social Problems* 33: 81–93.

LaFree, G., Day, K., & O'Day, P. (1992). Race and crime in postwar America: Determinants of African American and white rates. *Criminology* 30: 157–88.

Land, K., McCall, P., & Cohen, L. (1990). Structural covariates of homicide rates: Are there any invariances across time and space? *American Journal of Sociology* 95: 922–63.

Lander, B. (1954). *Toward an Understanding of Juvenile Delinquency.* New York: Columbia University Press.

Lash, T., Sigal, H., & Dudzinski, D. (1980). *State of the Child: New York City, II.* New York: Foundation for Child Development.

Laub, J. H., & Sampson, R. J. (1988). Unraveling families and delinquency: A reanalysis of the Gluecks' data. *Criminology* 26: 355–80.

Leighton, B. (1988). The community concept in criminology: Toward a social network approach. *Journal of Research in Crime and Delinquency* 25: 351–74.

Liebow, E. (1967). *Tally's Corner.* Boston: Little, Brown.

Loeber, R. (1982). The stability of antisocial child behavior: A review. *Child Development* 53: 1431–46.

Loeber, R., & Stouthamer-Loeber, M. (1986). Family factors as correlates and predictors of juvenile conduct problems and delinquency. In eds., M. Tonry & N. Morris, *Crime and Justice: An Annual Review of Research, Vol. 7.* Chicago: University of Chicago Press, pp. 29–150.

Logan, J., & Molotch, H. (1987). *Urban Fortunes: The Political Economy of Place.* Berkeley, CA: University of California Press.

Maccoby, E. E., Johnson, J. P., & Church, R. M. (1958). Community integration and the social control of juvenile delinquency. *Journal of Social Issues* 14: 38–51.

Massey, D., & Eggers, M. (1990). The ecology of inequality: Minorities and the concentration of poverty, 1970–1980. *American Journal of Sociology* 95: 1153–88.

Mauer, M. (1990). Young black men and the criminal justice system: A growing national problem. Washington, D.C.: The Sentencing Project.

McCord, J. (1991). Family relationships, juvenile delinquency, and adult criminality. *Criminology* 29: 397–418.

McCord, M., & Freeman, H. (1990). Excess mortality in Harlem. *New England Journal of Medicine* 322: 173–75.

Merton, R. (1938). Social structure and anomie. *American Sociological Review* 3: 672–82.

   (1964). Anomie, anomia, and social interaction: Contexts of deviant behavior. In ed., M. Clinard, *Anomie and deviant behavior.* New York: Free Press, pp. 213–42.

Messner, S., & Sampson, R. J. (1991). The sex ratio, family disruption, and rates of violent crime: The paradox of demographic structure. *Social Forces* 69: 693–713.

Olds, D. (1980). Improving formal services for mothers and children. In eds., J. Garbarino & S. Stocking, *Protecting Children from Abuse and Neglect.* San Francisco: Jossey-Bass, pp. 173–97.

Olweus, D. (1979). Stability of aggressive reaction patterns in males: A review. *Psychological Bulletin* 86: 852–75.

Osofsky, J. (1990). Gender issues in the development of deviant behavior: The case for teenage pregnancy. Paper presented at the "Workshop on Gender Issues in the Development of Deviant Behavior," Program on Human Development and Criminal Behavior, Radcliffe College, June 1990.

Park, R. E., Burgess, E. W., & McKenzie, R. (1925). *The City.* Chicago: University of Chicago Press.

Patterson, G. R. (1982). *Coercive Family Process.* Eugene, OR: Castalia.

Prothrow-Stith, D. (1991). *Deadly Consequences.* New York: HarperCollins.

Rainwater, L. (1970). *Behind Ghetto Walls: Black Families in a Federal Slum.* Chicago: Aldine.

Recktenwald, W., & Morrison, B. (1990). Guns, gangs, drugs make a deadly combination. *Chicago Tribune,* July 1, Section 2, p. 1.

Reiss, A. J., Jr. (1986a). Why are communities important in understanding crime? In eds., A. J. Reiss, Jr., & M. Tonry, *Communities and Crime.* Chicago: University of Chicago Press, pp. 1–33.

   (1986b). Co-offender influences on criminal careers. In eds., A. Blumstein, J. Cohen, J. Roth, & C. Visher, *Criminal Careers and "Career Criminals."* Washington, D.C.: National Academy Press, pp. 121–60.

Robins, L. N. (1966). *Deviant Children Grown Up.* Baltimore: Williams and Wilkins.

Rutter, M., & Giller, H. (1983). *Juvenile Delinquency: Trends and Perspectives.* New York: Guilford Press.

Sampson, R. J. (1985). Neighborhood and crime: The structural determinants of personal victimization. *Journal of Research in Crime and Delinquency* 22: 7–40.

(1987). Urban black violence: The effect of male joblessness and family disruption. *American Journal of Sociology* 93: 348–82.

(1991). Linking the micro and macro level dimensions of community social organization. *Social Forces* 70: 43–64.

(1992). Family management and child development: Insights from social disorganization theory. In ed., Joan McCord, *Facts, Frameworks, and Forecasts: Advances in Criminological Theory, Vol. 3.* New Brunswick, NJ: Transaction, pp. 63–93.

(1993). Community and family-level influences on delinquency: A contextual theory and strategies for research testing. In eds., D. Farrington, R. J. Sampson, & P. O. Wikström, *Integrating Individual and Ecological Aspects on Crime.* Stockholm, Sweden: National Council for Crime Prevention, pp. 153–68.

(1996). Structural contexts of informal social control: A multi-level investigation of Chicago neighborhoods, 1990–1995. Paper presented at the joint international meeting of the Law and Society Association and the Research Committee on Law, International Sociological Association, Glasgow, Scotland.

Sampson, R. J., & Groves, W. B. (1989). Community structure and crime: Testing social-disorganization theory. *American Journal of Sociology* 94: 774–802.

Sampson, R. J., & Laub, J. H. (1992). Crime and deviance in the life course. *Annual Review of Sociology* 18: 63–84.

Sampson, R. J., & Lauritsen, J. L. (1994). Violent victimization and offending: Individual-, situational-, and community-level risk factors. In eds., Albert J. Reiss, Jr., & Jeffrey Roth, *Understanding and Preventing Violence: Social Influences, Vol. 3.* (National Research Council.) Washington, D. C.: National Academy Press, pp. 1–114.

(1996). Racial and ethnic disparities in crime and criminal justice in the United States. In ed., Michael Tonry, *Crime and Justice, Vol. 22.* Chicago: University of Chicago Press, pp. 1–64.

Sampson, R. J., & Wilson, W. J. (1995). Toward a theory of race, crime, and urban inequality. In eds., John Hagan & Ruth Peterson, *Crime and Inequality.* Stanford, CT: Stanford University Press, pp. 37–56.

Shaw, C. R., & McKay, H. D. (1942). *Juvenile Delinquency and Urban Areas.* Chicago: University of Chicago Press.

(1949). Rejoinder. *American Sociological Review* 14: 614–17.

(1969, revised edition). *Juvenile Delinquency and Urban Areas.* Chicago: University of Chicago Press.

Short, J. F., Jr. (1963). Introduction to the abridged edition. In ed. F. Thrasher,

The Gang: A Study of 1,313 Gangs in Chicago. Chicago: University of Chicago Press, pp. xv–liii.

(1985). The level of explanation problem in criminology. In ed., R. Meier, *Theoretical Methods in Criminology.* Beverly Hills, CA: Sage, pp. 51–74.

Short, J. F., Jr., & Strodtbeck, F. (1965). *Group Process and Gang Delinquency.* Chicago: University of Chicago Press.

Simcha-Fagan, O., & Schwartz, J. E. (1986). Neighborhood and delinquency: An assessment of contextual effects. *Criminology* 24: 667–704.

Skogan, W. (1986). Fear of crime and neighborhood change. In eds., A. J. Reiss, Jr., & M. Tonry, *Communities and Crime.* Chicago: University of Chicago Press, pp. 203–29.

Smith, D. R., & Jarjoura, G. R. (1988). Social structure and criminal victimization. *Journal of Research in Crime and Delinquency* 25: 27–52.

Steinberg, L., & Darling, N. (1994). The broader context of social influence in adolescence. In eds., R. Silbereisen & E. Todt, *Adolescence in Context.* New York: Springer-Verlag, pp. 25–45.

Struening, E., Wallace, R., & Moore, R. (1990). Housing conditions and the quality of children at birth. *Bulletin of the New York Academy of Medicine* 66: 463–78.

Sullivan, M. (1989). *Getting Paid: Youth Crime and Work in the Inner City.* Ithaca, NY: Cornell University Press.

Suttles, G. (1968). *The Social Order of the Slum.* Chicago: University of Chicago Press.

Taylor, R. B., & Covington, J. (1988). Neighborhood changes in ecology and violence. *Criminology* 26: 553–90.

Taylor, R. B., Gottfredson, S., & Brower, S. (1984). Block crime and fear: Defensible space, local social ties, and territorial functioning. *Journal of Research in Crime and Delinquency* 21: 303–31.

Thrasher, F. (1963). *The Gang: A Study of 1,313 Gangs in Chicago* (Revised Edition). Chicago: University of Chicago Press.

Tienda, M. (1991). Poor people and poor places: Deciphering neighborhood effects on poverty outcomes. In ed., J. Huber, *Macro–micro Linkages in Sociology.* Newbury, CA: Sage, pp. 244–62.

U.S. Department of Justice. (1985). *The Risk of Violent Crime.* Washington, D. C.: U.S. Government Printing Office.

Wacquant, L. (1991). The specificity of ghetto poverty: A comparative analysis of race, class, and urban exclusion in Chicago's Black Belt and the Parisian Red Belt. Paper prepared for presentation at the Chicago Urban Poverty and Family Life Conference, University of Chicago.

Wallace, R. (1990). Urban desertification, public health and public order: "Planned shrinkage," violent death, substance abuse and AIDS in the Bronx. *Social Science and Medicine* 31: 801–13.

Wallace, R., & Wallace, D. (1990). Origins of public health collapse in New York

City: The dynamics of planned shrinkage, contagious urban decay and social disintegration. *Bulletin of the New York Academy of Medicine* 66: 391–434.

Warren, D. (1975). *Black Neighborhoods: An Assessment of Community Power.* Ann Arbor, MI: University of Michigan Press.

Whyte, W. F. (1943). *Street Corner Society: The Social Structure of an Italian Slum.* Chicago: University of Chicago Press.

Widom, C. S. (1989). The cycle of violence. *Science* 244: 160–6.

Wilbanks, W. (1986). Criminal homicide offenders in the U.S.: Black vs. white. In ed., D. Hawkins, *Homicide Among Black Americans.* Lanham, MD: University Press of America, pp. 43–56.

Wilson, W. J. (1987). *The Truly Disadvantaged: The Inner City, the Underclass, and Public Policy.* Chicago: University of Chicago Press.

  (1991). Studying inner-city social dislocations: The challenge of public agenda research. *American Sociological Review* 56: 1–14.

Wilson, W. J., Aponte, R., Kirschenman, J., & Wacquant, L. (1988). The ghetto underclass and the changing structure of American poverty. In eds., F. Harris & R. W. Wilkins, *Quiet Riots: Race and Poverty in the United States.* New York: Pantheon, pp. 123–54.

Wolfgang, M., & Ferracuti, F. (1967). *The Subculture of Violence.* London: Tavistock.

Placing American Urban Violence in Context*

JOAN MCCORD

American cities are more violent than those in other developed nations. This chapter focuses on understanding the high degree of urban violence in terms of American history, public policies, and national culture. The chapter also presents information relevant to understanding dimensions of urban violence – where it occurs, by whom, and against whom. The discussion describes how rates of violence reflect political decisions about whom to count as victims and what to count as crimes. The core of the chapter considers macrolevel explanations for violence in urban America. It explains why American cities have high rates of violence but not why particular city dwellers contribute to violence.

Claims that the frontier ethic or immigrants account for America's violence are rebutted. I argue that cultural conditions and historical pressures have strong – and underappreciated – explanatory roles to play in unearthing the causes of violence in American cities.

Many types of violence have been considered acceptable throughout the history of the United States. Violence has been used by the powerful to protect their interests, and violence has been used by the less powerful when peaceful methods of persuasion failed. Violence has also been used simply for pleasure.

In the United States, the historical record also includes persistently discriminatory policies that have isolated poor blacks in cities. Despite the democratic promise of equality, for many American urban blacks discrimi-

*This chapter has been much improved through the suggestions and cogent criticisms of Mark H. Haller, Professor of History at Temple University. I thank him most gratefully. In addition, I would like to thank Karen Colvard, Joel Wallman, and the Board of The Harry Frank Guggenheim Foundation for their insightful comments.

natory policies have blocked opportunities for legitimate success. Some urban violence appears to be displaced rage in response to unfair treatment.

The chapter is divided into six sections. The first summarizes rates of violent crime in the United States. The second sets American violence in cross-national perspective. The third section depicts violence in culturally diverse urban settings and provides grounds for rejecting both a frontier explanation and one that focuses on immigrants. The fourth discusses explanations for violence that are based on urban conditions of tolerance for deviance and lack of social control. The fifth describes policies that exacerbated criminogenic urban conditions and isolated poor black Americans in urban ghettos. The sixth and final section proposes cultural grounds for understanding current rates of violence, especially among blacks living in the inner cities of America.

Violent Crime Rates

The popular press often implies that America is more violent now than ever before. That common belief is probably wrong (Bell, 1960; Covey, Menard, & Franzese, 1992; Gurr, 1981, 1989; Lane, 1969/1970, 1989; Pepinsky, 1976; Reiss & Roth, 1993). Infanticide and drunken violence, murders and riots punctuated urban life during the mid-nineteenth century (Gurr, 1979; Lane, 1980, 1986; Wade, 1972). Although rates of violent crime known by police have risen during the last thirty years, declining rates of violence accompanied the rapid industrialization and urbanization of the late nineteenth and early twentieth centuries (Lane, 1980, 1989; Lodhi & Tilly, 1973; Monkkonen, 1981).

Rates of violence are particularly difficult to measure. Recorded rates depend partly on how society evaluates victims. At various periods in American history, widespread killings of sheepherders, Mexicans, native American Indians, blacks, Mormons, and Chinese – among others – were not counted as criminal acts (Frantz, 1969/1970; Hershberg, 1973; Hofstadter, 1970/1971; Hollon, 1974; Lane, 1976). It is unknown, therefore, whether present violence has reached the level of earlier days.

Rates of violence depend also on how data on behavior involving intentional injury have been collected. To get a picture of the various forms of data available for estimating rates of violence, let us consider the sources of these rates in contemporary America.

The Federal Bureau of Investigation Index counts murder and nonnegligent manslaughter, forcible rape, robbery, and aggravated assault as violent crimes. Since 1933, police departments have been reporting crimes in their districts to the FBI. The FBI converts the data to crime rates and publishes them under the title "Uniform Crime Reports." These reports show a general decline from that year until 1941, with a jagged, but overall rise until 1963 (National Commission on the Causes and Prevention of Violence, 1969). In the *Uniform Crime Report of 1963*, J. Edgar Hoover (1964) indicated that rates for murder, forcible rape, robbery, and aggravated assault had risen 12% since 1958. The urban murder rate, however, had changed little over that period and had declined by about two-thirds since the early 1930s. The rates for violent crimes between 1960 and 1992 have been variously described, partly depending upon the length and timing of the perspective taken. Dips in rates of reported violent crimes occurred from 1975 to 1976, between 1980 and 1984, and from 1986 to 1987. Nevertheless, the rates of violent crimes reported to the FBI have been generally increasing, an increase due largely to rising rates of aggravated assault (Maguire & Pastore, 1994). The data are presented in Figure 3.1 (adapted from Maguire & Pastore, 1994, Table 3.94).

The Uniform Crime Reports capture only part of the crime picture, one that reflects political reality as well as popular beliefs about police efficacy and proper behavior (Biderman & Reiss, 1967; Richardson, 1980). Politicians seeking increasing funds to fight crime or wanting to show success in campaigns against crime influence how police departments record and transmit information. Citizens who believe the police will do nothing about their complaints have few incentives to call the police, and people who believe that they deserve the injuries they receive (for example, in cases of domestic violence) will not seek police involvement. These sources of unreliability, plus known difficulties in ascertaining the population to use as a denominator in computing crime rates, led to a second national effort to collect data about violence.

In 1965–6, The National Opinion Research Center (NORC) undertook a study of households to determine the feasibility of gathering data on crimes from victims and other members of their households. NORC asked 10,000 randomly selected adult informants whether they or any other member of the household had been victims of a variety of crimes included in the Uniform Crime Reports. Among the crimes of violence, only homicide had a lower rate than the official Uniform Crime Reports figures. Victims' reports uncovered approximately twice as much forcible rape, robbery, and aggravated assault as had been reported to police (Ennis, 1967).

To measure crimes not reported to the police, the federal government

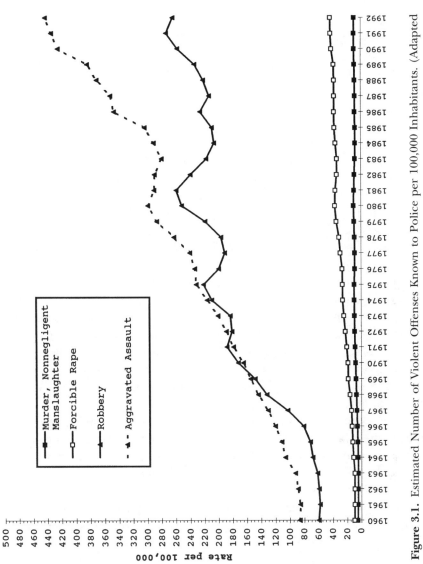

Figure 3.1. Estimated Number of Violent Offenses Known to Police per 100,000 Inhabitants. (Adapted from Maguire & Pastore, 1994, Table 3.94.)

now collects information about victimization through household surveys. These surveys inquire about crimes committed against respondents over the age of eleven. Between 1973 (the first year of record) and 1992, for every 100,000 eligible residents, between 2,810 and 3,450 people reported being victims of rape, robbery, or assault (Bureau of Justice Statistics, 1994). No clear trend in rates of reported victimization is discernible over those years.

The contrast between trends in violent crimes known by the police and those reported to interviewers could be due to a number of factors. To check on one, respondents were asked whether they had reported the incidents of victimization to the police. Throughout the twenty-year period, victims said that they reported to the police less than half the crimes of violence described to the interviewers. The reporting rate for violent crimes ranged from 44.2% in 1978 to 49.8% in 1992 (Bureau of Justice Statistics, 1994). Thus, changes in reporting rates fail to account for the difference. More likely, the difference is due to a combination on the one hand of subtly changing police attitudes toward recording as offenses those acts of violence over which they have discretion and on the other hand, memory "telescoping" that would tend to reduce changes in rates of crime reported retrospectively. The former would tend to produce an increase in violent crimes reported to police coincident with rising consciousness of the rights of minorities, women, and children. The latter would tend to reduce the amount of detectable change in criminality.

The two sources of information – from the police and from victims over the age of eleven – give a more complete picture of crime in the United States than either does alone. Even when combined, however, they overlook nonlethal child abuse, most incidents of domestic violence, and victimization during riots.

Risk is not equally distributed throughout the population. According to figures from the Centers for Disease Control and Prevention, homicide rates for 1989–90 show that black males were nearly eight times as likely as white males and black females were nearly five times as likely as white females to die as victims of intentional violence (Fingerhut, 1993). According to the victim survey of 1992, blacks were approximately 69% more likely than whites to be victims of violent crimes.

A study of age differences in relation to victimization showed that between 1985 and 1988, teenagers were more than twice as likely as adults to be victims of violent crimes. Black teenagers were more likely than white teenagers to be victims of robbery, aggravated assault, and murder. About three out of four of the white teenage victims were attacked by white offenders, and about four out of five of the black teenage victims were attacked by black offenders (Whitaker & Bastian, 1991).

Ten states have reported their number of court cases per 1,000 youths between the ages of ten and seventeen. Figures from these states show increases for every age from 1985 through 1989. In 1989, the rate of cases for blacks was four times greater than the rate for whites (Butts & Conners-Beatty, 1993). In 1990, 114,200 youths under the age of eighteen were arrested for indexed crimes of violence. These arrests accounted for 16% of the arrests for violent crimes (Snyder, 1992).

In recent years, rates of violence have been higher in urban than in suburban or rural areas. In 1992, for example, there were approximately 871 violent crimes known to the police per 100,000 people living in large cities, whereas in smaller cities the rate was 486, and in rural areas the violent crime rate was 220 per 100,000 (Flanagan & Maguire, 1992). The household survey of victims, too, shows higher rates of violent crimes (for victims over the age of eleven, excluding homicide and nonnegligent manslaughter) in urban than in suburban or nonmetropolitan areas. See Figure 3.2.

Of course, only a minority of city residents are violent. Conventionally, sex and racial descriptors have been used to identify groups at risk. The results show that black males are most likely to be both victims and perpe-trators of violence (Gurr, 1989; Lane, 1979; Wilson, 1987). According to the Committee on the Status of Black Americans, "Homicide is the leading cause of death for black males aged 15–34" (Jaynes & Williams, 1989, p. 419).

In summary, this section has shown that historical trends describing rates for violent crimes are untrustworthy, especially because much of the vio-lence was not counted. Nevertheless, reasonable evidence points to declin-ing rates of violence from the last half of the nineteenth century through the early twentieth century. Police records suggest increasing violence over the last thirty years, a trend not confirmed through victim surveys. Com-pared to whites, females, adults, and nonurban residents, black male ado-lescents living in central cities were the most likely candidates to be victims and perpetrators of violent crimes. The following section takes a broader view, comparing violence in the United States with that found in other countries.

American Violence in Cross-National Perspective

In 1968, in the wake of major urban riots, President Johnson created a National Commission on the Causes and Prevention of Violence. That

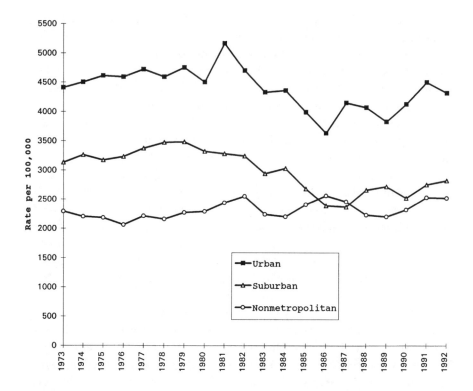

Figure 3.2. Estimated Number of Violent Offenses Reported by Victims over 11 Years in Age per 100,000 Inhabitants. (Adapted from *Criminal Victimization in the U.S.: 1973–92 Trends,* BJS Technical Report, NCJ–147006, 1994, Table 5.)

commission reported, "The United States is the clear leader among modern stable democratic nations in its rates of homicide, assault, rape, and robbery, and it is at least among the highest in incidence of group violence and assassination" (National Commission on the Causes and Prevention of Violence, 1969, p. 2). More than two decades later, the Committee on Law and Justice of the National Research Council sponsored a Panel on Understanding and Control of Violent Behavior. The summary report of the recent panel acknowledges, "Homicide rates in the United States far exceed those in any other industrialized nation" (Reiss & Roth, 1993, p. 3). This section examines some of the evidence for these claims.

Comparisons across cultures are difficult because countries define crimes differently and collect data in different ways (Archer & Gartner, 1984; van Dijk & Mayhew, 1993). For example, in reports of intentional homicide, Sri Lanka includes motor vehicle accidents and accidental deaths from firearms in addition to all deaths resulting from criminal acts. Some countries count crimes if anyone reports them and others only if additional investigations indicate that a crime has occurred or a perpetrator has been found (Pepinsky, 1977; UNAFEI & AIC, 1990). Reporting practices vary also in relation to the availability of police and of the means to communicate with them.

Nevertheless, a variety of studies contribute to the conclusion that America is among the most violent of countries – more violent, in fact, than other industrialized countries. The Comparative Crime Data File contains information on homicide rates for twenty-four nations over roughly equivalent periods between 1961 and 1970 (Archer & Gartner, 1984). These rates placed the United States homicide rate of 6.62 homicides per 100,000 population in the top quartile, above Australia, Austria, Belgium, Finland, Guyana, India, Ireland, Japan, Kenya, the Netherlands, New Zealand, Northern Ireland, Rhodesia, Scotland, Sri Lanka, Spain, and Sudan – but below Mexico, Panama, the Philippines, Trinidad and Tobago, and Turkey.

Martin Killias (1990) compared the homicide rates of eleven countries, averaging the years from 1983 through 1986 (except for Finland, where the data came from the years 1970–79). The United States, with a homicide rate of 7.6 per 100,000 residents, clearly exceeded France (4.4), Finland (2.9), Canada (2.6), Australia (2.0), Belgium (1.9), West Germany (1.5), Switzerland (1.2), the Netherlands (1.2), Norway (1.2), and England and Wales (.7).

Although homicide is but one form of violence and depends partially on distance from good medical assistance (Giacopassi, Sparger, & Stein, 1992; Lane, 1979), homicide rates yield an index of violence somewhat less subject to reporting errors than rates for other types of crimes. Death certificates from the United States and reported deaths from nine other nations for 1989–90 show that the homicide rate in the United States was between three and twenty times as great as those of the following contrast nations (listed in decreasing order): Scotland, Hungary, Canada, Portugal, Austria, Switzerland, Denmark, Japan, and England/Wales (Fingerhut, 1993).

The Third United Nations Survey for 1986 gathered data for crimes reported to the police. Robbery, a personal violent offense, appeared to have been counted similarly among twenty-three of the reporting nations (Pease & Hukkila, 1990). Rates per 100,000 ranged from 1 in Cyprus to 223 in the United States. These rates are presented in Table 3.1.

Partly to overcome problems of comparing crime rates in different countries, a group of researchers, who began data collection in 1988,

Table 3.1. *United Nations survey*

Robbery Rates per 100,000 Population: 1986	
Austria	15
Bulgaria	7
Canada	93
Cyprus	1
Czechoslovakia	9
Denmark	36
Federal German Republic	48
Finland	33
France	92
German Democratic Republic	5
Hungary	15
Italy	44
Malta	12
The Netherlands	73
Norway	15
Poland	16
Portugal	33
Switzerland	20
USSR	16
United Kingdom	
England & Wales	60
Northern Ireland	138
Scotland	80
United States	223

Adapted from Pease and Hukkila, 1990, Table 1.

constructed the International Crime Survey on victimization. The surveys used standardized questions and most used similar sampling techniques. Like the data based on official records, these data are imperfect indicators of criminal violence (Block, 1993; Kury & Würger, 1993). They too, however, point to the United States as a violent country. Response rates were low, but the data suggested that residents of the United States were more likely to have been assaulted than were those living in Australia, West Germany, Spain, Scotland, Norway, Belgium, Northern Ireland, the Netherlands, France, Finland, England and Wales, or Switzerland (van Dijk, Mayhew, & Killias, 1991).

Table 3.2. *Urban violent crimes*

City	Population	Violent Crime Rates per 100,000 People Year	Rate
Tokyo, Japan	29,320,000	1983	3.1[a]
Bangkok-Thonburi, Thailand	5,331,402	1981	75.1[b]
Lagos, Nigeria	4,923,000	1981	37.5[c]
Bogota, Columbia	4,200,000	1983	114.6[d]
Singapore	2,500,000	1983	5.4[e]
Warsaw, Poland	1,641,300	1983	79.3[f]
Nairobi, Kenya	896,819	1980	2,187.4[g]
San José, Costa Rica	679,432	1984	48.9[h]

[a] known to police: murder (excluding traffic accidents), rape, robbery (excluding extortion).
[b] known to police: murder, attempted murder, assault, gang robbery, robbery, forcible rape.
[c] known to police: murder, attempted murder, assault, robbery, rape.
[d] reached judiciary: average frequency 1981–3 for homicide plus assault.
[e] recorded offences: crimes against the person plus violent property crimes.
[f] offences cleared: homicide, assault, rape, robbery
[g] known to police: murder, attempted murder, assault, robbery, rape, attempted rape.
[h] reached judiciary: homicide, attempted homicide, assault, rape (excluding statutory), attempted rape.
Compiled from data presented in Buendia, 1989, for each city.

A second victim survey in 1992 enlarged the sample so that comparative figures could be reported for twenty countries, including some from Eastern Europe (van Dijk & Mayhew, 1992). Excepting Spain and Poland, the proportion of respondents who had been victims of robberies was highest for the United States. The proportion of respondents who reported having been personally attacked or threatened by someone in a way that really frightened them was higher in the United States than in all other countries except New Zealand.

The United Nations' efforts to establish uniform crime reporting depicts violent crimes in the largest cities of eight countries (Buendia, 1989). Except for Nairobi's rate of 2,187 per 100,000 residents, none of the cities surveyed came close to the United States average of 638.9 violent crimes known to police in large cities for the comparable year of 1984 (Flanagan & McGarrell, 1986). See Table 3.2.

More recent data show that in 1992, New York City had a rate of violent crimes known to the police of 2,163.7 per 100,000 people; Atlanta's rate of violent crimes was 3,859.1; that for Miami was 3,730.7; and for Los Angeles it was 2,459.5. Even among those large cities – over 250,000 in population – which have relatively low rates of violent crimes known to the police, the rates exceed those found in the United Nations survey. Honolulu, with a rate of 272.1, and Virginia Beach, with a rate of 285.1, had the lowest rates (Maguire & Pastore, 1994). The comparisons across countries demonstrate greater urban violence in America than in the major cities of any other industrialized country.

The following section considers conditions that contribute to violence in urban America.

Violence as an American Phenomenon

Just as individuals can be understood by looking at patterns of their behavior, explanations for the extremely high rates of American urban violence today can be found by examining patterns in American history. Lawrence Friedman refers to violence as being "as American as apple pie . . . by tradition, by inheritance, by ingrained habit" (1993, p. 173). Reflecting on the history of American violence, Richard Hofstadter refers to the "historic amnesia" of Americans with regard to violence. He wrote,

> What is impressive to one who begins to learn about American violence is its extraordinary frequency, its sheer commonplaceness in our history, its persistence into very recent and contemporary times, and its rather abrupt contrast with our pretensions to singular national virtue (1970/1971, p. 7).

During the 1960s, three major commissions addressed issues of violence in America: the President's Commission on Law Enforcement and Administration of Justice (1965), the National Advisory Commission on Civil Disorders (1967), and the National Commission on the Causes and Prevention of Violence (1968). Although few of their recommendations were carried out, these commissions generated and publicized a considerable amount of useful research. Philip Taft and Philip Ross, who described American labor violence for the National Commission on the Causes and Prevention of Violence, for example, reached the conclusion that

> the United Stated has had the bloodiest and most violent labor history of any industrial nation in the world. . . . The precipitating causes have been attempts by pickets and sympathizers to prevent a plant on strike from being reopened with strikebreakers, or attempts of company guards, police, or even by National Guardsmen to prevent such interference (1969/1970, p. 281).

The violence appeared particularly incongruous because it occurred despite the fact that no American labor union openly favored the use of violence. Peter Rossi and Richard Berk discovered that police brutality as well as exploitation of blacks by retail merchants were "conditions underlying the civil disorders of the sixties" (1970, p. 126). "Only recently," wrote James F. Short, Jr., and Marvin E. Wolfgang, who codirected research for the third panel, "have scholars concerned with crime focused on the role of law enforcement agents and agencies as contributors to the very behavior they are ostensibly designed to eliminate" (1970, p. 2).

For purposes of exposing patterns of violence, Richard Maxwell Brown divided American violence into two types. Negative violence included "criminal violence, feuds, lynching, the violence of prejudice (racial, ethnic, and religious violence), urban riots, freelance multiple murder, and assassination" (1969/1970, p. 45). Constructive violence, on the other hand, included "some of the most important events of American history" (p. 46). Among the latter, Brown pointed to the "domestic violence" of the American Revolution, the violence engendered by the Civil War, fighting against American Indians, vigilante action "to establish order and stability on the frontier," agrarian violence to "ease the plight of the farmer," labor violence as part of the workers' "struggle to gain recognition and a decent life," and police violence "to protect society against the criminal and disorderly" (p. 46). Two decades later, Brown expressed his considered view of historical patterns of American violence when he wrote, "Given sanctification by the Revolution, Americans have never been loath to employ unremitting violence in the interest of any cause deemed a good one" (1989, p. 26).

Two inadequate theories have often been proposed as general explanations for high crime rates in America. The first rests on the assumption that

Americans embrace individualism and violence because they emanate from a frontier history (Gastil, 1971; Wolfgang & Ferracuti, 1967). The second rests on the notion that immigration brings people to America who do not share its values or cannot achieve its rewards (Gordon, 1964; Higham, 1955/1963; Lukoff & Brook, 1974; Park & Burgess, 1925/1967). Although these theories deserve consideration, they should be rejected.

The idea that American culture can best be understood in terms of a continuous conquering of a receding frontier became popular through the writing and teaching of Frederick Jackson Turner. Turner argued, "The existence of an area of free land, its continuous recession, and the advance of American settlement westward, explain American development" (1894, p. 199). Settling the frontier presented a repetitive set of conditions that rewarded strength, energy, independence, and physical prowess. The "crucible of the frontier" Americanized immigrants. According to this thesis, the frontier produced selfishness, individualism, and antipathy to control. The proponents of this argument also credited the expanding frontier for producing an American character which is optimistic, independent, inquisitive, and pragmatically materialistic.

The frontier explanation for violence has several problems. Friedman questioned whether the western frontier was ever particularly violent. Although the western frontier attracted "rootless, deracinated men . . . who carry the germ of violence" (1993, p. 176), Friedman noted that Norwegian farmers in North Dakota and German Mennonites in Kansas settled frontiers peacefully.

The claim that frontiersmen showed contempt for law seems to misrepresent the character of even some of the mining towns, where armed consenting adults frequently fought over real or imagined insults (McGrath, 1989). In such towns, there was little robbery, burglary, or theft, and both "ladies" and children were generally safe. Without denying that the history of every western state was "replete with lawlessness" (1974, p. vii), W. Eugene Hollon criticized the frontier-violence explanation because American violence "was well developed long before large numbers of settlers were ready to move into the Great Plains and the Far West" (p. 35).

Describing the history of urban violence, Richard Wade pointed out that "disorder and violence in our cities were not simply occasional aberrations, but rather a significant part of urban development and growth" (1972, p. 475). Wade attributed the violence to a combination of the speed of urban development, the absence of a tradition of obedience to local authority, the presence of a sizeable transient population, the shifting class lines, and the influx of new blood fueling the struggle for dominance. Citing the report of the National Commission on the Causes and Prevention of Violence as evidence that "violence in America has traditionally been an urban rather than a frontier problem" (1974, p. 194), Hollon suggested that the notion that a frontier culture accounted for American violence could be attributed, in part, to exaggeration promoted by disillusioned westerners whose lives in fact were filled with boredom.

Some critics of the frontier explanation for violence have noted the degree to which cooperation played a role in the settlement of frontier territories. Other critics of the individualism-as-cause theory note how American fashions of dress, speech, and behavior represent conformity as opposed to individualism. Another criticism appears to be particularly salient: Despite sharing a frontier orientation, Canadian cities have rates of violence considerably lower than those found in the United States.

The claim that immigrants are responsible for a good deal of criminal violence has been so widely held that it contributed to anti-immigration legislation (Handlin, 1950; Higham, 1955/1963; Hofstadter, 1955; Solomon, 1956; Ward, 1989). This opinion rested on the belief that deviant behavior provided immigrants with their only means for achieving success (Cloward & Ohlin, 1960; Ferdinand, 1967; Glazer & Moynihan, 1963). The fact that immigrants typically rose through the occupational hierarchy, leaving the place at the bottom to newer and poorer immigrant groups, has given credence to the belief (Steinberg, 1989; Thernstrom, 1973).

The immigration argument is worth considering because parallels have been drawn between the experiences of immigrants from Europe and the experiences of blacks who migrated to northern cities. The parallel provides a basis for believing that time and economic opportunities will heal the wounds now festering in urban areas.

Although violence was associated with some specific types of crime that were dominated by ethnic groups (Haller, 1971–72), the immigration argument is not supported by the evidence. Immigrants lived in areas of high criminal activity (Hawes, 1971; Hogan, 1985; Menninger, 1947; Shaw & McKay, 1942/1972; Tarde 1897/1969; Wade, 1959; Ward, 1989; Weber, 1899/1963), and yet immigrants themselves were not disproportionately responsible for the violence. For example, among families living in impoverished areas of Cambridge and Somerville, Massachusetts, during the 1930s, those who were immigrants or sons of immigrants were not more likely to be convicted of crimes of violence than were native-born men and their sons (McCord, 1995). Rates for murder, assault, and robbery in Boston declined between 1878 and 1951 during periods of enormous growth through immigration (Ferdinand, 1967). Homicide rates in Philadelphia from 1790 to 1810 were not lower than those in 1937, although large waves of immigration occurred during the intervening period (Hobbs, 1943). Between 1860 and 1900, with the exception of Italians, homicide rates among new immigrants and their offspring were *lower* than those among older stock in Philadelphia (Lane, 1979).

To summarize: In comparison with other industrialized countries, the United States has exceptionally high rates of criminal violence. These high rates are due neither to frontier values nor to the behavior of immigrants. It therefore seems appropriate to look more closely at American culture, taking account of the pattern of urban development.

Violence and Cities

Wilbur R. Miller described New York in 1845 as "a violent city, whose disorder seemed to be steadily outstripping a police force plagued by manpower shortages and disciplinary problems" (1975, p. 94). New York City slums "swarmed with thieves, murderers, pickpockets, beggars, harlots, and degenerates of every type. . . . [I]t has been estimated that for almost fifteen years the Old Brewery averaged a murder a night" (Asbury, 1927, p. 15). Describing conditions for free blacks in the 1850s, Lerone Bennett, Jr., wrote, "Most free blacks at this juncture lived along the docks and wharves and in alleys. Wherever they lived, people wanted them to go away. . . . Time and time again, immigrants, fresh from the boats, cracked their skulls and burned their homes and churches" (1962/1993, p. 181). Crimes of violence in Philadelphia included teenage loungers who "pelted the citizenry with snowballs, rocks, or bricks" and inflicted beatings on those who objected (Johnson, 1973, p. 97). David R. Johnson described roaming gangs who fought with fists and pistols for pleasure, adding that "unprovoked assaults occurred with distressing frequency on the city's south side and in the less densely settled areas to the north" (p. 100). In antebellum Philadelphia, "[S]ome blacks were killed, many beaten, and others run out of town" (Hershberg, 1973, p. 113). Late in the nineteenth century, juries convicted fewer than half of all those indicted for murder, because "[m]iddle-class juries were fully aware that drunken violence was commonplace in the City of Brotherly Love" (Lane, 1980, p. 94).

In short, violence in urban America is not new. Perhaps the urban environment attracts violent people or perhaps conditions of urban living are conducive to violence. Of course these are not mutually exclusive alternatives. They have worked in conjunction with governmental policies that have helped to create pockets of poverty and of potential violence within American cities (Bartelt, 1993; Drake & Cayton, 1945/1962; Jaynes & Williams, 1989; Trotter, 1993; Wade, 1972; Yancey, Ericksen & Juliani, 1976).

Several studies have shown that urban residents and those who migrate to cities are more likely to be tolerant of people different from themselves than are those who never lived in cities (Abrahamson & Carter, 1986; Fischer, 1971; Tuch, 1987; Wilson, 1991). Tolerance is likely to make a city attractive to those who are unconventional. Thus, cities tend to gather individuals who differ in habits, values, and attitudes. Differences in the aggregate tend to produce conditions for subcultural affiliation (Fischer, 1975). Once subcultures have been differentiated, once a critical mass of "deviant" people has been collected, subcultures develop internal cohesion and generate both competition and conflict with outsiders (Fischer, 1975; Haller, 1973; Taylor, 1979; Yancey, Ericksen, & Juliani, 1976).

Although subcultural affiliations ameliorate the isolation of city living, urban dwellers spend much of their time surrounded by those who do not know them (Fischer, 1973; Skogan, 1979). Anonymity weakens both social control and *social support*, the availability of people to provide help when help is wanted. Lack of social support characterizes neighborhoods at high risk for spousal and child abuse (Earls & Barnes, this volume; Garbarino & Sherman, 1980; Sampson, this volume). Witnessing aggression and being abused as a child, in turn, increase the risks for becoming violent (McCord, 1988; Widom, 1989).

Urban life may also contribute to violence because it is difficult to supervise children in crowded areas where people can easily hide or disappear. The problem is particularly acute for poor families, both because adult caretakers work and because there are few attractive places for children to play (Anderson, this volume). Unsupervised children so commonly roamed the streets during the last half of the nineteenth century that returning lost children was an important part of urban policing (Lane, 1967; Monkkonen, 1981). Through the early decades of the twentieth century, criminal justice agencies used child-placing in families outside cities as a crime prevention strategy for those children who lacked "proper supervision and right personal direction" (Slingerland, 1919, p. 66; see also Brace, 1872; Hawes, 1971; Mennel, 1973; Platt, 1969/1977). Mark H. Haller (1972) credited lack of supervision in urban environments as a factor in the development of a separate youth culture.

Contemporary research shows that lack of supervision is a predictor of delinquency (Lizotte, Thornberry, Krohn, Chard-Wierschem, & McDowall, 1994; Loeber & Stouthamer-Loeber, 1986; Wilson, 1987) and of subsequent crimes against persons (McCord, 1979). Residents in high-density housing also tend to be single mothers. The failure of single-parent families to provide supervision may partially account for a strong ecological relation between areas with many single-parent families and violence (Gelles, 1989; Sampson, 1987; this volume).

In summary, American cities have a long history of violence. That violence appears to be promoted by subcultures that develop cohesion in an environment that attracts the unconventional. The cohesive subcultures encourage differentiation and, often, conflict between themselves and others. Furthermore, city life impedes social controls both by permitting anonymity among adults and by reducing the probability that youths in poor families will be supervised.

The next section reviews some of the developments of cities in America and shows how government policies have, perhaps unintentionally, exacerbated conditions that contribute to urban violence.

Policies and Urban America

Inner-city ghettos have been created by a series of government policies appended to the uncontrolled expansion of urban centers. These policies pertain to housing, zoning ordinances, tax incentives, decisions about transportation, loan policies, job opportunities, and the decentralization of taxing power. The policies were designed to promote industrial development and support economic progress. Their effects must be understood in the light of a history that included rapid urban expansion, industrialization, racial discrimination, and suburbanization.

Policies that have helped isolate the poor in American cities can be traced, in part, to governmental support for migration from population centers to their outskirts. By way of contrast, in Europe, governments protected land and restricted suburban development. European taxes supported public mass transportation and, in many older cities, public housing was constructed at the outskirts rather than in the center of cities (Jackson, 1985).

During the nineteenth century, city culture spread across America, "bringing urban ways into areas that knew no cities" (Barth, 1980, p. 233). Prejudice and exclusionary rules prevented blacks from benefiting in terms of either housing or employment from their own diligent efforts (Bennett, 1962/1993; Lane, 1986; Wade, 1972).

City life had become dominant in the West by 1829, a region that included Pittsburgh, Cincinnati, Lexington, and Louisville as well as Portland and San Francisco (Wade, 1959). During the first half of the century, cities were walking size. Many of the poor and blacks lived on the periphery, in suburbs, amid such distasteful businesses as slaughterhouses and tanneries (Jackson, 1985; Wade, 1964).

The last half of the nineteenth century was a period of enormous urban growth and mobility (Barth, 1980; Blumin, 1973; Park & Burgess, 1925/ 1967; Thernstrom, 1964/1970). Mass transportation facilitated centralization of industries (Warner, 1962/1978; Yancey, Ericksen, & Juliani, 1976). Gangs of white boys made it a practice to attack blacks, many of whom carried weapons for their own protection (Lane, 1986). Both the poor and the unemployed migrated from city to city, with only about 40% of the urban residents remaining in a single city for two decennial census enumerations; an estimated 10%–20% of the urban population lived in families that had a member who tramped in search of work at some time (Sugrue, 1993). Bands of wanderers and crowded conditions for workers contributed to urban disorganization.

Around the same time, romantic notions about country life promoted the building of a new type of suburb, where wealthy families could escape the turmoil of city living. Railroads and telegraph wires fostered the development. The middle classes followed the wealthy, buying homes built on smaller plots. Builders designed housing in economically – as well as racially – segregated suburbs (Barth, 1980; Sugrue, 1993; Ward, 1971; Warner, 1962/1978). Old city houses were turned into commercial properties or became homes to poorer families, often to be split into multiple-family dwellings (Johnson, 1973; Sugrue, 1993; Warner, 1962/1978; Yancey, Ericksen, & Juliani, 1976).

Between 1900 and 1915, three-quarters of the 14.5 million immigrants who arrived in the United States settled in cities, where rapid industrial growth enabled them to find employment and take over many of the skilled jobs in which blacks had been employed (Axinn & Levin, 1975; Bennett, 1962/1993; Lane, 1986; Ward, 1971).

During the period of rapid industrialization, blacks were excluded from the newly created positions and discriminated against in continuing older ones (Hershberg, Burstein, Ericksen, Greenberg, & Yancey, 1979; Lane, 1986). Those who did find work "stayed mired in unskilled, deadend, service jobs" (Lane, 1986, p. 141). Most unions refused to admit blacks. Employers fueled racial tensions by using or threatening to use blacks as strikebreakers (Lane, 1986; Olzak, 1989; Spear, 1967). Blacks were employed as strikebreakers in the steel mills of Pittsburgh in 1875, 1888, 1892, and 1909. In Chicago stockyards, where both blacks and Poles were strikebreakers in 1904 and 1905, the Poles kept their jobs and most of the blacks were fired (Spear, 1967; Trotter, 1993). Those few blacks able to afford comfortable housing found themselves subjected to violence when persuasion, blacklisting, and boycotting failed to convince them to live in designated black neighborhoods (Horton, 1993; Spear, 1967; Wade, 1972).

Automobiles transformed the relationship between cities and their suburbs (Stilgoe, 1988; Ward, 1971; Warner, 1962/1978). The Federal Highway Act of 1916 contributed to suburban growth. Public funds were used both to remove horses from the cities and to construct roads upon which automobiles could travel to and around the suburbs. In 1924, Henry Ford dropped the price of a Model T from $950 to $290, enabling the middle class to buy mass-produced automobiles. By 1929, every state had enacted a gasoline tax. Funds from these taxes were dedicated to the construction of highways and to providing support for private automobiles and trucks rather than for mass transportation and railroad hauling (Jackson, 1985). The choice to support highway construction in lieu of mass transportation involved supporting those who could afford automobiles without supporting forms of mobility available to the poor.

Zoning restrictions further contributed to separation of the social classes. Suburban residential zones promulgated restrictions stipulating required distances for street setbacks and separations between houses, as well as requirements for floor areas and minimum land-parcel sizes. These restrictions effectively produced affluent sanctuaries from which the poor were excluded as residents.

Federal loan policies created under the New Deal served to perpetuate segregated housing. These policies used racial criteria in deciding whether or not to approve loans.

Franklin D. Roosevelt signed a law creating the Home Owners' Loan Corporation on June 13, 1933. Using standardized and discriminatory appraisal policies, the Home Owners' Loan Corporation trained appraisers in every American city with a population greater than 25,000 (Jackson, 1985). The guidelines, transferred to the Federal Housing Authority during the 1940s, "show clearly that racial and ethnic characteristics of neighborhoods were an integral part of the decision to extend credit to some neighborhoods and deny it to others" (Bartelt, 1993, p. 147). Negative attitudes toward urban life were reflected in the appraisers' judgments, making it difficult for applicants to receive approval for a loan on urban property. Furthermore, neighborhoods with black residents never were given a rating above the fourth from highest (Jackson, 1985). The practice of downgrading housing with reference to ethnic composition of the neighborhood, known as redlining, continued until 1975.

After World War II, federally guaranteed loans made ownership in tract housing cheaper than many rentals. These loans distributed benefits to middle class families and encouraged their migration to the suburbs. Federal Housing Authority and Veterans Administration loans offered insurance only for new construction. They precluded constructions that would change a neighborhood's "character," a term used to refer to racial composition as well as land use (Adams et al., 1991; Bartelt, 1993; Jackson, 1985). Thus, blacks typically were forced to live in housing owned by absentee landlords who lacked incentives to improve their property.

Additional aid for the middle class and wealthy came through the tax deductions attached to home mortgages. Owners, but not renters, benefit from this tax relief for housing. The federal tax deduction for mortgage payments amounted to subsidies of billions of dollars a year (Bartelt, 1993).

After the end of World War II, highway construction and the availability of electrical energy contributed to an exodus of industries from cities. In the suburbs, plentiful land could be used for parking lots and for building relatively inexpensive single-story industrial structures. Tax laws allowing accelerated depreciation for new constructions favored abandonment of older urban buildings (Adams et al., 1991; Robinson, 1993). Passage of the federal Interstate Highway Act in 1956 further contributed to the migration of industries into the suburbs (Sugrue, 1993). Shopping malls and other services followed industries in the exodus. Effects of the shift can be seen in the Philadelphia area: In 1951, two-thirds of the job opportunities available in the region were city jobs, but by 1980, the city proportion had declined almost by half, to 38.6% (Adams et al., 1991).

Meanwhile, the black population in northern cities had increased dramatically. That increase was due, in part, to the effects of mechanization on southern farm ownership. Mechanization benefited those whose farms were large – in other words, whites – making it difficult for owners of smaller farms to compete. Gunnar Myrdal (1944) estimated that between 1909 and 1929, white farmers east of the Mississippi increased cotton production by 90,000 bales, while black-operated farms decreased production by 643,000 bales.

Black farmers, kept in the cotton fields before mechanization by Black Codes restricting their employment for higher wages elsewhere (Bennett, 1962/1993; Robinson, 1993), were encouraged to go north when their hands were no longer needed on the farms. Although blacks had filled approximately two-thirds of the skilled labor positions in the South prior to emancipation, after the war, "southern laws, licensing restrictions, and whites' refusal to work with blacks had denied them skilled employment in the South" (Robinson, 1993, p. 288).

In 1900, 80%–90% of American blacks lived in the rural South. Until 1910, blacks migrated only gradually to cities in the North, typically in search of better opportunities (Myrdal, 1944). In 1916 and 1917, with immigration halted by the war, prosperous northern industries recruited southern blacks, creating a massive stream of migration that "made race relations not just a provincial concern of the former Confederacy, but for the first time an urban and national concern" (Pettigrew, 1979, p. 121). By 1970, over 80% of American blacks lived in urban areas (Roof, 1979). Yet by 1970, relocation and transformation of industries had removed most of the job opportunities for blacks. "Jobs in the central city, mostly white-collar, were taken by whites driving in from suburban homes, financed by federally secured mortgages, over federally built roads" (Robinson, 1993, p. 303).

The northern migration of blacks brought about strenuous and often violent resistance to integrated housing. Middle-class blacks were unable to reap the fruits of their labor in terms of homes and schools for their children (Wade, 1972). Restrictive covenants institutionalized the separation between blacks and whites, confining blacks to areas in which the schools were poor, the roads badly maintained, and the public services inferior. In 1944, although powerless to change the situation, the Mayor's Committee of Chicago went on record in opposition to "conspiracies known as restrictive covenants" (Drake & Cayton, 1945/1962, p. 212). These covenants became illegal in 1948, with the Shelley vs. Kraemer decision, but "gentlemen's agreements" among realtors and mortgage policies by banks perpetuated practices that restricted most housing to whites only (Sugrue, 1993). Although the Civil Rights Act of 1968 banned discrimination in the sale or rental of housing, violations have rarely been prosecuted. Landlords elevated rents for black tenants trapped by housing restrictions, and grocery store owners raised their prices in black neighborhoods, often by as much as 30% (Robinson, 1993).

Until 1950, Federal Housing Authority regulations prohibited loans that would encourage or permit racial integration. As John M. Stahura pointed out, "Even after the formal regulations were changed in the early 1960s, the administrative practice of keeping blacks out of white areas continued" (1986, p. 133).

Housing segregation interacted with the policy of local taxes to exacerbate the struggles of urban residents. Prosperous suburbs could incorporate separately and devote few community resources to welfare. Taxes could be low and dedicated to such benefits as education and public lands. Low taxes attracted businesses, further reducing the tax base for urban areas. Kenneth T. Jackson described some of the effects of suburbanization: "As larger numbers of affluent citizens moved out, jobs followed. In turn this attracted more families, more roads, and more industries. The cities were often caught in a reverse cycle" (1985, pp. 284–5).

A policy of heavy reliance on local taxes left those least able to pay for them most responsible for supporting welfare, police, and urban services. Low income contributed to increased demand for public housing, health care, and social services. Increased taxes became necessary to provide these services, and increased taxes induced the middle class and affluent to migrate out of the cities – leaving the cities with even higher proportions of low-income residents.

During the period of rapid construction of the suburbs, public housing was largely restricted to already congested urban areas. In the United States, public housing required local authorization, which enabled residents to decide what kind of housing, if any, to permit in their neighborhoods. The very poor were encouraged to remain in congested areas by legislative tactics that permitted public housing as replacement only for existing slum dwellings. In 1980, public housing constituted only about 1% of the United States housing market; this can be compared with 46% in England/Wales and 37% in France (Jackson, 1985).

One result of residential segregation was the disappearance of what Eric Monkkonen (1977/1979) referred to as a common "grammar" of behavior. "The fundamental precondition for public order," wrote Ted Robert Gurr, "is congruence between the cultural values of the ordinary members of a society and the operating codes of order and opportunity maintained by political elites" (1976, p. 183). During the nineteenth century, daily contact brought about through close living in urban areas facilitated cooperation and development of shared values. Roger Lane suggested that urbanization resulted in a "settling, literally a civilizing, effect on the population involved" (1969/1970, p. 469). In rural America, he noted, no built-in checks restricted fits of violence or bouts of drunkenness. City living and employment, however, required coordination and "obedience to the rhythms of clock and calendar" (1969/1970, p. 477).

As a result of housing segregation, denigration of public transportation, and the movement of industries to the suburbs, the uneducated were separated from locations where they might obtain employment (Kasarda, 1989, 1992; Lichter, 1988; Wilson, 1991). They lacked what William Julius Wilson refers to as a "coherent organization of the present" (1991, p. 10).

Having a job creates a framework for eating, sleeping, and arranging activities. If Lane (1986) is correct about the civilizing influences of employment in industries, then there is reason to suspect that longstanding joblessness has taken a toll in terms of reducing inhibitions against personal displays of violence.

Even in neighborhoods where violence is prevalent, of course, one can find law-abiding citizens. Nevertheless, "a social context that includes poor schools, inadequate job information networks, and a lack of legitimate employment" leads to "a weak labor-force attachment" and increases pressure "to seek income derived from illegal or deviant activities" (Wilson, 1991, p. 10). Evidence fortifies Wilson's argument. In 1980, rates of violent crime in high poverty areas of Washington, D.C., were three times as great as those in nonpoverty neighborhoods. Between 1980 and 1988, the increase in rates for violent crime was more than four times as large in the high-poverty neighborhoods (Peterson & Harrell, 1992).

Illicit drugs, meanwhile, supply both lifestyle and financial support to the ghetto, with violence a not infrequent accompaniment (Dunlap, 1992; Fagan, 1992). Likening the attraction of drug dealing to that of bootlegging, Haller suggested that "young men from ethnic ghettos have assumed the risks of violence and of jails in pursuit of their version of the American dream" (1989, p. 158).

In summary, this section has shown how federal policies helped drain resources from American cities. Policies designed to contribute to growth outside the cities contributed also to isolating and emasculating poor and black urban residents.

The next and final section suggests ways in which American culture contributes to violence among some of those trapped in cities by circumstances beyond their control.

American Culture and Violence

Alexis de Tocqueville argued persuasively that American culture is permeated both by a rhetoric of equality and by a strong emphasis on personal success. He suggested the result was a disquieting emphasis on symbols of status presumed to be available to all. Tocqueville postulated that when

> the distinctions of ranks are obliterated and privileges are destroyed, when hereditary property is subdivided and education and freedom are widely diffused, the desire of acquiring the comforts of the world haunts the imagination of the poor, and the dread of losing them that of the rich (1835/1961, pp. 136–7).

Francis Joseph Grund, an immigrant from Vienna around 1827, reported that American society

> is characterized by a spirit of exclusiveness and persecution unknown in any other country. Its gradations not being regulated according to rank and titles, selfishness and conceit are its principal elements; and its arbitrary distinctions the more offensive, as they principally refer to fortune (1839/ 1959, p. 52).

Robert E. Park similarly observed, "The tenets of American democracy had done away with the aristocratic titles that ranked people in Europe. But in this professedly egalitarian society the modern city accepted a hierarchy in which money was the badge of distinction" (Park & Burgess, 1925/1967, p. 20). E. Digby Baltzell, analyzing a failure of the American educational system to engender commitment to public service among the upper class, attributed it to "a society which, ideologically and morally, places such an emphasis on material success" (1958, p. 314).

A presumption of equality underlies the belief that anyone can be successful. Being successful is, on this assumption, a sign of character and the proper basis for self-esteem and privilege (Weber, 1920/1958). What counts as success will differ, of course, in relation to where one is in a social hierarchy and what one considers as justified expectations.

Tocqueville (1835/1961) and Gunnar Myrdal (1944) were among the many reporters on America who deplored the unequal treatment of blacks and American Indians. "The Negro helped to make America what it was and what it is," noted Benjamin Quarles (1964, p. 7), a historian trying to correct the silence about contributions blacks have made to what is right in America. When the Civil War began, there were 488,070 free blacks. In Chicago, where a small pocket of free blacks had formed a community, "the laws of the state forbade intermarriage and voting by Negroes. Segregation on common carriers and in the schools and theaters was widespread" (Drake & Cayton, 1945/1962, p. 41). In Philadelphia between 1838 and 1860, while occupational opportunities for whites were increasing, "blacks were not only denied access to new jobs in the expanding factory system . . . they also lost their traditional predominance in many skilled and unskilled occupations" (Hershberg, 1973, p. 117; see also Hershberg et al., 1979; Ward, 1989). Even after the Civil War, blacks were largely excluded from educational institutions and factory as well as white collar occupations (Drake & Cayton, 1945/1962; Hershberg et al., 1979; Horton, 1993; Jones, 1993; Kirschenman & Neckerman, 1991; Lane, 1986; Steinberg, 1989; Thernstrom, 1973; Trotter, 1993).

There is another factor to be considered when attempting to understand violence – and that is the appearance of injustice (Carstairs, 1969/1970; Gans, 1988/1991; LaFree, Drass, & O'Day, 1992; Pettigrew, 1979; Smith, 1976; Taeuber, 1979). During the 1960s, the civil rights movement promised a better world, a world in which blacks would be given the opportunities so long denied them. That promise brought with it a new sense of injustice when discrimination continued (Jaynes & Williams, 1989).

The key to understanding high rates of violence may lie, as suggested by Hershberg (1973), in comprehending the urban context of discrimination and structural inequality facing black residents of American cities in a country promising equality for all. Sampson found that "the worst urban contexts in which whites reside with respect to poverty and family disruption are considerably better off than the *mean* levels for black communities" (1987, pp. 353–4, italics in original). Wacquant and Wilson suggested that

> the cumulative structural entrapment and forcible socioeconomic marginalization resulting from the historically evolving interplay of class, racial, and gender domination, together with sea changes in the organization of American capitalism and failed urban and social policies . . . explain the plight of today's ghetto blacks (1989, p. 25).

"It is not equality of *condition* but equality of *opportunity* that Americans have celebrated," wrote Stephan Thernstrom. He continued, "If careers are genuinely open to the talented, if all have an equal chance to compete for wealth, power, and prestige, the distribution that results is deemed just, however unequal" (1973, p. 256, italics in original). Democracy as practiced in America, however, has not made opportunities equally available to all. Nevertheless, because American culture has its roots in commitment to equality, differences in wealth or power give rise to moral tensions. The rich have reason to believe they are deserving (Thernstrom, 1964/1970). Those who are powerful tend to believe they earned their status and that their social status marks them as superior (Form & Rytina, 1969; Katz, 1993; Lubove, 1965/1980).

One result of moralizing differences in wealth is that the rich tend to treat the poor as undeserving. In doing so, they contribute to resentment among the poor. Resentment, rather than jealousy, seems to motivate some of the destruction accompanying modern urban riots, what seems to be pointless violence, and a good deal of juvenile delinquency.

At first consideration, perception of injustice may appear to have little to do with current urban violence because blacks so frequently are targets as well as perpetrators. Yet targets of violence often are not the source of anger. An angry person may hit the wall as a substitute for his opponent. A frustrated worker may kick the cat. Targets of anger may be hard to reach, but targets of aggression must be proximate. Although wealthy and powerful people are primary targets for this type of "justified" anger, segregation tends to make them unavailable as targets for aggression.

Albert K. Cohen described the dominant type of delinquency that arose from subcultures as "*non-utilitarian, malicious* and *negativistic*" (1955, italics in original, p. 25). He identified the process by which youngsters become delinquents as one in which a boy learns that he is not to be included in activities that more affluent and powerful peers make attractive. Cohen concluded, "It seems reasonable to assume that out of all this there arise feelings of inferiority and perhaps resentment and hostility" (p. 112).

Cohen considered improved status, a characteristic that depends on group responses, to be the primary goal for delinquency. More recently, the theory has been transformed to suggest that a desire for improved self-esteem (which can be seen as a product of having a certain status) motivates delinquency. Although attempts to show that delinquency results from desires to improve self-esteem have a mixed history (Bynner, O'Malley, & Bachman, 1981; Gold & Mann, 1972; Kaplan, 1980; McCarthy & Hoge, 1984; Wells & Rankin, 1983), the descriptive value of Cohen's work, particularly in the light of analyses of ghetto black culture, remains important.

In his interviews with violent men, Hans Toch (1969/1984) provided numerous examples of the types of perceived challenges that generate assaultive behavior, those situations that engendered resentment in the assailants. For example, quoting a male convict who had responded to a question about whether his victim had encouraged an assault, Toch wrote, "'He laughed, you know, he laughed. This righteously did make me angry cause he's more or less trying to floor show for the young ladies he's with'" (p. 21).

Jack Katz (1988) identified three features of typical homicides: self-righteousness, lack of premeditation, and the absence of a clear connection between the assailant's goals and the results of his actions. One of the problems an assailant addresses, argued Katz, is to "transform what he initially senses as an eternally humiliating situation into a rage. In rage, the killer can blind himself to his future, forging a momentary sense of eternal unity with the Good" (p. 19). Among the cases he reviewed, Katz also found that in "virtually all robberies, the offender discovers, fantasizes or manufactures *an angle of moral superiority* over the intended victim" (p. 169, italics in original).

High rates of societal violence seem partially explicable as reflections of an emphasis on presumed equality in the face of a reality that is exclusionary, coupled with concern for status differentiations and a learned tolerance for the use of violence. The long-term impact of racial inequality on black self-esteem and blacks' attitudes toward laws, John Davis suggested, produced the "bitterness turned inward" represented by high levels of violent crime committed by blacks against blacks (1976, p. 98). One consequence of this violence has been the tendency among whites to justify discriminatory practices. The absence of historical perspective encourages misunderstanding. Whereas racial discrimination contributed materially to criminalization of blacks who were "as fully ready as any group of urban newcomers to participate in the new industrial economy from which it was barred . . . the criminality created by racism has been used over time to justify racism, as the former black skills have become dissipated" (Lane, 1986, p. 171).

Inner-city residents, as Anderson (this volume) has shown, have little faith that their interests are protected by those who hold power in America. Recognizing the high degree of racial discrimination that continues, Herbert J. Gans argued that "racial minorities in the underclass will not be helped economically until white Americans become less fearful and hostile" (1988/1991, p. 152). Among other suggestions, Gans proposed using *pluralistic polling* to increase political representation of the varied perspectives of the urban poor. Some adjustments will be necessary in order to increase the benefits inner-city residents receive from the larger society or else they will not perceive that society as one with which they have a social contract.

Unless the governed perceive justice in the activities of government, they will have a difficult time believing in the legitimacy of its laws (Hartz, 1979; Silver, 1967; Tyler, 1990). As noted many years ago by Thomas Hobbes, ownership of property requires governing laws. Otherwise, physical possession amounts to ownership and there can be no such thing as theft. Without some degree of faith in legal protection, self-protection appears to be the only option. Private "justice" operates where there are no legitimate authorities. "Where there is no common Power, there is no Law: where no Law, no Injustice," wrote Hobbes (1651/1975, p. 188). Government requires, at a minimum, an exchange of benefits – be they merely protection or more complicated rights. A democracy requires more.

Adequate consideration of urban violence should take into account the processes of discrimination begun many years ago. These processes trapped blacks in cities that were themselves disadvantaged by government policies that supported development of suburbs and the migration of jobs away from cities. The policies that encouraged industrial migration stripped cities of a reasonable financial base and left many residents with little hope for better times to come.

Political rhetoric continues to emphasize equality of opportunities, and mass media have democratized expectations for the material benefits available from success. At least some of the poor know they are not being given the opportunities that have been promised. Rage comes easily. The history of unjust distribution of opportunities may well have undermined commitment to a social contract. If so, programs aimed simply at adjusting individuals to the present social system will not be sufficient. Redesign of the social contract may prove necessary in order to rebuild a civil society.

REFERENCES

Abrahamson, M., & Carter, V. J. (1986). "Tolerance, urbanization and region." *American Sociological Review* 51 (Apr.): 287–94.

Adams, C., Bartelt, D., Elesh, D., Goldstein, I., Kleniewski, N., & Yancey, W. (1991). *Philadelphia: Neighborhoods, Division, and Conflict in a Postindustrial City.* Philadelphia, PA: Temple University Press.

Anderson, E. (This volume). "Violence and the inner-city street code." In J. McCord (Ed.), *Violence and Childhood in the Inner City* (pp. 1–30). New York: Cambridge University Press.

Archer, D., & Gartner, R. (1984). *Violence & Crime in Cross-National Perspective.* New Haven, CT: Yale University Press.

Asbury, H. (1927). *The Gangs of New York: An Informal History of the Underworld.* New York: Alfred A. Knopf.

Axinn, J., & Levin, H. (1975). *Social Welfare: A History of the American Response to Need.* New York: Dodd, Mead & Co.

Baltzell, E. D. (1958). *Philadelphia Gentlemen: The Making of a National Upper Class.* New York: Free Press.

Bartelt, D. W. (1993). "Housing the 'underclass'." In M. B. Katz (Ed.), *The "Underclass" Debate* (pp. 118–60). Princeton, NJ: Princeton University Press.

Barth, G. (1980). *City People.* New York: Oxford University Press.

Bell, D. (1960). *The End of Ideology.* Glencoe, IL: Free Press.

Bennett, L., Jr. (1962/1993). *Before the Mayflower: A History of Black America, Sixth Edition.* New York: Penguin.

Biderman, A. D., & Reiss, A. J., Jr. (1967). "On exploring the 'Dark Figure' of crime." *The Annals of the American Academy of Political and Social Science* 374, 1–15.

Block, R. (1993). "Measuring victimizations risk: The effects of methodology, sampling, and fielding." In A. Alvazzi del Frate, U. Zvekic, & J. J. M. van

Dijk (Eds.), *Understanding Crime Experiences of Crime and Crime Control* (pp. 163–73). Rome: United Nations Publication.

Blumin, S. M. (1973). "Residential mobility within the nineteenth century city." In A. F. Davis & M. H. Haller (Eds.), *The Peoples of Philadelphia: A History of Ethnic Groups and Lower-Class Life, 1790–1940* (pp. 37–51). Philadelphia: Temple University Press.

Brace, C. L. (1872). *The Dangerous Classes of New York.* New York: Wynkoop & Hallenbeck.

Brown, R. M. (1969/1970). "Historical patterns of violence." In H. D. Graham & T. R. Gurr (Eds.), *The History of Violence in America* (pp. 45–83). New York: Bantam Books.

——— (1989). "Historical patterns of violence." In T. R. Gurr (Ed.), *Violence in America, Volume 2: Protest, Rebellion, Reform* (pp. 23–61). Newbury Park, CA: Sage Publications, Inc.

Buendia, H. G. (1989). *Urban Crime: Global Trends and Policies.* Hong Kong: The United Nations University.

Bureau of Justice Statistics. (1994). *Criminal Victimization in the United States: 1973–92 Trends.* Washington, D.C.: U.S. Department of Justice.

Butts, J. A., & Conners-Beatty, D. J. (1993). *The Juvenile Court's Response to Violent Offenders: 1985–1989.* Washington, D.C.: U.S. Department of Justice.

Bynner, J. M., O'Malley, P., & Bachman, J. G. (1981). "Self-esteem and delinquency revisited." *Journal of Youth and Adolescence* 10, 6, 407–41.

Carstairs, G. M. (1969/1970). "Overcrowding and human aggression." In H. D. Graham & T. R. Gurr (Eds.), *A History of Violence in America* (pp. 751–64). New York: Bantam Books.

Cloward, R. A., & Ohlin, L. E. (1960). *Delinquency and Opportunity.* New York: Free Press.

Cohen, A. K. (1955). *Delinquent boys.* Glencoe, IL: Free Press.

Covey, H. C., Menard, S., & Franzese, R. J. (1992). *Juvenile Gangs.* Springfield, IL: Charles C. Thomas.

Davis, J. A. (1976). "Blacks, crime, and American culture." *Annals of the American Academy of Political and Social Science* 423, 1, 89–98.

Drake, St. C., & Cayton, H. R. (1945/1962). *Black Metropolis: A Study of Negro Life in a Northern City.* New York: Harper & Row.

Dunlap, E. (1992). "Impact of drugs on family life and kin networks in the inner-city African-American single-parent household." In A. V. Harrell & G. E. Peterson (Eds.), *Drugs, Crime and Social Isolation* (pp. 181–208). Washington, D.C., The Urban Institute Press.

Earls, F., & Barnes, J. B. (This volume). "Understanding and preventing child abuse in urban settings." In J. McCord (Ed.), *Violence and Childhood in the Inner City* (pp. 207–55). New York: Cambridge University Press.

Ennis, P. H. (1967). *Criminal Victimization in the United States: A Report of a National Survey.* Washington, D.C.: U.S. Government Printing Office.

Fagan, J. A. (1992). "Drug selling and licit income in distressed neighborhoods: The economic lives of street-level drug users and dealers." In G. E. Peterson & A. V. Harrell (Eds.), *Drugs, Crime and Social Isolation: Barriers to Urban Opportunity* (pp. 99–142). Washington, D.C.: The Urban Institute Press.

Ferdinand, T. N. (1967). "The criminal patterns of Boston since 1848." *American Journal of Sociology* 78, 1, 84–99.

Fingerhut, L. A. (1993). "The impact of homicide on life chances: International, intranational and demographic comparisons." In C. R. Block & R. L. Block (Eds.), *Questions and Answers in Lethal and Non-lethal Violence 1993* (pp. 7–21). Washington, D.C.: National Institute of Justice.

Fischer, C. S. (1971). "A research note on urbanism and tolerance." *American Journal of Sociology* 76, 5, 847–56.

    (1973). "On urban alienation and anomie." *American Sociological Review* 38 (June), 311–26.

    (1975). "Toward a subcultural theory of urbanism." *American Journal of Sociology* 80 (May), 1319–41.

Flanagan, T. J., & McGarrell, E. F., eds. (1986). *Sourcebook of Criminal Justice Statistics 1985.* U.S. Department of Justice, Bureau of Justice Statistics. Washington, D.C.: U.S. Government Printing Office.

Flanagan, T. J., & Maguire, K., eds. (1992). *Sourcebook of Criminal Justice Statistics 1991.* U.S. Department of Justice, Bureau of Justice Statistics. Washington, D.C.: U.S. Government Printing Office.

Form, W. H., & Rytina, J. (1969). "Ideological beliefs on the distribution of power in the United States." *American Sociological Review* 34, 1, 19–30.

Frantz, J. B. (1969/1970). "The frontier tradition: An invitation to violence." In H. D. Graham & T. R. Gurr (Eds.), *Violence in America* (pp. 127–54). New York: Bantam Books.

Friedman, L. M. (1993). *Crime and Punishment in American History.* New York: Basic Books.

Gans, H. J. (1988/1991). *Middle American Individualism: The Future of Liberal Democracy.* New York: Oxford University Press.

Garbarino, J., & Sherman, D. (1980). "High-risk neighborhoods and high-risk families: The human ecology of child maltreatment." *Child Development* 51, 1 (Mar.), 188–98.

Gastil, R. (1971). "Homicide and a regional culture of violence." *American Journal of Sociology* 36 (June), 412–27.

Gelles, R. J. (1989). "Child abuse and violence in single-parent families: Parent absence and economic deprivation." *American Journal of Orthopsychiatry* 59, 4, 492–501.

Giacopassi, D. J., Sparger, J. R., & Stein, P. M. (1992). "The effects of emergency medical care on the homicide rate: some additional evidence." *Journal of Criminal Justice* 20, 249–59.

Glazer, N., & Moynihan, D. P. (1963). *Beyond the Melting Pot*. Cambridge, MA: MIT Press.

Gold, M., & Mann, D. (1972). "Delinquency as defense." *American Journal of Orthopsychiatry* 42, 3, 463–79.

Gordon, M. M. (1964). *Assimilation in American Life: The Role of Race, Religion, and National Origin*. New York: Oxford University Press.

Grund, F. J. (1839/1959). *Aristocracy in America*. New York: Harper & Row.

Gurr, T. R. (1976). *Rogues, Rebels and Reformers*. Beverly Hills, CA: Sage Publications, Inc.

(1979). "On the history of violent crime in Europe and America." In H. D. Graham & T. R. Gurr (Eds.), *Violence in America: Historical and Comparative Perspectives* (pp. 353–74). Beverly Hills, CA: Sage Publications, Inc.

(1981). "Historical trends in violent crimes: A critical review of the evidence." In M. Tonry & N. Morris (Eds.), *Crime and Justice, Volume 3* (pp. 295–353). Chicago: University of Chicago Press.

(1989). "Historical trends in violent crime: Europe and the United States." In T. R. Gurr (Ed.), *Violence in America, Volume 1: The History of Crime* (pp. 21–54). Newbury Park, CA: Sage Publications, Inc.

Haller, M. H. (1971–72). "Organized crime in urban society: Chicago in the twentieth century." *Journal of Social History* V (Winter), 210–34.

(1972). "Urban vice and civic reform: Chicago in the early twentieth century." In K. T. Jackson & S. K. Schultz (Eds.), *Cities in American History* (pp. 290–305). New York: Alfred A. Knopf.

(1973). "Recurring themes." In A. F. Davis & M. H. Haller (Eds.), *The Peoples of Philadelphia: A History of Ethnic Groups and Lower-Class Life, 1790–1940* (pp. 277–90). Philadelphia: Temple University Press.

(1989). "Bootlegging: The business and politics of violence." In T. R. Gurr (Ed.), *Violence in America, Volume 1: The History of Crime* (pp. 146–62). Newbury Park, CA: Sage.

Handlin, O. (1950). *Race and Nationality in American Life*. Garden City, NY: Doubleday Anchor Books.

Hartz, L. (1979). "A comparative study of fragment cultures." In H. D. Graham & T. R. Gurr (Eds.), *Violence in America: Historical and Comparative Perspectives* (pp. 119–32). Beverly Hills, CA: Sage.

Hawes, J. M. (1971). *Children in Urban Society: Juvenile Delinquency in Nineteenth-Century America*. New York: Oxford University Press.

Hershberg, T. (1973). "Free blacks in antebellum Philadelphia." In A. F. Davis & M. H. Haller (Eds.), *The Peoples of Philadelphia: A History of Ethnic Groups and Lower-Class Life, 1790–1940* (pp. 111–33). Philadelphia: Temple University Press.

Hershberg, T., Burstein, A., Ericksen, E., Greenberg, S., & Yancey, W. (1979). "A tale of three cities: Blacks and immigrants in Philadelphia, 1850–1880 and 1970." *The Annals of the American Academy of Political and Social Science: Race and Residence in American Cities* 441 (Jan.), 55–81.

Higham, J. (1955/1963). *Strangers in the Land: Patterns of American Nativism 1860–1925.* New York: Atheneum.

Hobbes, T. (1651/1975). *Leviathan.* Baltimore: Penguin.

Hobbs, A. H. (1943). "Criminality in Philadelphia: 1790–1810 compared with 1937." *American Sociological Review* 8, 198–202.

Hofstadter, R. (1955). *The Age of Reform: From Bryan to F.D.R.* New York: Alfred A. Knopf.

(1970/1971). "Reflections on violence in the United States." In R. Hofstadter & M. Wallace (Eds.), *American Violence: A Documentary History* (pp. 3–43). New York: Vintage Books.

Hogan, D. J. (1985). *Class and Reform: School and Society in Chicago, 1880–1930.* Philadelphia: University of Pennsylvania Press.

Hollon, W. E. (1974). *Frontier Violence: Another Look.* New York: Oxford University Press.

Hoover, J. E. (1964). *Crime in the United States.* Washington, D.C.: Federal Bureau of Investigation, Department of Justice.

Horton, J. O. (1993). *Free People of Color: Inside the African American Community.* Washington, D.C.: Smithsonian Institution Press.

Jackson, K. T. (1985). *Crabgrass Frontier: The Suburbanization of the United States.* New York: Oxford University Press.

Jaynes, G. D., & Williams, R. M., Jr. (Eds.) (1989). *A Common Destiny – Blacks and American Society,* by The Committee on the Status of Black Americans. Washington, D.C.: National Academy Press.

Johnson, D. R. (1973). "Crime patterns in Philadelphia, 1840–1870." In A. F. Davis & M. H. Haller (Eds.), *The Peoples of Philadelphia* (pp. 89–110). Philadelphia: Temple University Press.

Jones, J. (1993). "Southern diaspora: Origins of the northern 'underclass'." In M. B. Katz (Ed.), *The "Underclass" Debate* (pp. 27–54). Princeton, NJ: Princeton University Press.

Kaplan, H. B. (1980). *Deviant Behavior in Defense of Self.* New York: Academic Press.

Kasarda, J. D. (1989). "Urban industrial transition and the underclass." *The Annals: The Ghetto Underclass: Social Science Perspectives* 501 (Jan.), 26–47.

(1992). "The severely distressed in economically transforming cities." In A. V. Harrell & G. E. Peterson (Eds.), *Drugs, Crime and Social Isolation* (pp. 45–98). Washington, D.C., The Urban Institute Press.

Katz, J. (1988). *Seductions of Crimes: Moral and sensual attractions in doing evil.* New York: Basil Blackwell.

Katz, M. B. (1993). "The urban 'underclass' as a metaphor of social transformation." In M. B. Katz (Ed.), *The "Underclass" Debate* (pp. 3–26). Princeton, NJ: Princeton University Press.

Killias, M. (1990). "Gun ownership and violent crime: The Swiss experience in international perspective." *Security Journal* 1, 3, 169–74.

Kirschenman, J., & Neckerman, K. M. (1991). "We'd love to hire them, but . . .": The meaning of race for employers." In C. Jencks & P. E. Peterson (Eds.), *The Urban Underclass* (pp. 203–32). Washington, D.C.: The Brookings Institution.

Kury, H., & Würger, M. (1993). "The influence of the type of data collection method on the results of the victimization surveys." In A. Alvazzi del Frate, U. Zvekic, & J. J. M. van Dijk (Eds.), *Understanding Crime Experiences of Crime and Crime Control* (pp. 137–52). Rome: United Nations Publication.

LaFree, G., Drass, K. A., & O'Day, P. (1992). "Race and crime in postwar America: Determinants of African-American and White rates, 1957–1988." *Criminology* 30, 2, 157–85.

Lane, R. (1967). *Policing the City: Boston 1822–1885.* Cambridge, MA: Harvard University Press.

(1969/1970). "Urbanization and criminal violence in the 19th century: Massachusetts as a test case." In H. D. Graham & T. R. Gurr (Eds.), *Violence in America* (pp. 468–84). New York: Bantam Books.

(1976). "Criminal violence in America: The first hundred years." *The Annals of the American Academy of Political and Social Science: Crime and Justice in America: 1776–1976* 423 (Jan.), 1–13.

(1979). *Violent Death in the City.* Cambridge, MA: Harvard University Press.

(1980). "Urban homicide in the nineteenth century: Some lessons for the twentieth." In J. A. Inciardi & C. E. Faupel (Eds.), *History and Crime: Implications for Criminal Justice Policy* (pp. 91–110). Beverly Hills, CA: Sage Publications, Inc.

(1986). *Roots of Violence in Black Philadelphia 1860–1900.* Cambridge, MA: Harvard University Press.

(1989). "On the social meaning of homicide trends in America." In T. R. Gurr (Ed.), *Violence in America, Volume 1: The History of Crime* (pp. 55–79). Newbury Park, CA: Sage Publications, Inc.

Lichter, D. T. (1988). "Racial differences in underemployment in American cities." *American Journal of Sociology* 93, 4, 771–92.

Lizotte, A. J., Thornberry, T. P., Krohn, M. D. Chard-Wierschem, D. & McDowall, D. (1994). "Neighborhood context and delinquency: A longitudinal analysis." In I. G. M. Weitekamp & H.-J. Kerner (Eds.), *Cross-National Longitudinal Research on Human Development and Criminal Behavior* (pp. 217–27). Dordrecht, Netherlands: Kluwer.

Lodhi, A. Q., & Tilly, C. (1973). "Urbanization, crime, and collective violence in 19th century France." *American Journal of Sociology* 79, 2, 296–318.

Loeber, R., & Stouthamer-Loeber, M. (1986). "Family factors as correlates and predictors of juvenile conduct problems and delinquency." In M. Tonry & N. Morris (Eds.), *Crime and Justice, Volume 7* (pp. 29–149). Chicago: University of Chicago Press.

Lubove, R. (1965/1980). *The Professional Altruist: The Emergence of Social Work as a Career 1880–1930.* New York: Antheneum.

Lukoff, I. F., & Brook, J. S. (1974). "A sociocultural exploration of reported heroin use." In C. Winick (Ed.), *Sociological Aspects of Drug Dependence* (pp. 35–59). Cleveland: CRC.

Maguire, K., & Pastore, A. L., eds. (1994). *Sourcebook of Criminal Justice Statistics – 1993.* U.S. Department of Justice: Bureau of Justice Statistics. Washington, D.C.: U.S. Government Printing Office.

McCarthy, J. D., & Hoge, D. R. (1984). "The dynamics of self-esteem and delinquency." *American Journal of Sociology* 90, 2, 396–410.

McCord, J. (1979). "Some child-rearing antecedents of criminal behavior in adult men." *Journal of Personality and Social Psychology* 37, 1477–86.

⸻ (1988). "Parental behavior in the cycle of aggression." *Psychiatry* 51, 1, 14–23.

⸻ (1995). "Ethnicity, acculturation, and opportunities: A study of two generations." In D. F. Hawkins (Ed.), *Ethnicity, Race and Crime: Perspectives Across Time and Place* (pp. 69–81). Albany, NY: State University of New York Press.

McGrath, R. D. (1989). "Violence and lawlessness on the western frontier." In T. R. Gurr (Ed.), *Violence in America, Volume 1: The History of Crime* (pp. 122–145). Newbury Park, CA: Sage Publications, Inc.

Mennel, R. M. (1973). *Thorns and Thistles: Juvenile Delinquents in the United States 1825–1940.* Hanover, NH: The University Press of New England.

Menninger, W. C. (1947). "The role of psychiatry in the world today." *American Journal of Psychiatry* 104 (Sept.), 155–63.

Miller, W. R. (1975). "Police authority in London and New York City 1830–1870." *The Journal of Social History* (Winter), 81–101.

Monkkonen, E. (1977/1979). "Toward a dynamic theory of crime and the police: A criminal justice system perspective." In S. L. Messinger & E. Bittner (Eds.), *Criminology Review Yearbook, Volume 1* (pp. 335–43). Beverly Hills, CA: Sage Publications, Inc.

⸻ (1981). *Police in Urban America 1860–1920.* New York: Cambridge University Press.

Myrdal, G. (1944). *An American Dilemma: The Negro Problem and Modern Democracy, Volume 1.* New York: Harper & Row.

National Commission on the Causes and Prevention of Violence. (1969). *To Establish Justice, to Insure Domestic Tranquility: Final Report of the National Commission on the Causes and Prevention of Violence.* Washington, D.C.: U.S. Government Printing Office.

Olzak, S. (1989). "Labor unrest, immigration, and ethnic conflict in urban America, 1880–1914." *American Journal of Sociology* 94, 6, 1303–33.

Park, R. E., & Burgess, E. W. (1925/1967). *The City.* Chicago: University of Chicago Press.

Pease, K., & Hukkila, K. (1990). *Criminal Justice Systems in Europe and North America.* Helsinki, Finland: Helsinki Institute for Crime Prevention and Control.

Pepinsky, H. E. (1976). "The growth of crime in the United States." *The Annals of the American Academy of Political and Social Science: Crime and Justice in America: 1776–1976* 423 (Jan.), 23–30.

——— (1977). "The room for despotism in the quest for valid crime statistics: American crime measurement in historical and comparative perspective." In R. F. Meier (Ed.), *Theory in Criminology: Contemporary Views* (pp. 69–82). Beverly Hills: Sage Publications, Inc.

Peterson, G. E., & Harrell, A. V. (1992). "Inner-city isolation and opportunity." In A. V. Harrell & G. E. Peterson (Eds.), *Drugs, Crime and Social Isolation* (pp. 1–26). Washington, D.C.: The Urban Institute Press.

Pettigrew, T. F. (1979). "Racial change and social policy." *The Annals: Race and Residence in American Cities* 441 (Jan.), 114–31.

Platt, A. M. (1969/1977). *The Child Savers: The Invention of Delinquency, Second Edition, Enlarged.* Chicago: University of Chicago Press.

Quarles, B. (1964). *The Negro in the Making of America.* New York: Collier Books.

Reiss, A. J., Jr., & Roth, J. A., Eds. (1993). *Understanding and Preventing Violence.* Washington, D.C.: National Academy Press.

Richardson, J. F. (1980). "Police in America: Functions and control." In J. A. Inciardi & C. E. Faupel (Eds.), *History and Crime: Implications for Criminal Justice Policy* (pp. 211–24). Beverly Hills, CA: Sage Publications, Inc.

Robinson, C. D. (1993). "The production of black violence in Chicago." In D. F. Greenberg (Ed.), *Crime and Capitalism: Readings in Marxist Criminology* (pp. 279–333). Philadelphia, PA: Temple University Press.

Roof, W. C. (1979). "Race and residence: The shifting basis of American race relations." *Annals of the American Academy of Political and Social Science* 441, 1–12.

Rossi, P. H., & Berk, R. A. (1970). Local political leadership and popular discontent in the ghetto." *The Annals of the American Academy of Political and Social Science: Collective Violence* 391, 111–27.

Sampson, R. J. (1987). "Urban black violence: The effect of male joblessness and family disruption." *American Journal of Sociology* 93, 2, 348–82.

——— (this volume). "The embeddedness of child and adolescent development." In J. McCord (Ed.), *Violence and Childhood in the Inner City* (pp. 31–77). New York: Cambridge University Press.

Shaw, C. R., & McKay, H. D. (1942/1972). *Juvenile Delinquency and Urban Areas.* Chicago: University of Chicago Press.

Short, J. F., Jr., & Wolfgang, M. E. (1970). "On collective violence: Introduction and overview." *The Annals of the American Academy of Political and Social Science: Collective Violence* 391, 1–8.

Silver, A. (1967). "The demand for order in civil society: A review of some themes in the history of urban crime, police, and riot." In D. J. Bordua (Ed.), *The Police: Six Sociological Essays* (pp. 1–24). New York: John Wiley & Sons.

Skogan, W. G. (1979). "Crime in contemporary America." In H. D. Graham & T. R. Gurr (Eds.), *Violence in America: Historical and Comparative Perspectives* (pp. 375–92). Beverly Hills, CA: Sage Publications, Inc.

Slingerland, W. H. (1919). *Child-Placing in Families.* New York: Russell Sage Foundation.

Smith, D. C., Jr. (1976). "Mafia: The prototypical alien conspiracy." *The Annals of the American Academy of Political and Social Science: Crime and Justice in America: 1776–1976* 423, 75–88.

Snyder, H. N. (1992). *Arrests of Youth 1990.* Bureau of Justice Statistics, U.S. Department of Justice. Washington, D.C.: U.S. Government Printing Office.

Solomon, B. M. (1956). *Ancestors and Immigrants: A Changing New England Tradition.* Cambridge, MA: Harvard University Press.

Spear, A. H. (1967). *Black Chicago: The Making of a Negro Ghetto 1890–1920.* Chicago: University of Chicago Press.

Stahura, J. M. (1986). "Suburban development, black suburbanization and the Civil Rights Movement since World War II." *American Sociological Review* 51, 1, 131–44.

Steinberg, S. (1989). *The Ethnic Myth: Race, Ethnicity, and Class in America.* Boston: Beacon Press.

Stilgoe, J. R. (1988). *Borderland: Origins of the American Suburb, 1820–1939.* New Haven, CT: Yale University Press.

Sugrue, T. J. (1993). "The structures of urban poverty: The reorganization of space and work in three periods of American history." In M. B. Katz (Ed.), *The "Underclass" Debate* (pp. 85–117). Princeton, NJ: Princeton University Press.

Taeuber, K. E. (1979). "Housing, schools, and incremental segregative effects." *The Annals: Race and Residence in American Cities* 441 (Jan.), 157–67.

Taft, P., & Ross, P. (1969/1970). "American labor violence: Its causes, character, and outcome." In H. D. Graham & T. R. Gurr (Eds.), *The History of Violence in America* (pp. 281–398). New York: Bantam Books.

Tarde, G. (1897/1969). "Criminal youth." In T. N. Clarke (Ed.), *On Communication and Social Influence: Selected Papers* (pp. 255–73). Chicago: University of Chicago Press.

Taylor, R. L. (1979). "Black ethnicity and the persistence of ethnogenesis." *American Journal of Sociology* 84, 6, 1401–23.

Thernstrom, S. (1964/1970). *Poverty and Progress: Social Mobility in a Nineteenth Century City.* New York: Antheneum.

(1973). *The Other Bostonians: Poverty and Progress in the American Metropolis, 1880–1970.* Cambridge, MA: Harvard University Press.

Toch, H. (1969/1984). *Violent Men.* Cambridge, MA: Schenkman.

Tocqueville, A. de (1835/1961). *Democracy in America, Volume I.* New York: Schocken Books.

Trotter, J. W., Jr. (1993). "Blacks in the urban North: The 'underclass question' in historical perspective." In M. B. Katz (Ed.), *The "Underclass" Debate* (pp. 55–84). Princeton, NJ: Princeton University Press.

Tuch, S. A. (1987). "Urbanism, region, and tolerance revisited: The case of racial prejudice." *American Sociological Review* 52, 4, 504–10.

Turner, F. J. (1894). "The significance of the frontier in American history." *Annual Report for 1893* (pp. 199–227). Washington, D.C.: American Historical Association. (Reprinted in *Selected Essays of Frederick Jackson Turner: Frontier and Section.* Englewood Cliffs, N.J.: Prentice-Hall, 1961.)

Tyler, T. R. (1990). *Why People Obey the Law.* New Haven, CT: Yale University Press.

UNAFEI & AIC (1990). *Crime and Justice in Asia and the Pacific.* Tokyo: UNAFEI & AIC.

van Dijk, J. J. M., & Mayhew, P. (1992) *Criminal Victimization in the Industrialized World.* Netherlands: Ministry of Justice.

van Dijk, J. J. M., & Mayhew, P. (1993). Criminal victimization in the industrialized world: Key findings of the 1989 and 1992 international crime surveys. In A. Alvazzi del Frate, U. Zvekic, & J. J. M. van Dijk (Eds.), *Understanding Crime Experiences of Crime and Crime Control* (pp. 1–49). Rome: United Nations Publication.

(1991). *Experiences of Crime Across the World: Key Findings From the 1989 International Crime Survey,* Second Edition. Deventer, Netherlands: Kluwer.

Wacquant, L. J. D., & Wilson, W. J. (1989). "The cost of racial and class exclusion in the inner city." *Annals of the American Academy of Political and Social Science* 501, 8–25.

Wade, R. C. (1959). *The Urban Frontier: The Rise of Western Cities, 1790–1830.* Cambridge, MA: Harvard University Press.

(1964). *Slavery in the Cities: The South 1820–1860.* New York: Oxford University Press.

(1972). "Violence in the cities." In K. T. Jackson & S. K. Schultz (Eds.), *Cities in American History* (pp. 475–91). New York: Alfred A. Knopf.

Ward, D. (1971). *Cities and Immigrants.* New York: Oxford University Press.

(1989). *Poverty, Ethnicity, and the American City, 1840–1925.* New York: Cambridge University Press.

Warner, S. B., Jr. (1962/1978). *Streetcar Suburbs: The Process of Growth in Boston, 1870–1900.* Cambridge, MA: Harvard University Press.

Weber, A. F. (1899/1963). *The Growth of Cities in the Nineteenth Century: A Study in Statistics.* Ithaca, NY: Cornell University Press.

Weber, M. (1920/1958). *The Protestant Ethic and the Spirit of Capitalism* (translated by T. Parsons). New York: Charles Scribner's Sons.

Wells, L. E., & Rankin, J. H. (1983). "Self-concept as a mediating factor in delinquency." *Social Psychology Quarterly* 46, 1, 11–22.

Whitaker, C. J., & Bastian, L. D. (1991). *Teenage Victims: A National Crime Survey Report.* Washington, D.C.: U.S. Department of Justice.

Widom, C. S. (1989). "Child abuse, neglect, and adult behavior: Research design and findings on criminality, violence, and child abuse." *American Journal of Orthopsychiatry* 59, 3 (July), 355–67.

Wilson, W. J. (1987). *The Truly Disadvantaged.* Chicago: University of Chicago Press.

(1991). "Public policy research and the truly disadvantaged." In C. Jencks & P. E. Peterson (Eds.), *The Urban Underclass* (pp. 460–82). Washington, D.C.: The Brookings Institution.

Wolfgang, M. E., & Ferracuti, F. (1967/1982). *The Subculture of Violence.* Beverly Hills, CA: Sage Publications.

Yancey, W. L., Ericksen, E. P., & Juliani, R. N. (1976). "Emergent ethnicity: A review and reformulation." *American Sociological Review* 41, 3, 391–403.

Neuropsychology, Antisocial Behavior, and Neighborhood Context

TERRIE E. MOFFITT

Introduction

The belief that neuropsychological factors are among the causes of antisocial behavior is not new. For example, Benjamin Rush (1812, p. 360, cited in Elliott, 1978, p. 147) referred to the "total perversion of the normal faculties" in people who displayed "innate preternatural moral depravity." Rush proposed that "there is probably an original defective organization in those parts of the body which are occupied by the normal faculties of the mind" (p. 147). Since Benjamin Rush's day, quite a bit of research has been done to put his hypothesis to the scientific test. A relatively new field, called neuropsychology, has emerged to study the relations among "parts of the body" (the brain) and "faculties of the mind" (mental abilities and personality styles). Modern research methods have improved our ability to understand the role of neuropsychological factors in antisocial behavior.

Why should a chapter on neuropsychology be included in this book about childhood aggression in the inner city? In 1987, Sarnoff Mednick drew a connection between inner-city decay and research on biological and psychological correlates of criminal behavior. He wrote,

> We must not permit honest research efforts to be ignored simply because in the nineteenth century [eugenicist] Herbert Spencer twisted the theory of evolution to selfish, bigoted ends. Let us try to turn this sharp tool of knowledge to the correction of social injustice. Our cities, the strongholds of art, literature, music, and science, have decayed. Part of the reason for this decay is the fear of being assaulted or robbed. In many areas of many cities we have dropped below the level of societal conformity necessary for civilized human interaction. Understanding *all* the relevant characteristics of chronic offenders should be a high priority if we hope to control crime sufficiently to restore a minimal level of civilized interaction in our cities (p. x).

Encouraged by such remarks, neuropsychological researchers have labored to understand whether the very aggressive among us differ in "faculties of the mind." Some progress has been made, and that work will be described in this article.

Objectives of Neuropsychological Research. The objectives of neuropsychological research into antisocial behavior should not be misunderstood. First, the objective is not to show that head injuries cause most crimes. Head injuries or brain diseases are not the exclusive origins of the neuropsychological dysfunctions that are linked in theory to antisocial behavior. Any number of sources might be involved, including disrupted fetal brain development, deprivation of nutrition or stimulation during infancy, childhood exposure to toxic chemicals, fluctuating levels of transmitter chemicals within the brain, or heritable variation among brains.

Second, neuropsychological research does not endeavor to identify specific anatomical organs within the brain that cause delinquent behavior in a deterministic fashion. Instead, one of the aims of neuropsychological research on delinquency is to identify children whose neuropsychological problems place them at risk for maladaptive responses to the circumstances of their homes, neighborhoods, and schools. Neuropsychologists who are interested in antisocial behavior try to understand the ways in which neuropsychological abilities interact with social and environmental conditions to increase the chances that delinquent acts will occur.

Third, neuropsychological tests examine more than the mental abilities, such as intelligence, language, or memory, that are impaired after a brain injury or brain disease. Findings about the neural underpinnings of temperament, personality, social judgment, and interpersonal behavior have expanded the field of neuropsychological theory and inquiry. As used here, neuropsychology refers broadly to the study of the relationships between brain and behavior. Behavior includes both personality styles and cognitive functions. The goal of this research is to describe links between (a) the many different ways in which youngsters' brains process information and (b) their problem behaviors (Goldstein, 1987).

Neuropsychologists use a variety of neuropsychological measurement methods, including performance tests, the electroencephalogram, and brain-imaging technologies. To date, studies of samples of aggressive children have mainly emphasized data gathered with performance tests, probably because other methods are too costly and/or too invasive for use with general samples of children who have no demonstrable brain disease. The construct validity of these performance tests and the links between test scores and brain health have been established in several ways. For example, performance tests of self-control were originally designed to diagnose whether neurological patients had injury or disease in the frontal areas of the brain. In one such test, the patient is rewarded repeatedly for sorting a series of cards according to one characteristic that the cards share: color. But then the characteristic is covertly changed by the clinician to shape, and the clinician now mildly reprimands the patient who continues to sort by color. In this test, self-control is measured by observing how long it takes the head-injured patient to comply with the new "shape" rule. Patients with brain damage can understand the new rule, yet they find themselves unable to inhibit their first pattern of sorting so that they may sort according to the new rewarded pattern. During this test, the clinician examines the patient's reaction to six shifts from one characteristic to another, thereby generating a composite index of the patient's self-control problem that is quite reliable. (Antisocial individuals also experience difficulty in trying to inhibit behavior that they know is undesirable and to substitute new behavior in its place – ergo, the hypothetical relation between scores on this test and antisocial behavior.)

Such tests have a strong history of discriminating between hospitalized patients with frontal brain damage and patients with focal disease elsewhere in the brain (Lezak, 1983). Subsequently, research has shown that the test scores are linked to poor self-control among research participants who are not neurological inpatients. For example, prison inmates and hyperactive children, as well as adolescent boys who were drawn from the general population, have been tested. Within these research samples, subjects who perform poorly on tests of self-control also (1) show abnormalities in electroencephalographic recordings from electrode sites at the front of the head (Raine, 1988), (2) show poor blood flow to the frontal lobes of the brain in PET scan studies (Lou, Henriksen, & Bruhn, 1984), and (3) are described as impulsive by teachers, parents, and therapists (White, Moffitt, Caspi, Jeglum. Needles, & Stouthamer-Loeber, 1994). As another example of test validity, consider tests of verbal skills. For most people, verbal abilities are situated primarily in the left hemisphere of the brain. As expected, people who score below control levels on verbal neuropsychological tests also make more right-ear errors on dichotic listening tests, have higher rates of mixed- or left-handedness, show less metabolism of glucose in the left hemisphere on PET scans, and have difficulty learning to read and write in the classroom (Benson & Zaidel, 1985). Corroborative data from many different investigation methods provide evidence to support the interpretation of neuropsychological test findings.

This article reviews studies of antisocial youngsters' scores on neuropsychological tests. A total of 60 published reports were reviewed (reporting 57 different data bases). I attempted to identify reports exhaustively by conducting computerized searches of the literature in psychology and medicine from 1965 to 1992, by cross-reference checking, by reviewing 1980–92 program abstracts of the annual meetings of the International Neuropsychological Society, and by conducting a mail survey of selected researchers working in the field.

Most of the studies that I found on the neuropsychology of delinquency were plagued by problems that precluded drawing confident conclusions from their findings. Samples were small or highly selected, limiting generalization. Control groups were absent or were poorly matched to delinquent groups. Neuropsychological testing was often done after many years of antisocial involvement, raising concerns about causal order in the neuropsychology/delinquency relation; features of a delinquent lifestyle such as substance abuse, head injury, truancy, and incarceration might have lowered neuropsychological test scores. Antisocial behavior was defined via official delinquent adjudication, risking systematic sources of bias by race or class. Information was seldom provided about the reliability and validity of the neuropsychological measures. In some studies, the statistical treatment of the data failed to give protection against chance findings. Factors that might have confounded interpretation of test scores – such as gender, race, or social class – were typically not studied. Elsewhere, I have discussed in detail these methodological problems (Moffitt & Silva, 1988a; Moffitt, 1990b). But most important, studies published since the mid-1980s have corrected the earlier design problems, yet these better studies have reported the same patterns of results.

The many studies reviewed for this article used a wide variety of neuropsychological tests, and they employed many different methods of ascertaining antisocial behavior. Despite this diversity and despite the aforementioned methodological problems in this literature, the findings were fairly consistent. Across studies, antisocial youngsters were impaired in two specific neuropsychological domains: language skills and self-control. Thus, as a body, the literature paints a convincing picture. However, only a small selection of the better studies will be described in this chapter.

Unfortunately, none of the studies I reviewed compared the neuropsychological statuses of subjects from different neighborhood contexts. Thus, the available literature does not enlighten us with hard data about potential ways that neuropsychological factors interact with social context. However, almost all of the studies used samples of delinquents drawn from large cities (e.g., Boston, Philadelphia, Pittsburgh, and San Diego), and many samples contained children who were held in inner-city jails or urban psychiatric hospitals for their crimes. From these reports we do learn that the neuropsychology/delinquency relation pertains to poor children who grew up in the inner city.

The article follows the following format. First, I review the literature to establish the strength of the relation between neuropsychology and antisocial behavior. Second, I present an overview that locates ideas about the neuropsychology of antisocial behavior in the broader context of theory from the field of developmental psychopathology. Also, some specific hypotheses about verbal and self-control problems are extracted from the literature, and findings from a selection of the best-designed empirical studies are described. Third, near the end of the chapter, I present some new data from a new study designed to compare the link between neuropsychology and preteen delinquency across different types of neighborhoods. Where possible, literature will be cited that speaks to the relation between neuropsychological health and antisocial behavior in the context of poverty and disadvantage.

An Initial Appraisal of the Importance of Neuropsychology in the Study of Antisocial Behavior

Although the neuropsychological hypothesis is relatively old, the scientific evidence for it is relatively new. When prompted to recall correlates of crime, most Americans can readily nominate variables such as poverty, race, or delinquent friends. Few would think of neuropsychological factors; outside academic psychology, such factors are not famous correlates of delinquency. Thus, to invite the reader's interest in this article, I begin by documenting the strength of the association between antisocial behavior and neuropsychology. This is easily accomplished by citing data on one of the best measures of *overall* neuropsychological status: scores on tests of intelligence. An IQ test designed to tap into verbal and spatial functions forms the core of most neuropsychological test batteries. Moreover, IQ test scores bear moderate positive correlations with scores from most neuropsychological tests of all types of functions (see, e.g., Moffitt, 1988; White et al., 1994). Thus IQ may be used as an omnibus index of neuropsychological status.

How Strong is the Relation Between IQ and Delinquency? A critical mass of research has shown that IQ scores relate to delinquency about as strongly as do measures of class or race (Hirschi & Hindelang, 1977). One of the most robust findings in the study of antisocial behavior is that juvenile delinquents show an IQ deficit of one-half standard deviation – or about eight IQ points – when compared to their nondelinquent peers (Hirschi & Hindelang, 1977; Wilson & Herrnstein, 1985). When we evaluate the size of this statistical effect, it is important to remember that almost all studies have lumped together youths who are temporarily experimenting with mild delinquent acts and youths whose antisocial behavior is more serious, persistent, or physically aggressive. For example, in the representative sample of 536 New Zealand boys that I have studied, the 8-point IQ difference between delinquents and nondelinquents obtains, but we have discovered that it is the pooled result of a 1-point mean deficit for temporary adolescent-delinquents and a 17-point mean deficit for delinquents who were aggressive since childhood (Moffitt, 1990a). These findings suggest that compromised neuropsychological function may apply only to a subgroup of antisocial youngsters. For that subgroup, the strength of the relation may be stronger than previously thought. Although the neuropsychologically impaired subgroup may be small in numbers, its members warrant our concern because their antisocial behavior is especially severe and persistent.

Does the Relation Between Neuropsychological Variables and Antisocial Behavior Survive after Appropriate Scientific Controls are Applied? The relation between delinquency and IQ holds when IQ is assessed prospectively, well before the development of illegal behavior (Denno, 1989; Moffitt, 1990a; Moffitt, Gabrielli, & Mednick, 1981). IQ and delinquency share significant variance after controlling for socioeconomic status (Moffitt et al., 1981; Reiss & Rhodes, 1961; Wolfgang, Figlio, & Sellin, 1972), race (Lynam, Moffitt, & Stouthamer-Loeber, 1993; Short & Strodtbeck, 1965; Wolfgang et al., 1972), academic attainment (Denno, 1989; Lynam et al., 1993), and each child's motivation during the IQ test (Lynam et al., 1993). The relation between IQ and antisocial behavior is not an artifact of slow-witted delinquents being more easily detected by police; undetected delinquents who are identified by interviews have low IQ scores too (Moffitt & Silva, 1988a). Delinquent siblings have been shown to have lower IQs than nondelinquent siblings within the same families (Healy & Bronner, 1936; Shulman, 1929). Finally, the stability of individual children's low IQ scores has been shown to parallel the stability of their severe antisocial conduct problems when the same children are examined repeatedly from preschool through adolescence (Moffitt, 1990a).

Given the robustness of the IQ deficit, it may come as a surprise to learn that we still do not know *why* or *how* low IQ might influence the development of antisocial behavior. One way to approach those questions is to look beyond IQ. Neuropsychologists know that individuals with identical omnibus IQ scores may have *very* different patterns of mental strengths and weaknesses. Indeed, the IQ is only a crude indicator that conceals distinctive patterns of neuropsychological health and handicap. Such patterns can be measured with a battery of neuropsychological tests of specific brain functions. Two children with identical low IQ scores might suffer from different and relatively isolated problems such as impulsive social judgment, weak language processing, poor memory, or failure to synchronize visual information with motor actions (Lezak, 1988). Each distinct pattern of strengths and weaknesses could conceivably be better than the overall IQ at predicting conduct problems, but each would contribute to the development of conduct problems through a unique theoretical causal chain. Thus, findings from neuropsychological research can offer keys to the theoretical question of why cognitive impairment is linked to children's antisocial behavior problems.

Theoretical Perspectives from Developmental Psychopathology

Many explanations suggest that neuropsychological deficits are so proximally related to antisocial behavior that they are determinant at the moment of each incident of stealing or fighting. For example, it has been said that children with verbal deficits will rely more on physical modes of self-expression and will thus resort to hitting rather than discussion when disagreements arise. Alternately, it has been said that children with attentional deficits will neglect to reflect upon the consequences of each disobedient behavior before rushing into it. Such explanations are not concerned with development; they apply as well to a 30-year-old as to a 5-year-old. However, certain considerations suggest that such direct and immediate links should not be our only explanations for the association between neuropsychological deficits and antisocial behavior.

First, there is a seeming contradiction between the developmental courses of antisocial behavior and neurological damage: Antisocial behavior often grows worse over time (Loeber, 1988), whereas the frequent outcome for those suffering from neurological damage is improvement, if not recovery. Although recovery from childhood brain damage may be delayed in disadvantaged environments (but see Breslau, 1990), childhood brain damage is often compensated for by the remarkable plasticity of brain development (Rutter, 1983a). The test score deficits of delinquent samples are generally statistically significant, but they are clinically mild relative to the scores of neurological patients. Few, if any, antisocial children are readily identifiable as "severely brain damaged" by such clear signs as aphasia, sensory loss, limb paralysis, or gait disturbance.

Second, research is beginning to show that neuropsychological problems probably best predict a special sort of delinquency. Earlier in this chapter, I mentioned that IQ scores were particularly low among a relatively small subgroup of New Zealand delinquents whose behavior problems began early in childhood and who remained unusually aggressive from childhood throughout adolescence. More detailed neuropsychological testing revealed that a special pattern of strengths and weaknesses was linked to this form of aggression that begins at preschool ages and persists thereafter. Moreover, as children, these same boys suffered symptoms of impulsivity, poor attention, and motor hyperactivity. Subsequently, we showed that this finding also pertained to samples of black and white boys growing up in an American city. (These findings will be reviewed later in this article.) Apparently, neuropsychological problems are greatest for boys with serious behavior problems that begin precociously and remain stable across years.

These two observations suggest that neuropsychological problems may produce their effects early in the life-course. Perhaps the effects of early neuropsychological vulnerabilities are amplified over time as children interact with their environments, later culminating in behavior disorder. Consider one hypothetical cumulative sequence of interactions between boy and context. A preschooler who has special difficulty understanding language may resist his mother's efforts to read to him, because listening is frustrating to him. If his mother is overworked, a drug user, or does not read well herself, she may give up easily. This "interaction" delays the boy's readiness for school. When he enters school, the modal curriculum may not allow for teaching that is tailored to his delayed-readiness level, especially if the school is crowded and resources are poor. After a few years of school failure, the youth will be chronologically older than his classmates; perhaps he will feel socially rejected and wish for friends. He may be enrolled in a remedial class, containing pupils who have behavioral disorders as well as learning disabilities. There, daily association with conduct-disordered pupils brings familiarity with delinquent behaviors, and he may adopt delinquent ways to gain acceptance by peers.

This imaginary scenario is intended to illustrate how a relatively mild neuropsychological deficit might initiate an invidious sequence of interactions between individual characteristics and social contexts, culminating in a diagnosis of conduct disorder – or adjudication for a criminal offense. Neuropsychologists and developmental psychopathologists are collaborating to ask how dysfunction in the infant nervous system might influence behavior during infancy and very early childhood so as to get children "off on the wrong foot."

Beginnings: Neuropsychological Risk for Difficult Temperament and Behavioral Problems

If some individuals' antisocial behavior is stable from preschool to adulthood as the data imply, then we are compelled to look for its roots early in life – in factors that are present before or soon after birth. It is possible that the etiological chain begins with some factor capable of producing individual differences in the neuropsychological functions of the infant nervous system. Factors that influence infant neural development are myriad, and many of them have been empirically linked to antisocial outcomes.

One possible source of neuropsychological variation that is linked to problem behavior is disruption in the development of the fetal brain. Minor physical anomalies (such as very low-set ears or webbed toes) are thought to be observable markers for hidden anomalies in neural development because development of a fetus's external body features and internal brain structures may be disrupted together by a common insult. For example, physical anomalies co-occur with neuropsychological deficits in children with fetal alcohol syndrome. Minor physical anomalies have been found at elevated rates among violent offenders (Kandel, Brennan, & Mednick, 1989) and among subjects with antisocial personality traits (Fogel, Mednick, & Michelson, 1985; Paulhus & Martin, 1986). Neural development may be disrupted by maternal drug abuse, poor prenatal nutrition, or pre- or postnatal exposure to toxic agents such as lead (Needleman & Beringer, 1981; Rodning, Beckwith, & Howard, 1989; Stewart, 1983). Even brain insult suffered because of complications during a baby's delivery has been empirically linked to later violence and antisocial behavior in carefully designed longitudinal studies (Kandel & Mednick, 1991; Szatmari, Reitsma-Street, & Offord, 1986). In addition, some individual differences in neuropsychological health are heritable in origin (Borecki & Ashton, 1984; Martin, Jardine, & Eaves, 1984; Plomin, Nitz, & Rowe, 1990; Tambs, Sundet, & Magnus, 1984; Vandenberg, 1969). Just as parents and children share facial resemblances, they share some structural and functional similarities within their nervous systems.

After birth, neural development may be disrupted by neonatal depriva-
tion in such areas as nutrition, stimulation, and even affection (Cravioto &
Arrieta, 1983; Kraemer, 1988; Meany, Aitken, van Berkel, Bhatnagar, &
Sapolsky, 1988). Some studies of the histories of delinquents with
neuropsychological impairment have pointed to child abuse and neglect as
possible sources of brain injury (Lewis, Shanok, Pincus, & Glaser, 1979;
Milner & McCanne, 1991; Tarter, Hegedus, Winsten, & Alterman, 1984).
Clearly, one implication of this litany of sources of poor neuropsychological
health is that the risk is probably greater for infants born into poverty in the
inner city (compare Yudkin & Yudkin, 1968).

Neuropsychological Variation and the "Difficult" Infant. Before describing how neuropsychological variation might constitute risk for antisocial behavior, I think it is useful to define what is meant here by
neuropsychological. By combining "neuro" with "psychological," I refer
broadly to the extent to which anatomical structures and physiological
processes within the nervous system influence psychological characteristics
such as temperament, behavioral development, and/or cognitive abilities.
For example, individual variation in brain function may engender differences between children in activity level, emotional reactivity, or self-
regulation (temperament); speech, motor coordination, or impulse
control (behavioral development); and attention, language, learning,
memory, or reasoning (cognitive abilities).

Children with neurological difficulties severe enough to produce autism,
severe physical handicaps, or profound mental retardation are usually
identified and specially treated by parents and professionals. However,
other infants have subclinical levels of problems that make it difficult to
rear them; these problems are variously referred to as "difficult" temperament, language or motor "delays," or "mild cognitive impairments." Compromised neuropsychological functions are associated with a variety of
consequences for infants' cognitive and motor development, as well as for
their personality development (Rothbart & Derryberry, 1981). Toddlers
with subtle neuropsychological deficits may be clumsy and awkward, overactive, inattentive, irritable, impulsive, hard to keep on schedule, delayed in
reaching developmental milestones, poor at verbal comprehension, deficient at expressing themselves, or slow to learn new things (Rutter, 1977;
Rutter, 1983b; Thomas & Chess, 1977; Wender, 1971).

Hertzig (1983) has described an empirical test of the proposed relation
between neurological damage and difficult behavior in infancy. She studied
a sample of 66 low birth-weight infants from intact middle-class families.

Symptoms of brain dysfunction detected during neurological examinations were significantly related to an index of difficult temperament taken at ages one, two, and three (Thomas & Chess, 1977; the index comprised rhythmicity, adaptability, approach-withdrawal, intensity, and mood). The parents of these children with neurological impairment and difficult temperament more often sought help from child psychiatrists as their children grew up, and the most frequent presenting complaints were immaturity, overactivity, temper tantrums, poor attention, and poor school performance. Each of these childhood behavioral problems has been linked by research to later antisocial outcomes (Moffitt, 1990a; 1990b). Importantly, the impairments of the children with neural damage were not massive; their mean IQ score was 96 (only four points below the population mean). Hertzig's study shows that even subtle neurological deficits can influence infants' temperament and behavior, the difficulty of rearing them, and their behavioral problems in later childhood.

Child/Environment Covariation in Nature: A Contextual Source of Behavioral Continuity. Up to this point, this essay has emphasized the characteristics of the developing child, as if children's environments were held constant. But this book is about correlates of children's antisocial behavior in the *inner-city context*. Neuropsychologically vulnerable children might be found at elevated rates in inner-city neighborhoods because the sources of poor brain health are linked with institutionalized prejudice and poverty (Bronfenbrenner, Moen, & Garbarino, 1984; Department of Health and Human Services, 1986; Masten, 1991; National Institute of Drug Abuse, 1985; Sue, 1977). Among the inner-city poor, prenatal care is less available, low birth weight is more common, infant nutrition is poorer, and the incidence of fetal exposure to toxic and infectious agents is greater, placing infants at high risk for the nervous system problems that research has shown to interfere with optimal child development.

Unfortunately, children with cognitive and temperamental disadvantages are not generally born into supportive environments. Unlike the aforementioned infants in Hertzig's (1983) study of temperament and neurological symptoms, most low birth-weight infants are not born into intact, middle-class families. Vulnerable infants are disproportionately found in environments that will not be ameliorative because many sources of neural maldevelopment co-occur with family disadvantage or parental deviance.

Indeed, because some characteristics of parents and children tend to be correlated, parents of children who are at risk for antisocial behavior often inadvertently provide their children with criminogenic environments (Sameroff & Chandler, 1975). The intergenerational transmission of severe antisocial behavior has been carefully documented in a study of three generations (Huesmann, Eron, Lefkowitz, & Walder, 1984). In that study of 600 subjects, the stability of individuals' aggressive behavior from age 8 to age 30 was exceeded by the stability of aggression across the generations: from grandparent to parent to child. Thus, with regard to risk for persistent antisocial behavior, nature does not follow a "two by two" research design with equal numbers of children at all four cells. America's inner cities may constitute a "cell" wherein the most vulnerable children are exposed to the worst environmental circumstances.

Parents and children resemble each other in temperament and personality. Thus, parents of children who are difficult to manage often lack the necessary psychological and physical resources to cope constructively with a difficult child (Scarr & McCartney, 1983; Snyder & Patterson, 1987). For example, temperamental traits such as activity level and irritability are shared by parents and children because they are partially heritable (Plomin, Chipuer, & Loehlin, 1990). This suggests that children whose hyperactivity and angry outbursts might be curbed by firm discipline will tend to have parents who are inconsistent disciplinarians; the parents are impatient and irritable too. The converse is also true: Warm parents tend to have easy infants (Plomin et al., 1990).

Parents and children also resemble each other in cognitive ability. The known heritability of measured intelligence (Loehlin, 1989; Plomin, 1990) implies that children who are most in need of remedial cognitive stimulation will have parents who may be least able to provide it. Moreover, parents' cognitive abilities set limits on their own educational and occupational attainment (Barrett & Depinet, 1991). As one consequence, families whose members have below-average cognitive capacities may often be least able to escape the inner city. They may have difficulty financing professional interventions or optimal remedial schooling for their at-risk children.

Even the social and structural aspects of the environment may be stacked against children who enter the world at risk. Plomin and Bergeman (1991) have shown that there are genetic components to measures which are commonly used by developmental psychologists to assess socialization environments. For example, the HOME scale of family environments, the Moos Family Environment Scales, and the Holmes & Rahe scales of stressful life events all revealed the influence of heritable factors when they were examined with behavior genetic research designs (Plomin & Bergeman, 1991).

Apparently, people's characteristics have some influence on which environments they encounter or select. Vulnerable children are often subject to adverse homes and neighborhoods because their parents are vulnerable to problems too (see, e.g., Lahey et al., 1988).

It is significant that although examples from behavior genetics research have been cited in the previous three paragraphs, the perverse compounding of children's vulnerabilities with their families' imperfections does not require that the child's neuropsychological risk arises from any genetic disposition. In fact, for this inquiry into the complex relations between neuropsychological and environmental vulnerabilities, it is immaterial whether parent/child similarities arise from shared genes or shared homes. A home environment wherein prenatal care is unavailable, drugs are used during pregnancy, and infants' nutritional needs are neglected is a setting where sources of children's neuropsychological dysfunction that are clearly environmental coexist with a criminogenic social environment.

Problem Child/Problem Parent Interactions and the Emergence of Antisocial Behaviors. It is now widely acknowledged that personality and behavior are shaped in large measure by interactions between the person and the environment (compare Buss, 1987; Plomin, DeFries, & Loehlin, 1977; Scarr & McCartney, 1983). I believe that the juxtaposition of a vulnerable and difficult infant with an adverse rearing context sets the stage for the development of aggressive antisocial behavior. Subsequently, a process ensues in which the challenge of coping with a difficult child generates a chain of failed parent/child encounters (Sameroff & Chandler, 1975).

The assumption that children exert important effects upon their social environments is useful in understanding this hypothetical process of interaction between problem parent and problem child (Bell & Chapman, 1986). A difficult child's behavior may evoke distinctive and characteristic responses from parents and others, and the result is a continuous spiral of unpleasant and ineffective interactions (Caspi, Elder, & Bem, 1987).

Children with neuropsychological problems evoke a challenge to even the most resourceful, loving, and patient families. For example, Tinsley and Parke (1983) have reviewed literature showing that low birth-weight infants who were premature negatively influenced the behavior of their caretakers; they arrived before parents were prepared; and their crying patterns were rated as more relentlessly disturbing and irritating. Parents reported that they were less satisfying to feed, less pleasant to hold, and more demanding to care for than healthy babies. Many parents of pre-term infants hold unrealistic expectations about their children's attainment of developmental milestones, and these may contribute to later dysfunctional parent–child relationships (Tinsley & Parke, 1983). More disturbing, there is some suggestion that an infant's neurological health status may be related to risk for maltreatment and neglect (Friedrich & Boriskin, 1976; Frodi et al., 1978; Hunter, Kilstrom, Kraybill, & Loda, 1978; Milowe & Lowrie, 1964; Sandgrund, Gaines, & Green, 1974).

Numerous studies have shown that toddlers' problem behaviors may affect their parents' disciplinary strategies as well as their subsequent interactions with adults and peers (Bell & Chapman, 1986; Chess & Thomas, 1987). For example, children characterized as having a "difficult temperament" in infancy are more likely to resist their mothers' efforts to control them in early childhood (Lee & Bates, 1985). Similarly, mothers of "difficult" boys experience more problems in their efforts to socialize their children. Maccoby and Jacklin (1983) showed that over time, mothers of difficult infants reduce their efforts to guide and direct their children's behavior actively and become increasingly less involved in the teaching process. In a study of mothers and children, Anderson, Lytton, and Romney (1986) observed conduct-disordered and nonproblem boys interacting with mothers of conduct-disordered and nonproblem sons in unrelated pairs. The conduct-disordered boys evoked more negative reactions from both types of mothers than did normal boys, but the two types of mothers did not differ from each other in their negative reactions. It may well be that early behavioral difficulties contribute to the development of persistent antisocial behavior by evoking responses from the interpersonal social environment that exacerbate the child's tendencies (Goldsmith, Bradshaw, & Rieser-Danner, 1986; Lytton, 1990). "The child acts; the environment reacts; and the child reacts back in mutually interlocking evocative interaction" (Caspi et al., 1987, p. 308).

Such a sequence of interactions would be most likely to produce lasting antisocial behavior problems if caretaker reactions were more likely to exacerbate than ameliorate children's problem behavior. Students of child effects have not widely tested for interactions between child behavior and parental deviance or poor parenting, perhaps because very disadvantaged families are seldom studied with such designs. Nonetheless, some data suggest that children's predispositions toward antisocial behavior may be exacerbated under adverse rearing conditions. In the New Zealand longitudinal study, there was a significant interaction effect between children's neuropsychological deficit and family adversity on one type of delinquent act: aggressive confrontation with a victim or adversary. Among the 536 boys in the sample, the 75 boys who had *both* low neuropsychological test scores and adverse home environments earned a mean aggression score more than four times greater than that of boys with either neuropsychological problems or adverse homes alone (Moffitt, 1990b). The index of family adversity included parental characteristics such as poor mental health and low intelligence as well as low socioeconomic status, single parenting, and large family size. Behavior-genetic adoption studies of antisocial behavior often report a similar pattern of findings, wherein the highest rates of criminal outcomes are found for adoptees whose foster parents – as well as whose biological parents – were deviant (see, e.g., Mednick, Gabrielli, & Hutchings, 1984). Thus, children's predispositions may evoke exacerbating responses from the environment and may also render them more vulnerable to criminogenic environments.

Given the assumption that neuropsychologically vulnerable children are disproportionately subjected to high-risk environments, the remainder of this theoretical review will focus on "transactions, relationships over time, and the longitudinal development of behavior patterns in context" (Dodge, 1990, p. 698).

Hypotheses About Verbal Neuropsychological Deficits and Children's Antisocial Behavior

Several theorists have described ways in which neuropsychological deficits might produce children whose behavior poses a challenge to parenting. A. R. Luria (1961) as well as Luria and Hamskaya (1964) outlined a comprehensive theory of the importance of normal verbal memory and abstract reasoning for the development of self-control. According to Luria, deficits in these abilities impede socialization beginning with the earliest parent–child interactions. Luria tied the very young child's capacity for obedience to maturational development of the neuronal structures of the brain's frontal lobes and left cerebral hemisphere. He also outlined how language abilities are needed to convert parents' instructions and admonishments into children's internal tools for self-control. Luria did not discuss antisocial behavior in his writings, but the notion that deficient verbal mediation of behavior characterizes aggressive children has received some empirical support (Camp, 1977; Kopp, 1982).

Other writers have also commented on the influence of childhood language deficits on the development of antisocial behavior. Eysenck (1977), in his autonomic conditioning theory of antisocial personality disorder, stated that stimulus generalization should be enhanced when parents' verbally label their children's various misbehaviors as "naughty," "bad," or "wicked." But children with verbal-skill deficits might not profit from the labelling of a class of behaviors as punishment-attracting; they may have to learn by trial and error that different individual acts are wrong. Thus, verbally impaired children would attempt more misbehaviors and consequently be punished more often by their parents than verbally adept children – but with proportionately less result in curbing their problem behaviors. Consistent with Eysenck's prediction, Kaler and Kopp (1990) have demonstrated that much of problem toddlers' noncompliance can be explained by their poor verbal comprehension.

Tarter and his colleagues (Tarter, Hegedus, Alterman, & Katz-Garris, 1983; Tarter, Hegedus, Winsten, & Alterman, 1984) mention the intriguing notion that children with poor communication skills may elicit less positive interaction and more physical punishment from their parents, especially if the family lives in distressed conditions. Consistent with Tarter's prediction, McDermott and Rourke (cited in Rourke & Fiske, 1981) found fathers to be more negative, rejecting, and derogatory with their sons who had mild language deficits than with those boys' more verbally adept brothers. It follows from Tarter's speculation that poor verbal abilities may hinder the development of healthy parent–child relationships that might forestall problem behavior.

Wilson and Herrnstein (1985) suggest that low verbal intelligence contributes to a present-oriented cognitive style which, in turn, fosters irresponsible and exploitative behavior. Humans use language as the medium for abstract reasoning; we can keep things that are "out of sight" from also becoming "out of mind" by mentally representing them with words. Normal language development is thus an essential ingredient in prosocial processes such as delaying gratification, anticipating consequences of acts, and linking belated punishments with earlier transgressions.

In yet another account, Savitsky and Czyzewski (1978) speculate that a deficit in verbal skills may preclude children's ability to label their perceptions of the emotions expressed by others (victims or adversaries). Such deficits might also limit children's response options in threatening or ambiguous social situations, predisposing them to quick physical reactions rather than more laborious verbal ones. As such, children who feel uncomfortable or inept with verbal modes of communication may be more likely to strike out than to attempt to talk their way out of an altercation. If hitting gets them what they want, then they may enter the cycle of negative reinforcement for coercive behavior (Patterson, 1986a).

Empirical Evidence for a Verbal Deficit. Of course, none of these formulations is compelling unless there is good evidence that children who
ultimately become antisocial do suffer from deficits in verbal neuropsychological abilities. I have elsewhere reviewed and critiqued the large
available literature; existing research supports the conclusion that the link
between verbal impairment and antisocial outcomes is one of the largest
and most robust effects in the study of antisocial behavior (Moffitt, 1990b;
Moffitt & Henry, 1991; see also Hirschi & Hindelang, 1977). The verbal
deficits of antisocial children are pervasive, affecting their memory for
verbal material and their ability to listen and read, to solve problems, and
to speak and write.

The verbal problems of antisocial children constitute a specific *differential* deficit. That is, just as suspected by neuropsychologists, the overall IQ
concealed a special pattern of strengths and weaknesses that sets serious
delinquents apart from other children. Delinquents' visuo-spatial abilities
are generally unaffected, as evidenced by the oft-reported discrepancy
between their verbal and performance IQ scores (Moffitt, 1990b). Ever
since Wechsler (1944) remarked upon the diagnostic utility of a Performance IQ score greater than Verbal IQ score to identify delinquents, a
plethora of studies has been published on the "PIQ > VIQ" sign in delinquency. All of the subtests used to calculate the VIQ score are administered
orally, require an oral response, and are solved using language-based processing skills. Performance subtests, on the other hand, are administered
and solved in the visuo-spatial mode without the necessary use of language,
and they require a manual, not an oral, response. Prentice and Kelly
(1963) reviewed 24 reports that PIQ was greater than VIQ in delinquents;
West and Farrington (1973) reviewed still more studies, and the hypothesis
is still finding strong support (see, e.g., Haynes & Bensch, 1981; Lynam
et al., 1993; Walsh, Petee, & Beyer, 1987). Indeed, in all of the neuropsychological studies reviewed for this article that administered the
Wechsler IQ scales, delinquents' PIQs exceeded their VIQs. This impres-
sively replicable finding has been taken as strongly supporting a specific
deficit in language manipulation for delinquents. Because language functions are served by the left cerebral hemisphere in almost all individuals
(see Benson & Zaidel, 1985), the PIQ > VIQ findings have also been
interpreted as evidence for dysfunction of the left cerebral hemisphere in
the etiology of antisocial behavior.

Almost all of the neuropsychological studies reviewed for this article
provided some evidence of deficit on language-based tests for delinquents.
The following five studies were selected for detailed review because they

measured a representative sample of neuropsychological abilities, allowing for comparison of verbal and nonverbal functions.

Wolff, Waber, Bauermeister, Cohen and Ferber (1982) examined 56 adolescent males detained in an urban low-security facility. Comparison subjects were high school boys from poor neighborhoods. Delinquents scored significantly worse than comparison subjects on tests of reading, naming, vocabulary, and receptive language. Delinquents did not differ from comparison subjects on spatial or perceptual measures in this study.

Karniski, Levine, Clarke, Palfrey, and Meltzer (1982) tested 54 teenaged incarcerated urban boys using 29 tasks that were collapsed into composite measures of "neuromaturation, gross motor function, temporal-sequential organization, visual processing, and auditory-language function" (p. 151). A comparison group consisted of 51 boys from schools in a predominantly blue-collar urban community, who were screened for official delinquency. Notable mean group differences were obtained for two of the composite measures – visual processing and auditory-language function – but differences were greatest for the auditory–language area. When the tails of the distributions were examined, 29.6% of delinquents, but only 2% of comparison boys, scored two or more standard deviations below the comparison group's mean score on language skills.

Berman and Siegal (1976) administered the Halstead-Reitan Neuropsychological Battery (including the VIQ and PIQ tests) to 45 boys within one week of their first incarceration. The timing of the testing was selected to avoid institutionalization effects upon test scores. The Halstead-Reitan Battery contains tests of abstract reasoning, rhythmic sequencing, perception of speech sounds, sensory perception, motor response inhibition, and language skills, and it is designed to evaluate the functional integrity of the brain as a whole. It also includes several tests of sensory and manual functions that are repeated on the body's two sides (nonvisual manual problem-solving, finger tapping speed, grip strength, and sensory sensitivity to touch and sound) in order to reveal dysfunction in the brain's two hemispheres. The battery yielded 29 scores, which were analyzed using multiple t tests. If, in order to reduce the likelihood of chance error, only those t values statistically significant beyond $p = .001$ are considered, we find that delinquents were deficient on six of seven tests tapping verbal skills but on no tests of spatial skills.

Sobotowicz, Evans and Laughlin (1987) compared 50 incarcerated delinquents with 50 high school comparison subjects matched for age, race, and social class. Within each group, half the subjects had learning disabilities and half were normal learners, yielding four groups: Normal, JD (juvenile delinquent), LD (learning disabled), and JD+LD. On tests of verbal language skills, abstract verbal concept formation, and semantic and sequential memory, all three problem groups differed significantly from the comparison group. That the non-LD delinquents differed neuropsychologically from nondelinquents was unexpected, because the two groups were equal on mean full-scale IQ. In this study the three problem groups scored slightly *better* than nondelinquents on PIQ and other measures of nonverbal visuo-spatial skills. In a replication of the Sobotowicz et al. (1987) study, Henry, Moffitt, and Silva (1992) found that verbal deficits were evident in delinquents and learning disabled subjects but were especially severe in adolescents who were both delinquent and learning disabled.

Language-based measures were found to be more strongly associated with self-reported delinquency than were nonlanguage measures in our own longitudinal project in New Zealand. The New Zealand project is an important one for this field, because it was designed to correct many of the flaws in earlier research and to provide an "acid test" for the hypothesis that children with neuropsychological impairment are at risk for delinquency (Moffitt, 1988). Briefly, we avoided sampling bias by studying all 536 boys born in one town in 1972, assessing antisocial behavior at ages 3, 5, 7, 9, 11, 13, 15, and 18 via reports by parents, teachers, and boys' self-reports, as well as via police and court records. Tests of cognitive and motor abilities were given at ages 3, 5, 7, 9, and 11, and a neuropsychological test battery was administered near the boys' thirteenth birthday – in other words, before long-term drug and alcohol use could compromise neurological health. The neuropsychological findings from this prospective longitudinal study have been reported in several papers to date (Frost, Moffitt, & McGee, 1989; Henry, Moffitt, & Silva, 1992; Moffitt, 1990a,b; Moffitt & Henry, 1989; Moffitt & Silva, 1988a,b,c; White, Moffitt, Earls, Robins, & Silva, 1990; White, Moffitt, & Silva, 1989 & 1992).

In the New Zealand project, delinquent versus nondelinquent group differences were substantially greater for the tests of verbal and auditory-verbal memory skills than for tests of visual-motor integration or visuo-spatial skills. Specific language-based measures on which delinquents scored poorly relative to the sample norm were the Rey Auditory Verbal Learning Test (memorization of a word list), Verbal Fluency (rapid generation of a class of words), and the WISC-R VIQ subtests of Information, Similarities, Arithmetic, and Vocabulary. Findings were similar for girls and boys.

A subgroup of delinquent boys with past histories of Attention Deficit

Disorder with Hyperactivity (ADD-H) showed especially poor performance on the verbal and verbal memory factors, scoring a full standard deviation below nondelinquent boys (girls with ADD-H were too rare for reliable analysis). The delinquents with ADD-H had histories of extreme antisocial behavior that remained stable from age 3 to age 15. Apparently, their neuropsychological deficits were as longstanding as their antisocial behavior; at ages 3 and 5 these boys had scored more than a standard deviation below the age norm for boys on tests of motor coordination and on the Stanford-Binet test of cognitive performance. Contrast groups of boys with single diagnoses of either delinquent conduct problems of ADD-H did not have neuropsychological deficits or cognitive/motor problems, and neither were their behavior problems stable over time.

In a longitudinal study of the lives of these "delinquent+ADD-H" boys from age 3 to 15, Moffitt (1990a) showed that their conduct problems were exacerbated soon after they entered school. These boys had difficulty learning basic academic skills, such as reading and spelling. They also had many indicators of poor self-control, such as impulsivity and inattention, that may have interfered with their academic achievement (Hinshaw, 1992). In later years, these same boys were especially ill-prepared for the transition to high school; between ages 7 and 13, they fell further and further behind their peers on repeated tests of reading attainment. As adolescents, their acts of law-breaking were more aggressive than the acts of other delinquents who did not have a history of neuropsychological deficits and school failure.

Confounding Effects from Social Disadvantage and Reading Failure. The argument might well be made that delinquents score more poorly on tests requiring use of language skills than on nonlanguage tests because many verbal tests are more susceptible to the effects of sociocultural or educational disadvantage than are language-free tests. Delinquents, especially from officially-detected delinquent research samples, are predominantly from poor communities or from racial groups who typically score at a disadvantage on verbal tasks that depend on educational attainment. However, the specific verbal deficit has proven robust in studies where social class or family adversity effects were controlled (see, e.g., Moffitt, Gabrielli, & Mednick, 1981; Moffitt & Silva, 1988b; Sobotowicz et al., 1987). The delinquency-related verbal deficit has also been found within a single minority group (e.g., black subjects: see Denno, 1989; Lynam et al., 1993; Tarnopol, 1970), and in studies which have attempted to control statistically for the effects of race (Petee & Walsh, 1987).

Bryant and Bradley (1985), among others, have suggested that failure to learn to read handicaps children in their efforts to learn the sorts of information and thinking skills tapped by the subtests of the Verbal IQ. Children who fail to read may begin school with normal VIQ scores, but those scores might decline over time, with snowballing school failure (Share & Silva, 1988). In this view, the relatively low VIQ scores earned by delinquents might simply be a spurious effect of the disproportionately large numbers of reading disabled youngsters in officially detected delinquent research samples. Alternative views follow: (1) that low scores on verbal tests represent true information processing impairments that contribute to the development of both reading difficulty and antisocial behavior problems; or (2) that true cognitive impairment causes reading problems, which lead to school failure, which ultimately does contribute to delinquency.

Even if poor reading complicates interpretation of the relation between VIQ and conduct problems, this difficulty should have a smaller impact on many verbal neuropsychological tests than on subtests of the VIQ. VIQ tests specifically ask for information that is often gained through reading (e.g., Who invented the electric light bulb?), whereas many other verbal neuropsychological tasks do not. It is hard to imagine, for example, how reading failure might impede subjects from memorizing a list of digits. It is easier to imagine that both reading and memory for digits depend upon the cognitive ability to form mental symbol representations. Nevertheless, the possible reading confound remains an important issue for interpretation of many verbal test scores. In order to evaluate this possible confound using data from our New Zealand project, we retested for delinquent and nondelinquent group differences on the neuropsychological scores after entering reading achievement test scores as a covariate. Group differences remained significant at the .05 confidence level for the verbal factor, and they were significant beyond the .01 level for auditory–verbal memory. Also arguing against the reading confound are the aforementioned data from Sobotowicz et al. (1987), wherein delinquents who were screened for the absence of learning disabilities and matched to comparison subjects for full-scale IQ scored significantly below the comparison subjects on verbal neuropsychological tests.

Another way to challenge the proposed reading/VIQ confound is to search for prospective evidence that delinquents had verbal skill deficits before learning to read. Denno (1990) reported a causal structural longitudinal model of delinquency in which reading achievement at school was a strong predictor of later delinquency, but the model also showed that physicians' ratings of subjects' speech at age four and Stanford-Binet IQ at age four were strong predictors of school-age reading ability. Preliminary analyses of age three data from the New Zealand project show that delinquents with neuropsychological problems, but not all delinquents, first talked in sentences (by mother's diary record) a mean of five months later than nondelinquents. McMichael (1979) studied 198 boys in their first two years of school and reported that both antisocial behavior and deficits in tested skills such as visual discrimination, auditory discrimination, and vocabulary were present at school entry between ages $4\frac{1}{2}$ and $5\frac{1}{2}$ years, and that these problems preceded their learning to read. These analyses suggest that the verbal deficits found for delinquents studied cross-sectionally are not spurious consequences of reading failure.

Summary. A profile of relatively weaker verbal than visuo-spatial neuropsychological functions has been reported consistently in the majority of investigations of delinquents. This verbal deficit is pervasive, affecting receptive listening and reading, problem solving, expressive speech and writing, and memory for verbal material. Effects on neuropsychological scores from reading failure and from social disadvantage were considered. Data were provided that suggest that the verbal problems of persistent delinquents appear to be too robust to be wholly discounted by these confounding factors.

Hypotheses About Neuropsychological Self-Control Deficits and Children's Antisocial Behavior

The evidence is conclusive that verbal deficits are linked to the kind of aggressive antisocial behavior that begins in childhood and is sustained for lengthy periods. But verbal deficits are not the only neuropsychological sources of children's difficult behavior. Children who become antisocial may also have deficiencies in the brain's self-control functions. These mental functions are commonly referred to by neuropsychologists as "executive" functions. They include sustaining attention and concentration; abstract reasoning and concept formation; formulating goals; anticipating and planning; programming and initiating purposive sequences of behavior; self-monitoring and self-awareness; taking the perspective of others; inhibiting unsuccessful, inappropriate, or impulsive behaviors; and interrupting ongoing behavior patterns in order to shift to a more adaptive alternative behavior.

Three separate lines of research have now established that these various executive functions are primarily served by the frontal lobes of the brain and by connective pathways between the frontal lobes and other brain systems. Links between self-control of behavior and frontal brain structures have been found in research with animals whose brains have been experimentally damaged (for review, see Mark & Ervin, 1970), in clinical case studies of brain-damaged humans (Stamm & Kreder, 1979; Stuss & Benson, 1986), and with in-vivo neural imaging studies of the brains of children who have behavior disorders (Cohen et al., 1988; Lou, Henriksen, & Bruhn, 1984).

Indeed, one historical rationale for early neuropsychological research with delinquents was the apparent resemblance between criminal behavior and the disinhibited antisocial symptoms of patients with injury to the frontal lobes of the brain (Eiliott, 1978). Pontius (1972), Gorenstein (1982), and Yeudall (1980) have developed theories based on the observed similarity between the behavior of delinquents and pseudopsychopathic patients with frontal-lobe brain injuries. Gorenstein and Newman (1980) also described similarities between disinhibited antisocial human behavior and the behavior of experimental animals with damage to the structures of the frontal lobes and limbic system of the brain.

According to neuropsychological theory, executive dysfunctions should interfere with children's ability to control their own behavior, thus producing inattentive, impulsive individuals who are handicapped when considering the future implications of their acts. Such children should have difficulty understanding the negative impact their behavior has on others, they should fail to hold in mind abstract ideas of ethical values and future rewards, and they should fail to inhibit inappropriate behavior or adapt their behavior to changing social circumstances. Executive deficits may thus give rise to early childhood behavior problems that in turn set the stage for emerging antisocial behavior as the child grows physically older, although not necessarily more cognitively mature. Case studies of adults who sustained injury to the brain's frontal lobes as infants show this clinical picture, sometimes referred to as a "comportmental learning disability" (Price, Daffner, Stowe, & Mesulam, 1990). Interestingly, many patients with frontal brain damage who show extreme changes – from their original personality toward disinhibited antisocial behavior – have no IQ deficit at all.

Pontius (1972) suggested a number of neuropsychological tests that should be administered to delinquents with the objective of assessing executive functions:

1. The Wisconsin Card Sorting Test (WCST) measures abstract concept formation and the ability to inhibit a previously rewarded but now incorrect response. The WCST requires the subject to sort a deck of cards according to a characteristic, such as the color or the number of symbols on the cards. He or she must guess the characteristics, which are frequently changed covertly by the examiner.

2. The Stroop Color-Word Test requires inhibition of an over-learned automatic response. The subject views a list of color names, which are printed in colored inks that do not match their names. For example, where the word "red" is printed in green ink, the subject must say the name of the ink color and suppress the over-learned habit of reading the word.

3. In the Trail-Making Test, Form B, the subject must sustain attention to two competing sequences of letters and numbers on a page, while drawing a connect-the-dots line that alternates between them and inhibiting out-of-turn responses.

4. Halstead's Category Test is a task wherein the subject reasons inductively from categorical examples and uses this abstract information to classify new cases into categories.

Clinical frontal-lobe test batteries typically also include tests such as Verbal Fluency (in which the subject generates words within a category, such as animal names, as quickly as possible without uttering any words outside the category), Porteus or WISC-R Mazes (requiring sustained fine motor control and planning), and other tasks requiring similar motor programming and self-control abilities. Lezak (1983) provides detailed descriptions of these tests and cites validity studies for each.

Empirical Evidence for a Self-Control Deficit. Several studies that have applied batteries of formal tests of executive functions to delinquent subjects have now shown that the test scores can discriminate (albeit weakly) between antisocial and non-antisocial adolescents (see Moffitt, 1990b, and Moffitt & Henry, 1991, for detailed reviews). In addition, there is some evidence that the persistent and impulsive behaviors characteristic of conduct-disordered children and adults with antisocial personality disorder may be associated with executive deficits, particularly those relating to self-control of attention (Newman, 1987; Newman & Howland, 1989; Newman & Kosson, 1986; Raine, 1988; Shapiro, Quay, Hogan, & Schwartz, 1988).

In one of the better studies, Skoff and Libon (1987) compared the scores of 22 incarcerated delinquents to published test norms for the Wisconsin Card Sorting Test, Porteus Mazes, Trails B, Verbal Fluency, and four additional executive tasks. One-third of their subjects scored in the impaired range on the battery as a whole. Other studies, while not focusing specifically upon executive functions, have reported data from individual measures typically included in frontal-lobe batteries. These studies, taken together, provide additional support for the association between delinquency and executive deficit. Berman and Siegal (1976) found that delinquents scored poorly on Halstead's Category Test and Trails B. Wolff et al. (1982) reported delinquency-related impairments on tests of selective attention and on the Stroop Color-Word Test. Krynicki (1978) found that delinquent subjects performed similarly to subjects with documented organic brain damage on the Verbal Fluency test and on a test of motor perseveration, which indicates difficulty inhibiting an inappropriate response on command. Four studies showed delinquents to score poorly on various tests requiring them to organize complex sequences of motor behavior (Brickman, McManus, Grapentine, & Alessi, 1984; Hurwitz, Bibace, Wolff, & Rowbotham, 1972; Karniski et al., 1982; Miller, Burdg, & Carpenter, 1980).

In the New Zealand study, delinquent adolescent boys who exhibited coexisting persistent aggression and hyperactivity scored more poorly on neuropsychological tests of executive functions than their peers who had experienced either adolescent-onset delinquency or hyperactivity (Moffitt & Henry, 1989; Moffitt & Silva, 1988c). The Wisconsin Card Sorting Test, Verbal Fluency, Trails B, Porteus Mazes, and a measure of whether the child used a planned strategy to approach the task of copying a complex drawing (the Rey Osterreith Complex Figure Test) – as opposed to copying the drawing impulsively – were administered to the subjects. Multivariate analysis of variance demonstrated that a linear combination of these executive test scores significantly discriminated self-reported early delinquents from nondelinquents in the cohort, even after the effects of overall IQ were statistically controlled.

In a study designed to improve on measurement of executive functions (White et al., 1994), data were gathered on "self-control and impulsivity" for 430 inner-city Pittsburgh youths. Twelve measures were taken from multiple sources (mother, teacher, self, observer) via multiple methods (rating scales, neuropsychological tests, computer games, Q-sorts, and videotaped observations). A linear composite of the impulsivity measures was strongly related to the three-year longevity of antisocial behavior, even after controlling for IQ, race, and social class. Both black and white boys who were very delinquent from ages 10 to 13 scored significantly higher on impulsivity than either their nondelinquent or their temporarily delinquent age mates.

Taken together, the New Zealand and Pittsburgh longitudinal studies suggest that neuropsychological dysfunctions that manifest themselves as poor scores on tests of language and self-control – and as the inattentive, overactive and impulsive symptoms of ADD-H – are linked with the early childhood emergence of aggressive antisocial behavior and with its subsequent persistence.

Neuropsychological Studies of Violent Juveniles

The notion that brain dysfunction might relate specifically to violent behavior was popularized by Mark and Ervin in their book, *Violence and the Brain* (1970). Mark and Ervin were able to elicit rage attacks in human patients experimentally by electrically stimulating the brain's limbic system. The concept of a brain-based defect in control over aggressive impulses is an appealing one. The connection has often been framed as a variation on the theme of suppression by the neocortex of primitive aggressive and predatory instincts that have allegedly been retained in subcortical limbic structures (often called the phylogenetically "old" or "reptilian" brain). It has been said that evolution has added brain tissue in the frontal lobes that enables primates to engage in complex prosocial behavior; the frontal lobes mind our manners. But underneath, the old structures we share with reptiles remain, and this old brain is still capable of attack behavior if not modulated by the new brain. If the inhibiting processes of the frontal cortex are disrupted, or if there is damage to inhibiting neural pathways connecting the cortex and limbic system, it is posited that latent aggression is likely to be released, especially under certain aggression-eliciting circumstances. The neuropsychology of aggression is far more complex than implied by this simple theory; yet the theory stimulated research on the test performance of violent offenders. A few exemplary studies will be reviewed here, but a more complete review has been previously published (Moffitt & Henry, 1991).

The peak age for violent offending in most western nations is in the early twenties (Moffitt, Mednick, & Gabrielli, 1989; Wilson & Herrnstein, 1985). One natural consequence of the predominantly adult-age distribution of violent offending is that there are relatively fewer neuropsychological studies of violent juveniles than of violent adults. One point is made frequently in the adult studies that may have implications for the study of violence in juveniles: Repeatedly assaultive violent offenders are neuropsychologically different from offenders who commit a single isolated violent incident. Because juveniles will not have had much time in which to commit repeated acts of violence, it might be difficult to distinguish one-time from recidivistic violent offenders in juvenile samples. Therefore, we might expect somewhat attenuated results from neuropsychological studies of violence in juveniles – and that is what we find.

On the basis of a large battery of neuropsychological tests, Spellacy (1977) compared 40 nonviolent and 40 violent adolescents, who were classified according to their assaultive behavior while incarcerated at a training school. He reported that he was able to classify 83% of the subjects correctly on the basis of a discriminant function analysis using five of the test scores. Impairments were primarily in verbal and memory functions. Using the Luria-Nebraska Neuropsychological Test Battery, Brickman et al. (1984) also found that violence was differentially related to memory and verbal skill deficits. They studied 71 incarcerated youths, 63% of whom had committed at least one act of violence.

Tarter and his colleagues have conducted a series of interesting studies utilizing a very thorough battery of tests to evaluate boys referred from the juvenile court for neuropsychiatric evaluation. In the first study (1983), 73 boys were divided on the basis of their concurrent offense into violent, nonviolent, and sexual offenders (guilty primarily of rape). Statistically significant, though small (.22 to .39), correlations were obtained between a measure of severity of the concurrent violent offense and six neuropsychological measures. Comparison of the offender group means against test norms suggests that all three groups would probably have differed significantly from nondelinquents on most of the test scores if such boys had been studied.

In a second study, Tarter, Hegedus, Goldstein, Shelly, and Alterman (1984) compared 27 delinquents with histories of child abuse to 74 without abuse. The abused delinquents scored more poorly than the remainder on 6 of 47 tests, 5 of which were related to verbal and attentional skills. In addition, 44% of the abused group, but only 16% of the nonabused group had committed assault. In this group, therefore, some relation between assaultive behavior and cognitive deficit was seen, but its interaction with abuse history is unclear. The authors posited that verbally impaired children may be more susceptible to abuse and then may model their parents' abusive style of interaction under stress. It is also possible that head injuries incurred as a result of child abuse may impair neuropsychological function.

Lewis et al. (1979) dichotomized 97 incarcerated boys as "less violent" and "more violent." The more violent group had a greater frequency of abnormal EEG readings, neurological soft signs, and paranoid symptomatology, and they also reported histories of abuse, but there was only one group difference obtained from 14 tests of cognitive function (the Arithmetic subtest of the WISC). Other studies reported by this productive group (see, e.g., Lewis et al., 1985, 1988) have detailed the presence of neurological and neuropsychiatric abnormalities among adolescents who later murdered and among adolescents sentenced to death in the United States. The richness of the descriptive clinical data from these studies is an advantage. A disadvantage is that the subjects are generally highly selected and have something to gain by presenting themselves as psychiatrically or neurologically impaired.

The best extant study of cognitive factors in the violence of juveniles was conducted by Denno (1989). She conducted a longitudinal study of 987 black subjects from low-income black families in Philadelphia. Neuropsychological measures were taken in early childhood before the onset of violent delinquency. In that inner-city sample, no intellectual or achievement variables discriminated between violent offenders and recidivistic property offenders (offenders were designated as violent or not based on their cumulative offense records). Both delinquent groups scored significantly lower than nonarrested controls and one-time offenders on Verbal IQ, the Digit Span test of attention and short-term auditory memory, and on several achievement measures that had been taken prospectively in childhood. Denno's results imply that *recidivism*, regardless of offense type, may be the important correlate of neuropsychological deficit. Most violent adolescents are recidivists; they have a lengthy history of property crimes.

Causal Chains of Person–Environment Interactions: Failures in Discipline, Attachment, and Achievement

Granting that neuropsychological deficits characterize many children who show precocious behavior problems, how might neuropsychological risk initiate an antisocial style that is sustained over years? I argued earlier in this article that neuropsychological differences among infants are manifested as differences in behavioral styles and abilities and that children with difficult characteristics may evoke dysfunctional reactions from adults, especially from parents who are distressed, antisocial, or addicted to drugs. When difficult children keep company over time with difficult parents, and when both live in the difficult circumstances of the inner city, then cumulative sequences of negative interactions may ensue. Such sequences may elaborate what began as mere difficult characteristics into antisocial conduct problems by late childhood.

Along the way, important developmental tasks that should be negotiated jointly by small children and their caretakers risk failure. The sequences of events that build any given antisocial career will be "multifactorial," following several overlapping pathways through family, peer, and academic domains. It is not essential that every aggressive child follow all of the possible pathways or fail at every developmental task. As will be argued in the following sections, however, when the antisocial style invades more and more domains of functioning, the probability of change diminishes.

In this section, I shall describe for the reader some examples of sequential pathways by which neuropsychological problems might become channeled into antisocial behavior problems over time. For purposes of illustrating how sequences of person–environment interaction might work, I have selected three childhood tasks that have especially important implications for future adult adjustment: practicing social skills, establishing healthy interpersonal attachments, and achieving at school.

Cumulative Social Learning. As part of their ongoing longitudinal study of ego and cognitive development, Block and Block (1980) used an actometer to measure activity level in their subjects when the children were three and four years old. Observations of subsequent family interactions, when the children were five years old, revealed that parents of highly active children had become impatient with and hostile to their children and frequently got into power struggles with them (Buss, 1981). Moreover, when the children were seven years old, they were described by their teachers as aggressive, manipulative, noncompliant, and more likely to push limits and stretch the rules in many social encounters (Buss, Block, & Block, 1980). How were active children transformed to aggressive ones?

Research on aggressive children at the Oregon Social Learning Center has shown in elegant detail how evocative person–environment interactions can create and sustain destructive and aversive patterns of behavior (Patterson, 1982; 1986a; Patterson & Bank, 1990). By recording moment-to-moment interactions in families of antisocial boys, Patterson and his colleagues have been able to identify the peculiar reinforcement arrangements that typify the coercive family process. It appears that children's oppositional behaviors often provoke adult family members and force them to counter with highly punitive and angry responses; such interactions often escalate to an ever-widening gulf of irritation until the parents of such children eventually withdraw from aversive interactions with their children.

One outcome of such *negative reinforcements* is that children who coerce parents into providing short-term payoffs in the immediate situation may thereby learn an interactional style that continues to "work" in similar ways in later social encounters and with different interaction partners. Antisocial children learn to construct their social interactions to maximize their short-term payoffs; they get what they want by relying on offensive tactics. The immediate reinforcement not only short-circuits the learning of more prosocial interactional styles that might have greater adaptability in the long run, but it also increases the likelihood that coercive behaviors perfected at home will be extended to other people at other times. For example, children who are coercive with one family member are likely to be coercive with other family members (Patterson, 1986b). Analyses of sibling interactions show that here too reinforcement contingencies serve to strengthen the antisocial child's style (Patterson, 1986c; Snyder, 1977). Beginning the coercive cycle early increases the risk that it will generalize to other relationships; there is some evidence that a coercive style must be initiated well before the age of six if it is to influence later interactions (Eron, Huesmann, & Zelli, 1991). See Guerra (this volume) for an in-depth analysis of social learning effects on aggression.

The long-term costs associated with these short-term rewards are great. Early coercive family interactions have been found to portend deteriorated family management practices when antisocial children reach adolescence (Patterson, Capaldi, & Bank, 1991). At this point, parents of antisocial adolescents are less likely to supervise and monitor their sons; their inept disciplinary strategies, in turn, predict persistent and progressively more serious delinquency among their sons (Laub & Sampson, 1988; Loeber & Stouthamer-Loeber, 1986). In these ways, early dysfunctional social learning may help to initiate a persistent pattern of antisocial behavior.

Cumulative Attachment Failure. Children with subtle cognitive deficits or problem temperaments are not merely difficult to manage; they are sometimes difficult to love. The cross-sectional association between juvenile delinquency and weak attachment bonds to parents is well known (Hirschi, 1969); less is known about the *developmental course* of antisocial children's attachment bonds. One possibility is that neuropsychological problems may disrupt the initial formation of healthy parent–infant bonds. Kagan, Reznick, and Snidman noted that "[a]n excessively irritable, labile, or fearful infant is harder to nurture than a calm, stable, happy baby" (1990, p. 220; also see Goldsmith et al., 1986).

Indeed, Waters, Vaughan, and Egeland (1980) found that aspects of neonatal adaptation that are typically included in infant neuropsychological examinations (such as orientation and motor maturity) predicted the quality of later infant–mother attachment. Irritable infant temperament has been shown to predict weak parent–child attachment prospectively (measured by the toddler's resistance to reunion with his mother after a separation from her), *especially* when the mother lacked her own supportive relationships in the neighborhood (Crockenberg, 1981). Another study suggests that child–parent interactions influence attachment. Rodning, Beckwith, and Howard (1991) found that only 11% of a sample of prenatally drug-exposed toddlers were securely attached; the insecure children appeared dazed, aimless, confused, and unclear when communicating; at the same time, when interacting with their children, substance-abusing mothers displayed signs of rejection and insensitivity, and they provided little opportunity for physical contact. Although the data are still very sparse, they indicate that an infant's neuropsychological health may combine with parent and community characteristics (Sampson, this volume) to influence attachment bonds (Kagan, 1984).

Theorists such as Bowlby (1973; 1988) and Ainsworth (1973) have proposed that failure to form secure relationships with parents during infancy has far-reaching implications for the capacity to form affectionate, trusting friendships and stable family relationships in later life. If first relationships constitute a working model for subsequent relationships, then childhood experiences of neglect, rejection, or conflict might be expected to color subsequent attitudes toward peers, spouses, employers, and even potential victims of crimes. Such harmful childhood experiences appear to be typical in the backgrounds of persistent antisocial persons. Thus, the working model of a persistent antisocial person would predict a series of short-lived and exploitative relationships, relationships that are void of any deep affection. Compounding the problem, executive neuropsychological deficits such as impulsivity and poor judgment might strain antisocial persons' relationships too.

Absence of loyal friendships, unstable marital bonds, callous treatment of others, and irresponsible behavior toward one's offspring are the hallmarks of the antisocial personality. Indeed, Cleckley (1976) listed "incapacity for love" as a defining attribute of the psychopath. This construct has since been operationalized as the inability to maintain enduring attachments to a sexual partner, the existence of a poor marital history, the tendency to sexual promiscuity, a lack of close friendships, the failure to function as a responsible parent, and a history of repeated violent confrontations with others, all of which are among the diagnostic criteria for antisocial personality disorder (American Psychiatric Association, 1987; Robins, 1966).

No empirical studies have yet linked prospective measures of parent–child attachment during the infant period with delinquent or criminal outcomes in later life. A few studies predicting childhood behavior problems from infant–mother attachment have been done, but findings are mixed (see, e.g., Fagot & Kavanaugh, 1990; Lewis, Feirling, McGuffog, & Jaskir, 1984; Lieberman, 1977). The implications of these studies are unclear because they have used small and/or middle-class samples in which the base rates of insecure attachment, poor parenting, and conduct problems are low. The studies have operationalized the quality of attachment via the Strange Situation procedure, yet the heuristic value of Bowlby's theory for this analysis of antisocial behavior need not be clouded by debate over the validity of the Strange Situation classification system. The study that is perhaps most pertinent to this review is the longitudinal Minnesota Mother–Child Study, which has examined outcomes of weak attachment in a poor urban sample involving individuals at high risk for poor parenting. In that sample, avoidant attachment measured in infancy was significantly correlated with boys' aggressive behavior in elementary school. A combination of avoidant child attachment, maternal hostility, and negative child affect explained almost one-third of the variance in the children's aggressive outcomes (Renken, Egeland, Marvinney, Mangelsdorf, & Sroufe, 1989).

Earlier, I described how a coercive style that develops within the family might spread beyond the family to peers and others. A parallel pathway can be envisaged for attachment relationships. Studies show that insecure family relationships are associated with later maladaptive peer relationships (Hartup, 1983). It is notable that most of the aggressive behaviors measured among insecurely-attached youngsters by Renken et al. (1989) were directed toward peers at school. Young children who persistently aggress toward their peers are often rejected and have few friends (Coie, Belding, & Underwood, 1988). Thus, the lack of affectional ties may spread to potential relationships beyond the family.

There is also some evidence that poor parent/child bonds can predict antisocial behavior beyond childhood. An exhaustive review of family studies concluded that compared to all other aspects of family life and childrearing that have been systematically studied, neglect by parents was the strongest predictor of later criminal careers (Loeber & Stouthamer-Loeber, 1986). Similarly, McCord (1983a) and Eron et al. (1991) found that parental rejection was more strongly related to later criminal outcomes than other parenting practices (including discipline). Conversely, parental warmth and affection served to buffer boys who incurred risk for crime from other environmental disadvantages (McCord, 1983b).

A now-classic study of 500 urban delinquents lends some credence to the notion that weak family bonds discriminate the particular subgroup of aggressive delinquents who have neuropsychological problems from other delinquents. Hewitt and Jenkins (1946) concluded that parental rejection was characteristic of unsocialized aggressive delinquents (who were assaultive, cruel, defiant, malicious, and lacked guilt) but not of socialized delinquents (who engaged primarily in truancy and theft with peers). The unsocialized aggressive group had become delinquent at an earlier age and had lower IQ scores than the socialized group. Thus, the unsocialized individuals seem to fit the subtype of delinquents with verbal and self-control deficits. Parental rejection was defined on the basis of case records showing that the child had been illegitimate, unwanted, or rejected after delivery; that the child had lost contact with both natural parents; or that the mother was "sexually unconventional" or openly hostile to the child.

The research evidence cited above suggests that abnormal parent–child relationships in early life may be related to a persistent pattern of antisocial behavior in later years. In fact, disrupted affectional ties seem to be more influential than other family factors (e.g., social class, family structure, disciplinary strategies) in predicting long-term antisocial outcomes. It is conceivable that these early relational difficulties may have at least partial roots in children's neuropsychological endowments. This brief analysis of the theoretical long-term implications of disrupted attachments suggests the provocative hypothesis that delinquents who lack the capacity to form strong bonds with other people will more readily engage in antisocial behaviors of an interpersonal nature. If true, then neuropsychologically impaired delinquents, relative to other offenders, should be willing to engage in more violent or predatory confrontations with victims. And they may be less discriminating about whom they prey upon, finding victims among their "friends" and families as well as strangers.

Cumulative Academic Failure. The perspectives introduced in the last two sections have emphasized neuropsychological effects on early parent–child interactions. Other theorists point to the limits placed on school achievement by neuropsychological impairment. For example, Hirschi's

(1969) version of social control theory predicts that differences in intellectual capacity will have implications for how children experience school, a crucial agency in the transfer of children's respect and obedience from their parents to society and its laws. Cognitively-able children are likely to receive rewards at school and to develop bonds to this social institution as a consequence. Less able children may experience school as stressful and hence fail to form the social ties that are thought to prevent illegal behavior. Children with neuropsychological deficits have difficulty learning basic academic skills (Knights & Bakker, 1976; Rourke, 1985), and the formative educational experience of many children with even subtle, mild, cognitive impairments includes frustration, failure, and humiliation (Maloney & Ward, 1976).

Cognitive deficits may encourage antisocial behavior if they increase the likelihood that children will spend time in the company of already-delinquent pupils. Discussing the effects of individual differences on peer affiliation, Rowe and Osgood (1984) pointed out that scholarly students and failing students probably lack a common vocabulary and common interests. Thus, underachieving students would feel more comfortable with peers of low verbal ability, and we have seen that such children are likely to be antisocial. More worrisome is systematic concentration of antisocial students in classrooms as an unintended side-effect of ability tracking. Kellam (1990) demonstrated that tracking produces segregation by antisocial behavior. Some first-grade classrooms had no aggressive pupils, but in other classrooms, as a result of tracking by pupils' reading-readiness scores, as many as 70% of the pupils were aggressive.

Regardless of social experiences at school, cognitive deficits do interfere with youngsters' mastery of reading, writing, and arithmetic. Young adults who cannot read or understand basic mathematics will find few rewarding alternatives to crime in the job market. Consistent with this prediction, in a follow-up study of men who had been retarded readers as children, Maughan, Gray, and Rutter (1985) reported that poor reading was linked with low pay, unskilled jobs, and unemployment – and also with participation in criminal offending.

It must be said that there is controversy over the causal direction of the documented relation between measures of cognitive ability and antisocial behavior. Numerous studies conclude that antisocial behavior arises from cognitive deficit; others conclude that cognitive development is impeded by antisocial behavior. Hinshaw (1992) reviewed the evidence, and he pointed out that the entire data base for the controversy is correlational and thus can never be conclusive. In fact, both causal relations probably occur sequentially in a series of person–environment interactions. Such a model is consistent with the aforementioned data from the New Zealand sample (Moffitt, 1990a). In 5% of the boys, difficult behavior and low scores on cognitive and motor tests coincided at age three. Their antisocial behavior was exacerbated at the time of school entry, suggesting an effect of ability on behavior. From age 7 to age 13 their antisocial behavior remained stable, whereas their reading attainment fell further and further behind their peers, suggesting an effect of behavior on ability. As adolescents, they were more aggressive than other delinquents, and their performance on neuropsychological tests was poorer. In light of their abject reading failure, I predict poor employment prospects and continued delinquency, an effect of ability on behavior.

Summary. Although the three exemplary pathways described above make somewhat different predictions, they share the assumption that the child's complement of neuropsychological strengths and weaknesses is present very early in life, and their influence on personality and behavioral development begins to unfold with the child's earliest social interactions. If children who "step off on the wrong foot" remain on their ill-starred paths, subsequent stepping-stone experiences may culminate in persistent and aggressive antisocial behavior. For some antisocial individuals, deviant behavior patterns later in life may thus reflect early neuropsychological problems that are perpetuated or exacerbated by interactions with the social environment: first, at home; later, in the neighborhood and at school. To the extent that the urban family's bonds have been loosened and poor urban parents are under stress, high-risk infants should tend to develop the weak attachment bonds that, according to the research, predisposes them to aggressive interpersonal behavior. To the extent that poor urban children attend disadvantaged schools, there is less chance for correction of the learning disabilities that again according to the research, contributes to underemployment and recidivistic crime. Thus, for poor urban children, the snowball of cumulative continuity is anticipated to begin rolling earlier, and it rolls faster downhill.

But inauspicious beginnings do not complete the story. In the New Zealand study, for example, a combination of preschool measures of antisocial behavior and cognitive ability was able to predict 70% of the cases of conduct disorder at age 11 – but at the cost of a high false positive rate (White et al., 1990). Many children whom we expected to become antisocial did not. The next section explores some specific interactional processes that nourish and augment the persistent antisocial style beyond childhood.

Maintenance and Elaboration over the Life Course: Narrowing Options for Change

I have described some of the patterns of interaction between neuropsychologically impaired youths and their social environments that may promote antisocial continuity across time and across life domains. In addition, two more sources of continuity deserve mention here, because they narrow the options for change. These processes are:

1. failing to learn conventional prosocial alternatives to antisocial behavior
2. becoming ensnared in a deviant lifestyle by crime's consequences.

These concepts have special implications for the questions of why some antisocial youths fail to desist from delinquency when most other young adults do, and why this small group is so impervious to intervention.

A Restricted Behavioral Repertoire. This theoretical review asserts that the causal sequence begins very early for children with neuropsychological deficits and that the formative years are dominated by chains of cumulative continuity. Ongoing neuropsychological deficits can limit youngsters' ability to profit from experience. Furthermore, the inner-city context may offer limited opportunity structures (Sampson, this volume). As a consequence, little opportunity is afforded for the persistent antisocial individual to learn a behavioral repertoire of prosocial alternatives. Thus, one overlooked and pernicious source of continuity in antisocial behavior is simply a lack of recourse to any other options. In keeping with this prediction, Vitaro, Gagnon, and Tremblay (1990) have shown that aggressive children whose behavioral repertoires consist almost solely of antisocial behaviors are less likely to change over years than are equally aggressive children whose repertoires comprise some prosocial behaviors as well.

Persistent antisocial youths miss out on opportunities to acquire and practice prosocial alternatives at each stage of development. Children with poor self-control and aggressive behavior are often rejected by peers and adults (Coie, Belding, & Underwood, 1988; Dodge, Coie, & Brakke, 1982; Vitaro, Gagnon, & Tremblay, 1990). In turn, children who have learned to expect rejection are likely in later settings to withdraw or strike out preemptively, precluding opportunities to affiliate with prosocial peers (Dodge & Frame, 1982; Dodge & Newman, 1981; LaFrenier & Sroufe, 1985; Nasby, Hayden, & dePaulo, 1980). Such children are deprived of chances to practice conventional social skills. Or consider this commonly occurring sequence of narrowing options: Behavior problems at school and failure to attain basic math and reading skills place a limit on the variety of job skills that can be acquired and thereby cut off options to pursue legitimate employment alternatives to the underground economy (Farrington, Gallagher, Morley, Ledger, & West, 1986; Maughan, Gray, & Rutter, 1985; Moffitt, 1990a). Simply put, if social and academic skills are not learned in childhood, it is very difficult later to recover lost opportunities. This chapter argues that youngsters with neuropsychological deficits who grow up in the inner city have fewer opportunities than other children for learning important skills.

Becoming Ensnared by Consequences of Antisocial Behavior. Neuropsychological characteristics such as poor self-control, impulsivity, and inability to delay gratification increase the risk that antisocial youngsters will make irrevocable decisions that close the doors of opportunity. Teenaged parenthood, addiction to drugs or alcohol, school dropout, disabling or disfiguring injuries, patchy work histories, and time spent incarcerated are snares that diminish the probabilities of later success by eliminating opportunities for breaking the chain of cumulative continuity (Cairns & Cairns, 1991; Wilson & Herrnstein, 1985). Or once a poor male youth has discovered high earning potential or social status in the underground economy, he may be understandably reluctant to return to the sorts of poorly paid legitimate jobs available to inner-city males (Anderson, this volume). The contrast between opportunities in the underground versus legitimate economies is probably greater for young men who read poorly because of verbal deficits than for good readers. Similarly, labels accrued early in life can foreclose later opportunities; an early arrest record or a bad reputation may rule out lucrative jobs, higher education, or an advantageous marriage (Farrington, 1977; Klein, 1986; West, 1982). In short, the behavior of neuropsychologically impaired antisocial persons is increasingly maintained and supported by narrowing options for conventional behavior.

The Reason for Persistence: Traits, Environments, and Developmental Processes. According to some accounts of behavioral continuity, an everpresent underlying trait generates antisocial outcomes at every point in the lifespan (see, e.g., Gottfredson & Hirschi, 1990). By other accounts, antisocial behavior is sustained by environmental barriers to change (see, e.g., Bandura, 1979, pp. 217–24). In this neuropsychological theory of the rare form of antisocial behavior that persists across the life-course, neither traits nor environments fully account for continuity.

This theory begins with a trait – variation between individuals in their constellations of neuropsychological abilities – which is truly "underlying" insofar as it seldom comes to anyone's attention unless an infant is challenged by formal examinations; it is manifested behaviorally as variability in infant temperament, developmental milestones, and cognitive abilities.

Next, the theory brings environments into play. Parents and other people respond to the child's difficult temperaments and developmental deficits. In vigilant nurturing environments, the toddler's problems are often corrected. But in disadvantaged homes, schools, and neighborhoods, such as those found in America's inner cities, the responses are more likely to exacerbate than amend. Under such detrimental circumstances, difficult behavior is gradually elaborated into conduct problems and a dearth of prosocial skills. Thus, over the years, an antisocial personality is slowly and insidiously constructed. Likewise, deficits in language and reasoning are incrementally elaborated into academic failure and a dearth of job skills. Over time, accumulating consequences of the youngster's personality problems and academic problems prune away the options for change. As a result of this developmental process, relatively subtle childhood variations in neuropsychological health can be transformed into an antisocial style that pervades many domains of adolescent and adult behavior. It is this infiltration of the antisocial disposition into the multiple domains of a life that diminishes the likelihood of change.

Is there a point in the life-course when the potential for change dwindles to nil for some antisocial people? Is the potential for change from antisocial to conventional behavior always there, or are stronger interventions needed to produce change at older ages? I have argued that interactions between persons and their environments are needed before it is possible to predict emerging antisocial behavior. But how many interactions between individuals and their environments must accumulate before the persistent antisocial pattern becomes virtually set? Is the trajectory of cumulative antisocial development accelerated in the inner city? Answers to these questions are critical for prevention efforts. Answers to these questions will inform the optimal timing and intensity of interventions.

The well-documented resistance of antisocial personality disorder to treatments of all kinds seems to suggest that the persistent antisocial style is fixed sometime before age 18 (Suedfeld & Landon, 1978). Studies of crime careers reveal that if an adult is going to be strongly antisocial, the pattern must be established by late adolescence (Elliott, Huizinga, & Menard, 1989). Research has shown that adult-onset crime tends to be low-rate and nonviolent (Blumstein & Cohen, 1987), and it is generally not accompanied by the many complications that attend a long-term antisocial lifestyle (Farrington et al., 1990). At the same time, efforts to predict antisocial outcomes from childhood conduct problems yield many errors (see, e.g., White et al., 1990). These errors seem to suggest that antisocial styles become set sometime after late childhood.

Unfortunately, the extant longitudinal data base does not yet provide a basis for confident conclusions. Typically, research reports describe childhood behavior problems that were assessed at only one time point from a single source, thereby lumping the many children who are temporarily or situationally aggressive with the very few children who are on a persistent and pervasive aggressive trajectory. Outcomes are also typically assessed at a single point, most often during late adolescence. In adolescent samples, teens who experiment briefly with delinquency are inadvertently lumped with future adult criminal persisters, muddling research findings (Moffitt, 1993). Only recently have the original subjects of a handful of longitudinal studies of childhood aggression matured to adulthood, and neighborhood context has *never* been considered in a study of the continuity of an individual's aggression across the life-course. Future analyses should ask: Do childhood behavior problems and neuropsychological deficits predict antisocial outcomes among adults strongly in some environments but weakly in others?

Neuropsychology, Delinquency, and Neighborhood Context

This article has reviewed evidence from neuropsychological tests that brain dysfunction is a correlate of a form of persistent antisocial behavior that afflicts about 5% of males. Most of the studies I reviewed reported consistent findings of neuropsychological deficits for antisocial samples, particularly in verbal and self-control functions. Neuropsychological tests were shown statistically to predict variance in delinquent behavior independently of appropriate control variables. These findings argue that neuropsychological variables warrant further study as possible risk factors for aggression.

I have argued here that the traditional notion that neuropsychological deficits influence antisocial behavior in the moment preceding each individual act may not be a complete explanation. Neuropsychological test scores are not very impressive univariate predictors of general delinquency; they probably work in the context of interactions between person and environment over the course of development, and they probably apply to only a small subgroup of offenders. Despite a growing consensus that family and neighborhood adversity mediate the relations between neuropsychology and antisocial outcomes, no theories specify the family and neighborhood links in the developmental chains between early brain function and later antisocial syndromes. We have not progressed very far toward understanding how neuropsychological characteristics might interact with circumstances of family poverty and neighborhood disorganization. There is a great need for empirical data about how neuropsychological variables relate to delinquency in different types of neighborhoods.

New Data from the Pittsburgh Youth Study. To begin to address some of the questions raised by prior research, I examined data from a study designed to study the development of antisocial behavior in different neighborhood contexts: the Pittsburgh Youth Study. I compared the relation between neuropsychological test scores and delinquent behavior in two groups of black boys from different types of urban neighborhoods: one "good" and one "disadvantaged."

The boys were members of the Pittsburgh Youth Study, a longitudinal study of the development of delinquent behavior (more information about the Pittsburgh Youth Study is available from a publication prepared by its principal investigators, Loeber, Stouthamer-Loeber, Van Kammen, & Farrington, 1989). The boys were enrolled in the study in the late 1980s, when they were selected to represent all fourth grade boys in the Pittsburgh city public schools. As in all Pittsburgh classrooms, 54% of the sample boys were black. The sample began with 508 boys, and although some families dropped out from the study over time, our analyses show that the remainder are still representative of the original sample.

When the boys were 12–13 years old, their delinquent behavior was measured by asking them to self-report their experience with a roster of illegal behaviors during the past six months. Their reports were supplemented with reports from their parents and teachers to yield a reliable measure of preteen delinquent involvement. At the same time, each boy's neighborhood was categorized as "disadvantaged" or "good" by the Pittsburgh Youth Study principal investigators, who used data from the 1980 U.S. Census. Disadvantaged neighborhoods were those that were in the worst 25% in measures of median household income, unemployment, families below the poverty level, density of males aged 10–14, female-headed households, or rate of separation/divorce. Good neighborhoods were not extreme on any of these census factors. According to this definition, none of the white boys lived in a disadvantaged neighborhood. As a result, cross-neighborhood comparisons could not be made among white boys, so only the data for the black boys were analyzed for this chapter. Among black boys, 111 lived in disadvantaged neighborhoods and 81 lived in good neighborhoods. Most of the black boys (60%) were not delinquent.

When the boys were 12–13 years old, we administered to them a battery of performance measures of executive functions. Good scores required strong self-control and low impulsivity. We calculated a reliable measure that we labelled "cognitive impulsivity" by combining scores from four tests (Trail-Making, Stroop Color-Word, Time Perception, Circle Tracing) and two computer games that were played for money (Newman's Card-Playing Game and the Delay of Gratification Game). Two methodological studies showed that the cognitive impulsivity score was a valid indicator of each boy's self-control style. Observers who were blind to the goals of our study watched videotapes of the test sessions, rating each boy's approach to the games; these ratings showed that low motivation did not compromise test scores. In addition, cognitive impulsivity scores earned in our laboratory statistically predicted the boys' impulsive behaviors at home and school, as illustrated by a correlation of .53 with reports from parents and teachers. (For details of this research see Lynam et al., 1993; and White et al., 1994.)

To anticipate the results of the study: Scores on self-control tests were associated with the seriousness of delinquent behavior in both types of neighborhoods. Of greater interest was an unexpected finding: The good neighborhoods seemed to protect boys from delinquency, but only if they were neuropsychologically healthy. Boys with neuropsychological problems, even if they lived in good neighborhoods, were more likely to be delinquent.

We found that cognitive impulsivity scores were significantly correlated with delinquency scores in boys from both good ($r = .29$) and disadvantaged ($r = .19$) neighborhoods. On average, the nondelinquents' cognitive impulsivity scores were one-half standard deviation better than the delinquents' scores. On average, cognitive impulsivity scores were significantly worse, and delinquency scores significantly higher, among boys from disadvantaged neighborhoods. These findings are cross-sectional correlations, so they cannot be used to infer any causal sequence of effects. However, they are consistent with the chapter's thesis that neuropsychological deficit and delinquency coexist among individuals in disadvantaged inner-city environments.

The interaction between neuropsychology and environment was tested by comparing delinquency scores of boys who scored above versus below the mean on cognitive impulsivity; the samples were categorized further by good versus disadvantaged neighborhood. The statistical significance of this interaction effect was borderline ($p = .06$). When interpreted, the interaction was somewhat surprising. Boys with cognitive impulsivity scored one quarter standard deviation above the black boys' norm on delinquency, regardless of what kind of neighborhood they lived in. This finding echoes results reported by Breslau (1990), who found that children with neurological disorders were more likely than healthy children to show symptoms of depression, inattention, and impulsivity as teenagers; but the prevalence of symptoms was no greater if their families scored low on "family cohesion." It appeared that cognitive impulsivity may be a general risk factor for preteen delinquent involvement among Pittsburgh-Youth-Study boys across environments.

However, the picture differed for boys who were not cognitively impulsive. The ones from disadvantaged neighborhoods had average delinquency scores; their delinquency was typical for the full sample of black urban boys. By contrast, nonimpulsive boys who lived in good neighborhoods scored a full half standard deviation *below* the sample mean on delinquency. When individual cases were examined, it was found that all of the 42 nonimpulsive boys from good neighborhoods had reported no experience with delinquent offending at all. One possible interpretation for this interaction is that good urban environmental conditions can exert a powerful protective effect for boys who are neuropsychologically healthy. If true, efforts to improve children's neurological health should be an important ingredient of crime-prevention programs designed to improve inner-city conditions.

This presentation must be accompanied by a strong caution. The analyses presented here are useful, because they are the first effort to compare neuropsychological findings across different types of urban neighborhoods. However, the bases on which boys were grouped for comparison were relatively crude. The findings were modest, if not borderline. They are merely a beginning point for better research. An essential first step is to follow the lead of chapters in this book to develop more sensitive and rich measures of the many dimensions of a child's neighborhood. It is hoped that this chapter will encourage more neuropsychological research with designs that combine longitudinal study of development across time with comparative study of development across settings.

REFERENCES

Ainsworth, M. D. S. (1973). The development of infant-mother attachment. In B. M. Caldwell & H. N. Ricciuti (Eds.). *Review of child development research (Vol. 3)* (pp. 1–95). Chicago: University of Chicago Press.

American Psychiatric Association. (1987). *Diagnostic and statistical manual of mental disorders, Revised (DSM–III–R)*. Washington, DC: APA.

Anderson, A. (This volume). Violence and the inner-city street code. In J. McCord (Ed.). *Violence and childhood in the inner city* (pp. 1–30). New York: Cambridge University Press.

Anderson, K. E., Lytton, H., & Romney, D. M. (1986). Mothers' interactions with normal and conduct-disordered boys: Who affects whom? *Developmental Psychology* 22, 604–9.

Bandura, A. (1979). The social learning perspective: Mechanisms of aggression. In H. Toch (Ed.). *Psychology of crime and criminal justice* (pp. 193–236). Prospect Heights, IL: Waveland Press.

Barrett, G. V., & Depinet, R. L. (1991). A reconsideration of testing for competence rather than for intelligence. *American Psychologist* 46, 1012–24.

Bell, R. Q., & Chapman, M. (1986). Child effects in studies using experimental or brief longitudinal approaches to socialization. *Developmental Psychology* 22, 595–603.

Benson, D. F., & Zaidel, E. (1985). *The dual brain*. New York: Guilford Press.

Berman, A., & Siegal, A. W. (1976). Adaptive and learning skills in juvenile delinquents: A neuropsychological analysis. *Journal of Learning Disabilities* 9, 51–8.

Block, J., & Block, J. H. (1980). The role of ego-control and ego-resilience in the organization of behavior. In W. A. Collins (Ed.). *Minnesota symposia on child psychology (Vol. 13)* (pp. 39–101). Hillsdale, NJ: Erlbaum.

Blumstein, A., & Cohen, J. (1987). Characterizing criminal careers. *Science* 237, 985–91.

Borecki, I. B., & Ashton, G. C. (1984). Evidence for a major gene influencing performance on a vocabulary test. *Behavior Genetics* 14, 63–80.

Bowlby, J. (1973). *Attachment and loss: Vol. 2. Separation*. New York: Basic Books.
    (1988). Developmental psychiatry comes of age. *American Journal of Psychiatry* 145, 1–10.

Breslau, N. (1990). Does brain dysfunction increase children's vulnerability to environmental stress? *Archives of General Psychiatry* 47, 15–20.

Brickman, A. S., McManus, M. M., Graptentine, W. L., & Alessi, N. (1984). Neuropsychology assessment of seriously delinquent adolescents. *Journal of the American Academy of Child Psychiatry* 23, 453–7.

Bronfenbrenner, U., Moen, P., & Garbarino, J. (1984). Child, family, and community. In R. Parke (Ed.). *Review of child development research: Vol. 7. The family* (pp. 283–328). Chicago: University of Chicago Press.

Bryant, P., & Bradley, L. (1985). *Children's reading problems.* Oxford: Basil Blackwell, Ltd.

Buss, D. M. (1981). Predicting parent-child interactions from children's activity level. *Developmental Psychology* 17, 59–65.

Buss, D. M. (1987). Selection, evocation, and manipulation. *Journal of Personality and Social Psychology* 53, 1214–21.

Buss, D. M., Block, J. H., & Block, J. (1980). Preschool activity level: Personality correlates and developmental implications. *Child Development* 51, 401–8.

Cairns, R. B., & Cairns, B. D. (1994). *Lifelines and risks.* New York: Cambridge University Press.

Camp, B. W. (1977). Verbal mediation in young aggressive boys. *Journal of Abnormal Psychology* 86, 145–53.

Caspi, A., Elder, G. H., & Bem, D. J. (1987). Moving against the world: Life-course patterns of explosive children. *Developmental Psychology* 23, 308–13.

Chess, S., & Thomas, A. (1987). *Origins and evolution of behavior disorders: From infancy to early adult life.* Cambridge, MA: Harvard University Press.

Cleckley, H. (1976). *The mask of sanity.* St. Louis: Mosby.

Cohen, R. M., Semple, W. E., Gross, M., Holcomb, H. H., Dowling, M. S., & Nordahl, T. E. (1988). Functional localization of sustained attention: Comparison to sensory stimulation in the absence of instruction. *Neuropsychiatry, Neuropsychology, and Behavioral Neurology* 1, 3–20.

Coie, J. D., Belding, M., & Underwood, M. (1988). Aggression and peer rejection in childhood. In B. Lahey & A. Kazdin (Eds.). *Advances in clinical child psychology* (Vol. 2). New York: Plenum Press.

Cravioto, J., & Arrieta, R. (1983). Malnutrition in childhood. In M. Rutter (Ed.). *Developmental neuropsychiatry* (pp. 32–51). New York: Guilford Press.

Crockenberg, S. (1981). Infant irritability, mother responsiveness and social support influences on the security of infant/mother attachment. *Child Development* 52, 857–65.

Denno, D. (1989). *Biology, crime and violence: New evidence.* Cambridge, MA: Cambridge University Press.

(1990). *Biology and violence: From birth to adulthood.* Cambridge, MA: Cambridge University Press.

Department of Health and Human Services. (1986). *Report on the secretary's task force on black and minority health.* Washington, D.C.: DHHS.

Dodge, K. A. (1990). Nature versus nurture in childhood conduct disorder: It is time to ask a different question. *Developmental Psychology* 26, 698–701.

Dodge, K. A., Coie, J. D., & Brakke, N. P. (1982). Behavior patterns of socially rejected and neglected preadolescents: The roles of social approach and aggression. *Journal of Abnormal Child Psychology* 10, 389–410.

Dodge, K. A., & Frame, C. L. (1982). Social cognitive biases and deficits in aggressive boys. *Child Development* 53, 620–35.

Dodge, K. A., & Newman, J. P. (1981). Biased decision-making process in aggressive boys. *Journal of Abnormal Psychology* 90, 375–9.

Elliott, D. S., Huizinga, D., & Menard, S. (1989). *Multiple problem youth: Delinquency, substance use, and mental health problems.* New York: Springer-Verlag.

Elliott, F. A. (1978). Neurological aspects of antisocial behavior. In W. H. Ried (Ed.). *The psychopath* (pp. 146–89). New York: Brunner/Mazel.

Eron, L. D., Heusemann, L. R., & Zelli, A. (1991). The role of parental variables in the learning of aggression. In D. Pepler & K. Rubin (Eds.). *The development and treatment of childhood aggression* (pp. 171–88). Hillsdale, NJ: Erlbaum.

Eysenck, H. J. (1977). *Crime and personality.* London: Routledge & Kegan Paul.

Fagot, B. I., & Kavanaugh, K. (1990). The prediction of antisocial behavior from avoidant attachment classifications. *Child Development* 61, 864–73.

Farrington, D. P. (1977). The effects of public labelling. *British Journal of Criminology* 172, 112–25.

Farrington, D. P., Gallagher, B., Morley, L., Ledger, R. J., & West, D. J. (1986). Unemployment, school leaving and crime. *British Journal of Criminology* 26, 335–56.

Farrington, D. P., Loeber, R., Elliott, D. S., Hawkins, D. J., Kandel, D. B., Klein, M. W., McCord, J., Rowe, D., & Tremblay, R. (1990). Advancing knowledge about the onset of delinquency and crime. In B. Lahey & A. Kazdin (Eds.). *Advances in clinical child psychology* (Vol. 13, pp. 231–342). New York: Plenum Press.

Fogel, C. A., Mednick, S. A., & Michelson, N. (1985). Minor physical anomalies and hyperactivity. *Acta Psychiatrica Scandinavia* 72, 551–6.

Friedrich, W. N., & Boriskin, J. A. (1976). The role of the child in abuse. *American Journal of Orthopsychiatry* 46, 580–90.

Frodi, A. M., Laub, M. E., Leavitt, L. E., Donovan, W. L., Neff, C., & Sherry, D. (1978). Fathers' and mothers' responses to the faces and cries of normal and premature infants. *Developmental Psychology* 14, 490–8.

Frost, L. A., Moffitt, T. E., & McGee, R. (1989). Neuropsychological correlates of early adolescent psychopathology: Abstract. *Journal of Clinical and Experimental Neuropsychology* 10, 72.

Goldsmith, H. H., Bradshaw, D. L., & Rieser-Danner, L. A. (1986). Temperament as a potential developmental influence on attachment. In J. V. Lerner & R. M. Lerner (Eds.). *Temperament and social interaction during infancy and childhood* (pp. 5–34). San Francisco: Jossey Bass.

Goldstein, G. (1987). Neuropsychiatry: Interfaces between neuropsychology and psychopathology. *The Clinical Neuropsychologist* 4, 355–80.

Gorenstein, E. E. (1982). Frontal lobe functions in psychopaths. *Journal of Abnormal Psychology* 91, 368–79.

Gorenstein, E. E., & Newman, J. P. (1980). Disinhibitory psychopathology: A new perspective and a model for research. *Psychological Review* 87, 301–15.

Gottfredson, M., & Hirschi, T. (1990). *A general theory of crime.* Stanford, CA: Stanford University Press.

Guerra, N. (This volume). Intervening to prevent childhood aggression in the inner city. In J. McCord (Ed.). *Violence and childhood in the inner city* (pp. 256–312). New York: Cambridge University Press.

Hartup, W. W. (1983). Peer relations. In P. Mussen (Ed.). *Carmichael's manual of child psychology* (pp. 103–96). New York: Wiley.

Haynes, J. P., & Bensch, M. (1981). The P > V sign of the WISC–R and recidivism in delinquents. *Journal of Consulting and Clinical Psychology* 49, 480–1.

Healy, W., & Bronner, A. F. (1936). *New light on delinquency and its treatment.* New Haven, CT: Yale University Press.

Henry, B., Moffitt, T. E., & Silva, P. A. (1992). Disentangling delinquency and learning disability: Neuropsychological function and social support. *The International Journal of Clinical Neuropsychology* 13, 1–6.

Hertzig, M. (1983). Temperament and neurological status. In M. Rutter (Ed.). *Developmental Neuropsychiatry* (pp. 164–80). New York: Guilford Press.

Hewitt, L. E., & Jenkins, R. L. (1946). *Fundamental patterns of maladjustment: The dynamics of their origin.* Chicago: State of Illinois.

Hinshaw, S. P. (1992). Externalizing behavior problems and academic under-achievement in childhood and adolescence: Causal relationships and underlying mechanisms. *Psychological Bulletin* 111, 127–55.

Hirschi, T. (1969). *Causes of delinquency.* Berkeley, CA: University of California Press.

Hirschi, T., & Hindelang, M. J. (1977). Intelligence and delinquency: A revisionist review. *American Sociological Review* 42, 571–87.

Huesman, L. R., Eron, L. D., Lefkowitz, M. M., & Walder, L. O. (1984). Stability of aggression over time and generations. *Developmental Psychology* 20, 1120–34.

Hunter, R. S., Kilstrom, N., Kraybill, E. N., & Loda, F. (1978). Antecedents of child abuse and neglect in premature infants: A prospective study in a newborn intensive care unit. *Pediatrics* 61, 629–35.

Hurwitz, I., Bibace, R. M. A., Wolff, P. H., & Rowbotham, B. M. (1972). Neurological function of normal boys, delinquent boys and boys with learning problems. *Perceptual and Motor Skills* 35, 387–94.

Kagan, J. (1984). *The nature of the child.* New York: Basic Books.

Kagan, J., Reznick, J. S., & Snidman, N. (1990). The temperamental qualities of inhibition and lack of inhibition. In M. Lewis & S. M. Miller (Eds.). *Handbook of developmental psychopathology* (pp. 219–26). New York: Plenum.

Kaler, S. R., & Kopp, C. B. (1990). Compliance and comprehension in very young toddlers. *Child Development* 61, 1997–2003.

Kandel, E., Brennan, P., & Mednick, S. A. (1989). Minor physical anomalies and parental modeling of aggression predict to violent offending. *Journal of Consulting and Clinical Psychology* 78, 1–5.

Kandel, E., & Mednick, S. A. (1991). Perinatal complications predict violent offending. *Criminology* 29, 519–30.

Karniski, W. M., Levine, M. D., Clarke, S., Palfry, J. S., & Meltzer, L. J. (1982). A study of neurodevelopmental findings in early adolescent delinquents. *Journal of Adolescent Health Care* 3, 151–9.

Kellam, S. (1990). Developmental epidemiological framework for family research on depression and aggression. In G. R. Patterson (Ed.). *Depression and aggression in family interaction* (pp. 11–48). Hillsdale, NJ: Lawrence Erlbaum.

Klein, M. W. (1986). Labelling theory and delinquency policy. *Criminal Justice and Behavior* 13, 47–79.

Knights, R. M., & Bakker, D. J. (1976). *The neuropsychiatry of learning disorders.* Baltimore: University Park Press.

Kopp, C. B. (1982). Antecedents of self-regulation: A developmental perspective. *Developmental Psychology* 18, 199–214.

Kraemer, G. W. (1988). Speculations on the developmental neurobiology of protest and despair. In P. Simon, P. Soubrie, & D. Widlocher (Eds.). *Inquiry into schizophrenia and depression: Animal models of psychiatric disorders* (pp. 101–47). Basel: Karger.

Krynicki, V. E. (1978). Cerebral dysfunction in repetitively assaultive offenders. *Journal of Nervous and Mental Disease* 166, 59–67.

LaFrenier, P., & Sroufe, L. A. (1985). Profiles of peer competence in the preschool: Interrelations between measures, influence of social ecology and relation to attachment history. *Developmental Psychology* 21, 56–69.

Lahey, B., Hartdagen, S. E., Frick, P. J., McBurnett, K., Connor, R., & Hynd, G. W. (1988). Conduct disorder: Parsing the confounded relation to parental divorce and antisocial personality. *Journal of Abnormal Psychology* 97, 334–7.

Laub, J. H., & Sampson, R. J. (1988). Unraveling families and delinquency: A reanalysis of the Glueck's data. *Criminology* 26, 355–80.

Lee, C. L., & Bates, J. E. (1985). Mother-child interaction at age two years and perceived and difficult temperament. *Child Development* 56, 1314–23.

Lewis, D. O., Moy, E., Jackson, L. D., Aaronson, R., Restifo, N., Serra, S., & Simos, A. (1985). Biopsychosocial characteristics of children who later murder: A prospective study. *American Journal of Psychiatry* 142, 1161–67.

Lewis, D. O., Pincus, J. H., Bard, B., Richardson, E., Prichep, L. S., Feldman, M., & Yeager, C. (1988). Neuropsychiatric, psychoeducational and family characteristics of 14 juveniles condemned to death in the United States. *American Journal of Psychiatry* 145, 584–9.

Lewis, D. O., Shanok, S. S., Pincus, J. H., & Glaser, G. H. (1979). Violent juvenile delinquents: Psychiatric, neurological, psychological and abuse factors. *Journal of the American Academy of Child Psychiatry* 2, 307–19.

Lewis, M., Feirling, C., McGuffog, C., & Jaskir, J. (1984). Predicting psychopathology in six-year-olds from early social relations. *Child Development* 55, 123–36.

Lezak, M. D. (1983). *Neuropsychological assessment.* New York: Oxford University Press.

——— (1988). IQ: RIP. *Journal of Clinical and Experimental Neuropsychology* 10, 351–61.

Lieberman, A. F. (1977). Preschoolers' competence with a peer: Influence of attachment and social experience. *Child Development* 48, 1277–87.

Loeber, R. (1988). The natural histories of conduct problems, delinquency, and associated substance abuse. In B. B. Lahey & A. E. Kazdin (Eds.). *Advances in clinical child psychology* (Vol. II, pp. 73–124). New York: Plenum.

Loeber, R., & Stouthamer-Loeber, M. (1986). Family factors as correlates and predictors of juvenile conduct problems and delinquency. In M. Tonry & N. Morris (Eds.). *Crime and Justice* (Vol. 7). Chicago: University of Chicago Press.

Loeber, R., Stouthamer-Loeber, M., Van Kammen, W., & Farrington, D. (1989). Development of a new measure for self-reported antisocial behavior for young children: Prevalence and reliability. In M. Klein (Ed.). *Cross-national research in self-reported crime and delinquency* (pp. 203–26). Boston: Kluwer-Nijhoff.

Loehlin, J. C. (1989). Partitioning environmental and genetic contributions to behavioral development. *American Psychologist* 44, 1285–92.

Lou, H. C., Henriksen, L., & Bruhn, P. (1984). Focal cerebral hypoperfusion in children with dysphasia and/or attention deficit disorder. *Archives of Neurology* 41, 825–9.

Luria, A. R. (1961). *The role of speech in the regulation of normal and abnormal behavior.* New York: Basic Books.

Luria, A. R., & Homskaya, E. D. (1964). Disturbance in the regulative role of speech with frontal lobe lesions. In J. M. Warren & K. Akert (Eds.). *The frontal granular cortex and behavior* (pp. 353–71). New York: McGraw-Hill.

Lynam, D., Moffitt, T. E., & Stouthamer-Loeber, M. (1993). Explaining the relation between IQ and delinquency: Class, race, test motivation, school failure or self-control. *Journal of Abnormal Psychology* 102, 187–96.

Lytton, H. (1990). Child and parent effects in boys' conduct disorder: A reinterpretation. *Developmental Psychology* 26, 683–97.

Maccoby, E. E., & Jacklin, C. N. (1983). The "person" characteristics of children and the family as environment. In D. Magnusson & V. L. Allen (Eds.). *Human development: An interactional perspective* (pp. 75–92). New York: Academic Press.

Maloney, M. P., & Ward, M. P. (1976). *Psychological assessment: A conceptual approach.* New York: Oxford University Press.

Mark, V., & Ervin, F. R. (1970). *Violence and the brain.* New York: Harper & Row.

Martin, N. G., Jardine, R., & Eaves, L. J. (1984). Is there only one set of genes for different abilities? *Behavior Genetics* 14, 355–70.

Masten, A. S. (1991). Homeless children in the United States: Development in jeopardy. Paper presented at the Science and Public Policy Seminars of the Federation of Behavioral, Psychological and Cognitive Sciences, Washington, D.C.

Maughan, B., Gray, G., & Rutter, M. (1985). Reading retardation and antisocial behavior: A follow-up into employment. *Journal of Child Psychiatry and Psychology* 26, 741–58.

McCord, J. (1983a). A longitudinal study of aggression and antisocial behavior. In K. T. Van Dusen & S. A. Mednick (Eds.). *Prospective studies of crime and delinquency* (pp. 269–79). Boston: Kluwer-Nijhoff.

(1983b). A forty-year perspective on the effects of child abuse and neglect. *Child Abuse and Neglect* 7, 265–70.

McMichael, P. (1979). The hen or the egg? Which comes first – Antisocial emotional disorders or reading disability? *British Journal of Educational Psychology* 49, 226–38.

Meany, M. J., Aitken, D. H., van Berkel, C., Bhatnagar, S., & Sapolsky, R. M. (1988). Effect of neonatal handling on age-related impairments associated with the hippocampus. *Science* 239, 766–8.

Mednick, S. A. (1987). Preface. In S. A. Mednick, T. E. Moffitt, & S. A. Stack (Eds.). *The causes of crime: New biological approaches* (pp. ix–x). New York: Cambridge University Press.

Mednick, S. A., Gabrielli, W. F., & Hutchings, B. (1984). Genetic factors in criminal behavior: Evidence from an adoption cohort. *Science* 224, 891–3.

Miller, L., Burdg, N. B., & Carpenter, D. (1980). Application of recategorized WISC–R scores of adjudicated adolescents. *Perceptual and Motor Skills* 51, 187–91.

Milner, J. S., & McCanne, T. R. (1991). Neuropsychological correlates of physical child abuse. In J. S. Milner (Ed.). *Neuropsychology of aggression* (pp. 131–45). Boston: Kluwer Academic Publishers.

Milowe, I. D., & Lowrie, R. S. (1964). The child's role in the battered child syndrome. *Journal of Pediatrics* 65, 1079–81.

Moffitt, T. E. (1988). Neuropsychology and self-reported early delinquency in an unselected birth cohort: A preliminary report from New Zealand. In T. E. Moffitt & S. A. Mednick (Eds.). *Biological contributions to crime causation* (pp. 89–112). New York: Martinus Nijhoff Press.

(1990a). Juvenile delinquency and attention-deficit disorder: Developmental trajectories from age three to fifteen. *Child Development* 61, 893–910.

(1990b). The neuropsychology of delinquency: A critical review of theory and research. In N. Morris & M. Tonry (Eds.). *Crime and justice* (pp. 99–169). Chicago: University of Chicago Press.

(1993). "Life-course-persistent" and "adolescence-limited" antisocial behavior: A developmental taxonomy. *Psychological Review* 100, 674–701.

Moffitt, T. E., Gabrielli, W. F., & Mednick, S. A. (1981). Socioeconomic status, IQ, and delinquency. *Journal of Abnormal Psychology* 90, 152–6.

Moffitt, T. E., & Henry, B. (1989). Neuropsychological assessment of executive functions in self-reported delinquents. *Development and Psychopathology* 1, 105–18.

(1991). Neuropsychological studies of juvenile delinquency and juvenile violence. In J. S. Milner (Ed.). *The neuropsychology of aggression* (pp. 67–91). Boston: Kluwer Academic Publishers.

Moffitt, T. E., Mednick, S. A., & Gabrielli, W. F. (1989). Predicting criminal violence: Descriptive data and predispositional factors. In D. Brizer & M. Crowner (Eds.). *Current approaches to the prediction of violence* (pp. 13–34). New York: American Psychiatric Association Press.

Moffitt, T. E., & Silva, P. A. (1988a). Neuropsychological deficit and self-reported delinquency in an unselected birth cohort. *Journal of the American Academy of Child and Adolescent Psychiatry* 27, 233–40.

(1988b). IQ and delinquency: A direct test of the differential detection hypothesis. *Journal of Abnormal Psychology* 97, 330–3.

(1988c). Self-reported delinquency, neuropsychological deficit, and history of Attention Deficit Disorder. *Journal of Abnormal Child Psychology* 16, 553–69.

Nasby, W., Hayden, B., & dePaulo, B. M. (1980). Attributional bias among aggressive boys to interpret unambiguous social stimuli as displays of hostility. *Journal of Abnormal Psychology* 89, 459–68.

National Institute of Drug Abuse. (1985). *Drug abuse among minorities.* Rockville, MD: ADAMHA.

Needleman, H. L., & Beringer, D. C. (1981). The epidemiology of low-level lead exposure in childhood. *Journal of Child Psychiatry* 20, 496–512.

Newman, J. P. (1987). Reaction to punishment in extroverts and psychopaths: Implications for the impulsive behavior of disinhibited individuals. *Journal of Research in Personality* 21, 464–80.

Newman, J. P., & Howland, E. (1989). The effect of incentives on Wisconsin Card-sorting task performance in psychopaths. Unpublished manuscript: University of Wisconsin.

Newman, J. P., & Kosson, D. S. (1986). Passive avoidance learning in psychopathic and nonpsychopathic offenders. *Journal of Abnormal Psychology* 95, 257–63.

Patterson, G. R. (1982). *Coercive family process.* Eugene, OR: Castalia.

(1986a). Performance models for antisocial boys. *American Psychologist* 41, 432–44.

(1986b). Maternal behavior: Detriment or product for deviant child behavior? In W. Hartup & Z. Rubin (Eds.). *Relationships and development* (pp. 73–94). Hillsdale, NJ: Erlbaum.

(1986c). The contribution of siblings to training for fighting. In D. Olweus,

J. Block, & M. Radke-Yarrow (Eds.). *Development of prosocial and antisocial behavior* (pp. 235–62). Orlando, FL: Academic Press.

Patterson, G. R., & Bank, L. (1990). Some amplifying mechanisms for pathologic processes in families. In M. R. Gunnar & E. Phelen (Eds.). *Systems and development: The Minnesota Symposia on Child Psychology* (Vol. 22, pp. 167–209). Hillsdale, NJ: Erlbaum.

Patterson, G. R., Capaldi, D., & Bank, L. (1991). An early starter model for predicting delinquency. In D. Pepler & K. Rubin (Eds.). *The development and treatment of childhood aggression* (pp. 139–68). Hillsdale, NJ: Erlbaum.

Paulhus, D. L., & Martin, C. L. (1986). Predicting adult temperament from minor physical anomalies. *Journal of Personality and Social Psychology* 50, 1235–39.

Petee, T. A. & Walsh, A. (1987). Violent delinquency, race and the Wechsler performance-verbal display. *Journal of Social Psychology* 127(3), 353–4.

Plomin, R. (1990). The role of inheritance in behavior. *Science* 248, 183–8.

Plomin, R., & Bergeman, C. S. (1991). The nature of nurture: Genetic influence on "environmental" measures. *Behavioral and Brain Sciences* 14, 373–86.

Plomin, R., Chipuer, H. M., & Loehlin, J. C. (1990). Behavioral genetics and personality. In L. Pervin (Ed.). *Handbook of personality* (pp. 225–43). New York: Guilford Press.

Plomin, R., DeFries, J. C., & Loehlin, J. C. (1977). Genotype-environment interaction and correlation in the analysis of human behavior. *Psychological Bulletin* 84, 309–22.

Plomin, R., Nitz, K., & Rowe, D. C. (1990). Behavioral genetics and aggressive behavior in childhood. In M. Lewis & S. M. Miller (Eds.). *Handbook of developmental psychopathology* (pp. 119–33). New York: Plenum.

Pontius, A. A. (1972). Neurological aspects in some types of delinquency, especially among juveniles: Toward a neurological model of ethical action. *Adolescence* 7, 289–308.

Prentice, N. M., & Kelly, F. J. (1963). Intelligence and delinquency: A reconsideration. *Journal of Social Psychology* 60, 327–37.

Price, B. H., Daffner, K. R., Stowe, R. M., & Mesulam, M. M. (1990). The comportmental learning disabilities of early frontal lobe damage. *Brain* 113, 1383–93.

Raine, A. (1988). Evoked potentials and antisocial behavior. In T. E. Moffitt, S. A. Mednick, & S. A. Stack (Eds.). *Biological contributions to crime and causation* (pp. 14–39). Dordrecht, The Netherlands: Martinus Nijhoff Publishers.

Reiss, A. J., Jr., & Rhodes, A. L. (1961). The distribution of juvenile delinquency in the social class structure. *American Sociological Review* 26, 720–32.

Renken, B., Egeland, B., Marvinney, D., Mangelsdorf, S., & Sroufe, L. A. (1989).

Early childhood antecedents of aggression and passive-withdrawal in early elementary school. *Journal of Personality* 57, 257–81.

Robins, L. N. (1966). *Deviant children grown up.* Baltimore: Williams and Wilkins.

Rodning, C., Beckwith, L., & Howard, J. (1989). Charateristics of attachment organization and play organization in prenatally drug-exposed toddlers. *Development and Psychopathology* 1, 277–89.

(1991). Quality of attachment and home environments in children prenatally exposed to PCP and cocaine. *Development and Psychopathology* 3, 351–66.

Rothbart, M. K., & Derryberry, D. (1981). Development of individual differences in temperament. In M. E. Lamb & A. L. Brown (Eds.). *Advances in developmental psychology* (pp. 37–66). Hillsdale, NJ: Erlbaum.

Rourke, B. P. (1985). Statistical analysis of large neuropsychological data bases: Methodological and clinical considerations. *Journal of Clinical and Experimental Neuropsychology* 7, 631.

Rourke, B. P., & Fiske, J. L. (1981). Socio-emotional disturbances of learning disabled children: The role of central processing deficits. *Bulletin of the Orton Society* 31, 77–88.

Rowe, D. C. & Osgood, D. W. (1984). Heredity and sociological theories of delinquency: A reconstruction. *American Sociological Review* 49, 526–40.

Rush, B. (1812). *Medical injuries and observations upon the diseases of the mind,* Philadelphia: Kimber & Richardson.

Rutter, M. (1977). Brain damage syndromes in childhood: Concepts and findings. *Journal of Child Psychology and Psychiatry* 18, 1–22.

(1983a). Issues and prospects in developmental neuropsychiatry. In M. Rutter (Ed.). *Developmental neuropsychiatry* (pp. 32–51). New York: Guilford Press.

(1983b). *Developmental neuropsychiatry.* New York: Guilford Press.

Sameroff, A., & Chandler, M. (1975). Reproductive risk and the continuum of caretaking casualty. In F. Horowitz, M. Hetherington, S. Scarr-Salapatek, & G. Seigel (Eds.). *Review of child development research* (pp. 187–244). Chicago: University of Chicago Press.

Sampson, R. (This volume). The embeddedness of child and adolescent development. In J. McCord (Ed.). *Violence and childhood in the inner city* (pp. 31–77). New York: Cambridge University Press.

Sandgrund, A. K., Gaines, R., & Green, A. H. (1974). Child abuse and mental retardation: A problem of cause and effect. *American Journal of Mental Deficiency* 79, 327–30.

Savitsky, J. C., & Czyzewski, D. (1978). The reaction of adolescent offenders and nonoffenders to nonverbal emotional displays. *Journal of Abnormal Child Psychology* 6, 89–96.

Scarr, S., & McCartney, K. (1983). How people make their own environments:

A theory of genotype to environment effects. *Child Development* 54, 424–35.

Shapiro, S. K., Quay, H. C., Hogan, A. E., & Schwartz, K. P. (1988). Response perseveration and delayed responding in undersocialized conduct disorder. *Journal of Abnormal Psychology* 97, 371–3.

Share, D. L., & Silva, P. A. (1988). Language deficits and reading retardation: Cause or effect? *British Journal of Disorders of Communication* 22, 219–26.

Short, J. F., Jr., & Strodtbeck, F. L. (1965). *Group process and gang delinquency.* Chicago: University of Chicago Press.

Shulman, H. M. (1929). *A study of problem boys and their brothers.* Albany, NY: New York State Crime Commission.

Skoff, B. F., & Libon, J. (1987). Impaired executive functions in a sample of male juvenile delinquents. *Journal of Clinical and Experimental Neuropsychology* 9, 60.

Snyder, J. J. (1977). A reinforcement analysis of interaction in problem and non-problem families. *Journal of Abnormal Psychology* 86, 528–35.

Snyder, J. J., & Patterson, G. R. (1987). Family interaction and delinquent behavior. In H. C. Quay (Ed.). *Handbook of juvenile delinquency* (pp. 216–43). New York: Wiley.

Sobotowicz, W., Evans, J. R., & Laughlin, J. (1987). Neuropsychological function and social support in delinquency and learning disability. *The International Journal of Clinical Neuropsychology* 9, 178–86.

Spellacy, F. (1977). Neuropsychological differences between violent and non-violent adolescents. *Journal of Clinical Psychology* 33, 966–9.

Stamm, J. S., & Kreder, S. V. (1979). Minimal brain dysfunction: Psychological and neuropsychological disorders in hyperkinetic children. In M. Gazzaniga (Ed.). *Handbook of behavioral neurology: Vol. 2. Neuropsychology* (pp. 119–52). New York: Plenum.

Stewart, A. (1983). Severe perinatal hazards. In M. Rutter (Ed.). *Developmental neuropsychiatry.* New York: Guilford.

Stuss, D. T., & Benson, D. F. (1986). *The frontal lobes.* New York: Raven Press.

Sue, S. (1977). Community mental health services to minority groups: Some optimism, some pessimism. *American Psychologist* 37, 616–28.

Suedfeld, P., & Landon, P. B. (1978). Approaches to treatment. In R. Hare & D. Schalling (Eds.). *Psychopathic behaviour* (pp. 347–76). New York: Wiley.

Szatmari, P., Reitsma-Street, M., & Offord, D. (1986). Pregnancy and birth complications in antisocial adolescents and their siblings. *Canadian Journal of Psychiatry* 31, 513–16.

Tambs, K., Sundet, J. M., & Magnus, P. (1984). Heritability analysis of the WAIS subtests: A study of twins. *Intelligence* 8, 283–93.

Tarnopol, L. (1970). Delinquency and minimal brain dysfunction. *Journal of Learning Disabilities* 3, 200–7.

Tarter, R. E., Hegedus, A., Goldstein, G., Shelly, C., & Alterman, A. I. (1984).

Adolescent sons of alcoholics: Neuropsychological and personality characteristics. *Alcoholism: Clinical and Experimental Research* 8, 330–3.

Tarter, R. E., Hegedus, A. M., Alterman, A. I., & Katz-Garris, L. (1983). Cognitive capabilities of juvenile violent, nonviolent and sexual offenders. *Journal of Nervous and Mental Disease* 171, 564–67.

Tarter, R. E., Hegedus, A. M., Winsten, N. E., & Alterman, A. I. (1984). Neuropsychological, personality and familial characteristics of physically abused delinquents. *Journal of the American Academy of Child Psychiatry* 23, 668–74.

Thomas, A., & Chess, S. (1977). *Temperament and development*. New York: Brunner/Mazel.

Tinsley, B. R., & Parke, R. D. (1983). The person-environment relationship: Lessons from families with preterm infants. In D. Magnusson & V. L. Allen (Eds.). *Human development: An interactional perspective* (pp. 93–110). New York: Academic Press.

Vandenberg, S. G. (1969). A twin study of spatial ability. *Multivariate Behavioral Research* 4, 273–94.

Vitaro, F., Gagnon, C., & Tremblay, R. E. (1990). Predicting stable peer rejection from kindergarten to grade one. *Journal of Clinical Child Psychology* 19, 257–64.

Walsh, A., Petee, T. A., & Beyer, J. A. (1987). Intellectual imbalance and delinquency: Comparing high verbal and high performance IQ delinquents. *Criminal Justice and Behavior* 14(3), 370–9.

Waters, E., Vaughan, B., & Egeland, B. (1980). Individual differences in infant-mother attachment: Antecedents in neonatal behavior in an urban economically disadvantaged sample. *Child Development* 51, 208–16.

Wechsler, D. (1994). *The measurement of adult intelligence*, 3rd edition. Baltimore: Williams & Wilkins.

Wender, P. H. (1971). *Minimal brain dysfunction in children*. New York: Wiley.

West, D. J. (1982). *Delinquency, its roots, careers and prospects*. Cambridge, MA: Harvard University Press.

West, D. J., & Farrington, D. P. (1973). *Who becomes delinquent?* London: Heinemann Educational Books.

White, J., Moffitt, T. E., Caspi, A., Jeglum, D., Needles, D., & Stouthamer-Loeber, M. (1994). Measuring impulsivity and examining its relation to delinquency. *Journal of Abnormal Psychology* 103, 192–205.

White, J., Moffitt, T. E., Earls, F., Robins, L. N., & Silva, P. A. (1990). How early can we tell? Predictors of childhood conduct disorder and adolescent delinquency. *Criminology* 28, 507–33.

White, J., Moffitt, T. E., & Silva, P. A. (1989). A prospective replication of the protective effects of IQ in subjects at high risk for juvenile delinquency. *Journal of Consulting and Clinical Psychology* 57, 719–24.

(1992). Neuropsychological and socio-emotional correlates of specific arithmetic disability. *Archives of Clinical Neuropsychology* 7, 1–16.

Wilson, J. Q., & Herrnstein, R. J. (1985). *Crime and human nature.* New York: Simon & Schuster.

Wolff, P. H., Waber, D., Bauermeister, M., Cohen, C., & Ferber, R. (1982). The neuropsychological status of adolescent delinquent boys. *Journal of Child Psychology and Psychiatry* 23, 267–79.

Wolfgang, M. E., Figlio, R. M., & Sellin, T. (1972). *Delinquency in a birth cohort.* Chicago: University of Chicago Press.

Yeudall, L. T. (1980). A neuropsychological perspective of persistent juvenile delinquency and criminal behavior. *Annals of the New York Academy of Sciences* 347, 349–55.

Yudkin, S., & Yudkin, G. (1968). Poverty and child development. *Developmental Medicine and Child Neurology* 10, 569–79.

Psychological Mediators of Violence in Urban Youth

RONALD G. SLABY

A single mother who grew up and currently lived in a working class urban community proudly told her pediatrician the following story of how she taught her child to deal with violence (Stringham, 1993, personal communication):

> When her 5 year old daughter complained that another girl had been hitting her on the way home from school, the mother told her to hit the other girl back. The daughter replied, "No, Mom, I can't. She's bigger than me and I'm afraid of her." The mother had grown up in an urban housing project where as a child she had experienced a great deal of violence as a witness, a victim, and a perpetrator. Drawing from her childhood experience, she decided to teach her daughter a lesson in dealing with violence. So she walked her outside, locked the door, and told her through the screen door, "You won't get back into this house until you come back with the other girl's two front teeth."
>
> More than an hour later, her daughter came back, knocking on the door softly and crying. She didn't know if her mother would let her back into the house because she had only one-half of a tooth from the other girl to present to her mother. She had broken it off with a rock. The mother agreed to let her daughter back into the house.
>
> Soon afterwards, the mother got a phone call from the irate mother of the girl with the broken tooth. While her daughter listened to her responses, the mother screamed at the other mother and threatened her by saying, "If you get me, I'll get you." She proudly reported to her pediatrician that so far, the other mother had not bothered her again and the other girl had not hit her daughter again.

This true story simultaneously illustrates a number of important issues that will be discussed in this chapter on the development of violence in urban youth, including

171

- the early learning of patterns of violence through their roles as aggressors, victims, and witnesses.
- the enduring influence of childhood experiences with violence on one's behavior patterns as an adult.
- the direct and sometimes coercive influence of an adult on the violent behavior of a child (in the case cited above, the mother's demand that her daughter become a perpetrator of violence under the threat of banishment).
- the indirect influence of an adult on a child through modeling of violence-related behaviors (the mother's modeling of violent threats on the phone in the presence of her daughter).
- the perpetuation of many cycles of violence
    (a) across phases of an individual's life (from mother's childhood to her adulthood).
    (b) across generations (from mother to her child).
    (c) across settings (from home to playground).
    (d) across roles (from victim to aggressor).
- the escalation of retaliatory violence (from one child hitting with a fist to another child hitting with a rock; from one mother's irate remarks to another mother's screaming threat).
- the immediate social rewards for violent threats and behaviors such as
    (a) ending banishment (from the house).
    (b) regaining approval (of her mother).
    (c) stopping further hitting (by the other girl).
    (d) preventing enactment of the phone threat (by the other mother).
- the anticipated social approval for using violence to deal with conflicts (a mother's anticipated approval from her pediatrician)

One can only speculate about what enduring effects this event might have on the behavior of these two children at different phases in their lives and what further violence might yet result from this event if the second family decides to retaliate and escalates the level of violence.

This story also illustrates several common psychological factors that contribute to violent behavior – learned patterns of thought that mediate the use of violence. These learned patterns of thought include:

1. a sense of being victimized or challenged by hostile adversaries
2. a set of beliefs that violence provides a legitimate, effective, and socially approved means of defending oneself and maintaining respect
3. an inability to keep a cool head
4. an incomplete use of fundamental problem-solving skills (for example,

defining the problem in an unbiased way, seeking relevant information, generating a full range of alternative solutions, anticipating the consequences of these solutions for self and others, prioritizing the suitability of the solutions for the situation, and choosing the most effective response)

Thus, violence often derives from learned patterns of thought that simultaneously provide support for the use of violence while failing to engage fully those problem-solving skills that could lead to effective, nonviolent solutions.

The Question of Why

Youth violence in America often seems to defy explanation. We hear about young children killing other children over minor disputes and showing no remorse. We hear reporters characterizing violence as "senseless, random acts." We can indeed describe violence. We can identify its common external risk factors and social contexts. We can even point to some intervention strategies that have found some success in reducing violence. But can we explain *why* violence occurs? Can we identify the learned and internalized psychological factors that may indicate who is likely to engage in violence and under what circumstances? Can we explain how these factors may be changed to reduce an individual's likelihood of engaging in violence? In this chapter the question of *why* will be explored by considering the developing child growing up in urban America.

Psychological research brings a half century of findings, formulations, and strategies to the question of what causes violence and what we can do about it (American Psychological Association, 1993; Eron, Gentry, & Schlegel, 1994). As we will see, these research findings and formulations ultimately fall short of providing a full explanation of youth violence. Nevertheless, this body of research provides some meaningful conceptual vehicles, points of departure, and signposts along a journey toward understanding how youth violence develops and how to prevent or alter its use. Rather than providing a comprehensive review of the literature that describes children's developing patterns of violent behavior, this analysis will selectively address those key research findings and strategies that might help to explain these patterns.

To address the question of *why* most directly, this analysis will depart in several ways from previous reviews of the topic of the development of youth aggression. Although these works have provided a broad foundation for this analysis (see, e.g., American Psychological Association, 1993; Parke & Slaby, 1983; chapters in Pepler & Rubin, 1991; Pepler & Slaby, 1994; Slaby & Roedell, 1982), they have commonly

1. focused on the aggressor, without examining the contributing roles of the victim, the bystander, and the nonviolent problem solver
2. viewed children primarily as recipients of social experiences that may lead to involvement with violence rather than also as active architects or meaning-makers of their own social experiences
3. examined agents of social transmission separately (e.g., parents, peers, the media) rather than considered the interconnections among the spheres of influence through which children navigate on a daily basis
4. dealt primarily with the aggressive child's social experiences rather than with the developing child's internal psychological mediators, those that play a pivotal role in providing the meaning for these experiences as well as the motivation to translate them into either violent or nonviolent actions.

Growing up in America today, young children often face many experiences that contribute to an involvement with violence (e.g., suffering child abuse or neglect, witnessing violence, viewing media violence, having access to firearms, becoming involved with drugs, experiencing socioeconomic inequality, and facing discrimination) (American Psychological Association, 1993). The child growing up in an inner-city community may encounter these factors at particularly high levels due to the failure of many inner-city community structures to "realize the common values of [the inner-city's] residents and maintain effective social controls" (see Sampson, this volume).

Although the list of experiences that may contribute to violence is long, none of these external factors inevitably leads to violence. Some children who experience high levels of such "toxins" become involved in violence as aggressors, victims, or bystanders, whereas others who experience the same toxins do not. The difference may lie in the extent to which children have developed an "immune system" in the form of patterns of thought and action that protect them against involvement with violence. Such an immune system may provide substantial psychological resilience in the face of these violence toxins. This analysis will therefore focus on the developing psychological mediators of violence in urban youths. It will examine what learning experiences and interventions may provide young children with strong and enduring protection against the effects of those social experiences that usually contribute to violence.

Aggressor, Victim, and Bystander Involvement with Violence

Most behavioral science research on the development of aggression and violence has focused almost exclusively on the aggressor. Such a focus is inadequate to the search for explanations of violence among urban youths. To understand the ways in which urban youths may become involved in violence, we need to broaden this traditional focus on the aggressor by considering the distinct but interrelated roles of victims of violence and bystanders who contribute to violence (Slaby & Stringham, 1994).

Acts of interpersonal violence rarely involve a random connection between aggressor, victim, and bystander. Most acts of interpersonal violence involve an aggressor and a victim who know each other, often quite well. Not only do aggressors and victims commonly know each other, but they usually share common background factors such as age, gender, area of residence, socioeconomic status, educational level, psychological profile, and reliance on weapons (Cook, 1986; Dennis, 1980). In addition, urban youths who become participants in violent encounters often share the common psychological bond of adopting "the code of the streets" while rejecting "the code of decency" (as described by Anderson, this volume).

Violent encounters among urban youths often occur in the presence of others – on school grounds, in parks, or on the streets. Thus, violent encounters often involve bystanders (i.e., third-party participants), who may provide direct or indirect social support for violence by instigating, encouraging, or passively accepting violence. Of course, individuals who are originally just bystanders may also become first- or second-party participants in violence – by "aiding and abetting" the aggressor, by becoming a co-perpetrator, or by becoming a victim of violence. The inner-city public environment often makes it difficult to maintain one's public image and avoid "being bothered," disgraced, or "dissed" (disrespected) in front of others (Anderson, this volume). The mere presence of bystanders often increases both the volatility and the stakes of an encounter between two individuals by defining it as a *public* encounter. For individuals who are invested in the code of the streets, a public encounter may require them to defend their image by using violence. Many such youths are literally willing to lose their own lives or to take the life of another to uphold their perceived right to be shown public respect.

As a conflict escalates toward violence, the participants often seem to take turns auditioning for the roles of aggressor, victim, and bystander, as though they were involved in a game of "musical roles." When a gun fires, the music suddenly stops. Then, and perhaps forever after, the individual holding the gun has been cast in the role of an aggressor, the one on the ground is a victim, and the one who has been encouraging the violent encounter is a bystander who has contributed to violence (Slaby & Stringham, 1994).

Although some individuals may eventually play each of these roles in violent encounters, young children are often particularly well prepared to play one of these roles repeatedly: either aggressor, victim, or bystander. The habitual patterns of thought and behavior that characterize each of these roles may be learned and developed throughout childhood. Although these patterns of involvement with violence can be altered through intervention, if left untreated they are likely to lead young children down a developmental pathway to violence.

Aggressors

In early childhood, some boys and girls begin to show patterns of aggressive behavior in their family, in their schools, in their interaction with peers, or in their activities in the community. They pick fights with their brothers and sisters, scream at their parents, verbally attack their teachers, bully their peers, and intimidate younger children in the neighborhood. Some young children also begin to reveal their attraction to aggressive behavior through their play with weapons and their media choices and responses.

Individuals who engage in violence show early patterns of behavior that are distinctive. Evidence indicates that young children's early patterns of aggressive behavior are likely to

1. transfer from one social setting to another (e.g., from home to school to street settings) (Parke & Slaby, 1983; Patterson, 1982; Straus, 1991).
2. persist and become increasingly predictable from one year to the next, beginning in early childhood and extending into adulthood (Eron, Huesmann, Dubow, Romanoff, & Yarmel, 1987; Farrington, 1993; Huesmann, Eron, Lefkowitz, & Walder, 1984; Olweus, 1979).
3. escalate in level of severity (Loeber, Wung, Keenan, Giroux, Stouthamer-Loeber, Van Kammen, & Maughan, 1993).
4. broaden into a wider range of aggressive and violent behaviors (Patterson, Reid, & Dishion, 1992).

Violence does not simply appear full-blown and without precedent in an adolescent. Meta-analyses of longitudinal investigations of aggression indicate that in the absence of intervention, an individual's aggressive behavior commonly shows considerable continuity and predictability over major portions of the lifespan (Olweus, 1979; 1982). For example, the aggressive behavior of boys in early childhood has been found to be predictive of serious antisocial behavior in adulthood 22 years later, including criminal offenses, spousal abuse, and a tendency to punish one's children severely (Huesmann, Eron, Lefkowitz, & Walder, 1984). The aggressive behavior of boys and girls is about equally predictable from one year to the next. The predictability of individuals' aggressive behavior across substantial portions of their lifespan is on a par with that of IQ (Olweus, 1979). Aggression and IQ are often negatively correlated (Moffitt, this volume), but the high predictability of aggression remains even when IQ is statistically held constant (Huesmann, Eron, Lefkowitz, & Walder, 1984).

The best predictor of chronic delinquent offending and violence in adolescence is aggressive and antisocial behavior in childhood (Capaldi & Patterson, 1993). Young boys who have followed a developmental pathway toward violence have been found to engage in a developmental sequence of escalating types of aggressive behavior toward peers. They typically progress in three steps, from (1) annoying or bullying others during the period from 8 to 14 years of age, to (2) fighting with individuals or gangs, and eventually to (3) perpetrating violence (e.g., attacking, strong-arming, or forcing sex) (Loeber et al., 1993).

Given the developmental continuity and patterns of escalation in aggressive behavior, the aggression of young children can be regarded as a possible indicator of later violent behavior as well as an opportunity to initiate corrective intervention before violence becomes habitual. As we will see, however, early and repeated victimization of young children can also be regarded as an early predictor of both further victimization and violent behavior in later life.

Victims

It is important to address the problem of the development of violence from the perspective of the victim for several reasons (Finkelhor & Dziuba-Leatherman, 1994; Slaby & Stringham, 1994):

1. Compared to adults, children and youths are more often the victims of such violence as physical punishment, sibling assaults, bullying, sexual abuse, and rape; the only possible exception to this rule is homicide (Finkelhor & Dziuba-Leatherman, 1994).
2. Victims of a violent attack suffer the immediate consequences of psychological injury, pain, physical injury, or death.

3. Victims of one act of peer violence are often repeatedly victimized by their peers, and children are often physically punished or abused repeatedly by their parents (Olweus, 1993a; Straus, 1991).
4. Victims of repeated bullying by peers or repeated physical punishment or abuse by parents often suffer long-term consequences of depression, impaired self-esteem and suicide ideation (Olweus, 1993a; Straus, 1995).
5. Victims of violence often become perpetrators of violence by responding to a perceived threat with a preemptive violent attack, by retaliating against their victimizer, or by perpetrating violence against others (Fattah, 1993; McCord, 1983; Straus, 1991; Straus, Gelles, & Steinmetz, 1980; Widom, 1989a).
6. Perpetrators of violence often feel as though they are primarily victims (Slaby & Guerra, 1988).
7. Interventions that focus on preventing victimization may be more acceptable and effective for both potential aggressors and victims because they reduce the implicit blame that usually characterizes interventions that focus on the aggressor alone (Slaby & Stringham, 1994).

Aggressors often select their victims carefully and then shape the victim's patterns of thought and behavior through repeated and escalating episodes of threats, coercion, and aggression (see, e.g., Patterson, Littman, & Bricker, 1967). Little is known about how victims' patterns of thought and action may specifically influence the probability, intensity, and duration of aggression by peers. In a review of research on victimization (Perry, Kusel, & Perry, 1988), however, acts of peer aggression were generally found to increase if the victim:

1. is perceived by the aggressor as deliberately provocative (Mallick & McCandless, 1966).
2. resembles others whom the aggressor has seen victimized (Berkowitz, 1970).
3. has generally yielded to the aggressor in the past (Patterson, Littman, & Bricker, 1967).
4. fails to emit signs that normally inhibit aggression (e.g., signs of intense pain) (Camras, 1980; Ginsburg, Pollman, & Wauson, 1977; Perry & Perry, 1974).

In the most comprehensive investigations of young victims to date, one involving 150,000 school children is Scandinavia, Olweus (1978; 1993b) found that typical victims of repeated peer bullying, teasing, and attacks are generally anxious, lacking in self-esteem, socially isolated, physically weak, and afraid to defend themselves. During the school years in which children have relatively little control over their choice of associates, children's victimization is often repetitive, persistent, and predictable for particular individuals. During the school years, child victims may face considerable difficulty in controlling their own social environment in ways that permit them to avoid becoming repeatedly victimized.

A recent follow-up investigation of children victimized during the school years indicated, however, that childhood victimization did *not* predict harassment at age 23, although it often predicted depression in adulthood (Olweus, 1993b). This lack of continuity of victimization experiences from childhood to adulthood may be an indication of the greater freedom that adults have to choose their social and physical environments.

These findings highlight the importance of clarifying how, to what extent, and in which circumstances children may make a transition from being primarily involuntary recipients of social experiences associated with violence to becoming active controllers of these social experiences. Although young children often have considerable control over particular aspects of their environments (e.g., television viewing), they often have relatively little control over their choices of associates, less control perhaps than any other segment of the population besides prisoners (Finkelhor & Dziuba-Leatherman, 1994). Children's limited control over people and environments may affect their vulnerability to victimization in the home, the school, and the street.

Bystanders

Bystanders may play a pivotal role in violent encounters. As mentioned earlier, they may contribute to violence through direct instigation, active encouragement, passive acceptance, or mere presence. Alternatively, they may help to prevent violence or to stop it through preventive intervention, active encouragement to solve the problem nonviolently, or withdrawal of their social support or their presence.

Bystander research of the past (see, e.g., Latane & Darley, 1970; Siegel & Kohn, 1959; Staub, 1974) has recently been invoked in an examination of the bystander role in the current problem of violence in America (see, e.g., Slaby, Wilson-Brewer, & DeVos, 1994; Staub, 1989). Siegel and Kohn (1959) have shown, for example, that the mere presence of an adult bystander who passively watched preschool boys behaving aggressively in one play session increased their aggressive behavior in the next play session, presumably because children interpreted the adult's nonresponse as tacit approval of their aggression. We are only beginning to understand what leads some children to accept passively or provide active bystander support for violence while others refuse to support it or even take active steps to prevent peer violence.

Preadolescent children named by their peers as commonly providing bystander support for violence through active encouragement or passive acceptance have been found to share with aggressors and victims a number of social experiences and patterns of thought (Slaby, Wilson-Brewer, & DeVos, 1994). For example, bystanders who support violence have been found to share with aggressors several beliefs that favor the use of aggression, including the beliefs that aggression is a legitimate response, that it leads to approval from others, and that it is often the only alternative to being victimized; they also share the "none your business" belief that violence does not concern nonparticipants (Slaby, Wilson-Brewer, & DeVos, 1994). In addition, bystanders who support violence often share with both aggressors and victims strong social rejection by their classmates, as indicated in peer ratings. In contrast, individuals who are recognized as nonviolent problem solvers commonly receive strong peer acceptance as friends and playmates.

It is noteworthy, however, that these findings of peer rejection for aggressors, victims, and bystanders derive from peer ratings among students in grades 5–8 in urban and suburban middle-school classrooms, where the code of decency presumably dominates over the code of the street. (For a description of the code of the street, see Anderson, this volume). In contrast, several studies suggest that aggressive children tend to be popular in aggressive environments and among aggressive peers (Cairns, Cairns, Neckerman, Gest, & Gariepy, 1988; Feltham, Doyle, Schwartzman, Serbin, & Ledingham, 1985; Olweus, 1977). Among those urban youths who become invested in the code of the street, whose norms are often consciously opposed to those of mainstream society, it may be that peer acceptance and approval is accorded to aggressors, to bystanders who support violence, and even to victims who become victimized in the service of defending their right to be shown public respect.

Social Experiences that Contribute to Violence

As children develop, they face a variety of social experiences that may lead them down a developmental pathway toward involvement with violence – either as aggressors, victims, or bystanders. The social experiences that serve as violence toxins are often highly concentrated in urban communities, and they include:

1. suffering violence (child abuse, physical punishment, being bullied, or being battered)
2. witnessing violence
3. viewing or interacting with media violence (television, movies, videos, videogames, or radio)
4. having unsupervised access to firearms
5. using or trafficking alcohol and other drugs
6. experiencing socioeconomic inequality (living under survival conditions while others have plenty)
7. facing discrimination, verbal abuse, or harassment because of membership in a social group (discriminatory practices based on race, ethnic group, sexual orientation, or gender) (American Psychological Association, 1993; Centers for Disease Control and Prevention, 1992; Eron & Slaby, 1994).

When children experience one or several of these factors, violence is more likely, but it is not an inevitable outcome.

The physical and social-environmental characteristics of poor urban communities often contribute to the delivery of high concentrations of these and other violence toxins to young children (Goldstein, 1994). For example, the social structural disorganization of many urban communities is a condition which often interferes with the creation of interpersonal resources and contributes to the breakdown of family management in ways that generate community-level concentrations of child abuse, infant mortality, low birth weight, cognitive impairment, and other adjustment problems; these conditions, in turn, constitute major risk factors for later delinquency and violence (Sampson, this volume). Neighborhood composition and attitudes have also been found to influence the recidivism rates of released criminal offenders (Gottfredson & Taylor, 1988).

Although environmental risk factors at the community and neighborhood levels influence the developing child's behaviors, their influence is typically delivered to the child through day-to-day social interactions with adults, peers, and the media (Patterson, Reid, & Dishion, 1992; Simcha-Fagan & Schwartz, 1986). The influence of these external socialization experiences is further mediated through the developing child's internal psychological resources for understanding the meanings, uses, and alternatives to violence (Parke & Slaby, 1983; Slaby & Roedell, 1982).

Children's patterns of involvement with violence presumably develop from an interaction of both internal factors that reside within the individual and external factors in the individual's environment. Analyses that focus solely on the external factors that contribute to violence at the community level or at the socialization level often do not attempt to explain:

1. observed patterns of difference in the behavior of individuals who have been subjected to the same violence toxins.
2. observed patterns of both consistency in individuals' involvement with violence across settings and continuity over major portions of the lifespan.

What accounts for both the distinctiveness and consistency in individuals' patterns of violent behavior? The answer probably lies not so much in the objective experiences themselves as in the way the child organizes, interprets, and emotionally responds to these factors. Several sources of social interaction often play a central organizing role in this process, and they do so not only by delivering to children or shielding them from these violence toxins, but also by shaping habitual patterns of thought and emotional response that mediate between these external experiences and behavioral outcomes.

We will first examine the *sources of social interaction related to violence* that are provided by adults, peers, and the media. Special emphasis will be given to the interconnections among these sources, as well as to the influence of each one on the developing child's learned habits of thought and emotional response that contribute to the development and maintenance of patterns of violence. Following this discussion, we will address the *development of psychological mediators of violence* that provide the rationale and motivation for engaging in violence or the reasons for stopping or preventing it.

Sources of Social Interaction Related to Violence

Adults, peers, and the media provide primary sources of influence on the developing child's involvement with violence. The child typically navigates among these social worlds on a daily basis, and the social influences within one domain clearly affect children's behavior in other domains. The highest levels of cohesiveness and long-term continuity in behavior would be expected for those whose social worlds provide relatively concordant, overlapping, or mutually supportive social influences, as suggested by Hartup (1979). However, particularly in urban settings beset by social disorganization, these social worlds may impart to a young child a contradictory set of social messages regarding violence. For example, many inner-city families attempt to impart a code of decency to their young children. At the same time, however, through their peer-group interaction, media exposures, and contact with street-oriented adults who follow the code of the street, these children may receive a contradictory set of messages that support the use of violence.

For most children, the social world of adults (e.g., parents, grandparents, relatives, friends of the family, and teachers) provides their first and most important source of influence. Besides having an immediate effect on children's behavior, the parental behaviors that children experience can also have important long-term influences. The parental behaviors of aggressiveness, conflict, and low supervision have been found to predict the criminal violent behavior of males 30 years later (McCord, 1979). Children are also influenced by peers and the media, and these social influences generally increase as the child develops (Hartup, 1970).

Children generally navigate daily through the social worlds of adult, peer, and media influences, and these sources can have separate and interacting effects on the children's development of aggression (Parke & Slaby, 1983). Several models have been advanced to investigate the extent to which these social worlds may ultimately provide relatively concordant, overlapping, or mutually supportive socialization influences that could contribute to continuity in children's aggressive behavior (see, e.g., Hartup, 1979).

According to the social-interactional model proposed by Patterson and his colleagues, the primary contexts for children's social learning may typically shift in importance at successive phases in their development (e.g., Patterson, 1982; Patterson, DeBaryshe, & Ramsey, 1989; Patterson, Reid, & Dishion, 1992; Reid & Patterson, 1989). While recognizing that broad factors such as parental criminality, socioeconomic disadvantage, child temperament, and marital conflict can influence the development of children's aggressive behavior, these investigators argue that the influence of these factors is determined by the degree to which they manifest themselves in the child's daily interactions with parents.

According to this model, maladaptive parent–child interaction patterns and ineffective parenting practices are key determinants of young children's coercive and aggressive behavior. During the elementary years, children's learned coercive and aggressive patterns of behavior often transfer to other contexts, such as the school, where children's aggressive behavior patterns may interfere with academic achievement and the development of positive relationships with peers. During late childhood or early adolescence, aggressive children's academic failure and peer rejection often lead to increased risk for depression and involvement in a deviant peer group. Thus, the social-interactional model suggests that as children develop, their primary source of influence on patterns of aggression may shift from parents to schools and then to deviant peer groups. At the same time, children's learned patterns of aggressive behavior may transfer from one context to another (Pepler & Slaby, 1994).

Adult Influences on Violence

The family usually provides children with their first and potentially most intense learning experiences, and parents play a particularly influential role in the development of children's aggression. The wide variety of parental variables that have been implicated in the etiology of aggression, as indicated in a review by Eron, Huesmann, and Zelli (1991) include: parental aggression, parental conflict and disharmony, lack of parental supervision, inconsistent parental disciplinary practices, parental rejection, harsh punishment, parental modeling, lack of parental supervision, and family history of antisocial behavior (Andrew, 1981; Farrington, 1983; Farrington & West, 1971; McCord, 1979; Neapolitan, 1981; Olweus, 1980; Osborn & West, 1979; Patterson & Stouthamer-Loeber, 1984; Robins, West, & Herjanic, 1975; Wadsworth, 1979; West & Farrington, 1973).

Whether by design or by default, parents and other adults frequently serve as *teachers*, *models*, and *supervisors* for their children's learning about violence.

Adults as Teachers. Parents and other adults influence children's understanding and use of aggression through direct interaction. Although family members frequently provide one another with physical and emotional support, the rights and responsibilities that they feel toward each other can result in the use of "justified violence." Family members often feel that they have the right to compel each other to behave in particular ways and that resistance to such coercive attempts can justifiably be countered with various forms of aggression (Straus, Gelles, & Steinmetz, 1980). Family experiences found to contribute to the developing child's risk of involvement with violence include:

1. physical abuse or neglect (see, for example, Earls & Barnes, this volume; Egeland, Sroufe, & Erickson, 1983; Widom, 1989a, 1989b)

2. heavy use of physical punishment (see, e.g., Engfer & Schneedwind, 1982; Martin, 1975; Slaby & Roedell, 1982; Straus, 1991)
3. parental permissiveness for aggression (Olweus, 1979)
4. active encouragement of the use of aggression outside of the home (Bandura & Walters, 1959)
5. high levels of coercive family interaction (Patterson, 1982).

In a direct test of the hypothesis that violence breeds violence across generations, Widom (1989a) found that physical abuse in childhood is linked to later violent criminal behavior, even when other relevant demographic variables such as age, sex, and race are held constant. Documented childhood neglect was also found to lead to later violent criminal behavior. At the same time, the link between childhood abuse or neglect and adult criminal violence was found to be far from inevitable, since almost 90% of the individuals victimized as children showed no evidence of arrest for violent criminal acts. This finding suggests the need to understand further the possible mediating factors that may act to buffer abused or neglected children against developing violent criminal behavior as adults.

Observations of family interactions reveal that a great deal of coercive behavior occurs on a daily basis in most families. Furthermore, in families that include a highly aggressive child, it is often the case that virtually every member of the family shows unusually high levels of coercive behavior and unusually low levels of approval (Patterson, 1979). One of the most reliable and generalizable predictors of children's aggression is the parents' heavy use of harsh, punitive discipline and corporal punishment (Greven, 1990; Martin, 1975; Straus, 1991). When parents use hitting as a means of coercing or punishing the behavior of a child, young children may learn the implicit lesson that "might makes right." Parental punitiveness is often one component of a general pattern of intercorrelated parental behaviors that influences children's aggressive behavior. This pattern includes permissiveness for aggression, negativism or lack of warmth, low use of reasoning, and inconsistent application of discipline (Olweus, 1979; Sears, Maccoby, & Levin, 1957).

Parents presumably choose to use physical punishment based on their belief that this technique will effectively correct the misbehavior to which it is applied. Although physical punishment is sometimes effective in stopping aggressive behavior temporarily, it often is counterproductive, stimulating further aggression in the long term (Straus, 1991). Patterson (1979) and others have detailed how these counterproductive patterns of coercive family interaction operate and lead to an escalation of aggression within the family. (As Slaby and Roedell have noted, for example).

> A coercive pattern of interaction occurs when one family member presents an aversive behavior (e.g., teasing, whining, yelling, hitting), and another family member attempts to alter it by presenting a second aversive behavior. The coercive interchange often continues, escalates in intensity, and draws in other family members until one member backs down and withdraws his or her aversive behavior, thereby breaking the cycle of aversive interchange for the moment. However, since the others have been "negatively reinforced" or rewarded by successfully stopping the aversive behavior of one family member, they will be even more likely to use highly aversive behaviors and to direct them at the submitting family member again in the future. Through this process children can quickly learn to become both initiators and victims of aggression while inadvertently training their parents to become highly punitive and even abusive (1982, p. 112).

As the previous example of the mother who required her young daughter to knock out two front teeth of her playmate illustrates, parents can also have a major effect on children by teaching them ways of resolving a conflict with peers that either increases or decreases the risk of violence. The advice that parents give their children who face conflict with peers has been found to differentiate male adolescent violent offenders from their nonaggressive counterparts who grew up in similar neighborhoods. For example, the father of a boy who as an adolescent was arrested for violently attacking someone had previously told his young son, "You're going to whip these boys or else I'm going to whip you" (Bandura & Walters, 1959, p. 107).

In contrast, a mother of a boy who had become a nonviolent adolescent told him, "It takes a bigger man to keep from getting into a fight than it does to pick a fight. Anybody can fight." (Bandura & Walters, 1959, p. 114). Parents of nonviolent adolescents had also previously encouraged their young sons to understand the perspective of others, to maintain their own standards and principles, to assert themselves in socially acceptable ways, and to view the use of hostile aggression as a sign of weakness.

Adults as Role Models. There is growing evidence that for children, the witnessing of violence among adults in the family and the community is associated with aggression and victimization. The childhood experience of witnessing marital violence has been found to be a risk factor for both perpetration of violence and victimization by one's spouse or intimate partner in later life (Hotaling & Sugarman, 1986; Jaffe, Wolfe,

Wilson, & Zak, 1986; Rosenberg & Rossman, 1990). Increasingly, in urban communities throughout America, children are also becoming involved both as victims of and as eyewitnesses to episodes of violence outside the family. Although some efforts are being made to reduce the number of injuries and deaths associated with the growing levels of violence, relatively little attention has been paid to the psychological consequences of children living in what are often chronically and desperately violent circumstances.

Recent findings of the National Institute of Mental Health Community Violence Project provide an initial portrait of children's exposure to violence and its consequences (Richters & Martinez, 1993). In an inner-city community in Washington, D.C., parents and their children, ages six to nine, independently reported the frequency with which the children had been victimized by, had witnessed, or had heard about the many forms of violence and violence-related activities in the community. For each reported episode, parents were asked about where the violence took place, who perpetrated the violence, who (if not the child) was victimized, and when the incident occurred. Children were given a structured interview that probed their exposure to similar violence and violence-related themes in an age-appropriate format. Teacher ratings of the stability and violence of the homes of each child were also collected and compared to the reports of parents and children.

Reports indicated that although a disturbing number of children had been direct victims of violence in their homes or neighborhoods, they were more than twice as likely to have witnessed violence to others and/or violence-related scenes involving others. For example, among children in the fifth and sixth grades, 72% had witnessed some form of violence against others (including shootings, stabbings, murders, suicides, or the viewing of a dead body outside of the home), whereas 32% had been a victim of violence.

Many domains of children's cognitive, social-emotional, and psychological functioning can be affected by exposure to violence. Children who witness violence are likely to manifest a variety of distress symptoms, particularly if the violence they have witnessed involves family members, friends, or acquaintances. Symptoms may include depression, withdrawal, extreme fear, anxiety, affect disregulation, blunted affect, dissociative reactions, intrusive thoughts, flashbacks, and aggression (Richters, 1993).

The ways in which parents help their children cope with the high levels of violence they face in chronically violent communities presumably has a major impact on children's reactions to this exposure. However, evidence indicates that parents of children in high violence inner-city communities greatly underestimate their children's exposure to violence, as well as the effects of such exposure.

It is unclear to what extent these underestimates by parents represent an intentional minimization, a lack of parental monitoring and awareness, or an unconscious denial of the problem (Richters & Martinez, 1993). Regardless of its source, parental underestimates of their children's exposure to violence and its consequences may result in both an inadequate response to symptoms that may arise from exposure and a failure to deal preventively with the real risks of violence that their children may face.

Adults as Supervisors. In addition to these direct and modeling contributions to the development of children's orientation toward violence, the family plays an important role, particularly in the early childhood years, in mediating their developing children's access to and orientation toward other risk factors; these factors include the children's involvement with peer groups that endorse the code of the street, exposure to media violence, access to firearms, involvement with alcohol and other drugs, strategies for solving social problems, endorsement of beliefs that support the use of violence, techniques for controlling emotions and impulses, and development of prejudiced or egalitarian beliefs.

Parents of aggressive children often lack the supervisory skills and the family or community support to manage their children effectively within and outside of the home. Several programs in parent management training have been systematically developed and thoroughly investigated over the past several decades by Patterson and his colleagues (see, e.g., Patterson, 1982; 1986; Patterson, Reid, Dishion, 1992). Founded on the view that coercive interaction patterns in the family inadvertently contribute to the development, maintenance, and escalation of violence both within and outside of the family, these programs have focused on training parents of young children (ages 3 to 12) to define and respond to coercive behavior in the home in new, noncoercive ways. Parents are also trained to increase their skills in monitoring, guiding, and supervising children's activities.

Although the usefulness of parent management training programs is limited by the heavy demand it places on parents to develop skills, these programs have demonstrated some success in reducing violence both within and outside the home (Kazdin, 1987). The utility of such programs would be strengthened by developing interconnections with systems of social support outside of the home and by investigating the long-term effectiveness of this treatment in reducing violence.

Media Influences on Violence

Media influences on the developing child's involvement with violence deserve to be considered on a par with the influences of family and peers. The connections between children's exposure to media violence and their involvement with real-life violence have been extensively reviewed (see, e.g., Comstock, 1991; Comstock & Paik, 1990; Condry, 1989; Donnerstein, Slaby, & Eron, 1994; Huston et al., 1992; Liebert & Sprafkin, 1988; Parke & Slaby, 1983). This analysis will focus on three effects of exposure to media violence: the *aggressor effect*, the *victim effect*, and the *bystander effect*. The ways in which these effects may prepare children for participation in violence and stimulate their appetite for increased exposure to violence will be discussed.

Children are exposed to a great deal of violence from television as well as from a wide variety of other media sources (e.g., movies, videos, video games, radio, compact discs, and comic books). Children typically watch a great deal of television, particularly in the preschool and elementary school years (more than 25 hours per week) (Nielsen, 1992). Much of American programming contains violence, and children's programming in America typically portrays more violence than any other category of programming (TV Guide, 1992). Children from lower socioeconomic-status homes generally watch more television and more violent programs than children from more affluent homes. African-American children generally watch more television and more violent programs than white children at the same levels of socioeconomic status (Lyle, 1972).

American television glorifies violence and presents many unrealistic, misleading, and harmful lessons about violence. "Entertainment violence" commonly teaches us that interpersonal violence is prevalent, legitimate, justified, socially approved, rewarded, effective, clean, and inconsequential. Sometimes violence is portrayed as heroic, manly, funny, and even pleasurable. Even when violence is presented in nonfictional programs (e.g., in the news), it generally fails to reflect reality. Death by interpersonal violence in such programs is often sensationalized, given top billing, presented as random acts rather than as predictable and preventable acts, and overrepresented (Johnson & Russell, 1990), whereas incidents more prevalent in real life are underrepresented (e.g., death by self-directed violence such as suicide and death due to forms of injury or disease). Children's exposure to these unrealistic and glorified portrayals of violence on television has recently increased dramatically with the greater availability of video, satellite, cable, and interactive video game technologies.

All viewers, and particularly children, learn skills, beliefs, and behaviors from the media. Watching violence on television or in films does not inevitably lead to real-life effects. Nevertheless, several effects of viewing media violence have been confirmed.

Aggressor Effect. Viewers of television violence, particularly those who strongly identify with the aggressor, generally become more likely than nonviewers to show meanness, aggressive behavior, and even a tendency to engage in serious violence and criminal violence toward others (Comstock & Paik, 1990). Besides the potential for a single exposure to have immediate effects on the viewer, there appear to be long-term cumulative effects as well. The amount of violence that children watch on television has been found to predict the frequency with which they engage in and the extent of their later involvement in criminal acts of violence as long as 22 years later; this correlation remains after the effects of background factors were removed (Huesmann, Eron, Lefkowitz, & Walder, 1984). It appears that watching violence on television in childhood can contribute to the building of aggressive habits that may continue to affect an individual's behavior for many years. In general, children from lower socioeconomic homes and African-American children would presumably be at higher risk for this aggressor effect, since they commonly choose to watch particularly high levels of violent television programming (Lyle, 1972).

Victim Effect. Some viewers of television violence, particularly those who identify with the victim, are more likely to show fearfulness, mistrust, and self-protective behavior, such as carrying a gun (which, paradoxically, greatly increases one's risk of becoming victimized). Those who watch a great deal of television violence often show a distorted set of perceptions of the real world that have been described as the "mean world syndrome" (Gerbner, Gross, Eleey, Jackson-Beeck, Jeffries-Fox, & Signorielli, 1977), and this effect appears to be stronger with children than with adults (Gerbner, Gross, Jackson-Beeck, Jeffries-Fox, & Signiorelli, 1978). As might be expected, the distortions in television's portrayal of violence greatly affect the beliefs of heavy viewers of such violence; they are more likely than light viewers to hold an exaggerated mistrust of others and an exaggerated view of both the prevalence of violence and the appropriateness of its use (Gerbner et al., 1977).

Bystander Effect. Heavy viewers of television violence are more likely than light viewers to be callous toward victims of violence and behaviorally indifferent toward perpetrators of violence in real life, perhaps because they have been desensitized into accepting it. Thus, those who view television violence are more likely than nonviewers to show lower levels of emotional arousal to portrayals of violence (as measured by skin conductance) (see, e.g., Osborn & Endsley, 1971). In an experimental study, children who watched a violent program were afterwards far less likely than children who watched a neutral program to intervene or to call for an adult to intervene when younger children for whom they were "babysitting" began to fight (see, e.g., Thomas & Drabman, 1975; Thomas, Horton, Lippincott, & Drabman, 1977). Particularly when violence is portrayed as acceptable and justifiable, the experience of watching violence on television appears to undermine the viewer's feelings of concern, empathy, or sympathy toward victims of real-life violence (Donnerstein, Slaby, & Eron, 1994).

In summary, media violence is largely unrealistic, overrepresented, distorted, and glorified, and it tends to misguide viewers in their preparations for dealing with real-life conflict. Watching such portrayals of violence on television may contribute to real-life violence by cultivating viewers' meanness, fearfulness, and callousness toward violence in their own lives. Each of these effects serves in different ways to increase the individual's acceptance of the use of violence in real life. Although no one seems to be immune to these effects, some individuals are clearly more susceptible than others, and individuals show differential responses to these effects. The major research questions have moved from asking whether there is such an effect (or several different effects) from watching violence on television to examining who is most susceptible, under what conditions, and through what means – as well as to examining how these effects can be reduced, prevented, or even reversed. Since television is an effective teacher with regard to violence, it also has the capability of reversing its current effects by teaching instead a broad variety of potentially effective solutions to society's violence (Slaby, 1994).

Susceptibility to Media Effects. Children are generally more susceptible to media effects than adults because they lack real-world experience and the critical judgment needed to evaluate the ways in which media violence portrayals are unrealistic, distorted, and glorified. Boys and girls appear to be equally susceptible to media violence effects (Comstock & Paik, 1990).

However, boys and girls may show different kinds of effects because of the different ways in which male and female characters are portrayed on television and because of the common tendency for viewers to identify more strongly with same-sex characters than with other-sex characters (Henchman, 1994; Hendrix, 1990).

For example, since television portrays males behaving aggressively far more often than females, boys (who typically identify with male characters more strongly than do girls) may be more likely than girls to show the aggressor effect after viewing typical portrayals of television violence. When television portrays female characters engaging in violence, they are disproportionately shown as victims (Signorielli, 1993), and viewers who identify with the victim character may be more susceptible to the victim effect of increased fear and mistrust (Hendrix, 1990). Thus, differential effects have been found among viewers of a violent episode in accordance with their gender-based identification with the characters depicted as aggressor or victim (Henchman, 1994; Hendrix, 1990).

Several social-cognitive mediators of television violence effects have been identified. Three factors which were found to enhance viewers' susceptibility to the effects of watching violence on television are the viewers' identification with the characters, their perception that the portrayed violence is realistic and representative of real life (Huesmann, Langerspetz, & Eron, 1984), and their fantasies of engaging in violence (Huesmann & Eron, 1986). Children's susceptibility to the effects of watching violence on television is also influenced by their experiences in real world social interactions. For example, boys who watch high levels of violence on television were found to be particularly likely to engage in criminal behavior if they also experienced parental abuse (Heath, Kruttschnitt, & Ward, 1986).

The interconnection among these internal social-cognitive and external social-interaction factors, which were identified by Huesmann (1986), suggests a reciprocal process through which watching violence on television and aggressive behavior perpetuate each other. Donnerstein, Slaby, and Eron write,

> Children who are heavy viewers of television violence will see characters solving interpersonal problems by behaving aggressively. To the extent that these children identify with the aggressive characters they observe and believe the aggression is realistic, they will fantasize about and encode in memory the aggressive solutions they observe. If aggressive behaviors are emitted in the appropriate situations, the aggressive behaviors will be reinforced with desirable outcomes. But, if aggressive behavior becomes ha-

bitual, it will interfere with social and academic success. The more aggressive child will become less popular at school with peers and especially with teachers. These academic and social failures may lead to aggression, but just as importantly they may also lead to more regular television viewing. It is hypothesized that children might obtain satisfactions that they are denied in their social lives from television and might be better able to justify their own aggressive behavior after seeing more aggression in the media. The self-perpetuating cycle of aggression, academic and social failure, violence viewing, and fantasizing which mutually facilitate each other then continues (1994, pp. 234–35).

Although parents can have important influences on children's learning from the media, they often relinquish their teaching, modeling, and supervisory roles regarding media violence. Parents and teachers can help their children interpret and critically evaluate the meaning of, the authenticity of, the real-life relevance of, the acceptability of, and the alternatives to the violence they view. For example, when co-viewing adults make disapproving comments about televised violence, children are subsequently less likely to behave aggressively in the absence of the adult (see, e.g., Collins, Sobol, & Westby, 1981; Grusec, 1973; Hicks, 1968). When teachers asked children to compose and to read on videotape persuasive essays explaining how television is not like real life and why it would be harmful for other children to watch too much television and imitate the violent characters, these activities were successful in changing children's attitudes about television violence and in modifying their aggressive behavior (Huesmann, Eron, Klein, Brice, & Fischer, 1983).

Not surprisingly, children's habits of watching television are heavily influenced by their parents' habits, since their parents serve as models. In many homes, however, the television set is operating continuously from early in the morning until late at night. When parents make direct attempts to supervise and regulate their children's television viewing diet, they are often successful, particularly during the preschool years (Stein & Friedrich, 1972). Yet, few parents put restrictions on either the amount or the content of television that their children watch (Lyle & Hoffman, 1972), usually treating television as a "children's medium" for which the young have become the resident experts (Comstock, 1978). Since television has become an electronic member of virtually every American family, an investigation is needed on the potential interactive effects tying exposure to television violence to other risk factors within and outside of the family. In addition, an investigation is needed on the ways that parents and teachers can both reduce the effects of television violence on young children and stimulate the development of new television programs and educational strategies that contribute to the prevention of violence.

Psychological Mediators of Violence

As we have seen, a variety of social experiences may contribute to violence. These experiences are delivered to the developing child through his or her social interactions with adults, peers, and the media. Yet none of these social experiences or sources of social interaction, singly or in combination, will inevitably lead to violent behavior for all individuals. Rather, the effect of these experiences on an individual's behavior derives from the ways in which that individual organizes, interprets, and translates these experiences into patterns of cognitive and emotional response. Much like a physiological immune system, learned patterns of psychological mediation are capable of succumbing to, neutralizing, or counteracting the impact of social experiences that act as violence toxins.

Systematic investigation of psychological mediating factors may help to explain how and why external events affect behavioral outcomes. Psychologists have long recognized the importance of mediating variables, even though the systematic search for their influence has been limited. Baron and Kenny (1986) provide a conceptual, strategic, and analytic basis for defining mediator variables. They point out that learning theorists as diverse as Woodworth, Hull, Tolman, and Lewin have recognized that "the effects of stimuli on behavior are mediated by various transformational processes internal to the organism" (p. 1176). Psychological mediators may operate in defining, interpreting, organizing, processing, and translating social experiences in ways that direct the behavioral response.

The way in which cognitive factors mediate a connection between children's experience of physical abuse and their subsequent aggressive behavior is illustrated in several studies. For example, physical abuse in the home leads some young children to aggressively attack their peers or teachers in the classroom (George & Main, 1979). But not all children who are victimized in this way perpetuate the cycle of violence by becoming perpetrators of aggression against others. The mechanisms by which physical abuse in childhood may lead to the development of aggressive behavior was examined in a prospective study of five-year-old children who had been physically harmed at home (Dodge, Bates, & Pettit, 1990). Neither family-ecological factors (such as poverty, marital violence, and family instability) nor child-biological factors (such as early health problems and temperament) proved to be critical. The experience of physical abuse was found to increase the risk of children's chronic aggressive behavior independent of the influence of the ecological or biological factors.

The experience of being physically abused was found to be predictive of hostile bias and deficient patterns of solving social problems. Specifically, abused children were more likely than nonabused children to show a failure to attend to relevant cues, a tendency to attribute hostile intentions to others, and a lack of effective nonviolent strategies to solve social problems. These biased and deficient patterns of thought, in turn, were found to mediate children's subsequent aggressive behavior toward their peers in the classroom. Among the abused children, those who refrained from translating their own victimization experience at home into violent attacks on peers at school were those who had acquired the cognitive skills needed to solve social problems nonviolently. These findings suggest that particular patterns of thought may serve as either risk factors or protective factors by guiding children to establish or to break the cycle of violence.

Patterns of Thought Supporting Violence

Through various phases of development, highly aggressive children have been found to differ dramatically from their low aggression peers in their patterns of thought (see, e.g., Dodge & Frame, 1982; Guerra & Slaby, 1989; Perry, Perry, & Rasmussen, 1986; Shure & Spivack, 1988; Slaby & Guerra, 1988). Nevertheless, patterns of thought can be changed through direct intervention, and such changes lead to corresponding changes in the subsequent level of aggressive behavior (Guerra & Slaby, 1990; Kazdin, 1987). Components of an individual's patterns of thought include:

1. *processes of thought*, or how one thinks (e.g., as measured by one's cognitive skills in solving social problems).
2. *contents of thought*, or what one thinks (e.g., as measured by one's beliefs supporting the use of violence).
3. *style of thought*, or the way in which one connects and deploys the process and content of thought (e.g., as in the impulsive style of making quick, incomplete, and erroneous responses, or in the reflective style of making slow, thorough, and accurate responses).

Processes of Thought. Beginning in the preschool years and throughout development into adulthood, highly aggressive or violent individuals have been found to show patterns of thought that reflect deficits in their skills, particulary in their ability to process social information and solve social problems. When faced with a social problem with a peer, aggressive individuals often define the problem in a hostilely biased way, adopt a hostile goal, seek few additional facts that may be helpful in solving the problem, think of few alternative solutions to the problem, anticipate few consequences for an aggressive solution, and choose ineffective solutions as their "best" and "second best" options (see, e.g., Dodge, 1986; Parke & Slaby, 1983; Shure & Spivack, 1988; Slaby & Guerra, 1988).

Contents of Thought. Combined with their deficits in social problem-solving skills, aggressive children and violent adolescent offenders commonly hold general beliefs that support the use of aggression. Highly aggressive individuals often believe that aggression is a legitimate response, that it increase one's self-esteem, that it helps to avoid a negative image, that it does not lead to suffering by the victim, and that it leads to successful outcomes and material rewards (Guerra & Slaby, 1989; Perry, Perry, & Rasmussen, 1986; Slaby & Guerra, 1988).

Particularly in inner-city communities, children have many opportunities to adopt beliefs supporting violence. They may be exposed outside of their homes to an oppositional street culture whose norms are often consciously opposed to those of mainstream society and supportive of a code of violence. Within their own homes or the homes of their peers, inner-city children may interact with so-called street parents who also model and teach their children a code of violence (see Anderson, this volume). The example of the mother who required her daughter to break the teeth of her playmate illustrates the way in which the belief that violence is needed to prevent victimization may be passed on from one generation to the next. The media's unrealistic and glorified portrayals of violence are so abundant and attractive that a young child may have difficulty rejecting them, particularly if the child associates with others who endorse such glorified portrayals of violence.

Style of Thought. Highly aggressive individuals often respond to provocation from a peer in a hot-headed and impulsive way. Under conditions of high emotional arousal, aggressive individuals are likely to default almost automatically to learned stereotypic patterns of behavior that are often both violent and inappropriate for the situation (see for example, Slaby & Stringham, 1994).

Many interventions to prevent violence include some component designed to foster impulse control, frustration tolerance, or anger management and redirection (see, e.g., Guerra & Slaby, 1990). For example, in the Think Aloud program, aggressive boys who were found to be unable to use covert verbalization (i.e., talking to themselves) to control their behavior effectively were taught to verbalize aloud as a means of considering alternative responses and controlling their aggressive behavior (Camp & Bash, 1981). Another strategy for teaching control of anger is the stress-innoculation approach (Novaco, 1986). Individuals are taught nonviolent ways of responding to anger-provoking situations by exposing them to manageable levels of stressors that emotionally arouse but do not overwhelm their defenses, while simultaneously teaching a variety of cognitive and behavioral coping skills.

Conclusion

Many factors at the societal level, the community level, the interpersonal level, and the individual level contribute to a developing child's propensity to become involved in violence – as an aggressor, a victim, or a bystander who supports violence. Individuals develop their own distinct and consistent patterns of response to the same external events. The external experiences to which individuals often respond differentially and consistently include frustrations, provocations, conflicts, coercive encounters, victimizations, witnessed violent events, and exposure to violent images in the media. Violence is not an inevitable consequence of these external experiences, in part because they are mediated and responded to in accordance with the way in which an individual has learned to elicit, perceive, make meaning from, justify, generate alternative responses to, and anticipate others' reactions to the external events. Learned psychological mediators for violence have been variously described as a "code of the streets" (Anderson, this volume), "cognitive scripts" (Huesmann & Eron, 1989), and "habits of thought" (Slaby & Stringham, 1994).

This analysis leads to several assumptions that may be examined in future research. It is suggested that children acquire, internalize, and utilize these psychological mediators largely through their interactions with adults, peers, and the media. Once learned and repeatedly used, these patterns of thought may become cohesive, consistent, and enduring psychological mediators of violence. The mediational patterns that underlie violent behavior appear to be learned early in childhood and are largely applied in a nonmindful fashion. However, because they are learned, they may be unlearned, or conditions can be changed so that they are not acquired in the first place. Much like habits of behavior, patterns of psychological mediation may be potentially modifiable through direct intervention.

Children growing up in the inner city typically encounter an abundance of social experiences that contribute to involvement with violence, and they interact with many individuals who accept, model, and even teach the use of violence. Beyond demonstrating the clear need to reduce or eliminate many of these toxic experiences for violence, this analysis suggests the need to strengthen the child's antiviolence immune system. Resources are needed to enable parents, educators, health professionals, and media professionals to teach children the skills, beliefs, and strategies by which to solve social problems safely, effectively, and nonviolently. It is our hope that through early, continual, and systematic intervention, children can be taught how to protect themselves from involvement with violence, how to resolve conflicts constructively, and how to become actively involved in passing on their own constructive resources to others in their homes and communities.

REFERENCES

American Psychological Association. (1993). *Violence and youth: Psychology's response. Vol. I: Summary of the American Psychological Association Commission on Violence and Youth.* Washington, D.C.: American Psychological Association.

Anderson, E. (this volume). Violence and the inner-city street code. In J. McCord (Ed.), *Violence and childhood in the inner-city* (pp. 1–30). New York: Cambridge University Press.

Andrew, J. M. (1981). Delinquency: Correlating variables. *Journal of Clinical Child Psychology* 10, 136–40.

Bandura, A., & Walters, R. H. (1959). *Adolescent aggression.* New York: Ronald Press.

Baron, R. M., & Kenny, D. A. (1986). The moderator-mediator variable distinction in social psychological research: Conceptual, strategic, and statistical considerations. *Journal of Personality and Social Psychology* 51, 1173–82.

Berkowitz, L. (1970). The contagion of violence: An S–R mediational analysis of some effects of observed aggression. In W. J. Arnold & M. M. Page (Eds.), *Nebraska Symposium on Motivation* (pp. 95–135). Lincoln: University of Nebraska Press.

Cairns, R. B., Cairns, B. D., Neckerman, H. J., Gest, S. D., & Gariepy, J. L. (1988). Social networks and aggressive behavior: Peer support or peer rejection? *Developmental Psychology* 24, 815–23.

Camp, B. W., & Bash, M. A. S. (1981). *Think aloud: Increasing social and cognitive skills – A problem-solving program for children.* Champaign, IL: Research Press.

Camras, L. A. (1980). Children's understanding of facial expressions used during conflict encounters. *Child Development* 51, 879–85.

Capaldi, D. M., & Patterson, G. R. (1993). The violent adolescent male. Specialist or generalist? Paper presented at the Biennial Meeting of the Society for Research in Child Development, New Orleans (March).

Centers for Disease Control (1992). Prevention of violence and injuries due to violence. In *Injury control: Position papers from the third national injury control conference: Setting the national agenda for injury control in the 1990s* (pp. 159–254). Atlanta, GA: Centers for Disease Control, U.S. Department of Health and Human Services.

Collins, W. A., Sobol, B. L., & Westby, S. (1981). Effects of adult commentary on children's comprehension and inferences about a televised aggressive portrayal. *Child Development* 52, 158–63.

Comstock, G. (1978). The impact of television on American institutions. *Journal of Communication* 28, 12–28.

(1991). *Television and the American child.* New York: Academic Press.

Comstock, G., & Paik, H. (1990). The effects of television violence on aggressive behavior: A meta-analysis. A Preliminary Report to the National Research Council for the Panel on the Understanding and Control of Violent Behavior. Unpublished manuscript, Syracuse University, Syracuse, N.Y. 13244.

Condry, J. (1989). *The psychology of television.* Hillsdale, NJ: Erlbaum.

Cook, P. J. (1986). The demand and supply of criminal opportunities. In M. Tonry & N. Morris (Eds.), *Crime and justice. Vol. 7* (pp. 1–27). Chicago: University of Chicago Press.

Dennis, R. E. (1980). Homicide among black males: Social costs to families and communities. *Public Health Report* 95 (6), 556.

Dodge, K. A. (1986). A social information-processing model of social competence in children. In M. Perlmutter (Ed.), *Minnesota symposium on child psychology. Vol. 18* (pp. 77–125). Hillsdale, NJ: Erlbaum.

Dodge, K. A., Bates, J. E., & Pettit, G. S. (1990). Mechanisms in the cycle of violence. *Science* 250, 1678–83.

Dodge, K. A., & Frame, C. L. (1982). Social cognitive biases and deficits in aggressive boys. *Child Development* 53, 629–35.

Donnerstein, E., Slaby, R. G., & Eron, L. D. (1994). The mass media and youth aggression. In L. D. Eron, J. Gentry, & P. Schlegel (Eds.), *Reason to hope: A psychological perspective on violence and youth* (pp. 219–50). Washington, D. C.: American Psychological Association.

Earls, F., & Barnes, J. (this volume). Understanding and preventing child abuse in urban settings. In J. McCord (Ed.), *Violence and childhood in the inner-city* (pp. 207–55). New York: Cambridge University Press.

Egeland, B., Sroufe, L. A., & Erickson, M. (1983). The developmental consequences of different patterns of maltreatment. *Child Abuse and Neglect* 7, 459–69.

Engfer, A., & Schneedwind, K. A. (1982). Causes and consequences of harsh parental punishment. *Child Abuse and Neglect* 6, 129–39.

Eron, L. D., Gentry, J. H., & Schlegel, P. (1994). *Reason to hope: A psychosocial perspective on violence and youth.* Washington, D.C.: American Psychological Association.

Eron, L. D., Huesmann, L. R., Dubow, E., Romanoff, R., & Yarmel, P. (1987). Aggression and its correlates over 22 years. In D. G. Crowell, I. M. Evans, & C. R. O'Donnell (Eds.), *Childhood aggression and violence: Sources of influence, prevention, and control* (pp. 249–62). New York: Plenum Press.

Eron, L. D., Huesmann, L. R., & Zelli, A. (1991). The role of parental variables in the learning of aggression. In D. J. Pepler & K. H. Rubin (Eds.), *The development and treatment of childhood aggression* (pp. 169–88). Hillsdale, NJ: Erlbaum.

Eron, L. D., & Slaby, R. G. (1994). Introduction. In L. D. Eron, J. Gentry, & P. Schlegel (Eds.), *Reason to hope: A psychological perspective on violence and youth* (pp. 1–22). Washington, D. C.: American Psychological Association.

Farrington, D. P. (1983). Offending from 10 to 25 years. In K. T. Von Desen & S. A. Mednick (Eds.), *Prospective studies of crime and delinquency* (pp. 17–37). Boston: Kluwer-Nijhoff.

(1993). Childhood origins of teenage antisocial behavior and adult social dysfunction. *Journal of the Royal Society of Medicine* 86, 13–16.

Farrington, D. P., & West, D. J. (1971). A comparison between early delinquents and young aggressives. *British Journal of Criminology* 11, 341–58.

Fattah, E. A. (1993). Doing unto others: The revolving roles of victim and victimizer. *Simon Fraser University Alumni Journal* 11, 12–17.

Feltham, R. F., Doyle, A. B., Schwartzman, A. E., Serbin, L. A., & Ledingham, J. E. (1985). Friendship in normal and socially deviant children. *Journal of Early Adolescence* 5, 371–82.

Finkelhor, D., & Dziuba-Leatherman, J. (1994). Victimization of children. *American Psychologist* 49, 173–83.

George, C., & Main, M. (1979). Social interactions of young abused children: Approach, avoidance and aggression. *Child Development* 50, 306–18.

Gerbner, G., Gross, L., Eleey, M. F., Jackson-Beeck, M., Jeffries-Fox, S., & Signorielli, N. (1977). TV violence profile No. 8: The highlights. *Journal of Communication* 27, 171–80.

Gerbner, G., Gross, L., Jackson-Beeck, M., Jeffries-Fox, S., & Signorielli, N. (1978). Violence profile No. 9: Cultural indicators. *Journal of Communication* 28, 176–207.

Ginsburg, H. J., Pollman, V. A., & Wauson, M. S. (1977). An ethological analysis of nonverbal inhibitors of aggressive behavior in male elementary school children. *Developmental Psychology* 13, 417–18.

Goldstein, A. P. (1994). *The ecology of aggression.* New York: Plenum.

Gottfredson, S., & Taylor, R. B. (1988). Community contexts and criminal offenders. In T. Hope, & M. Shaw (Eds.), Communities and crime reduction (pp. 62–82). London: Her Majesty's Stationery Office.

Greven, P. (1990). *Spare the child: The religious roots of punishment and the psychological impact of physical abuse.* New York: Knopf.

Grusec, J. E. (1973). Effects of co-observer evaluations on imitation: A developmental study. *Developmental Psychology* 8, 141.

Guerra, N. G., & Slaby, R. G. (1989). Evaluative factors in social problem solving by aggressive boys. *Journal of Abnormal Child Psychology* 17, 277–89.

(1990). Cognitive mediators of aggression in adolescent offenders: 2. Intervention. *Developmental Psychology* 26, 269–77.

Hartup, W. W. (1970). Peer interaction and social organization. In P. H. Mussen (Ed.), *Carmichael's manual of child psychology*, Vol. 2, 3rd ed. (pp. 103–96). New York: Wiley.

(1979). The social worlds of childhood. *American Psychologist* 34, 944–50.

Heath, L., Kruttschnitt, C., & Ward, D. (1986). Television and violent criminal behavior: Beyond the Bobo doll. *Victims and Violence* 1 (3), 177–90.

Henchman, K. G. (1994). Sex-typing as a predictor of adolescent responses to television violence. Doctoral Dissertation, Harvard University, Graduate School of Education: Cambridge, MA.

Hendrix, K. (1990). Cognitive mediation of television violence in adolescents. Doctoral Dissertation, Harvard University, Graduate School of Education: Cambridge, MA.

Hicks, D. I. (1968). Effects of co-observer's sanctions and adult presence on imitative aggression. *Child Development* 39, 303–9.

Hotaling, G. T., & Sugarman, D. (1986). An analysis of risk markers in husband to wife violence: The current state of knowledge. *Violence and Victims* 1, 101–24.

Huesmann, L. R. (1986). Psychological processes promoting the relation between exposure to media violence and aggressive behavior by the viewer. *Journal of Social Issues*, 42 (3), 125–40.

Huesmann, L. R., & Eron, L. D. (1986). *Television and the aggressive child: A cross-national comparison.* Hillsdale, NJ: Erlbaum.

(1989). Individual differences and the trait of aggression. *European Journal of Personality* 3, 95–106.

Huesmann, L. R., Eron, L. D., Klein, R., Brice, P., & Fischer, P. (1983). Mitigating the imitation of aggressive behaviors by changing children's attitudes about media violence. *Journal of Personality and Social Psychology* 44, 899–910.

Huesmann, L. R., Eron, L. D., Lefkowitz, M. M., & Walder, L. O. (1984). The stability of aggression over time and generations. *Developmental Psychology* 20, 1120–34.

Huesmann, L. R., Langerspetz, I., & Eron, L. D. (1984). Intervening variables in the TV violence-aggression relation: Evidence from two countries. *Developmental Psychology* 20, 1120–34.

Huston, A. C., Donnerstein, E., Fairchild, H., Feshbach, N. D., Katz, P. A., Murray, J. P., Rubinstein, E. A., Wilcox, B. L., & Zuckerman, D. (1992). *Big world, small screen: The role of television in American society.* Lincoln, NE: University of Nebraska Press.

Jaffe, P., Wolfe, D., Wilson, S., & Zak, L. (1986). Similarities in behavior and social maladjustment among child victims and witnesses to family violence. *American Journal of Orthopsychiatry* 56, 142–6.

Johnson, R., & Russell, G. (1990). Paper presented at the World Conference of the International Society for Research on Aggression, Banff, Canada (June).

Kazdin, A. E. (1987). Treatment of antisocial behavior in children: Current status and future directions. *Psychological Bulletin* 102, 187–203.

Latane, B., & Darley, J. M. (1970). Social determinants of bystander intervention in emergencies. In J. Macaulay & L. Berkowitz (Eds.), *Altruism and helping behavior* (pp. 13–27). New York: Academic Press.

Liebert, R. M., & Sprafkin, J. (1988). *The early window: Effects of television on children and youth.* New York: Pergamon Press.

Loeber, R., Wung, P., Keenan, K., Giroux, B., Stouthamer-Loeber, M., Van Kammen, W. B., & Maughan, B. (1993). Developmental pathways in disruptive child behavior. *Developmental Psychopathology* 5, 103–33.

Lyle, J. (1972). Television in daily life: Patterns of use. In E. A. Rubinstein, G. A. Comstock, & J. P. Murray (Eds.), *Television and social behavior. Vol. 4. Television in day-to-day life: Patterns of use* (pp. 1–32). Washington, D.C.: U.S. Government Printing Office.

Lyle, J., & Hoffman, H. (1972). Children's use of television and other media. In E. A. Rubinstein, G. A. Comstock, & J. P. Murray (Eds.), *Television and social behavior. Vol. 4. Television in day-to-day life: Patterns of use* (pp. 129–256). Washington, D.C.: U.S. Government Printing Office.

McCord, J. (1979). Some child rearing antecedents of criminal behavior in adult men. *Journal of Personality and Social Psychology* 37, 1477–86.

(1983). A forty year perspective on effects of child abuse and neglect. *Child Abuse and Neglect* 7, 265–70.

Mallick, S. K., & McCandless, B. R. (1966). A study of catharsis of aggression. *Journal of Personality and Social Psychology* 4, 591–6.

Martin, B. (1975). Parent-child relations. In F. D. Horowitz (Ed.), *Review of child development research. Vol. 4* (pp. 463–540). Chicago: University of Chicago Press.

Moffitt, T. E. (This volume). Neuropsychology, antisocial behavior, and neighborbood context. In J. McCord (Ed.), *Violence and childhood in the inner city* (pp. 116–70). New York: Cambridge University Press.

Neapolitan, J. (1981). Parental influences on aggressive behavior: A social learning approach. *Adolescence* 16, 831–40.

Nielsen, A. C. (1992). Nielsen television index. National audience demographics reports. Northbrook, IL: A. L. Nielsen Co.

Novaco, R. W. (1986). Anger as a clinical and social problem. In R. J. Blanchard & D. C. Blanchard (Eds.), *Advances in the study of aggression. Vol. 2* (pp. 1–67). Orlando, FL: Academic Press.

Olweus, D. (1977). Aggression and peer acceptance in adolescent boys: Two short-term longitudinal studies of ratings. *Child Development* 48, 1301–13.

(1978). *Aggression in the schools: Bullies and whipping boys.* Washington, D.C.: Hemisphere (also Wiley).

(1979). Stability and aggressive patterns in males: A review. *Psychological Bulletin* 86, 852–75.

(1980). Familial and temperamental determinants of aggressive behavior in adolescent boys: A causal analysis. *Developmental Psychology* 16, 644–60.

(1982). Continuity in aggressive and inhibited withdrawn behavior patterns. *Psychiatry and Social Science* 1, 141–59.

(1993a). Victimization by peers: Antecedents and long-term outcomes. In K. H. Rubin & J. B. Asendorf (Eds.), *Social withdrawal, inhibition, and shyness in childhood* (pp. 315–41). Hillsdale, NJ: Erlbaum.

(1993b). *Bullying at school: What we know and what we can do.* Cambridge, MA: Basil Blackwell.

Osborn, D. K., & Endsley, R. C. (1971). Emotional reactions of young children to TV violence. *Child Development* 42, 321–31.

Osborn, S. G., & West, D. J. (1979). Conviction records of fathers and sons compared. *British Journal of Criminology* 19, 120–3.

Parke, R. D., & Slaby, R. G. (1983). The development of aggression. In P. H. Mussen (Series Ed.), *Handbook of child psychology.* 4th Ed., *Vol. 4* (pp. 547–641). New York: Wiley.

Patterson, G. R. (1979). A performance theory for coercive family interaction. In R. B. Cairns (Ed.), *The analysis of social interactions: Methods, issues and illustrations* (pp. 119–62). Hillsdale, NJ: Erlbaum.

(1982). *A social learning approach to family intervention: Coercive family processes.* Eugene, OR: Castalia Press.

(1986). Performance models for antisocial boys. *American Psychologist* 44, 329–35.

Patterson, G. R., DeBaryshe, B. D., & Ramsey, E. (1989). A developmental perspective on antisocial behavior. *American Psychologist* 44, 329–35.

Patterson, G. R., Littman, R. A., & Bricker, W. (1967). Assertive behavior in children: A step toward a theory of aggression. *Monographs of the Society for Research in Child Development* 32 (5), Serial No. 113.

Patterson, G. R., Reid, J. B., & Dishion, T. J. (1992). *Antisocial boys.* Eugene, OR: Castalia Press.

Patterson, G. R., & Stouthamer-Loeber, M. (1984). The correlation of family management practices and delinquency. *Child Development* 55, 1299–1307.

Pepler, D. J., & Rubin, K. H. (Eds.). (1991). *The development and treatment of childhood aggression.* Hillsdale, NJ: Erlbaum.

Pepler, D. J., & Slaby, R. G. (1994). Theoretical and developmental perspectives on youth and violence. In L. D. Eron, J. Gentry, & P. Schlegel (Eds.), *Reason to hope: A psychological perspective on violence and youth* (pp. 27–58). Washington, D.C.: American Psychological Association.

Perry, D. G., Kusel, S. L., & Perry, L. C. (1988). Victims of peer aggression. *Developmental Psychology* 24, 807–14.

Perry, D. G., & Perry, L. C. (1974). Denial of suffering in the victim as a stimulus to violence in aggressive boys. *Child Development,* 45, 55–62.

Perry, D. G., Perry, L. C., & Rasmussen, P. (1986). Cognitive social learning mediators of aggression. *Child Development* 57, 700–11.

Reid, J. B., & Patterson, G. R. (1989). The development of antisocial behavior patterns in childhood and adolescence. *European Journal of Personality* 3, 107–20.

Richters, J. E. (1993). Community violence and children's development: Toward a research agenda for the 1990s. *Psychiatry* 56, 3–6.

Richters, J. E., & Martinez, P. (1993). The NIMH Community Violence Project: I. Children as victims of and witnesses to violence. *Psychiatry* 56, 7–21.

Robins, L. N., West, P. A., & Herjanic, B. I. (1975). Arrests and delinquency in two generations: A study of black urban families and their children. *Journal of Child Psychology and Psychiatry* 15, 125–40.

Rosenberg, M. S., & Rossman, B. B. R. (1990) The child witness to marital violence. In R. T. Ammerman & M. Herson (Eds.), *Treatment of family violence: A sourcebook* (pp. 183–210) New York: Wiley.

Sampson, R. J. (this volume). The embeddedness of child and adolescent development. In J. McCord (Ed.), *Violence and childhood in the inner city* (pp. 31–77). New York: Cambridge University Press.

Sears, R. R., Maccoby, E. E., & Levin, H. (1957). Patterns of child rearing. Evanston, IL: Row, Peterson.

Shure, M. B., & Spivack, G. (1988). Interpersonal cognitive problem solving. In R. G. Price, E. L. Cowen, R. P. Lorion, & J. Ramos-McKay (Eds.), *14 ounces of prevention: A casebook for practitioners* (pp. 69–82). Washington, D.C.: American Psychological Association.

Siegel, A. E., & Kohn, L. G. (1959). Permissiveness, permission, and aggression: The effects of adult presence or absence on aggression in children's play. *Child Development* 36, 131–41.

Signorielli, N. (1993). Personal communication.

Simcha-Fagan, O., & Schwartz, J. E. (1986). Neighborhood and delinquency: An assessment of contextual effects. *Criminology* 24, 667–99.

Slaby, R. G. (1994). Combating television violence. *The Chronicle of Higher Education. Vol. XL,* No. 18 (pp. B1–B2).

Slaby, R. G., & Guerra, N. G. (1988). Cognitive mediators of aggression in adolescent offenders: 1. Assessment. *Developmental Psychology* 24, 580–8.

Slaby, R. G., & Roedell, W. C. (1982). Development and regulation of aggression in young children. In J. Worell (Ed.), *Psychological development in the elementary years* (pp. 97–149). New York: Academic Press.

Slaby, R. G., & Stringham, P. S. (1994). Prevention of peer and community violence: The pediatrician's role. *Pediatrics* 94, (supplement).

Slaby, R. G., Wilson-Brewer, R., & DeVos, E. (1994). *Aggressors, victims, and bystanders: An assessment-based middle school violence prevention curriculum.* Final Report of Grant #R 49/CCR103559 from the Centers for Disease Control and Prevention, Atlanta, GA. (Available from *National Technical Information Service,* 5285 Port Royal Road, Springfield, VA 22161.)

Staub, E. (1974). Helping a distressed person: Social, personality, and stimulus determinants. In L. Berkowitz (Ed.), *Advances in experimental social psychology. Vol.* 7 (pp. 293–344). New York: Academic Press.

 (1989). *The roots of evil: The origins of genocide and other group violence.* New York: Cambridge University Press.

Stein, A. H., & Friedrich, L. K. (1972). Television content and young children's behavior. In J. P. Murray, E. A. Rubinstein, & G. A. Comstock (Eds.), *Television and social behavior. Vol. 2: Television and social learning* (pp. 202–317). Washington, D.C.: U.S. Government Printing Office.

Straus, M. A. (1991). Discipline and deviance: Physical punishment of children and violence and other crime in adulthood. *Social Problems* 38, 133–54.

 (1995). Corporal punishment of children and adult depression and suicidal ideation. In J. McCord (Ed.), *Coercion and punishment in long-term perspectives* (pp. 59–77). New York: Cambridge University Press.

Straus, M. A., Gelles, R. J., & Steinmetz, S. K. (1980). *Behind closed doors: Violence in the American family.* Garden City, NY: Anchor Press.

Stringham, P. (1993). Personal Communication, East Boston Neighborhood Health Center, Boston, MA.

Thomas, M. H., & Drabman, R. S. (1975). Toleration of real-life aggression as a function of exposure to television violence. *Merrill-Palmer Quarterly* 21, 227–32.

Thomas, M. H., Horton, R. W., Lippincott, E. C., & Drabman, R. S. (1977). Desensitization to portrayals of real-life aggression as a function of exposure to television violence. *Journal of Personality and Social Psychology* 35, 450–8.

TV Guide. (1992). Is TV violence battering our kids? New study, new answers. *TV Guide* (August 22). New York: NY.

Wadsworth, M. (1979). *Roots of delinquency: Infancy, adolescence, and crime*. New York: Harper & Row.

West, D. J., & Farrington, D. P. (1973). *Who becomes delinquent? Second report of the Cambridge study in delinquent development*. London: Heinemann Educational Books.

Widom, C. S. (1989a). The cycle of violence. *Science* 244, 160–6.

  (1989b). Does violence beget violence? A critical examination of the literature. *Psychological Bulletin* 106, 3–28.

Understanding and Preventing Child Abuse in Urban Settings

FELTON EARLS

JACQUELINE BARNES

Introduction

Of all forms of violence, child abuse is the most invidious. At once, it demands an immediate response and introduces its victims to one loop in a spiral of aggression and violence linking generations. The dependent status of children requires society to intervene in a manner unlike that for other forms of violence. However, a dilemma exists. The dilemma is portrayed in its starkest (and commonest) form when the abuser is a parent. We ask, "Is it necessary to protect the child by removal from the primary source of support and care, or can the family be spared this fracture and undergo needed repair with the child present?" More fundamentally, the question is, "When does the positive freedom of the child to develop normally supersede the negative freedom of the family to socialize the child?"[1] Unfortunately, the roles of law, social welfare, and health care are complex, imprecise, and often at odds. We aim to show in this paper that the balance between children's rights and the integrity of the family as the most basic unit of socialization is upset in the context of urban poverty and social disorganization. Of fundamental importance in efforts to control violence against children is the need to reverse the trend toward

---

[1] Amartya Sen defines positive freedom as the capability of individuals to function normally. Here we adopt the term to describe the right – or freedom – of a child to develop without injury or restraint. By contrast, negative freedom involves placing a constraint on others so that individuals can exercise a right, as in freedom of speech [see A. Sen, *Resources, Values and Development* (Cambridge, MA: Harvard University Press, 1984), pp. 314–15]. In *Making All the Difference* (Ithaca, NY: Cornell University Press, 1990, pp. 283–311), Martha Minnow provides a broad-ranging discussion of the complexities involved in interpreting children's rights in the context of family relationships.

deteriorating urban environments. Our focus on the topic of child abuse underscores this reality.

Children who are victims of violence and neglect are more likely to behave in aggressive ways with their peers, and as they mature, they are likely to become abusive and violent with their own children. In this sense, child abuse embodies the double jeopardy of both a short-term and long-term impact on society. This is not new information, and many experts have highlighted the intergenerational effects of child maltreatment. Yet as our review of the literature will demonstrate, the topic has not been examined in appropriate depth with regard to life in American cities – and particularly with regard to those individuals who are most disadvantaged in such contexts. It is just this liability, characteristic of life in the central areas of many American cities, that strains human existence and threatens the integrity of families and children.

What we wish to accomplish in this chapter is to evaluate existing knowledge within a framework based on public health theory and methodology. Our ultimate aim is to advance new ways of enhancing life for families who live in conditions of urban disadvantage. If successful, this approach has the promise of resolving the child/family dilemma by promoting the family's welfare as a preventive measure and, at the same time, of reducing the number of children growing up with a vulnerability to becoming aggressive and violent themselves.

The Public Health Approach

A national commission, which was organized to recommend action to reduce the exponential increase in cases of child abuse and neglect over the past two decades, put the problem in this context. It wrote,

> During the year in which the worst epidemic of poliomyelitis occurred in the United States – an epidemic which stimulated a national "Mothers' March on Polio" – 3,145 children died and 21,269 others were paralyzed. In 1989, at least 1,200 and perhaps as many as 5,000 children died as a result of maltreatment, and over 160,000 children were seriously harmed (U.S. Department of Health and Human Services, 1990a, p. 15).

The analogy is apt only insofar as it elicits a sense of proportion. Child abuse and neglect is tolerated in a way that would not be permitted for many other problems that exact a lesser toll on children's health. There are perhaps two major reasons for the absence of a more determined effort to reduce the incidence of child maltreatment. One is the status of the family as a unit beyond reproach. It is assumed to be the bedrock of society; thus, there are reservations about the degree to which we should expose its failures. The other reason relates to the nonrandom distribution of the most serious forms of violence in the society at large. The distribution of homicide is heavily concentrated in relatively small geographic areas of large American cities, areas known for high levels of poverty, unemployment, and social disorganization (Earls, 1991; Sampson, this volume). Such neighborhoods are also inhabited by ethnic minorities. It is not surprising, therefore, that nonfatal forms of violence, including child abuse, reflect the same pattern as these fatalities (Zuravin & Taylor, 1987).

In this paper we will describe and analyze the problem of child abuse and neglect, combining an ecological theory of human development with public health strategies for evaluation and intervention. The evidence that public health systems are targeting child abuse is shown in national health objectives for intentional injury.[2] By the year 2000, the Public Health Service has proposed to reduce the rate of child abuse 15%–20% (National Commission on Children, 1991). Considering the epidemic proportion of this problem in some communities, this may seem like a modest proposal. Yet the strategies for accomplishing this objective are completely untested and, for the most part, novel to public health practitioners. The specific strategies to reduce the risk are:

1. nurse-home visitation programs (or other home-visitor programs) for high risk infants.
2. educational interventions for children, for example, teaching nonviolent interpersonal problem-solving skills, social skills, and appropriate norms of nonviolent behavior.
3. timely crisis intervention for families under stress and at risk for violence.
4. development of media programs that foster nonviolent behavior.

What remains to be seen is whether risk can be reduced through such strategies. In many cases, the introduction of straightforward environmental change has had a dramatic impact on morbidity and mortality. The use of safety caps on medicines has significantly reduced childhood poisonings,

[2] Intentional injury is a category that includes homicide, suicide and attempted suicide, spousal abuse, child abuse, elder abuse as well as other patterns of fatal and nonfatal injury. In the current system of classifying public health problems, this category is differentiated from unintentional injuries (or accidents).

and the use of seatbelts and bicycle helmets has likewise reduced the incidence of serious injuries (Cataldo et al., 1986; Faber, 1986). It is much more difficult to envision how such simple procedures could be adapted for the prevention of child abuse or other forms of violence within the family.

Definitions of Child Abuse and Neglect

Definitions of harm to children constitute a major source of concern in any discussion of child maltreatment, and we aim to provide a sense of some of the complexities that characterize the ways these definitions are being handled in society. Direct physical injury to a child represents only part of a spectrum of harmful encounters that children experience as victims. Sexual abuse and parental negligence in providing for the basic physical, emotional, and intellectual needs of children are other areas. Psychological abuse – or efforts to embarrass or torture children and undermine their self-esteem – must also be considered in the spectrum of harm. For both parental negligence and sexual abuse, definitions are more subjective than they are for situations in which there is objective evidence of physical injury. Nonetheless, definitional debates are commonplace for all aspects of abuse and neglect (Cicchetti, 1991; Dubowitz, Black, Starr, & Zuravin, 1993; McGee & Wolfe, 1991). It is also important to articulate definitions within a societal context, and this applies particularly to identification of neglect, which is likely to be influenced by the level of prosperity and basic services available in a society (Graham, Dingwall, & Wolkind, 1985).

There are no standard definitions of abuse or neglect across societies – or even within one society such as the United States. Since children rarely report themselves as harmed, existing definitions depend on the observations and interpretation of others, usually adults. These definitions carry legal significance, because they indicate the circumstances in which society justifiably should intervene to protect a child from physical or psychological harm. In many cases, they set limits on the types of evidence that are required for the state to assume custody of a child. The most varied lists of definitions are presented by individual states. The Child Abuse and Neglect Prevention Act of 1974 mandates that every state establish criteria for abuse and designate an agency to receive and process reports of abuse. The definitions vary considerably in the range of conditions encompassed and in their specificity. The state of California, for example, has a particularly broad definition that considers child abuse as a situation in which a child suffers from any one or more of the following: 1) serious physical injury inflicted . . . by other than accidental means, 2) harm by reason of intentional neglect . . . , 3) going without necessary and basic physical care, 4) willful mental injury, negligent treatment . . . , and 5) any condition which results in the violation of the rights or physical, mental or moral welfare of a child or jeopardizes a child's present or future health, opportunity for normal development or capacity for independence (U.S. Department of Health and Human Services, 1988).

This definition of abuse includes all the forms of maltreatment described above. But contrast this definition of abuse with Maryland's: "the sustaining of physical injury by a child as the result of cruel or inhumane treatment" (U.S. Department of Health and Human Services, 1988). Arizona includes a clause in its laws on child abuse and neglect justifying the use of corporal punishment "when reasonable, necessary; and appropriate to maintain discipline" (U.S. Department of Health and Human Services, 1988). The Pennsylvania legal code requires direct observation of a child to register a report of abuse, whereas the Colorado law will accept the oral report of an adult. This difference in the law itself appears to result in a much lower rate of reported abuse in Pennsylvania than in Colorado (Kalichman & Brosig, 1992). In general, the definitions of sexual abuse are more elaborate and varied than are those concerning the variations in physical abuse and neglect.

Although it is beyond the scope of this paper to discuss the administrative strategies used to implement child protective services, it is quite clear that the law permits a broad degree of leeway as to what constitutes abuse or neglect. With this in mind, it should be assumed that significant variations exist from jurisdiction to jurisdiction.

The threshold between what is a commonly accepted norm and what constitutes danger takes us into the central dilemma of defining and responding to child abuse. Since the use of physical punishment is widespread in American society – even compared to other societies – the question of degree or seriousness of harm becomes a paramount concern (Graziano, Lindquist, Kunce, & Munjal, 1992). In the 1985 survey conducted by Straus and Gelles (1986), although the majority of parents admitted to the use of some form of physical punishment, 11% reported using techniques that would be considered very serious (beating up, using a blunt instrument, and so on). The distinction that must be kept in mind is between the number of children at risk for abuse because they are subject to coercive and physically punitive disciplinary practices and the number actually subject to injury as a consequence of such behavior.

Prevalence

The National Center for Children in Poverty (1990) estimates that in 1989 there were about 13 million children under the age of 18 and 5 million under the age of 6 who lived in families below the poverty line (defined as $9,890 for a family of 3 and $12,675 for a family of 4). Within this group there should be some 6 to 7 million children living in central urban areas. It is this group of children who represent the denominator in estimates of child abuse that are relevant to this paper.

One of the most important sources of information is the National Study of the Incidence and Severity of Child Abuse and Neglect. The first survey was completed in 1979 (NIS–1) and a second more detailed study in 1986 (NIS–2; Sedlak, 1988; 1991). In these studies data from all potential administrative sources (law enforcement, schools, social service agencies, and hospitals and medical clinics) were obtained in a sample of 28 counties in 19 states; this sample was then weighted statistically to be representative of the entire U.S. population. The studies have used an operational definition in which an injury or impairment had to be in the moderate-to-severe range to be classified as maltreatment. Using this same definition, the researchers who conducted these studies found that the rate of substantiated cases increased from 10.5 per 1,000 in the NIS–1 to 14.8 per 1,000 in 1986. The 1986 study also included a broadened definition of abuse and neglect to account for children at substantial risk of serious maltreatment although not meeting the criteria of moderate or severe injury. The prevalence rose to 22.6 per 1,000 with this expanded definition. Given the narrower definition, researchers found that cases of abuse were somewhat more common than neglect, but cases of neglect were much more common when using the broader definition.[3]

The best estimates of the distribution of child abuse and neglect by age, sex, ethnicity, and income are derived from the NIS study. The results show that abuse is somewhat more common than neglect except during infancy and late adolescence, when neglect is more common. In general, there is a steady, although not steep, increase of abuse and neglect with age. Females have a slightly higher rate than males. It should come as no surprise that the

---

[3] The American Humane Association, by aggregating data from child protective services in many states, provided another commonly referenced source of data on prevalence for the period from 1976 to 1987. However, these data provided no standard criteria for case selection, included both unsubstantiated and duplicated cases, and were obtained only from child protective services.

severity of abuse is also related to poverty (National Research Council, 1993). No doubt a reflection of this condition is the finding that black children are five times more likely to die as a consequence of abuse and neglect than are white children (National Research Council, 1993).

Recent efforts to develop an improved national system for reporting child abuse have generated findings that are in keeping with these past estimates. The National Child Abuse and Neglect Data System was created by the National Center on Child Abuse and Neglect (NCCAN) to decrease duplication in counting cases by giving each child a unique identifier and to standardize procedures for deleting unsubstantiated cases from files (U.S. Department of Health and Human Services, 1990b). In 1991, 2.7 million cases of children under the age of 18 were reported, and of these 1.6 million were substantiated, making for a prevalence of 25 per 1,000 (National Commission on Children, 1991). If the estimate of 6 to 7 million given earlier and the above prevalence estimates for children living in central urban areas are accurate, the number of children at serious risk of abuse would be in the 450,000–600,000 range.

All the above data reflect what should be termed administrative prevalence to distinguish it from the true prevalence. Estimates of true prevalence are derived from samples that are known to be representative of either the entire U.S. population or clearly delineated local population groups. The most frequently cited data are derived from telephone interviews rather than face-to-face assessments or official records (Straus & Gelles, 1986). In this survey, conducted in 1975 and again in 1985, the prevalence of abuse was six to seven times higher than what estimates from administrative data show. The results of these surveys are treated cautiously because of the way in which abuse was defined, because of the changes made in sampling and methodology between the two surveys, and because of the uncertain validity of telephone interviews (National Research Council, 1993). Of particular note are findings from these two surveys suggesting that the prevalence of abuse was declining over the decade during which all administrative sources indicated dramatic increases in both reported and substantiated cases of abuse and neglect.

In the absence of data on true national prevalence, methods of estimating rates for local areas are needed. In fact, such estimates are more useful to urban areas that differ in ethnic and social class status – and to areas where the population is undergoing dynamic change – than are efforts to extrapolate from national samples.

There has been discussion about the possibility that reports of abuse increase as a function of the public attention directed to them and as laws on mandated reporting are more strictly established. A 20-year study of a county of 120,000 residents in Indiana distinguished the total number of reported cases from those that had been substantiated. All reports to the Child Protective Services were studied, from the first logged contact to the final disposition, as determined by child welfare/child protective services. Data were collected from 1965, the year in which mandated reporting for medical professionals was introduced, through 1984. The results show that the increase in administrative prevalence of abuse probably reflects a true increase in incidence (Knudsen, 1988). From 1965 to 1984 the rate of substantiated reports increased for both preschool and school-age children by factors of three to five times. For example, the rate for preschool children increased from 4.55 per 1,000 children in the 1964–73 period to 23.59 in the 1979–81 period to 31.91 in the 1982–84 period. If an increased sensitivity to and the reporting of suspected abuse and neglect had occurred because of legal requirements and heightened public awareness, the expectation would be for there to be an increase in milder cases overall and a change in the profile of perpetrators and victims. Furthermore, the increase in milder cases would be expected to reduce the proportion of substantiated cases following an investigation. The fact that these characteristics were not found by those examining these long-term trends supports the assumption of an increase in true prevalence.

Although there may not be a strong bias toward overreporting abuse in children, there do remain other sources of bias which may well have been present throughout the recent period during which an overall rate increase has occurred. Low social class and minority status are among the prominent sources of a bias toward overreporting (Hampton, 1987; Lindholm & Willey, 1986). At least two factors might explain these biases. Since poor urban neighborhoods are broadly perceived to be more violent than others, residents of such areas may be subject to more intensive surveillance by police and social workers. Alternatively, caseworkers and police officers may receive inadequate training to be culturally sensitive and to respond appropriately to families living in urban communities.

Risk Factors

Risk factors for abuse and neglect are manifold. Some are attributes of the child or parent; others point to the broader family context or to the societal/cultural environment. Establishing the relative importance of any specific risk factor is not easy given the nature of the studies that are available. There are problems in seeking evidence that poverty is a specific risk for abuse. Little direct evidence has been collected about the factors that increase risk for abuse among the urban poor. Evidence about risk factors has typically been gathered by studying working- and middle-class families. Furthermore, few studies have included nonabusing families for comparisons. With poverty, overcrowding, and poor health combined in urban pockets, factors that increase risk for abuse may not resemble risk factors identified under less stressful conditions.

The type of abuse experienced and the way it is defined are relevant to interpreting the literature on risk factors. It is not always clear what kind of abuse specific risks pertain to, or whether the choice of target group is conceptually or pragmatically driven. For example, neglect is less often included in reports, because it is much more difficult to document, and the line between sexual abuse and physical violence may be drawn arbitrarily. For the sake of clarity, we will discuss risk factors for all types of abuse, but we will make reference to physical abuse, neglect, and sexual abuse if they have been noted in a particular study.

In reviewing the literature on risk factors, we are searching for ways to broaden our understanding of the mechanisms that underlie abuse, a strategy which will ultimately assist in providing for more focused intervention efforts. From a public health orientation toward control and prevention of violence toward children, risk factors should be modifiable. Demographic indicators can direct attention to high risk groups; longitudinal data collection and more detailed analysis can then make the mechanisms that determine abusive behavior more explicit. We will look in particular at any studies that have included inner-city populations or tried to understand the particular risks inherent in those groups.

Many investigators have sought to clarify risk factors associated with child abuse. Some characteristics of children are thought to raise the likelihood that they will be abused. Low birth weight or prematurity (Searight & Handal, 1986), HIV infection (Jason, 1991), and disability (Diamond & Jaudes, 1983; Westcott, 1991) have been thought to increase the risk for abuse.

Each of these conditions is found with greater frequency among the urban poor than among the rest of the American population. There are higher rates of low birth weight (Boston Department of Health and Hospitals, 1992; Fink, Yano, & Goya, 1992), inadequate prenatal care (St. Peter, Newacheck, & Halfon, 1992), and HIV infection (Van Dyke, 1991) in families living within inner-city areas, compared with those in suburban or rural communities. Nevertheless, a recent review concludes that although children with circumscribed difficulties (such as multiple handicapping conditions and concomitant behavior problems) may add to risk in families already under stress, there is no compelling argument that child factors in isolation contribute to the risk for abuse (Ammerman, 1991). Ammerman suggested that it is more useful to ask about how circumstances that are proximal to the child contribute to the overall likelihood of abuse than to attempt to identify specific child characteristics (or situational factors) that may be risk markers.

Psychiatric and psychological studies have traditionally looked at the family environment in terms of specific characteristics of abusers. Although many separate aspects of parents and the family have been studied, it may be fallacious to conceptualize them separately. Most could be placed within a model that associates child maltreatment with family stress (Whipple & Webster-Stratton, 1991). Young and/or single parents, particularly those living in impoverished conditions and in contexts that do not provide adequate social support and guidance from other adults, represent a high risk group (Sack, Mason, & Higgins, 1985; Schloesser, Pierpoint, & Poertner, 1992). Much of the information comes from official statistics (Gelles, 1989), and the overrepresentation of single parents among reported cases of child abuse has led to intervention studies targeting single and young mothers (Olds, Henderson, Chamberlin, & Tatelbaum, 1986; Schinke, Schilling, Barth, & Gilchrist, 1986).

Population samples can clarify the issues in that they avoid biases inherent in official statistics, although they usually rely on the researchers' definitions of abuse; unfortunately, such definitions may be very different from criteria used by social service workers, making comparisons of rates problematic. Sack, Mason, and Higgins (1985) interviewed a probability sample of adults 18 and older, asking retrospectively how they had been punished as children up to the age of 16. The interview employed a scale from 0 to 4, where 0 represented "no abuse" (spanking only or no physical discipline, 52%), 1 represented "possible abuse" (e.g. severe whipping not on the buttocks, 42%) and 2, 3, and 4 signified "well established abuse" (e.g. hit with fist, knocked unconscious, 6%). Well-established abuse was found nearly twice as frequently among those reared in single-parent households (9%) than among those from two-parent families (5%). Marital status was also a risk factor in that those single parents who had been married but were divorced had the highest abuse rate, implicating extended periods of family discord or reaction to changes in circumstances rather than the condition of being a single parent. These retrospective accounts may, however, have been biased by recall of family discord. Gelles

(1989) studied discipline in the Second National Family Violence Survey, a probability sample of more than 6,000 households. Although he did not find that single parents differed from two-parent families in the overall reported use of violent discipline by parents, he did find that single-parent families were more likely to use severe violence (behaviors likely to cause injury such as kicking, hitting with something, burning). Nonetheless, the difference was related to parent gender. The use of severe violence during discipline was at a similar level for mothers whether in single- or dual-parent homes, but fathers who were single used violent strategies significantly more often than fathers in two-parent homes. A similar effect was seen when the sample was divided into those families living in poverty (with incomes below $10,000) and those living above the poverty line (with incomes greater than $10,000). The discipline of mothers in the low income families was similar, whether or not they lived in single- or two-parent families. In contrast, men living in poverty who were single parents were more likely to use severe violence than men living in poverty but in two-parent homes.

It has been suggested that maternal mental health problems, in particular depression (Stoneman, Brody, & Burke, 1989; Webster-Stratton & Hammond, 1988) and alcoholism and other substance abuse (Famularo, Stone, Barnum, & Wharton, 1986; Murphy, Jellinek, Quinn, Smith, Poitrast, & Goshko, 1991) are associated with abusive parenting. Depressed caregivers are likely to use a style of parenting that could easily lead to neglect or physical abuse. For instance, Webster-Stratton and Hammond (1988) found that depressed mothers were more likely to be rejecting, to be harsh and critical, and to use frequent physical punishment. It has also been shown that abusive parents are more likely to report clinical levels of depression (Whipple & Webster-Stratton, 1991).

Yet it has not been clearly demonstrated that maternal depression precedes documented child maltreatment. In reviewing the relationship between child maltreatment and parental isolation, Seagull (1987) pointed to the association between maternal depression and poor social support, suggesting that this factor may be an important mediator in the relationships found between single-parent status and abuse. She suggested that many intervention strategies have been too narrowly conceived about the potential benefits of providing social support, because they have not taken into account the underlying problems that parents may be experiencing.

Neither has parental alcoholism been clearly identified as a risk factor that precedes abuse (Orme & Rimmer, 1981). In reviewing the literature,

Orme and Rimmer highlighted the overrepresentation of low-income-class families in samples demonstrating an association between child abuse and parental alcoholism. The higher rates of many types of problems and stresses could be associated with poverty rather than with alcoholism.

Some more recent work has attempted to address this issue. Famularo, Stone, Barnum, and Wharton (1986) compared a random sample of parents who had been referred to the court for child abuse with a control group whose children had been admitted to a local pediatric hospital. By completing psychiatric interviews, they established that parents who were referred for abuse were more likely to have a history of alcoholism, although not necessarily at the time of presentation to the court. Parents with a history of alcoholism more often suffered from major depression. It could be that depression is the primary explanatory factor; alcoholism would then be a secondary factor, providing a way for parents to relieve or cope with depressive symptomatology. This may be particularly likely when parents lack the financial resources to obtain health care for mental health problems.

McCord (1983) looked at the outcome for 97 youths from the Cambridge-Somerville Youth Study who had experienced abuse or neglect. Forty-four (labelled "vulnerable") later became criminals, alcoholics, or mentally ill, or they had died before age 35; 53 had none of these indicators of poor outcome. She found that paternal alcoholism, although not related to the occurrence of child abuse, appeared to increase the likelihood that abuse or neglect would be detrimental to future development. Significantly, more of the vulnerable group had alcoholic or criminal fathers. Murphy et al. (1991) examined 206 consecutive cases of child abuse or neglect brought before a Boston juvenile court, excluding cases of sexual abuse, and they found that 50% of the parents had abused alcohol, heroin, or cocaine. Unfortunately, there was no mention of how prevalent cocaine or alcohol abuse was in the population from which the parents were drawn. They did find that the presence of parental alcoholism was associated with a larger number of prior child abuse reports and that alcoholic parents were more likely to reject court-ordered services and to eventually lose custody of their children; these findings were consistent with McCord's earlier (1983) findings that parental alcoholism is predictive of poor child outcome.

The complex interaction among multiple risks is highlighted by studies of parents in families who are homeless or migrant and who are identified as at risk as perpetrators of child abuse (Larson, Doris & Alvarez, 1990;

Woods, Valdez, Hayashi, & Shen, 1990). Larson, Doris, and Alvarez (1990) direct attention to the possibility that both poverty and minority status could lead to inequitable treatment of migrant families by child protective systems. Farm workers tend to have frequent contact with mandated reporters such as health care providers, whose tendency to report incidents of abuse and neglect is influenced by the race and social class of the alleged perpetrator (Hampton & Newberger, 1985). Since migrant farm workers are primarily of minority status and living in abject poverty, these characteristics may influence rates of reporting abuse. Detailed studies of migrant workers that are based on mobility differences have revealed variations within that group. Children of migrant workers who stay within one state have higher rates of child abuse than farm-working families who travel between states (Larson, Doris, & Alvarez, 1990).

The authors suggest that those who are interstate migrants may be less isolated because they travel together and thus may have more access to dependable social support from extended family and government programs. Garbarino (1977) identified social isolation as a major family risk indicator for child abuse, and subsequent studies have confirmed this idea (Cohen & Adler, 1986; Dunst, Trivette, & Cross, 1986; Gaudin & Pollane, 1983). Social isolation is certainly pertinent to an understanding of the risk of child abuse in homeless families. Homeless mothers more often describe spousal violence, mental health problems, alcohol abuse, abuse in their own childhoods, and poor social support networks, all of which would heighten the risk for abuse (Bassuk & Rosenberg, 1988; Goodman, 1991; Robertson, 1991; Woods, Valdez, Hayashi, & Shen, 1990).

Gelles (1987) provides a useful analysis of the family's role in child abuse. He sees the structure and function of the family group as central, and he commented that no one factor can explain the presence or absence of abuse. Beyond family characteristics such as social stress, poverty, and social isolation, he examined some alternative theories, including the sociocultural explanation that the social context of the United States supports violence as a response to stress. Garbarino's model for understanding child abuse, which builds on Bronfenbrenner's (1979) ecological approach to human development (Garbarino, 1977; Garbarino, 1981), also set the family within a broader context. Garbarino moved attention beyond characteristics of a child or parent to characteristics of the neighborhood, hypothesizing that the detrimental influence of living in a weak or high-risk neighborhood on family life will be greater for families who lack economic resources. This attention to multiple levels of influence and the incorporation of personal and social resources makes Garbarino's approach an effective method for understanding risk factors within specific groups such as the urban poor (see Sampson, this volume).

Foster placement, although more commonly discussed in terms of its use as a treatment following abuse, may also be a risk factor. Many children, who have experienced gross abuse and neglect in situations where drug dealing, interpersonal violence, and crack, cocaine, and alcohol use are commonplace, are at highest risk for developing psychiatric problems. The nation's foster care system is under duress, faced with ever increasing cases (rising 29% between 1986 and 1989) and a smaller pool of suitable foster placements. Documents issued by the Children's Defense Fund (1991) and the U.S. Department of Health and Human Services (1990a) point to deficits of the system, reporting that in some states, both the children who are placed and the foster families who take them do not know the name of the caseworker; in addition, it is reported that social workers may not be able to provide foster parents with the necessary support to care for the increasingly difficult youngsters they are placing into families (Fanshel, Finch, & Grundy, 1992; Kurland & Salmon, 1992). Foster parents who are unprepared or unwilling to cope with symptoms such as hoarding food, defecating on the floor, and other signs of behavior regression may themselves be abusive to children placed in their care (Dugger, 1992a; 1992b; 1992c).

Negative Consequences and Developmental Mechanisms

Inherent in a public health approach to child abuse and neglect are two important ideas: There are negative consequences for the child's development, and increased understanding of the mechanisms involved will make it possible to plan more effective strategies for reducing abusive or neglecting parental behavior. The most obvious and clearly demarcated outcome of abuse is death. Disadvantaged urban children are at heightened risk of death as an outcome of abuse, because emergency health care is inadequate or else it is inaccessible without health insurance. Nevertheless, population patterns of mortality associated with child abuse and neglect are not easy to study because accurate quantification relies on the ability of medical personnel to identify abuse as a cause of death. Using FBI records, McClain, Sacks, Froehlke, and Ewigman (1993) determined that about 85% of child abuse and neglect deaths in the United States for children aged 17 or younger between 1979 and 1988 were not recorded as such on the death certificate, leading to the conclusion that surveys relying on official reports of child abuse fatalities are gross underestimates. It is worth noting that both neglect and physical violence may lead to death (Margolin, 1990), and the former will be the most difficult to identify.

McClain et al. (1993) do not consider possible causes of bias in completing death certificates, but Hampton and Newberger (1985) showed that medical personnel are influenced by the race, social class, and social or other skills of the adult involved when making decisions about reporting suspected abuse. As part of the National Study of the Incidence and Severity of Child Abuse and Neglect (NIS), the hospital emergency room staff at 70 hospitals spread through ten states completed reports identifying children who were thought to have been abused. These forms were only available to research staff and not to local Child Protective Services. Comparison of rates of abuse with those obtained through child protection agencies revealed that disproportionate numbers of unreported cases (identified to researchers but not filed) came from white families of higher income and from those where the mother was the alleged perpetrator. The researchers concluded that hospitals failed to report large numbers of cases and that the label "child-abuser" was more problematic when applied to parents who were closer in socioeconomic status to the nurses and physicians.

We will not attempt to provide a comprehensive review of all outcomes of abuse. A number of reviews are available, including those relating to the long- and short-term effects of sexual abuse (Beitchman, Zucker, Hood, daCosta, & Akman, 1991; Beitchman, Zucker, Hood, daCosta, Akman, & Cassavia, 1992; Browne & Finkelhor, 1986); the effects of abuse and neglect (Ammerman, Cassisi, Hersen, & Van Hasselt, 1986; Conaway & Hansen, 1989); the consequences of physical violence (Widom, 1989c); and the intergenerational transmission of abusive behavior (Kaufman & Zigler, 1987). Focused reviews have considered the role of abuse in developmental or academic problems (Augoustinos, 1987; Heilig, 1987; Houck & King, 1989), psychological problems (McLaren & Brown, 1989) and delinquency (Koski, 1987). We aim to give an overview of the effects of abuse, including more detailed information about the effects of physical abuse and neglect than about the effects of sexual abuse. Our particular focus will be on effects that are relevant to the development of aggression and on scientific evidence that can illuminate ways to plan prevention programs, particularly in the context of urban poverty.

Outcomes of abuse may be perceived as part of an escalating spiral of influence throughout development – from childhood and into adulthood, with long-term effects that will contribute to an intergenerational pattern of family violence as the abuse victim becomes a parent. There are many potentially detrimental effects which can be identified early in life, including problems with social relationships and aggressive or other problematic child behavior. These outcomes are likely to interact with such precipitating factors as parental coercive behavior or alcoholism to produce a more severe outcome. To understand the contribution that a preventive, public health model can make, we must first examine the mechanisms underlying different consequences; we must pay particular attention to the individual differences in outcomes among children who have experienced similar abuse or other maltreatment. Why is it that some children who experience severe neglect will later be prone to suicidal behavior or alcoholism, whereas others are overtly aggressive, and still others appear to develop normally?

Abuse of children is seen by developmentalists as an opportunity to answer important questions about individual responses to conditions that would on ethical grounds be impossible to manipulate experimentally (Cicchetti, 1989). Prospective studies can elucidate mechanisms of resilience; this is important for planning prevention strategies. The effects of abuse are particularly relevant for those seeking to understand the ways in which violent and aggressive behavior develops (Dodge, Bates, & Pettit, 1990; Widom, 1989a); but these effects are also relevant to a wide range of other developmental disruptions in diverse areas of functioning, including communicative ability (Allen & Oliver, 1982), peer relations (Kaufman & Cicchetti, 1989), sense of self (Allen & Tarnowski, 1989; Kaufman & Cicchetti, 1989), morality (Smetana, Kelly, & Twentyman, 1984), depression (Allen & Tarnowski, 1989), and substance abuse (Dembo, Dertke, LaVoie, Borders, Washburn, & Schmeidler, 1987; Dembo et al., 1990).

Unlike epidemiological studies of risk factors, many smaller scale developmental studies of families who have abused or neglected their children include information that is relevant to families living in poverty. Many developmental studies include comparison families who are not abusive but who are from urban areas and from low-income groups (Allen & Oliver, 1982; Jaffe, Wolfe, Wilson, & Zak, 1986; Smetana et al., 1984).

Reflecting the theoretical perspective expounded by Sroufe and Rutter (1984), much of the recent developmental research on children experiencing abuse and neglect has examined outcomes that are considered stage-salient. Attachment, the formation of secure relationships with one or more adults who are seen regularly, is explored in the first 12 months. The development of autonomy and self-reliance is thought to be crucial from 12 to 30 months; the establishment of peer relations in early childhood; and the integration of attachment, autonomy, and peer relationships in the form of internalizing standards, assuming responsibilities, and expressing multiple emotions in late childhood (Cicchetti, 1989; Cicchetti & Schneider-Rosen, 1986). We will use these development guideposts in reviewing what is currently known about the effects of abuse and neglect.

Infancy and Preschool

Egeland and Sroufe (1981) studied parent–child relations in a group of 267 primiparous women receiving prenatal care through public assistance, enrolling them in the last trimester of pregnancy. Home visits were made at three monthly intervals through the first year, and an "inadequate care" scale was completed that involved evidence of violence in the household, poor physical care, unsanitary conditions, and neglect (such as not changing diapers or clothing, or not providing the infant with a place to sleep). By the age of 12 months, 31 mothers had been identified as seriously neglecting or abusing their infants, the majority (24) involving cases of severe neglect. The Ainsworth Strange Situation (Ainsworth, Blehar, Waters, & Wall, 1978) was used at 12 months to evaluate the quality of the infant's relationship with the mother. This procedure involves seven 3-minute sequences in which the infant's exploration of a novel environment in the presence of the mother, reaction to separation from her, and subsequent reunion are observed. Infants are rated as "secure" if they explore while returning briefly to their mother for reassurance, if they are upset when she leaves the room, and if they seek out reassurance from her upon her return. Some infants are judged to be insecure if they display other kinds of behavior, such as lack of distress on the mother's departure, avoidance of her when she returns (called "anxious-avoidant"), or failure to explore in the mother's presence and failure to be comforted by her after the separation (called "anxious-resistant"). Infants whose mothers were identified as providing inadequate care were more often observed to be insecurely attached than a group of 33 whose mothers were judged to be providing excellent care. Differences between the groups in the proportion rated as insecure were less pronounced by 18 months, but it was more likely that the attachment rating of the maltreated infants was different at 18 months than it had been at 12, whereas attachment ratings of the nonmaltreated children were likely to be the same at both assessments.

The two samples were similar in terms of poverty due to initial sample selection criteria, but the mothers in the inadequate care group were younger (mean age 19 years versus 24 years) and less well educated, and more were unmarried (82% vs 40%). These differences may have contributed to the variation in parent–child relationships, but other studies are consistent in finding that children who experience maltreatment early in life are more likely to demonstrate insecure attachment (Cicchetti & Barnett, 1991; Schmidt & Eldridge, 1986), and identifiable effects of abuse and neglect are evident throughout the preschool period (Youngblade & Belsky, 1989).

The majority of studies show that many (but, importantly, not all) mal-treated children are anxious and insecure about the ways in which adults might behave, and their behavior in laboratory settings, such as in the Ainsworth Strange Situation, is less stable from one age to another between infancy and the preschool years than that of nonmaltreated children, probably reflecting their own inconsistent experiences. The methodology for evaluating attachment is continually being refined in ways that have particular relevance for understanding the effects of abuse and neglect. The initial Ainsworth coding has been extended by the addition of a new category labelled "disorganized" attachment. Disorganized children are those who behave inconsistently with caregivers during the episodes of separation and reunion in the Ainsworth Strange Situation. At some points they may seek comfort, at others avoid the caregiver, and at others appear inconsolably distressed. This pattern of disorganized behavior is found to be typical of many abused children (Carlson, Cicchetti, Barnett, & Braunwald, 1989; Main & Hesse, 1989). It has been suggested that the infants in the disorganized group represent a greater degree of maladapta-tion in their relationships than insecure children, putting them at highest risk of continued difficulties.

The categorization of children into those who are securely attached, those who are insecure (anxious or avoidant), or those who are disorga-nized in their use of a caregiver for comfort and security has been adapted to incorporate more of the behaviors typical of preschool age children in the Ainsworth Strange Situation (Cassidy & Marvin, 1991). Cicchetti and Barnett (1991), using this technique, found that at 30 months, maltreated children (a nonspecific group whose members were abused and/or ne-glected) showed more disorganized and other atypical patterns of behavior than matched controls. Nevertheless, the difference was not identified at later ages (36 and 48 months). Refinement of the techniques may clarify some of the ways in which abused and neglected children differ from nonabused children in the development of internal representations of the behavior of their caregivers.

Crittenden (1985) found that abused infants were more difficult and angry when stressed, and neglected children tended to be more passive and helpless. This differentiation between abuse and neglect is less evident during interactions with peers. Both abused and neglected children tend to be either highly aggressive or withdrawn and shy, responding to aggression with aggression but failing to respond to friendly overtures (Dodge, Bates, & Pettit, 1990; George & Main, 1979; Howes & Eldredge, 1985; Jacobson & Straker, 1982; Martin & Beezley, 1977). George and Main (1979) studied 20 children ranging from 1 to 3 years old, 10 of whom were placed in metropolitan day-care centers serving families who had been placed in protective services following identification of abuse, and 10 of whom were placed in centers for families under stress where participation was voluntary and no abuse was identified. Detailed observations of each target child over several days showed that children who had been abused were much more likely to avoid other children, to respond to friendly overtures by avoidance, and to be aggressive to other children. The abused children were also unlikely to respond to distress of peers, whereas 33% of the nonabused children responded with concern (Main & George, 1985). In contrast, most of the abused infants but only one of the controls responded with fear or aggression to the cries of peers.

Howes and Eldredge (1985) also found that the response to peers' distress differentiated abused and neglected children from nonmaltreated controls. Eighteen children between the ages of 14 and 33 months attending one day-care center were observed, 5 of whom had been physically abused and 4 neglected; 9 were matched controls who had not experienced maltreatment. Detailed sequential observations in free play and structured dyadic situations revealed that abused children responded more often than controls to peer distress with aggression and less frequently offered a helpful response. The abused and neglected groups were also more likely than controls to respond to peer aggression with retaliatory aggression, which was likely to accelerate conflicts. In contrast, the controls more often responded to aggression by crying. The lack of empathy toward peers and the use of retaliation rather than attempts at conflict resolution can be expected to lead to problems maintaining peer relationships in childhood.

Childhood

The cognitive aspect of interpersonal relationships, and in particular the development of an understanding of emotions expressed by peers, has been studied in relation to the effects of abuse and neglect. A laboratory study of children aged three to seven years, which looked at their ability to interpret the emotions of other children from photographs, provides some insight into underlying mechanisms (Camras, Ribordy, Hill, Martino, Spaccarelli, & Stefani, 1988). All the children were attending day-care centers that had child abuse prevention programs serving primarily low income status families. The abused children had been identified by Child and Family Services, and many had experienced both abuse and neglect.

Children were read stories in which different emotions were described (happiness, surprise, anger, sadness, fear, disgust) and were then asked to pose for a photograph in a way that represented that emotion. These photographs were then rated from 0 to 2 by graduate students to give an emotion-production score. Subsequently, the children were shown photographs of child models whose expressions represented one of these six emotions; some of the photos showed four "masked" emotions, in which anger, disgust, fear, and sadness were represented by smiling. Subjects were shown two pictures in each category, and they could gain a score from 0 to 2 for accurate identification of the emotion portrayed. Abused children gained significantly lower recognition and production scores than the nonabused group; furthermore, the ability of their mothers to produce recognizable emotions was significantly related to children's recognition score. The lower "posing" performance of both abused children and their mothers suggests that the family environment lacks sufficient information about the morphology and meaning of facial expressions and their attendant emotions.

The complexity of children's attributions about social situations is shown by Dean, Malik, Richards, and Stringer (1986). Maltreated and non-maltreated children who were between the ages of 6 and 14 years old and who were from low-income families were asked to tell stories about kind and unkind incidents, some child-to-child and some adult-to-child or child-to-adult (for example, "Tell me a story in which John does something nice for his mother"). After each story, they were asked what the recipient would do. Scoring covered reciprocity, context, content, and verbal fluency. Reciprocity was scored if the actor's initiative and the recipient's response were of the same type (e.g., both unkind, such as hit/hit or hit/curse; both kind, such as help/help). As predicted, there was a developmental lag in the emergence of prosocial reciprocity in peer relations for the maltreated children. The children in the younger (6–8-year-old) maltreated group were less likely than controls to describe prosocial reciprocity between peers in their stories, although control and maltreated groups in the older age groups responded similarly. Reflecting the tendency of abused children to take on a "parentified" role, at all ages they were more likely than the controls to compose stories in which children responded with kindness rather than reciprocal unkindness to adult unkindness. Maltreated children in the younger age group also included significantly more aggression in stories about peer interactions, and maltreated children of all ages told more stories that included physical aggression from adult to child and more that represented a "perfect parent–worthless child" model, with justification for adult unkindness by descriptions of children's bad behavior. Verbal fluency did not differentiate the maltreated children and controls.

Dodge et al. (1990) found that children with a history of abuse were not only more aggressive in their own behavior but also less attentive to social cues and more likely to ascribe hostility to the actions of others than a matched group who had not experienced abuse.

Other cognitive differences have been identified in groups of maltreated children, with important implications for subsequent aggression. When asked to imitate scenarios portrayed by puppets (e.g., doctor, nurse, patient), abused children between the ages of six and eight were able to imitate dyadic interactions, but nonabused controls could successfully copy more complex triadic exchanges among the puppets (Barahal, Waterman, & Martin, 1981); these results are interpreted as an indication that abused children have more trouble integrating alternative roles in social situations. Smetana, Kelly, and Twentyman (1984) found that three- to five-year-old abused and neglected children had a stronger tendency to judge the transgressions of other children as serious and in need of punishment than nonabused children. A three point visual scale showing three progressively exaggerated frowns was used; after the children were shown drawings of social-conventional (e.g. not listening to the teacher) and moral (e.g., biting) transgressions, they were asked how "bad" the behavior was and whether the transgressor (who was described sometimes as "himself" or "herself", and at other times as another child) should be punished. Although the mean seriousness scores of the abused, neglected, and control children were similar when they thought about themselves transgressing, the abuse and neglect groups rated transgression by others as more serious and needing more punishment than did the control children.

In central zones of large cities, daily exposure of young children to violent incidents in homes, streets, and neighborhoods is becoming more common (Groves, Zuckerman, Marans, & Cohen, 1993) and may influence attributions of behavior. If parents encourage children living in dangerous neighborhoods to be hypervigilant about their environment, to expect danger, and to distrust rather than trust people as a matter of course, then social attributions and perceptions of potential danger or hostile intent in the actions of others may not differentiate abused from nonabused children. Further studies using Dodge's methodology should be conducted to explore this idea before it can be concluded that abuse is associated with distorted attributions of intent for children who live in urban disadvantage.

Increasing attention is being paid to the influence of observing violence within the family, which has been associated both with aggression and internalizing behavior problems such as social isolation or depression (Fantuzzo, DePaola, Lambert, Martino, Anderson, & Sutton, 1991; Holden & Ritchie, 1991; Jaffe, Hurley, & Wolfe, 1990). Further work with children who experience daily violence within their communities – but not necessarily within their homes – should clarify whether exposure to daily scenes of aggression has a more powerful impact than being the recipient oneself.

Children who have experienced either verbal or physical abuse are said by mothers to have particularly high levels of aggressive behavior and school problems compared to those without a background of abuse (Jaffe, Wolfe, Wilson, & Zak, 1986; Ney, 1987; Vissing, Straus, Gelles, & Harrop, 1991). It is possible, nevertheless, that behavior ratings obtained from abusive parents may be biased toward describing children in negative terms. One study of families referred to pediatric clinics in a New York hospital showed that although children from families in which maltreatment had occurred had higher rates of general disturbance and poorer academic standing than children from control families, teachers differentiated between nonvictimized children in abusive families and the identified victim but parents did not (Salzinger, Kaplan, Pelcovitz, Samit, & Krieger, 1984). The overall problem ratings on the Conners Teacher Questionnaire were similar for control and nonvictimized children, and they were significantly higher for the victimized group, but maltreating parents rated victimized children and their siblings equivalently on the Child Behavior Checklist. Notwithstanding parental bias, children who had experienced abuse did have significantly more behavior problems, and observational studies (Hoffman-Plotkin & Twentyman, 1984; Kaufman & Cicchetti, 1989) confirm these findings.

Cognitive and language deficits have been noted in abused children (Augoustinos, 1987; Fantuzzo et al., 1991) but not consistently (Alessandri, 1991; Dean et al., 1986). The language measure used to compare groups, the inclusion in many studies of both physical abuse and neglect, or the age of the children may account for these results. Cicchetti (1989) emphasizes the importance of language in social context, proposing that deficits shown by abused children in their ability to use language during conversations illustrates how socioemotional difficulties such as insecure attachment may influence subsequent cognitive development. For example, he and his colleagues found that the communicative quality of maltreated 24-month-olds' speech was related to their attachment classification, securely attached children having more advanced language skills than those who were insecurely attached (Gersten, Coster, Schneider-Rosen, Carlson, & Cicchetti, 1986). Subsequent work by the same authors (Coster, Gersten, Beeghly, & Cicchetti, 1989) with slightly older children demonstrated that maltreated 30 month olds used less complex language than non-maltreated controls. The maltreated sample used more repetitive speech, had fewer descriptive utterances, and asked for less information than the control group. They also used shorter statements and terminated topics after brief exchanges.

Different influences depending on the type of maltreatment are suggested by Allen and Oliver (1982), who found that in comparing abused or neglected four year olds matched for socioeconomic status, those who had experienced neglect had delayed auditory comprehension and verbal ability, whereas physically abused children did not. This is an area of research that could be very informative for those trying to understand the long-term effects of early neglect, and it could aid in the development of appropriate intervention programs.

Adolescence

One of the challenges of late childhood and early adolescence is the development of a more elaborated sense of self. Several specific patterns of disrupted psychosocial development during adolescence have been linked with abuse – in particular, excessive use of controlled substances and alcoholism (Dembo et al., 1987; Dembo et al., 1990); depression (Allen & Tarnowski, 1989; Kazdin, Moser, Colbus, & Bell, 1985); and suicidal behavior (Anderson, 1981; Deykin, Alpert, & McNamara, 1985; Green, 1978). Kazdin et al. (1985) investigated the relationship between depression and abuse in a sample of child psychiatry inpatients, none of whom had been admitted because of abuse. Those who had experienced physical abuse exhibited more symptoms of depression and described lower self-esteem than those who did not have a history of abuse. Allen and Tarnowski (1989) studied children who were identified by child protective services and matched them with controls from the community, and they found similarly that abused children had significantly more depressive symptomatology. Neither of these samples was large, nor were they predominantly from inner-city locations, but it would seem that experiences of abuse are associated with increased vulnerability to depression in adolescence. Strategies designed to improve the peer relationships of abuse victims should take this into account.

Suicidal behavior is associated with marked difficulties in organization and regulation of personality, and it may be a consequence of the effects of early maltreatment on attachment to caregivers (Masten, Best, & Garmezy, 1990). Depressive thoughts about death or suicidal intent are relevant for an understanding of the ways in which early abuse may lead to self-directed aggression; other important factors include the child's gender, style of responding, and the availability of a support structure beyond the abusive family context. Drug abuse may be another facet of self-directed violence, in that it is detrimental to emotional and physical well-being. However, the association between adolescent suicide – or adolescent substance abuse – and abuse in early childhood has not been clearly demonstrated.

It has been proposed frequently that victims of child abuse, both physical and sexual, will go on to commit violent acts themselves, either against peers and victims within society or within their own families (Capell & Heiner, 1990; Garbarino & Gilliam, 1980); this is the so-called cycle of violence. Three decades ago, Curtis (1963) suggested that abused and neglected children would become tomorrow's murderers and violent criminals. Retrospective statistics and clinical studies repeatedly indicate that juvenile delinquents and adult criminals, both male and female, have a much higher rate of reported abuse as children than the general population (Lewis, Lovely, Yeager, & Femina, 1979; Vissing, Straus, Gelles, & Harrop, 1991). Department of Justice statistics released in 1991 revealed that 49% of women convicted of violent crimes say they were sexually or physically assaulted at some time in their lives (Boston Globe, 1991). But many of these reports, based on retrospective data from clinical or criminal samples, have methodological problems (Lane & Davis, 1987). Widom (1989a; 1989b) has carefully analyzed juvenile court cases of abuse and neglect from the late 1960s, looking at them prospectively to compare them with matched controls. The groups did not differ markedly, with 29% of the abused and 21% of the controls having criminal records. Although those who had been abused were more likely to exhibit criminal behavior, levels of violent crime did not significantly differentiate the groups. She emphasizes that the majority (71%) of individuals who had been abused had no criminal record, although of course there may have been many other ways that their behavior was problematic. Using factor analysis to study the family processes and environments of chronically violent delinquents, Fagan and Wexler (1987) found that although family interactions and especially family criminality and violence played an important role in explaining adolescent violence, the school environment and peer delinquency were also important. Although this study was cross-sectional and had no control group, it suggests the importance of using an integrated theory incorporating social context and family processes when attempting to predict the long-term outcome of childhood abuse.

It is possible to say with more confidence that within a group of juvenile offenders or adult criminals, those who have a history of abuse are more likely than nonabused delinquents to commit violent offenses (Tarter, Hegedus, Winsten, & Alterman, 1984). In a longitudinal study conducted in Great Britain, Farrington (1991) demonstrated that violent offending in an inner-city sample was associated both with harsh, authoritarian parenting and with neglect in the form of lack of supervision. Following up men who had been part of a study designed to prevent delinquency among youths living in urban disadvantage in the United States, McCord (1988) reported that those who had been reared by generally aggressive parents – that is, parents who exhibited violence against spouses and other family members – were more likely to commit such serious crimes as burglary, assault, rape, kidnapping, and murder; the men in this group were compared with those whose parents, although not generally aggressive, practiced a style of discipline which was harsh and punitive. This furthers the idea that witnessing violence and being the victim may have differing effects. Those who witness violence may express it themselves, but victims are more likely to suffer in their self-image and experience depression, social isolation, and other internalizing problems.

Parenthood

Parents who are abusive to their children, either sexually or physically, may themselves have been abused as children (Ney, 1989; Oliver, 1988; Zeanah & Zeanah, 1989). While it could seem logical to explain their behavior as adults by looking back to their experiences as children, there are many aspects of their life experiences that also should be taken into account; such factors as racial discrimination, extreme poverty, malnutrition, or inadequate health care and education could be associated with their current parenting problems. Additionally, the intergenerational link between abused and abuser has not been thoroughly studied within the context of urban poverty.

It cannot be doubted that experiences of abuse, neglect, or sexual victimization will influence individual development, but targeting preventive services to those individuals who were themselves exposed to abuse will be beneficial only if current circumstances and individual resilience are taken into account. Otherwise, parents who are coping well may be labeled as high-risk. Early adverse experiences may in some cases strengthen parenting skills. Some victims of abuse may be able to build on that disadvantage and work toward being better parents themselves, although less resilient; or more damaged men and women, and especially those living in situations of unending stress and poverty, may perpetuate the pattern, particularly in a society such as the United States, in which corporal punishment and aggressive ways of responding to stress are widely condoned.

Treatment and Preventive Interventions

Treatment for or prevention of child abuse is of great relevance to those interested in reducing aggression and violence in urban centers. If it can be shown that some treatments are more effective than others, the cycle of aggression may be broken. One major problem in addressing the literature on the treatment of child abuse is that close attention to rigorous methodological evaluations of treatments is exceptional (Pecora, Fraser, & Haapala, 1992). Opinions vary about the importance of evaluation. Schorr and Both (1991) suggest that the pursuit of elegant methodology has been detrimental to intervention programs for the disadvantaged; and that although depleted communities require comprehensive, multifaceted strategies in order to help youngsters move out of poverty and despair, evaluators prefer to design programs with one or two specific outcomes (in the interests of science). Others (Garbarino, 1986; McGuire & Earls, 1991) emphasize the importance of conducting rigorously designed and carefully planned evaluations, and of moving beyond comprehensive demonstration programs to more focused intervention strategies. Without careful evaluation, there is no good reason to believe that one program is more effective than another – or better than none.

There are several levels at which service agencies can intercede in cases of child abuse, ranging from treatment to secondary or primary prevention. Within the domain of treatment, responses can vary from providing support and guidance, through mandated educational activities, up to removal of children from their homes, usually to foster placement. Prevention programs such as intensive home visiting can be provided for parents thought to be at greatest risk of abusing their children – or for a whole community without pinpointing specific families. The previous review of risk factors demonstrates some of the problems in identifying at-risk parents. Defining at-risk communities may be more effective, and recent work has shown that this is possible (Garbarino & Kostelny, 1992).

During recent years, the relative effectiveness of intensive treatment, such as removal of the child from the family and prosecution of the abusive parent, has been weighed against supportive strategies. A concerted effort was made during the 1970s to improve the child protection systems, resulting in passage of the Child Welfare and Adoption Assistance Act (PL 96–272) in 1980. The effort succeeded in reducing the number of children in out-of-home care from 502,000 in 1977 to 275,000 in 1983. This dramatic decline was offset by a subsequent, equally rapid increase so that by 1989, the number of children in out-of-home care had climbed to 340,000 – and it is projected to reach over 550,000 by 1995. Although evidence is not available to support the conjecture, it is expected that the increased rate is largely due to children from central city areas. The increase in the number of drug-exposed and HIV-infected infants, a continuing increase in the number of single-parent families, and the growing poverty in this segment of American society make this a sound deduction. As we have already mentioned, foster placement of disturbed, developmentally delayed children may lead to additional abuse rather than to a beneficial outcome, giving more weight to the idea that abusing families may be more effectively helped by intensive in-home intervention than by placing the children in foster care. Information on the effectiveness of foster placement is equivocal. Fanshel, Finch, and Grundy (1989), describing a follow-up of children placed in foster care in New York and six western states, reported that those who remained in care did as well as those returned to their homes. They did, however, also point out that children from ethnic minorities, who were living in impoverished and chaotic circumstances, showed gains in foster care. More longitudinal studies are needed to determine whether placement experiences moderate the consequences of early victimization or exacerbate them, as well as how these processes influence adult violent behavior.

The National Commission on Children (1991) provides an informative review of the policies that have been in place since PL 96–272 was adopted. Although a huge increase in federal funding for child welfare services has occurred over the past decade – from $536 million in 1981 to $2.5 billion in 1992 – the federal strategy has shown a clear preference for out-of-home placements. It is estimated that 15% of the victims of maltreatment are placed in an unrelated foster home (American Humane Association, 1981;

Runyan, Gould, Trost, & Loda, 1981). However, it would be more consistent with a preventive public health model to direct more funding to the evaluation of strategies to prevent child abuse – that is, to the evaluation of those strategies that direct services to entire communities and as a consequence support and strengthen families. Such an approach would not target vulnerable families but would begin by identifying communities that are at the highest risk. A prevention program that is designed at the community level will be described in the next section along with ways in which the public health approach can be used to evaluate its effectiveness, but first some secondary interventions and treatments will be discussed.

There has been a major emphasis by service providers on refocusing resources to deal more comprehensively with the context in which families live. Schorr (1988) describes one new direction of policy: strengthening families by providing the social support and guidance that was traditionally gained from intergenerational family networks and neighbors but that is not available in the fragmented and impoverished circumstances of many urban environments today. Even when nuclear families were in the majority, extended families tended to be more successful (Sennett, 1970/1984). Schorr describes one model, "Homebuilders" (Kinney, Haapala, Booth, & Leavitt, 1990; Kinney, Madsen, Fleming, & Haapala, 1977), a treatment program that aims to reduce the number of children who have to be placed outside their families consequent to abuse or neglect. Homebuilders falls midway between a traditional caseworker treatment/foster placement model and community-based primary prevention through family support. Its originators, based in Tacoma, Washington (Kinney, Haapala, Booth, & Leavitt, 1990; Kinney, Masden, Fleming, & Haapala, 1977), believe that removal to a foster placement, group care, or a residential setting represents a bleak future replete with further disruptions and multiple placements (Schorr, 1988). Instead, Homebuilders offers intensive, home-based, 24 hour support, with an emphasis on tailoring services to each family for a short duration (4–6 weeks) and with a concentration on strengthening parenting skills without punitive and criminal sanctions.

Much of Schorr's enthusiasm for Homebuilders is based on anecdotal reports, and the strategy has apparently been successfully reproduced in the Bronx, New York, under conditions different from those found in urban areas of the state of Washington. Pecora, Fraser, and Haapala (1992) describe an attempt to quantify the effectiveness of the program using a "quasi-experimental design (one group pretest–posttest) with a partial 12-month follow-up period" (pp. 179–80), one which collected data from four sites in Washington and two in Utah. Unfortunately, the only outcome described is success/failure, success being defined as preventing the child from being placed outside the home with a nonrelative. Other measures of family functioning were collected but have not as yet been reported.

An example of a second level, proactive prevention strategy for a high-risk group was designed and evaluated by Olds (Olds & Henderson, 1989; Olds, Henderson, Chamberlin & Tatelbaum, 1986). This program is worthy of note because it was evaluated by a randomized clinical trial, and it was shown to reduce rates of reportable child abuse. Those targeted for service were primiparous, young, usually single, with low income, but to avoid stigmatizing the program as exclusively for the poor, the study design allowed for inclusion of any woman who asked to participate and who was expecting her first child. After enrollment in the study, women were randomly assigned to one of four groups. Two control conditions were established in order to separate the possible effects of treatment from those of clinic attendance: no services beyond assessments of the infants at one and two years, and assessments plus free transportation to regular prenatal and well-child clinics. In the third condition, a home health visitor was assigned during pregnancy and visited, on average, nine times, approximately every two weeks until the birth. For the fourth condition the same treatment as group three was given, but nurses continued to visit weekly for 6 weeks; from 6 weeks to 4 months every 2 weeks; from 4 to 14 months every 3 weeks; from 14 to 20 months every 4 weeks; and from 20 to 24 months every 6 weeks. Both treatment groups also received free transportation to all clinic visits. It was demonstrated that those mothers receiving the total service played more adequately with their infants, punished them more appropriately, had significantly fewer cases of abuse or neglect, and visited hospital emergency rooms (for poisoning and other accidents) less often. The effects were most marked for young women who had described feeling little control over their lives, suggesting that they had been helped to gain some feelings of competence.

This appears to be a successful technique for first-time parents with infants, and similarly designed studies are needed to evaluate the utility of strategies tailored to parents of older children or to those with large families. Given that abuse can have a major impact on development throughout childhood and into adulthood, it would be useful to examine the utility of this strategy with other age groups and in urban contexts. A British study designed to reduce child behavioral problems of preschool age children based in Leeds, a city in the north of England, found that supportive home visiting and family therapy within the home were less successful than providing services such as play groups and discussion sessions outside the home (Nicol, Stretch, Davidson, & Fundudis, 1984).

The preceding review indicates that there are many potential risk factors for abuse, and effective prevention needs to be planned with both a thorough knowledge of risk and an understanding of how the wider ecological context can interact with specific risk factors (Olds & Kitzman, 1990). Schorr (1988) argues that high-risk families living in urban decay need comprehensive and intensive services, but there has also been a move to direct the focus of assistance away from the family and toward the entire community, taking an ecological approach to risk (Bronfenbrenner, 1987). The Family Support Movement (Kagan, Powell, Weissbourd, & Zigler, 1987; Weissbourd & Kagan, 1989; Zigler & Black, 1989) combines the understanding that the family influences the capacity of individuals of all ages to learn and succeed with the knowledge that families have vulnerabilities that are inextricably bound up in their environmental context. Social support is seen as key to enhancing child health and development and to preventing various family dysfunctions such as abuse and neglect (Weiss, 1989). There are limitations to any prevention based exclusively on social support, since social isolation, identified as a risk for abuse, entails deficiencies in the parent's abilities to form relationships (Olds & Henderson, 1989).

Much of the interest in family support derives from programs that were not designed to influence child abuse but were akin to Head Start programs; the focus of such programs was on enhancing preschool children's intellectual, emotional, and physical development through a range of services including educational group activities, parent education, healthful meals, and behavioral strategies to modify behavior problems (Seitz, Rosenbaum, & Apfel, 1985). There are, however, some community-based strategies that are designed to influence levels of child abuse and the overall level of violence within urban communities. Belsky (1980) advanced the ecological framework of Bronfenbrenner (1979) to encompass the multiple interacting levels of risk (individual, family, the immediate social environment, the broader cultural context) that are required both to improve understanding of the causes of child abuse and neglect and to design effective interventions. Garbarino and colleagues (Garbarino, 1981; Garbarino & Kostelny, 1992; Garbarino & Sherman, 1980) have followed a similar line of reasoning, and Shay (1980) has described a strategy for organizing communities to deal with child abuse prevention. Despite the widespread appeal for using this model to guide research and practice, there have been surprisingly few well-documented efforts (Barry, 1992). In accordance with public health methodology, we propose that community- or neighborhood-level interventions may be the most appropriate for ameliorating child maltreatment in situations of urban poverty and social decay.

In the next section we describe a neighborhood program of this nature and methods to evaluate its effectiveness derived from public health strategies. It is of interest to note that neither process nor outcome evaluations have received the attention that they merit and that policy decisions may be made without being informed by evaluation results (Garbarino, 1986).

Research Strategy in a Disadvantaged Neighborhood

The Neighborhood

From 1950 to the present, the neighborhood of North Dorchester in Boston has been a prime exemplar of urban change; it has been marked by out-migration of lower- and middle-class white families and in-migration of poor black and Hispanic families, combined with a steady decline in the overall population. From the turn of the century to the 1960s, it was an area composed almost exclusively of white families. Since then, it has changed to become one that in 1990 was predominantly black, with a smaller Hispanic population and a few white residents. For instance, one of the five census tracts in which we work had a population in 1970 that was 7.8% black and 91.6% white, but by 1990 it had changed to 61% black and 14.3% white, with 21.5% of the families Hispanic. Another tract changed from having a population in which 99% were white in 1960 to one in which 3.4% were white in 1990 (U.S. Bureau of Census, 1950 to 1990). In just the three years after the most recent census was taken, more changes in the composition of the neighborhoods occurred. New immigrants from Southeast Asia arrived, settled in block areas, and established a presence.

At the same time that changes in ethnic composition were taking place, the total population of the area became smaller. In one of the five census tracts, the population went from 5,719 in 1950 to 3,648 in 1990, with a reduction of almost 50% in the number of families (from 1,475 in 1950 to 759 in 1990). The last decade shows evidence of a decline in the number of families with children. In 1980, families with a child under 18 represented 69% of all families; 34% of families in the census tract were officially classified as living in poverty; the proportion of residents under the age of 18 was 45%; and more than half (51%) of households with children under 18 were headed by a single parent. By 1990, households with children represented a smaller number (59%) of all households; the proportion of residents under the age of 18 was lower (36%); and more families with a child under 18 were headed by a single parent (60%).

The relative income of residents dropped gradually beginning in 1960; by 1980 residents of these census tracts on average earned about half the mean for the Standard Metropolitan Statistical Area. The decline in the proportion of families with children, combined with an overall decline in the population, suggest that the area is increasingly perceived as an undesirable place of residence, particularly for childrearing. One can easily imagine the accompanying decline in services, such as the absence of banks, restaurants, health clinics, shops, and other amenities, along with the deterioration of housing and concomitant increase in vacant lots, during that 20 year period.

The neighborhood contains sharp contrasts. At one end, elegant Victorian villas border a large green open space; several well-attended churches and an historic school stand on a hill; and trees provide shade for the children who play on the grass. Within two or three blocks, one can find a shopping street with vacant, boarded-up buildings, litter-filled gutters, and a vacant lot containing discarded furniture and bits of wood or metal which provide a space during the day for the many homeless individuals in the community and at night for the large number of youths who roam the neighborhood aimlessly. Street violence pervades the area. A brick wall still shows the chalk circle, made by police, identifying the end point of a bullet that recently killed a young man in a random, drive-by shooting. Children in the day-care center across the street regularly have to move away from the windows of their classroom at the sound of gunshots. All types of crime, violent and not, have risen dramatically in the past two decades.

The Prevention Initiative

The National Center on Child Abuse and Neglect is supporting a small number of community-based child abuse prevention initiatives, one of which is located in North Dorchester. Begun in 1990, its aim is to change the neighborhood rather than just place services within the community as some community programs have done (Barry, 1992). The program aims to bring together community organizations and residents to promote healthy family relationships and to give parents the support, education, and resources that they need. To accomplish this goal, an interagency continuum of family strengthening services is provided, ranging from those that can be seen as primary prevention (food pantry, clothing, home health visiting) through a secondary level (family nurturing program, family literacy, respite care) and finally to tertiary treatment (Department of Social Services referrals). The neighborhood-based multiservice center functions like a settlement house on one of the main thoroughfares of the neighborhood. The target area, initially one census tract, now includes four adjacent census tracts encompassing a population of about 15,000 residents. Since its inception, approximately 150 to 200 families have used the food pantry each week; on any single day, up to 60 residents attend English-as-a-second-language classes; more than 40 young mothers have received supportive home health visiting during the first two years of their child's life; approximately 40 parents and their 75 children have attended intensive 15-week workshops directed at improving parent–child relations; and a similar number of professionals from local agencies have attended the workshops to become trained group leaders themselves.

The Evaluation

The design of our evaluation aims to capture the degree to which the beneficial effects of the intervention actually permeate the neighborhood over time. The central hypothesis is that increased social organization in the neighborhood, brought about as a result of the intervention, will help reduce family violence, leading to a measurable reduction in harsh, punitive, and violent interactions with children. Much of our thinking about neighborhoods has been influenced by Sampson (1992; and this volume), whose theoretical work indicates that increases in social organization – growth in informal social networks and an increase in social capital – will yield a decrease in violence, including child abuse.

Our three-strategy approach includes community surveillance in the form of the monitoring of available population indicators as a means of tracking changes in the neighborhood (e.g., health indicators, crime rates, school achievement, reported cases of child maltreatment); repeated cross-sectional surveys of neighborhood families to assess the risk factors for child maltreatment; and a detailed study of parents who participate in the family nurturing programs.

Community Surveillance of Population Indicators. We have been developing ways to use population indicators to monitor the neighborhood characteristics and to distinguish variation at the census-tract level in statistics that are more often aggregated into larger districts. Health indicators such as infant mortality (18.3 per 1,000 births, from 1984–88 surveys of the Boston Department of Health and Hospitals [1992]) and low birth weight (13.4% of all newborns, from 1987–89 surveys of the Massachusetts Department of Public Health [1990]) demonstrate the vulnerability of families with young children in the neighborhood. Mapping at the census-tract level can demonstrate variations within areas that may otherwise be perceived as globally disadvantaged. For instance, nine adjacent census tracts in North Dorchester have low birth-weight rates that range from 6.4 per 1,000 births to 14.1. Similar information is being collated on crime and child abuse per census tract rather than on the larger units which most administrative systems use. The rate of violent crime in one of the five target census tracts was 1,544 per 100,000 in 1975, nearly doubling to 2,714 per 100,000 in 1991. Superimposing statistics of risk indicators underscores ways in which some neighborhoods experience multiple risks. The distribution of homicides in Boston for 1990 shows that 80% took place in or around the neighborhoods surrounding and including the target area. The close juxtaposition of the pattern of infant deaths in Boston with that of homicides illustrates how closely associated both are with deprivation and urban poverty (see Sampson in this volume).

Several aspects of our current work will be enhanced over the near term. We are interested in refining our capacity to map the geographic and demographic characteristics of the area using computer technology. One of the major difficulties with organizing statistics from different sources by geographical areas such as census tracts is the different operational definitions of neighborhoods by criminal justice, health, education, and social service organizations. A central focus of our present work is to establish common databases which enable us to accurately link child abuse reports with the other kinds of information about neighborhoods, particularly with other forms of violence. Most of the data collected so far have been from census documents and the police department.

Cross-Sectional Surveys. Random household surveys provide the opportunity to study change at the family level, but in a way that reflects those neighborhood characteristics which are expected to be modified by the presence of the intervention program. Households were selected by random sampling. Then the primary caretaker of young children within the home was interviewed about the ways that parents and other caregivers manage children; about perceptions of the neighborhood, including problems such as crime, danger, and disorder; about social networks within the community; about ways in which the neighborhood influences parenting; about feelings of personal efficacy; and about the mental or physical health problems of the parents. The interview used a combination of several existing questionnaires and some open-ended questions (see Earls, McGuire, & Shay, 1994 for full details of the methodology).

The responses to questions about the neighborhood reflect a picture similar to that obtained from the census data insofar as individuals did not express strong identification with the neighborhood and many seemed disinclined to stay. Only a small proportion (14%) assigned a name to the neighborhood; over half (64%) described their neighborhood as 10 blocks or less; and about half (51%) expected to stay in the neighborhood for less than three years.

Residents appeared to feel vulnerable within their neighborhood. Only about a third (32%) felt comfortable more than four blocks from home, and the majority (86%) said that it was risky to go out at night. Most (83%) were also personally afraid. Many kinds of violent incidents were believed to occur in the area. Most commonly mentioned were fights with weapons (58%), youth gang disturbances (42%), incidents where someone was wounded (38%), and arguments between neighbors (26%). Excessive public drinking, home burglaries, unemployed men hanging about in the street, the presence of drug addicts, and muggings or assaults were also said to be common in the neighborhood, suggesting a high level of social disorganization. When asked how the neighborhood differed from that of their own childhood, respondents most often mentioned dangers in the environment (22/71, 31%); next they cited higher levels of child misbehavior (20/71, 28%) and loss of adult authority (8/71, 11%).

Perceptions of danger within the neighborhood were significantly associated with ratings of the quality of the area as a place to live and raise children ($r = .64$, $p < .0001$) as well as a place that fostered a sense of belonging to the neighborhood ($r = .55$, $p < .0001$). Those parents who described more dangers in the neighborhood were more likely to employ parent-centered discipline methods ($r = .24$, $p < .05$) and more use of verbal aggression when disciplining ($r = .25$, $p < .05$). Nonetheless, perception of danger was not found to be associated with more use of physical violence in disciplining children.

It has been suggested that parents within dangerous urban neighborhoods use physical control to ensure their children's safety (Ogbu, 1985). We have found that methods of discipline are associated with the parents' place of birth, suggesting that Ogbu's hypothesis needs to be examined in relation not only to the level of danger but also the background of the families, their own childhood experiences, and their cultural values. Specifically, those born in Cape Verde reported much less verbal and physical violence than the other groups (Earls et al., 1994).

The survey data complement the aggregate sources of information derived from census level statistics by providing a more detailed understanding of how individual families contribute to the picture of change. A new wave of out-migration might occur during the five-year cycle of the ongoing intervention. On the other hand, if the intervention succeeds and existing social networks are enriched and new ones develop, the perception of the neighborhood may improve and out-migration may become viewed as less desirable.

Evaluation of Program Participants. A key component of the services relative to preventing violence is provision of a program designed to help parents avoid abusive discipline: the Nurturing Program for Parents and Children (Bavolek & Bavolek, 1986; Bavolek & Comstock, 1983). Activities focus on remediating four distinct patterns of inappropriate parenting that often lead to aversive interactions: inappropriate parental expectations of the child, lack of empathic awareness of child needs, valuing physical punishment, and parent–child role reversal. Parents may be referred by social service agencies, but the program is offered to anyone within the community who would like to attend. The hope is that some of the community members who are willing to learn can themselves be trained, after participating themselves, to be facilitators in subsequent sessions and role models within the community.

Evaluation of nurturing program participants has not yet taken place but will involve assessments of parenting, parent–child relationships, and organization of the home both pre- and postinvolvement in the program. In addition, ratings of participants' behavior during the groups (such as enthusiasm and level of active participation, regularity of attendance, behavior toward other group members) will be incorporated so that specific feedback can be given to the Nurturing Program group leaders to facilitate participation and learning. The interviews with program participants will follow a methodology similar to those used in community surveys in order to ensure that survey participants can be used as a random control group. We would expect the responses postparticipation to demonstrate less use of physical discipline, less hostility toward and criticism of children, and more social support than community controls.

Future Directions

Community-based intervention is broadly supported by both public health and social welfare constituencies as a major strategy in strengthening families and communities. The research methods employed in the first step of this long-term evaluation project indicate that systematic approaches to data collection using standardized instruments where feasible are important. By monitoring population indicators of change, the data collected in the repeated household surveys will permit more accurate and complete understanding of the effects of the intervention and the mechanisms of change as they apply at the neighborhood level. In using serial maps to depict neighborhood changes, we must remember that it is important to include some indicators which reflect contemporaneous events (e.g., 911 calls) and not just the more static measures which are accumulated over longer intervals.

At the same time that we are assessing impact of the intervention, we are monitoring the evolving nature of the intervention itself. The extent to which the intervention achieves its child-centered objectives and is responsive to the complex mosaic of ethnic groups making up the population would appear to be the cardinal ingredients of success from our current vantage.

It seems unlikely that interventions targeting high-risk individuals but disregarding the influence of neighborhood or wider community context will be successful in reducing the rate of child abuse. No doubt both approaches have a place, but in designing a comprehensive and multifaceted intervention strategy, it is essential, from our perspective, to ensure that changing the neighborhood context be the leading edge.

Conclusions

Poverty and social disadvantage, both characteristic of many urban neighborhoods, are contexts in which many human functions are compromised, including the rearing of children. The perspective that we advance is one which shifts the focus from individual abuser to the habitability of such environments. The intervention evolving from this standpoint is one that seeks ultimately to facilitate a process of community transformation and, through it, an enhancement of the social competence of its members. This, of course, will require long-term preventive strategies and an enduring commitment on the part of government to improve the quality of urban life. The more immediate goal for interventions in neighborhoods of the type in which we work is to help stabilize the resident population and strengthen families. If successful, this should lead to improved social organization. To what extent the dynamic ethnic composition of these neighborhoods, high unemployment rate, particularly among older males, and poverty undermine such potential remains to be seen. A primary purpose of public health science is to evaluate intervention strategies of the type that we have described in this chapter.

As an indication of where we currently are in the effort to understand and control child abuse and neglect, consider the absence of any good estimates of its true prevalence. We do not know if it is decreasing or increasing in the general population – let alone in high-risk groups such as disadvantaged urban dwellers. For this reason we are not in a position to figure the extent to which the various risk factors are associated with child abuse. Epidemiologists use the term "attributable risk" for this purpose – that is, the extent to which elimination of a specific risk factor is expected to decrease the incidence or prevalence of a condition. As this relatively new interest in public health matures, it is hoped that in the near future we will find ourselves with much more evidence – and of a higher quality – than presently exists to illuminate the problem of child abuse and neglect, and it is hoped that such evidence can confidently be used to suggest ways to control the problem.

REFERENCES

Ainsworth, M. D. S., Blehar, M. C., Waters, E., & Wall, S. (1978). *Patterns of Attachment: a Psychological Study of the Strange Situation.* Hillsdale, N.J.: Erlbaum.

Alessandri, S. M. (1991). Play and social behavior in maltreated preschoolers. *Development and Psychopathology* 3, 191–205.

Allen, D. M., & Tarnowski, K. J. (1989). Depressive characteristics of physically abused children. *Journal of Abnormal Child Psychology* 17 (1), 1–11.

Allen, R., & Oliver, J. M. (1982). The effects of child maltreatment on language development. *Child Abuse and Neglect* 6 (3), 299–305.

American Humane Association. (1981). *National Analysis of Child Neglect and Abuse Reporting,* 1979. Englewood, Colorado: American Humane Association.

Ammerman, R. T. (1991). The role of the child in physical abuse: A reappraisal. *Violence and Victims* 6, 2, 87–101.

Ammerman, R. T., Cassisi, J. E., Hersen, M., & Van Hasselt, V. B. (1986). Consequences of physical abuse and neglect in children. *Clinical Psychology Review,* 6 (4), 291–310.

Anderson, L. S. (1981). Notes on the linkage between the sexually a-bused child and the suicidal adolescent. *Journal of Adolescence* 4 (2), 157–62.

Augoustinos, M. (1987). Developmental effects of child abuse: Recent findings. *Child Abuse and Neglect* 11 (1), 15–27.

Barahal, R. M., Waterman, J., & Martin, H. P. (1981). The social cognitive development of abused children. *Journal of Consulting and Clinical Psychology* 49 (4), 508–16.

Barry, F. (1992). *Neighborhood based approach – what is it?* Background paper for the U.S. Advisory Board on Child Abuse and Neglect. Ithaca, NY: Cornell University, Family Life Development Center.

Bassuk, E. L., & Rosenberg, L. (1988). Why does family homelessness occur? A case-control study. *American Journal of Public Health* 78 (7), 783–8.

Bavolek, S. J., & Bavolek, J. D. (1986). Increasing the nurturing parenting skills of families in Head Start. Research Report, University of Utah, College of Health.

Bavolek, S. J., & Comstock, C. (1983). An innovative program for reducing abusive parent-child interactions. *Child Resource World Review* 2, 6–24.

Beitchman, J. H., Zucker, K. J., Hood, J. E., daCosta, G. A., & Akman, D. (1991). A review of the short-term effects of childhood sexual abuse. *Child Abuse and Neglect* 15, 537–56.

Beitchman, J. H., Zucker, K. J., Hood, J. E., daCosta, G. A., Akman, D., & Cassavia, E. (1992). A review of the long-term effects of child sexual abuse. *Child Abuse and Neglect* 16, 101–18.

Belsky, J. (1980). Child maltreatment: An ecological integration. *American Psychologist* 35 (4), 320–35.

Boston Department of Health and Hospitals (1992). *Health perspectives. Boston and its neighborhoods. A summary of health statistics for Boston, 1988.* Boston: Office of Health and Vital Statistics.

Boston Globe. (1991). Women in prison report past abuse. April 6, p. 5.

Bronfenbrenner, U. (1979). *The ecology of human development.* Cambridge, MA: Harvard University Press.

——— (1987). Foreword. Family support: The quiet revolution. In Kagan, S. L., Powell, D. R., Weissbourd, B., & Zigler, E. F., (Eds.), *America's family support programs.* New Haven, CT: Yale University Press, pp. vi–ix.

Browne, A., & Finkelhor, D. (1986). Impact of sexual abuse: A review of the research. *Psychological Bulletin* 99 (1), 66–77.

Camras, L. A., Ribordy, S., Hill, J., Martino, S., Spaccarelli, S., & Stefani, R. (1988). Recognition and posing of emotional expressions by abused children and their mothers. *Developmental Psychology* 24, 6, 776–81.

Cappell, C., & Heiner, R. B. (1990). The intergenerational transmission of family aggression. *Journal of Family Violence* 5 (2), 135–52.

Carlson, V., Cicchetti, D., Barnett, D., & Braunwald, K. (1989). Disorganized/

disoriented attachment relationships in maltreated infants. *Developmental Psychology* 25, 4, 525–31.

Cassidy, J., & Marvin, R., in collaboration with the MacArthur Working Group on Attachment (1991). *Attachment organization in three- and four-year-olds: Coding guidelines.* Unpublished manuscript, Pennsylvania State University.

Cataldo, M. F., Dershewitz, R. A., Wilson, M., Cristophersen, E. R., Finney, J. W., Fawcett, S. B., & Seekins, T. (1986). Childhood injury control. In N. A. Krasegor, J. D. Arasteh, & M. F. Cataldo (Eds.), *Child health behavior. A behavioral pediatrics perspective.* New York: Wiley, pp. 153–75.

Children's Defense Fund (1991). *The nation's investment in children. An analysis of the President's FY 1992 Budget Proposals.* Washington, D.C.: Children's Defense Fund.

Cicchetti, D. (1989). How research on child maltreatment has informed the study of child development: Perspectives from developmental psychopathology. In D. Cicchetti & V. Carlson (Eds.), *Child maltreatment. Theory and research on the causes and consequences of child abuse and neglect.* New York: Cambridge University Press, pp. 377–431.

—— (1991). Defining psychological maltreatment: Reflections and future directions. *Development and Psychopathology* 3 (1), 1–2.

Cicchetti, D., & Barnett, D. (1991). Attachment organization in maltreated preschoolers. *Development and Psychopathology* 3 (4), 397–411.

Cicchetti, D., & Schneider-Rosen, K. (1986). An organizational approach to childhood depression. In M. Rutter, C. Izard, & P. Read (Eds.), *Depression in young people: Clinical and developmental perspectives.* New York: Guilford Press, pp. 71–134.

Cohen, C. I., & Adler, A. (1986). Assessing the role of social network interventions with an inner-city population. *American Journal of Orthopsychiatry* 56 (2), 278–88.

Conaway, L. P., & Hansen, D. J. (1989). Social behavior of physically abused and neglected children: A critical review. *Clinical Psychology Review* 9 (5), 627–52.

Coster, W. J., Gersten, M. S., Beeghly, M., & Cicchetti, D. (1989). Communicative function in maltreated toddlers. *Developmental Psychology* 25 (6), 1020–29.

Crittenden, P. M. (1985). Maltreated infants: Vulnerability and resilience. *Journal of Child Psychology and Psychiatry and Allied Disciplines* 26 (1), 85–96.

Curtis, G. C. (1963). Violence breeds violence – perhaps? *American Journal of Psychiatry* 120, 386–7.

Dean, A. L., Malik, M. M., Richards, W., & Stringer, S. A. (1986). Effects of parental maltreatment on children's conceptions of interpersonal relationships. *Developmental Psychology* 22 (5), 617–26.

Dembo, R., Dertke, M., LaVoie, L., Borders, S., Washburn, M., & Schmeidler, J.

(1987). Physical abuse, sexual victimization and illicit drug use: A structural analysis among high risk adolescents. *Journal of Adolescence* 10, 13–33.

Dembo, R., Williams, L., LaVoie, L., Getreu, A., Berry, E., Genung, L., Schmeidler, J., Wish, E., & Kern, J. (1990). A longitudinal study of the relationships among alcohol use, marijuana/hashish use, cocaine use, and emotional/psychological functioning problems in a cohort of high-risk youths. *The International Journal of the Addictions* 25 (11), 1341–82.

Deykin, E. Y., Alpert, J. J., & McNamara, J. J. (1985). A pilot study on the effect of exposure to child abuse or neglect on adolescent suicidal behavior. *American Journal of Psychiatry* 142 (11), 1299–1303.

Diamond, L. J., & Jaudes, P. K. (1983). Child abuse in cerebral-palsied population. *Developmental Medicine* 25 (2), 169–74.

Dodge, K. A., Bates, J. E., & Pettit, G. S. (1990). Mechanisms in the cycle of violence. *Science* 250, 1678–83.

Dubowitz, H., Black, M., Starr, R., & Zuravin, S. (1993). A conceptual definition of child neglect. *Criminal Justice and Behavior* 20 (1), 8–26.

Dugger, C. W. (1992a). Shattered lives: When foster care fails. I. Troubled children flood ill-prepared care system. *New York Times*, Sept. 8.

(1992b). Shattered lives: When foster care fails. II. Fatal beating points up a system in crisis. *New York Times*, Sept. 9.

(1992c). Shattered lives: When foster care fails. III. A boy back from the brink: When love and care prevail. *New York Times*, Sept. 10.

Dunst, C. J., Trivette, C. M., & Cross, A. H. (1986). Mediating influences of social support: Personal, family, and child outcomes. *American Journal of Mental Deficiency* 90;4, 403–17.

Earls, F. (1991). A developmental approach to understanding and controlling violence. In H. E. Fitzgerald (Ed.), *Theory and Research in Behavioral Pediatrics Vol. 5.* New York: Plenum Press, pp. 61–88.

Earls, F., McGuire, J., & Shay, S. (1994). Evaluating a community intervention to reduce the risk of child abuse. Methodological strategies in conducting neighborhood surveys. *Child Abuse and Neglect* 18(5), 473–85.

Egeland, B., & Sroufe, L. A. (1981). Attachment and early maltreatment. *Child Development* 52, 44–52.

Faber, M. M. (1986). A review of efforts to protect children from injury in car crashes. *Personality and Individual Differences* 9, 25–41.

Fagan, J., & Wexler, S. (1987). Family origins of violent delinquents. *Criminology* 25 (3), 643–69.

Famularo, R., Stone, K., Barnum, R., & Wharton, R. (1986). Alcoholism and severe child maltreatment. *American Journal of Orthopsychiatry* 56 (3), 481–5.

Fanshel, D., Finch, S. J., & Grundy, J. F. (1989). Foster children in life-course perspective: The Casey Family Program experience. *Child Welfare* 68 (5), 467–78.

(1992). Serving the urban poor: A study of child welfare preventive services. *Child Welfare* 71 (3), 197–211.

Fantuzzo, J. W., DePaola, L. M., Lambert, L., Martino, T., Anderson, G., & Sutton, S. (1991). Effects of interparental violence on the psychological adjustment and competencies of young children. *Journal of Consulting and Clinical Psychology* 59, 258–65.

Farrington, D. P. (1991). Childhood aggression and adult violence: Early precursors and later-life outcomes. In D. J. Pepler & K. H. Rubin (Eds.), *The development and treatment of childhood aggression.* Hillsdale, NJ: Erlbaum, pp. 5–29.

Fink, A., Yano, E., & Goya, D. (1992). Review: Prenatal programs: What the literature reveals. *Obstetrics and Gynecology* 80 (5), 867–72.

Garbarino, J. (1977). The human ecology of child maltreatment: A conceptual model for research. *Journal of Marriage and the Family* 39, 721–36.

(1981). An ecological approach to child maltreatment. In L. H. Polton (Ed.), *The social context of child abuse and neglect.* New York: Human Sciences Press, pp. 228–67.

(1986). Can we measure success in preventing child abuse? Issues in policy, programming and research. *Child Abuse and Neglect* 10, 143–56.

Garbarino, J., & Gilliam, G. (1980). *Understanding Abusive Families.* Lexington, MA: Lexington Books.

Garbarino, J., & Kostelny, K. (1992). Child maltreatment as a community problem. *Child Abuse and Neglect* 16, 455–64.

Garbarino, J., & Sherman, D. (1980). High-risk neighborhoods and high-risk families: The human ecology of child maltreatment . *Child Development* 51, 188–98.

Gaudin, J. M., & Pollane, L. (1983). Social networks, stress and child abuse. *Children and Youth Services Review* 5 (1), 91–102.

Gelles, R. J. (1987). The family and its role in the abuse of children. *Psychiatric Annals* 17 (4), 229–32.

(1989). Child abuse and violence in single-parent families: Parent absence and economic deprivation. *American Journal of Orthopsychiatry* 59 (4), 492–501.

George, C., & Main, M. (1979). Social interactions of young abused children: Approach, avoidance, and aggression. *Child Development* 50 (2), 306–18.

Gersten, M., Coster, W., Schneider-Rosen, K., Carlson, V., & Cicchetti, D. (1986). The socio-emotional bases of communicative functioning: Quality of attachment, language development, and early maltreatment. In M. E. Lamb, A. L. Brown, & B. Rogoff (Eds.), *Advances in Developmental Psychology, Vol. 4.* Hillsdale, NJ: Erlbaum, pp. 105–51.

Goodman, L. A. (1991). The prevalence of abuse among homeless and housed poor mothers: A comparison study. *American Journal of Orthopsychiatry* 61 (4), 489–500.

Graham, P., Dingwall, R., & Wolkind, S. (1985). Research issues in child abuse. *Society for Scientific Medicine* 21 (11), 1217–28.

Graziano, A. M., Lindquist, C. M., Kunce, L. J., & Munjal, K. (1992). Physical punishment in childhood and current attitudes: An exploratory comparison of college students in the United States and India. *Journal of Interpersonal Violence* 7 (2), 147–55.

Green, A. H. (1978). Self-destructive behavior in battered children. *American Journal of Psychiatry* 135 (5), 579–82.

Groves, B. M., Zuckerman, B., Marans, S., & Cohen, D. J. (1993). Silent victims: Children who witness violence. *Journal of the American Medical Association* 269 (2), 262–4.

Hampton, R. L. (1987). Race, class and child maltreatment. *Journal of Comparative Family Studies* 18 (1), 113–26.

Hampton, R. L., & Newberger, E. H. (1985). Child abuse incidence and reporting by hospitals: Significance of severity, class, and race. *American Journal of Public Health* 75;1, 56–60.

Heilig, E. D. (1987). A review of the research on the relationship between child abuse and neglect and cognitive development and scholastic achievement. *Graduate Research in Urban Education and Related Disciplines* 18 (1–2), 34–52.

Hoffman-Plotkin, D., & Twentyman, C. T. (1984). A multimodal assessment of behavioral and cognitive deficits in abused and neglected preschoolers. *Child Development* 55, 794–802.

Holden, G. W., & Ritchie, K. L. (1991). Linking extreme marital discord, child rearing, and child behavior problems: Evidence from battered women. *Child Development* 62, 311–27.

Houck, G. M., & King, M. C. (1989). Child maltreatment: Family characteristics and developmental consequences. Special Issue: Family violence. *Issues in Mental Health Nursing* 10 (3–4), 193–208.

Howes, C., & Eldredge, R. (1985). Responses of abused, neglected, and nonmaltreated children to the behaviors of their peers. *Journal of Applied Developmental Psychology* 6 (2–3), 261–70.

Jacobson, R. S., & Straker, G. (1982). Peer group interaction of physically abused children. *Child Abuse and Neglect* 6 (3), 321–7.

Jaffe, P., Hurley, D. J., & Wolfe, D. (1990). Childrens' observations of violence: Critical issues in child development and intervention planning. *Canadian Journal of Psychiatry* 35 (6), 466–70.

Jaffe, P., Wolfe, D., Wilson, S., & Zak, L. (1986). Similarities in behavioral and social maladjustment among child victims and witnesses to family violence. *American Journal of Orthopsychiatry* 56 (1), 142–6.

Jason, J. M. (1991). Abuse, neglect, and the HIV-infected child. *Child Abuse & Neglect* 15, supplement 1, 79–88.

Kagan, S. L., Powell, D. R., Weissbourd, B., & Zigler, E. F. (Eds.). (1987). *America's family support programs.* New Haven, CT: Yale University Press.

Kalichman, S. C., & Brosig, C. L. (1992). The effects of statutory requirements on child maltreatment reporting: A comparison of two state laws. *American Journal of Orthopsychiatry* 62, 284–96.

Kaufman, J., & Cicchetti, D. (1989). Effects of maltreatment on school-age children's socioemotional development: Assessments in a day-camp setting. *Developmental Psychology* 25 (4), 516–24.

Kaufman, J., & Zigler, E. (1987). Do abused children become abusive parents? *American Journal of Orthopsychiatry* 57 (2), 186–92.

Kazdin, A. E., Moser, J., Colbus, D., & Bell, R. (1985). Depressive symptoms among physically abused and psychiatrically disturbed children. *Journal of Abnormal Psychology* 94 (3), 298–307.

Kinney, J. M., Haapala, D. A., Booth, C., & Leavitt, S. (1990). The Homebuilders model. In J. K. Whittaker, J. Kinney, E. M. Tracey, & C. Booth (Eds.), *Reaching high-risk families: Intensive family preservation in human services.* New York: Aldine de Gruyter, pp. 31–64.

Kinney, J. M., Madsen, B., Fleming, T., & Haapala, D. A. (1977). Homebuilders: Keeping families together. *Journal of Consulting and Clinical Psychology* 45 (4), 667–673.

Knudsen, D. D. (1988). Child maltreatment over two decades: Change and continuity. *Violence and Victims* 3, 129–44.

Koski, P. R. (1987). Family violence and non-family deviance: Taking stock of the literature. *Marriage and Family Review* 12 (1–2), 23–46.

Kurland, R., & Salmon, R. (1992). When problems seem overwhelming: Emphases in teaching, supervision, and consultation. *Social Work* 37 (3), 240–4.

Lane, T. W., & Davis, G. E. (1987). Child maltreatment and juvenile delinquency: Does a relationship exist? In J. D. Burchard & S. N. Burchard (Eds.), *Prevention of Delinquent Behavior.* New York: Sage Publications, pp. 122–38.

Larson, O. W., III, Doris, J., & Alvarez, W. F. (1990). Migrants and maltreatment: Comparative evidence from central register data. *Child Abuse & Neglect* 14 (3), 375–85.

Lewis, D. O., Lovely, R., Yeager, C., & Femina, D. D. (1979). Toward a theory of the genesis of violence: A follow-up study of delinquents. *Journal of the American Academy of Child and Adolescent Psychiatry* 28 (3), 431–6.

Lindholm, K. J., & Willey, R. (1986). Ethnic differences in child abuse and sexual abuse. *Hispanic Journal of Behavioral Sciences* 8 (2), 111–25.

Main, M., & George, C. (1985). Responses of abused and disadvantaged toddlers to distress in agemates: A study in the day care setting. *Developmental Psychology* 21 (3), 407–12.

Main, M., & Hesse, E. (1989). Parents unresolved traumatic experiences are related to infant disorganized attachment status: Is frightened and/or frightening parental behavior the linking mechanism? In M. T.

Greenberg, D. Cicchetti, & E. M. Cummings (Eds.), *Attachment in the preschool years: Theory, research, and intervention.* Chicago: University of Chicago Press, pp. 161–82.

Margolin, L. (1990). Fatal child neglect. *Child Welfare* 69 (4), 309–19.

Martin, H. P., & Beezley, P. (1977). Behavioral observations of abused children. *Developmental Medicine* 19 (3), 373–87.

Massachusetts Department of Public Health. (1990). Average infant mortality rates, low birth weight, inadequate and no prenatal care rates by census tract. Unpublished report.

Masten, A. S., Best, K. M., & Garmezy, N. (1990). Resilience and development: Contributions from the study of children who overcome adversity. *Development and Psychopathology* 2, 425–44.

McClain, P. W., Sacks, J. J., Froehlke, R. G., & Ewigman, B. G. (1993). Estimates of fatal child abuse and neglect, United States, 1979 through 1988. *Pediatrics* 91 (2), 338–43.

McCord, J. (1983). A forty-year perspective on effects of child abuse and neglect. *Child Abuse and Neglect* 7, 265–70.

(1988). Parental behavior in the cycle of aggression. *Psychiatry* 51, 14–23.

McGee, R. A., & Wolfe, D. A. (1991). Psychological maltreatment: Toward an operational definition. *Development and Psychopathology* 3 (1), 3–18.

McGuire, J., & Earls, F. (1991). Prevention of psychiatric disorders in early childhood. *Journal of Child Psychology and Psychiatry* 32 (1), 129–53.

McLaren, J., & Brown, R. E. (1989). Childhood problems associated with abuse and neglect. *Canada's Mental Health* 37 (3), 1–6.

Murphy, J. M., Jellinek, M., Quinn, D., Smith, G., Poitrast, F. G., & Goshko, M. (1991). Substance abuse and serious child mistreatment: Prevalence, risk, and outcome in a court sample. *Child Abuse & Neglect* 15 (3), 197–211.

National Center for Children in Poverty. (1990). *Five Million Children: A Statistical Profile of Our Poorest Citizens.* New York: School of Public Health, Columbia University.

National Commission on Children. (1991). *Final report. Beyond Rhetoric: A New American Agenda for Children and Families.* Washington, D.C.: U.S. Government Printing Office.

National Research Council. (1993). *Understanding Child Abuse and Neglect.* Washington, D.C.: National Academy Press.

Ney, P. G. (1987). Does verbal abuse leave deeper scars: A study of children and parents. *Canadian Journal of Psychiatry* 32 (5), 371–8.

(1989). Child mistreatment: Possible reasons for its transgenerational transmission. *Canadian Journal of Psychiatry* 34 (6), 594–601.

Nicol., A. R., Stretch, D. D., Davidson, I., & Fundudis, T. (1984). Controlled comparison of three interventions for mother and toddler problems: Preliminary communication. *Journal of the Royal Society of Medicine* 77, 488–91.

Ogbu, J. U. (1985). A cultural ecology of competence among inner-city blacks. In M. B. Spencer, G. K. Brookins, & W. R. Allen (Eds.), *Beginnings: The Social and Affective Development of Black Children.* Hillsdale, NJ: Erlbaum, pp. 45–66.

Olds, D. L., & Henderson, C. R., Jr. (1989). The prevention of maltreatment. In D. Cicchetti & V. Carlson (Eds.), *Child Maltreatment. Theory and research on the causes and consequences of child abuse and neglect.* New York: Cambridge University Press, pp. 722–63.

Olds, D. L., Henderson, C. R., Jr., Chamberlin, R., & Tatelbaum, R. (1986). Preventing child abuse and neglect: A randomized trial of nurse home visitation. *Pediatrics* 78 (1), 65–78.

Olds, D. L., & Kitzman, H. (1990). Can home visitation improve the health of women and children at environmental risk? *Pediatrics* 86 (1), 108–16.

Oliver, J. E. (1988). Successive generations of child maltreatment: The children. *British Journal of Psychiatry* 153, 543–53.

Orme, T. C., & Rimmer, J. (1981). Alcoholism and child abuse: A review. *Journal of Studies on Alcohol* 42, 273–87.

Pecora, P. J., Fraser, M. W., & Haapala, D. A. (1992). Intensive home-based family preservation services: An update from the FIT Project. *Child Welfare* 71 (2), 177–88.

Robertson, M. J. (1991). Homeless women with children: The role of alcohol and other drug abuse. *American Psychologist* 46 (11), 1198–204.

Runyan, D. K., Gould, C. L., Trost, D. C., & Loda, F. A. (1981). Determinants of foster care placement for the maltreated child. *Child Abuse* 6 (3), 343–50.

Sack, W. H., Mason, R., & Higgins, J. E. (1985). The single-parent family and abusive child punishment. *American Journal of Orthopsychiatry* 55 (2), 252–9.

Salzinger, S., Kaplan, S., Pelcovitz, D., Samit, C., & Krieger, R. (1984). Parent and teacher assessment of children's behavior in child maltreating families. *Journal of the American Academy of Child Psychiatry* 23 (4), 458–64.

Sampson, R. J. (1992). Family Management and Child Development: Insights from Social Disorganization Theory. In J. McCord (Ed.), *Facts, Frameworks, and Forecasts: Advances in Criminological Theory, Volume 3.* New Brunswick, NJ: Transaction, pp. 63–93.

(This volume). The embeddedness of child and adolescent development: A community-level perspective on urban violence. In J. McCord (Ed.), *Violence and Childhood in The Inner City.* New York: Cambridge University Press, pp. 31–77.

Schinke, S. P., Schilling, R. F., Barth, R. P., & Gilchrist, L. D. (1986). Stress-management intervention to prevent family violence. *Journal of Family Violence* 1 (1), 13–26.

Schloesser, P., Pierpont, J., & Poertner, J. (1992). Active surveillance of child abuse fatalities. *Child Abuse and Neglect* 16 (1), 3–10.

Schmidt, E., & Eldridge, A. (1986). The attachment relationship and child maltreatment. *Infant Mental Health Journal* 7 (4), 264–73.

Schorr, L. B. (1988). *Within our reach. Breaking the cycle of disadvantage.* New York: Anchor Press.

Schorr, L. B., & Both, D. (1991). Attributes of effective services for young children: A brief survey of current knowledge and its implications for program and policy development. In L. B. Schorr, D. Both, & C. Copple (Eds.), *Effective services for young children: Report of a workshop.* Washington, DC: National Academy Press, pp 23–47.

Seagull, E. A. W. (1987). Social support and child maltreatment: A review of the evidence. *Child Abuse and Neglect* 11, 41–52.

Searight, H. R., & Handal, P. J. (1986). Premature birth and its later effects: Towards preventive intervention. *Journal of Primary Prevention* 7 (1), 3–16.

Sedlak, A. (1988). Technical amendment to the study findings – National incidence and prevalence of child abuse and neglect: 1988. Report submitted to the National Center on Child Abuse and Neglect, 1990. Available from Westat, Inc. Rockville, MD.

   (1991). National prevalence of child abuse and neglect. Presented at the Conference on Child Welfare Reform Experiments, Washington, D.C., 1991. Available from Westat, Inc. Rockville, MD.

Seitz, V., Rosenbaum, L. K., & Apfel, N. H. (1985). Effects of family support intervention: A ten-year follow-up. *Child Development* 56, 376–91.

Sennett, R. (1970/1984). *Families against the city: Middle class homes of industrial Chicago 1872–1890.* Cambridge, MA: Harvard University Press.

Shay, S. W. (1980). Community council for child abuse prevention. In C. H. Kempe & R. E. Helfer (Eds.), *The Battered Child, Third Edition. Revised and Expanded.* Chicago: University of Chicago Press, pp. 330–46.

Smetana, J., Kelly, M., & Twentyman, C. T. (1984). Abused, neglected, and nonmaltreated children's conceptions of moral and social-conventional transgressions. *Child Development* 55 (1), 277–87.

Sroufe, L. A., & Rutter, M. (1984). The domain of developmental psychopathology. *Child Development* 55, 1184–99.

Stoneman, Z., Brody, G. H., & Burke, M. (1989). Marital quality, depression, and inconsistent parenting: Relationship with observed mother-child conflict. *American Journal of Orthopsychiatry* 59 (1), 105–17.

St. Peter, R. F., Newacheck, P. W., & Halfon, N. (1992). Original contributions: Access to care for poor children: Separate and unequal? *Journal of the American Medical Association* 267 (20), 2760–64.

Straus, M. A., & Gelles, R. J. (1986). Societal change and change in family violence from 1975 to 1985 as revealed in two national surveys. *Journal of Marriage and the Family* 48, 465–79.

Tarter, R. E., Hegedus, A. M., Winsten, N. E., & Alterman, A. I. (1984). Neuropsychological, personality, and familial characteristics of physically abused delinquents. *Journal of the American Academy of Child Psychiatry* 23, 668–74.

U.S. Department of Health and Human Services. (1988). *State Statutes Related to Child Abuse and Neglect.* Washington, DC: DHHS Pub. No. 06–88098.

(1990a). *Child Abuse and Neglect: Critical Steps in Response to a National Emergency.* Washington, DC. The U.S. Advisory Board on Child Abuse and Neglect, U.S. Government Printing Office Stock No. 017–092–00104–5.

(1990b). *National Child Abuse and Neglect Data System, Working Paper 1: Summary Data Component.* Washington, DC: DHHS Pub. No. (ACF) 92–30361.

Van Dyke, R. B. (1991). Pediatric human immunodeficiency virus infection and the acquired immunodeficiency syndrome. A health care crisis of children and families. *American Journal of Diseases of Children* 145 (5), 529–32.

Vissing, Y. M., Straus, M. A., Gelles, R. J., & Harrop, J. W. (1991). Verbal aggression by parents and psychosocial problems of children. *Child Abuse and Neglect* 15, 223–38.

Webster-Stratton, C., & Hammond, M. (1988). Maternal depression and its relationship to life stress, perceptions of child behavior problems, parenting behaviors, and child conduct problems. *Journal of Abnormal Child Psychology* 16 (3), 299–315.

Weiss, H. B. (1989). State family support and education programs: Lessons from the pioneers. *American Journal of Orthopsychiatry* 59 (1), 32–48.

Weissbourd, B., & Kagan, S. L. (1989). Family support programs: Catalysts for change. *American Journal of Orthopsychiatry* 59 (1), 20–30.

Westcott, H. (1991). The abuse of disabled children: A review of the literature. *Child Care, Health and Development* 17 (4), 243–58.

Whipple, E. E., & Webster-Stratton, C. (1991). The role of parental stress in physically abusive families. *Child Abuse and Neglect* 15 (3), 279–91.

Widom, C. S. (1989a). Child abuse, neglect, and adult behavior: Research design and findings on criminality, violence and child abuse. *American Journal of Orthopsychiatry* 59 (3), 355–66.

(1989b). The cycle of violence. *Science* 244, 160–9.

(1989c). Does violence beget violence? A critical examination of the literature. *Psychological Bulletin* 106 (1), 3–28.

Woods, D., Valdez, R. B., Hayashi, T., & Shen, A. (1990). Homeless and housed families in Los Angeles: A study comparing demographic, economic, and family function characteristics. *American Journal of Public Health* 80 (9), 1049–52.

Youngblade, L. M., & Belsky, J. (1989). Child maltreatment, infant-parent attachment security, and dysfunctional peer relationships in toddlerhood. *Topics in Early Childhood Special Education* 9 (2), 1–15.

Zeanah, C. H., & Zeanah, P. D. (1989). Intergenerational transmission of maltreatment: Insights from attachment theory and research. *Psychiatry* 52 (2), 177–96.

Zigler, E., & Black, K. B. (1989). America's family support movement: Strengths and limitations. *American Journal of Orthopsychiatry* 59 (1), 6–18.

Zuravin, S. J., & Taylor, R. (1987). The ecology of child maltreatment: Identifying and characterizing high-risk neighborhoods. *Child Welfare* 66 (6), 497–506.

Intervening to Prevent Childhood Aggression in the Inner City

NANCY G. GUERRA

"There's been more killing this year than I can ever remember, and I came to Chicago in '51," he said, He was a 61-year-old grandfather whose young adult son, Andre, had just been beaten to death by five young men, apparently because his son had chided one of them for taunting a young woman in the neighborhood. "We can go to the moon, but we can't do anything about these gangs and drugs and violence. Why? Why?" he asked insistently. "We've got a brain, and it is greater than any machine ever built, but we can't fix this," he said. "Why? If I could read, I'd read every book in the library until I found an answer." (Chicago Tribune, 1992).

The weekend of Andre's killing, 28 people were killed in the city of Chicago, most of them young, poor, and from West Side or South Side neighborhoods where killings have become routine and commonplace. These killings rarely make the news, because they are not news but rather everyday events – facts of life in the inner city. They are sometimes motivated by absurd reasons, such as a real or imagined insult. Victims often meet their fate simply by being "in the wrong place at the wrong time," for instance, by getting caught in crossfire during a clash between rival gangs.

It is not only the level but also the senselessness of the violence that perplexes us. Why would anyone kill someone over a few words? Why has violence overtaken some communities, creating an intricate web of aggression and retaliation whereby a sizable number of young men believe that their possessions, their status, and their standing in the community depend on their willingness to use violence (Anderson, this volume)? In the words of a young gang member, "Yo, young Lawrence is straight if we did shit def like the big fellas then people would respect us. We should start popping dudes if they look at us wrong, then everybody would give us big play and say them Loes is bad" (Taylor, 1989, p. 67).

"Popping dudes" is a euphemistic label for killing. Euphemistic labels frequently emerge where violence has been institutionalized. Such labels serve to disengage moral sanctions and relieve individuals of a sense of personal responsibility for their actions (Bandura, 1991). The language of war provides a compelling example – bombing attacks are "strikes" and dead civilians are "collateral damage." Today's inner cities have been compared to war zones, and researchers are beginning to consider children's development in this context by looking at war-related disturbances such as posttraumatic stress disorder (PTSD) (Garbarino, Kostelny, & Dubrow, 1991).

Statistics corroborate the chilling observation made by Andre's father. The incidence of aggressive and violent behavior in the United States has risen dramatically since the 1950s, and the modal age for various violent offenses has decreased (Blumstein, Farrington, & Moitra, 1985). In fact, the 1991 violent crime rate is the highest it has been in the last three decades (Uniform Crime Reports, 1992). There is also a strong positive relation between violent behavior and population density, with urban areas typically displaying violent crime rates 4–10 times higher than the national average. Within urban areas, violent crime rates are highest among African-American and Hispanic young men living in the lowest income, most disadvantaged inner-city neighborhoods (Fingerhut & Kleinman, 1990; Hammond & Yung, 1991; Shakoor & Chalmers, 1991).

For example, while African Americans make up about 12% of the population, they account for approximately 50% of the arrests for murder, rape, and robbery (Uniform Crime Reports, 1992). According to the most recent data, homicide is now the leading cause of death for African Americans between the ages of 15 and 24 (Centers for Disease Control and Prevention, 1991). While official statistics may reflect possible biases in arrests of low-income minority individuals, self-report studies have also found that the highest rates of serious and violent delinquency are reported by urban, lower-class minority adolescents (Elliott & Huizinga, 1980).

However, it is important to bear in mind that even in inner cities, not all children grow up to be seriously aggressive. Although violent crime has spiraled upward, only a relatively small percentage of children ultimately display habitual aggressive behavior. Nevertheless, an important component of prevention programs is their focus on preventing serious dysfunction before it occurs, and early intervention during childhood can postpone or thwart the development of more serious forms of violent and criminal behavior later in life. Given the higher rates of violence in the inner city, intervention during childhood seems warranted.

Habitual aggression refers to chronic and serious aggressive behavior, as distinguished from infrequent, age-typical aggressive actions. Although aggression has been defined conceptually and operationally in a multitude of ways, most definitions refer to intentional behavior that causes physical or psychological harm to another. Occasional displays of aggressive behavior are, in fact, quite common during childhood and adolescence. For most children in most settings, this behavior is part of the normal course of development and does not presage chronic aggressive and violent behavior in adolescence and adulthood. However, for some children, aggressive behavior becomes more chronic and serious and does not taper off. In fact, there is considerable evidence that children who develop such habitual aggressive behavior during childhood are likely to be aggressive as adults (Farrington, 1986; Huesmann & Eron, 1984; Olweus, 1979) and that they are also likely to have aggressive children (Huesmann, Eron, Lefkowitz, & Walder, 1984). Since this type of behavior typically co-occurs with other types of disruptive behaviors, it may be labeled alternately conduct disorder (when a psychiatric diagnosis has been applied), delinquency (when a legal designation based on adjudication has been invoked), or more generally antisocial or problem behavior. Although important distinctions can be made among these different classifications and although it is important to evaluate program outcome on aggression and violence, a broader perspective can be gained by considering aggression as part of a general class of antisocial and disruptive behaviors.

No single factor, by itself, can explain much of the variance in the extent and/or intensity of aggression in the population, much less predict who will engage in serious aggressive behavior. Rather, habitual aggression is best understood as a multiply-determined behavior which is influenced by a range of individual, situational, social-contextual, community, and societal factors (Eron, 1987; Loeber, 1991; Scholte, 1992; Seidman, 1991). A plethora of research has been conducted on each of these factors. However, only when there is a convergence of several factors is chronic or habitual aggressive or violent behavior likely to occur (Eron, 1990).

Complex problems demand sophisticated solutions. Not only is it easy to oversimplify the causes of aggression, but it is also tempting to oversimplify the solutions. Single-component programs provide valuable information about the relation of such components to aggression. For some people, such programs may be potent enough at a given point in time to significantly change the course of development of and prevent habitual aggression. Still, the fact that aggression is a multiply-determined behavior makes it unlikely that single-component programs will beget enduring changes in most children's behavior. It is particularly unlikely that such programs will be effective for inner-city children, since the chronic and persistent disadvantage that exists there increases the general level of risk for all children and exacerbates individual risk. The harsh realities of the inner city provide little cushion for the normal trials and errors of development.

The purpose of this chapter is to review intervention programs aimed at preventing habitual aggressive behavior in inner-city children. The majority of these programs are driven by psychological or sociological conceptions of aggression and antisocial behavior and provide therapeutic and/or educational services. The term prevention is applied to intervention efforts that occur prior to the application of a clinical diagnosis (e.g., conduct disorder) or legal classification (e.g., delinquency). Because only a limited number of intervention research studies specifically focused on the prevention of aggression have been carried out in the most distressed inner-city neighborhoods, it is necessary, at times, to discuss intervention studies conducted with children from less disadvantaged settings. Still, consideration is given to particular characteristics of the inner-city environment that both limit the applicability of many past interventions and provide direction for future efforts.

I begin by reviewing several critical issues in intervention programming. Next, I discuss the particular features of the inner-city environment that bear directly on prevention efforts, specifically the overall levels of stress and lack of resources, social disorganization, the prevalence of violence and the availability of guns, and the differing histories and cultural values of ethnic minority groups that intervention programs must consider. This is followed by a review of preventive intervention programs that focus on change across several developmental contexts, including the individual child and the child's family, peer group, and school. Finally, I attempt to integrate the extant developmental and intervention research in order to summarize the current state of the art and make recommendations for future prevention research and programs.

Critical Issues in Intervention Programming

Given the dramatic increase in aggression and violence in the United States over the last several decades, it is not surprising that interventions designed to prevent or ameliorate such behavior have proliferated. Such programs have emerged from a variety of traditions, including earlier social work programs such as the Child Saver Movement and Children's Aid Societies, as well as programs aimed at providing treatment services for identified or diagnosed at-risk or aggressive children. Most recently, a good deal of attention has focused on the prevention of aggressive behavior, since prevention is generally easier and more cost-effective than remediation or treatment.

The development of effective preventive interventions hinges on a number of factors. These include consideration of typologies for preventive interventions, the timing and context of intervention efforts, specification of the factors involved in the development of aggression and the relevant pathways leading to aggressive behavior, and an appreciation of implementation and evaluation issues related to applied research and service delivery. By way of providing a general framework for understanding preventive intervention programming and research, each of these factors is discussed separately.

Classifying Preventive Interventions

When we speak of prevention, we refer to intervention efforts that occur before behavioral problems have emerged. In relation to aggressive behavior, the goal of prevention is to reduce the incidence of such behavior or the number of new cases of children who display habitual aggression. There have been several approaches to classifying prevention efforts. These include the public health classification system of primary, secondary, and tertiary prevention, as well as more recent mental health classification systems identifying universal, selected, and indicated preventive interventions.

According to the public health model, primary prevention entails preventing such behavior from occurring before any signs of such behavior are noted through population-based or universal interventions. For example, a preschool enrichment program offered to all children in a community could be considered a primary prevention effort if one outcome objective was to reduce the onset of aggressive behavior in childhood. Secondary prevention consists of mitigating the further development of aggressive behavior in children who already display aggression and/or certain other risk factors associated with aggression. Tertiary prevention is really more akin to treatment, because interventions are conducted after behavioral problems are evident.

The problem with the public health classification is that it relies on "case" documentation and fails to differentiate prevention from treatment adequately. In the recent Institute of Medicine (1994) report, the term prevention was reserved for interventions that did not involve case identification. Like primary prevention, universal preventive interventions are programs targeted to the whole population, and they are programs which operate without prior identification of at-risk targets based on indices of risk. Selective preventive interventions are targeted toward subgroups of the population who are at higher than average risk but who show no evidence of specific behavioral problems. Finally, indicated preventive interventions are targeted toward individuals who are identified as having detectable symptoms but not the disorder, such as children who are referred for behavioral problems.

Because minority children living in the inner city can be considered an at-risk population, they may be identified as an initial population from which to draw children for selective prevention services. However, as mentioned previously, only a small percentage of these children will ultimately display habitual aggressive behavior, and the specification of additional individual risk factors may be necessary in order to be able to select children for more intensive services and to develop relevant interventions. Given that risk factors tend to co-occur, often interact with each other and with other variables, and vary over development, it is quite difficult to determine which factor or set of factors should be used to further identify children for interventions (Kazdin, 1990). One general approach that is consistent with the criteria for indicated preventive interventions is to identify children based on their early aggression, since this behavior is easily measurable and has been found to be remarkably stable over time across a wide range of cultural and community settings (Huesmann & Eron, 1984; Loeber, 1991; Olweus, 1979).

Of course, early aggression is only a broad marker for risk and provides limited direction for intervention programs. It is erroneous to assume that aggressive children are a homogeneous group, that all aggressive children share a common set of risk factors, and that the influence of such risk factors will be constant regardless of other factors such as age, gender, and ethnicity. Thus it is important to specify additional risk factors and to distinguish those that can be used to increase the accuracy of prediction as well as those that might be modified in order to prevent further dysfunction. Several additional risk factors have been identified, including neuropsychological dysfunction (Moffitt, this volume), poor academic functioning (Hawkins & Lishner, 1987), hyperactivity (Loeber, 1982), early aggression (Huesmann & Eron, 1986; Loeber & Dishion, 1983), social-cognitive deficits (Dodge, 1986; Guerra & Slaby, 1990), criminality of parents (Farrington, 1989), harsh and inconsistent parental disciplinary style (Loeber & Stouthamer-Loeber, 1986), coercive family management

(Patterson, 1982), and association with deviant peers (Farrington & Hawkins, 1991).

Timing and Context of Intervention Efforts

When and in what context should intervention efforts occur? Since some interventions are more likely to be suitable at particular times while others are better administered at other times, it is important to identify key periods for intervention efforts and the most appropriate social contexts for intervention at each key period. In terms of timing, one approach is to identify important developmental periods and provide programs during some or all of these periods. At least six major developmental periods can be identified. These include prenatal, infancy, early childhood (preschool), middle childhood (elementary school), early adolescence (middle school), and late adolescence (high school). Another approach is to identify critical transitions in children's lives and to build interventions around them, since such transitions are often accompanied by heightened stress that challenges children's coping skills. These transitions may be related to age, such as the transition from elementary school to middle school, or to particular life events, such as divorce or illness.

In addition to the question of when interventions should occur, the appropriate or ideal intervention context also varies. Intervention context is intended here to refer to a specific social system that influences the child's development rather than the particular setting or location where the intervention may take place. At least four intervention contexts can be identified as viable foci for preventive interventions: the individual child, the child's family, peers, and school. The variation in focus depends on whether programs attempt directly to teach children certain skills and behaviors either individually or in groups, or whether interventions work with families, peers, or schools to create systems and/or organizations that are effective at promoting the learning of nonaggressive, socially competent behaviors. There is often considerable overlap, and many programs provide at least some type of service across several contexts. In addition, it should be mentioned that other contexts such as neighborhood, community, and the political/legal system can and do impact the development of aggression and violence, although they are not addressed by most psychological or educational interventions.

Given the various developmental periods, life transitions, and multiple social systems that influence a child's development, it is evident that there are numerous possibilities for preventive interventions based on different combinations of timing and context. Some intervention programs attempt primarily to change individual factors during a specific developmental stage. For example, Head Start programs were designed primarily to provide enrichment experiences for individual children during the preschool years (although some programs also taught parents how to interact more effectively with their children). Other programs utilize more indirect methods of changing behavior over longer periods of time; one such program, the Comer School Intervention Model (Comer, 1980, 1989), advocates global organizational changes at the school level (such as parent involvement in decision making) that presumably filter into the community, the family, and the classroom – and ultimately affect individual student performance and behavior during the school years. As these examples illustrate, programs vary in both timing and context. However, programs designed to prevent childhood aggression tend to cluster around specific developmental periods and intervention contexts.

In terms of developmental timing, a popular notion among scholars is that prevention programs should begin early in development. This belief derives support from several complementary lines of research. First, since children's behavior is more malleable at younger ages, early interventions should be more successful than interventions at later periods in development (Loeber, 1990). Second, the relative intractability of aggressive behavior once established suggests that interventions should occur before such behavior becomes characteristic and habitual – at least as early as age eight (Huesmann & Eron, 1984). Third, a rather robust finding in the literature is that early onset of aggressive/antisocial behavior is highly predictive of the frequency, variety, and duration of subsequent offending, particularly in boys (Loeber & LeBlanc, 1990).

Thus, serious offenders are more likely to have been more aggressive as children and to have displayed specific types of aggressive and antisocial behavior earlier in development than their less seriously antisocial peers (Reitsma-Street, Offord, & Finch, 1985). For instance, it has been demonstrated that rates of offending are approximately two to three times higher for boys who begin their delinquency prior to ages 12 or 13 (Tolan, 1987). Although early onset does not unequivocally portend later delinquency, most serious offenders are characterized by early onset; late onset of aggression is relatively uncommon, and very few late-onset offenders become high-rate offenders. Thus, the effectiveness of early interventions can be measured both in terms of preventing the behavior from becoming habitual and characteristic as well as in terms of its success in delaying the age of onset of certain types of aggressive and antisocial behaviors.

There are, however, questions of just how early in development programs should begin. Some early intervention programs begin before birth, whereas others begin at different times during the preschool period. Although the first five years of life have been considered a particularly sensitive developmental period, issues of precise timing within this period have not been resolved. There are also limitations to an exclusive focus on early intervention. For instance, individual risk factors such as hyperactivity and difficult temperament clearly emerge early in development, while social-cognitive factors such as attitudes about aggression may crystallize later in development (Huesmann, Guerra, Miller, & Zelli, 1992; Huesmann, Guerra, Zelli, & Miller, 1992). Similarly, the impact of social contextual factors may vary with developmental period. There is some consensus that family variables are quite influential during the first years of life; in contrast, peer influences gain importance during preadolescence and adolescence, although family influences still remain important (Greenberg, 1992; Loeber, 1991; Patterson, DeBaryshe, & Ramsey, 1989). Less is known about the influence of schools and teachers on aggressive behavior, although early academic failure and lack of commitment to school are robust predictors of the maintenance of offending in adulthood (Farrington & Hawkins, 1991).

Scientific Approaches to Developing Preventive Interventions

As discussed above, interventions can occur in different contexts and at different stages of development. However, specifying *when* and *where* interventions take place does not address the issue of *what* interventions should be trying to accomplish. There are certainly more variations in program content than in developmental period or intervention context. Two leading scientific approaches to developing preventive interventions can be identified. The first approach draws on studies of *risk factors* to specify the content of the intervention approach. In addition, these interventions often aim to promote development of specific "protective factors" (for example, the ability to solve social problems) that may cancel the effects of risk factors. The second approach draws on *theoretical models* to drive programs – including specific theories about aggression, delinquency, and problem behavior – or more general theories of social development and behavior that are applied to aggression.

A complete review of the risk factor research or the various theoretical perspectives on the causes of aggressive behavior is beyond the scope of this chapter and can be found in some recent reviews (Kazdin, 1987, 1993). The multiplicity of views reflects the lack of consensus on the primary causes of aggressive behavior. As this diversity suggests, it is likely that many different factors operate in the development of aggression. As mentioned previously, there is no single causal factor, just as there is no single solution. How are we to decide which of these different factors should be targeted by preventive interventions or which theoretical framework best explains how aggression is learned and how it might be prevented? Furthermore, what factors are most critical when working with inner-city children?

Risk Factors. In risk factor research, a preliminary strategy involves differentiating those factors that are potentially modifiable by means of ethical intervention programs from those that are not modifiable. For example, factors such as birth order and temperament have been indicated as risk factors, and these risk factors may be quite useful in selecting individuals for secondary prevention efforts; but they do not provide direction for intervention programs. However, other factors have been implicated in the development of aggression that are amenable to change. In many cases, the effects of such risk factors have been demonstrated in a range of settings, including urban and inner-city environments. These risk factors can be broadly classified according to social systems that influence development and are similar to those specified as intervention contexts.

CHARACTERISTICS OF CHILDREN. Several child characteristics related to cognitive functioning have been identified as risk factors for aggression. As Moffitt (this volume) notes, there is strong research evidence that habitual aggressive behavior that begins in childhood is linked to hyperactivity, poor self-control, IQ deficits, academic deficiencies, and low verbal skills. To the extent that these factors are the result of neuropsychological impairment and are associated with the living conditions in the inner city (for example, poverty, inadequate health care, high rates of substance abuse, increased exposure to toxins), they increase the likelihood that inner-city children will be born with or develop such disorders early in life. In addition, given a resource-poor, unresponsive environment, a relatively mild individual impairment might also escalate into a more serious disorder, evoking a chain of failed person/environment encounters (Sameroff & Chandler, 1975). For instance, a minor learning disorder, if left uncorrected, might intensify into more serious academic difficulties, further increasing the child's risk for aggressive behavior later in life.

In addition to cognitive limitations, a number of child risk factors have been identified that involve the child's social status. Several recent studies have indicated that aggression and peer rejection often go hand in hand. For example, in a series of studies with elementary school children, Coie and his colleagues have found positive relations between early aggression, subsequent rejection, and later social isolation and increased aggression (Coie, Dodge, & Capotelli, 1982; Coie & Kupersmidt, 1983; Dodge, 1983). Similarly, Roff and Wirt (1984) reported a monotonic relation between decreased peer status, as measured by peer rejection, and increased risk of delinquency.

In our own work with inner-city and urban minority elementary school children, my colleagues and I have also found high correlations between aggression and rejection, typically above .75. However, in this sample we also found that extremely aggressive children are rejected; in contrast, moderate levels of aggression relate significantly to popularity rather than rejection (Huesmann, Guerra, & Eron, 1993). Clearly, an understanding of risk based on social status requires careful analysis of the particular social setting, because in some settings moderate levels of aggressive behavior may relate to popularity rather than rejection (Wright, Giammarino, & Parad, 1986). Furthermore, when deviant peer groups are firmly established, such as occurs during adolescence, peer acceptance by the deviant peer group may relate to increased aggressive and deviant behavior (Feltham, Doyle, Schwartzman, Serbin, & Ledingham, 1985).

A somewhat distinct body of research provides evidence that aggressive children are also likely to display deficits and biases in their cognitive processing and in their interpretations of social events. One line of investigation has focused on children's abilities to process information sequentially and generate multiple solutions to problematic social situations. Numerous studies have shown that aggressive children generate fewer and more aggressive solutions to social problems (Dodge, 1980; Dodge & Frame, 1982; Guerra & Slaby, 1990; Rubin, Bream, & Rose-Krasnor, 1991). However, in disadvantaged urban environments, generating more solutions may relate to generating more aggressive solutions, and both quality and quantity of solutions must be considered (see, e.g., Weissberg et al., 1981).

Along these lines, aggressive children have been shown to be more likely to attribute hostile intent to others when intent cues are ambiguous (Dodge & Somberg, 1987) as well as to endorse beliefs that aggression is a legitimate response across a range of social situations (Guerra, Huesmann, & Hanish, 1994; Slaby & Guerra, 1988). These biases and beliefs also appear to be consistent across children from different ethnic and economic status groups and have been implicated as factors in the development of aggression among inner-city youths (Guerra, Huesmann, Tolan, Van Acker, & Eron, 1995; Huesmann, Guerra, Miller, & Zelli, 1992; Huesmann, Guerra, Zelli, & Miller, 1992). Thus, it is likely that cognitive skills, biases, and beliefs play a role in the learning of and maintenance of aggression.

CHARACTERISTICS OF FAMILIES. At least three dimensions of family functioning have been studied as risk factors for aggression and possible targets for intervention. Parent management methods have been extensively studied, and several management techniques have been found to characterize parents of aggressive and delinquent children. These include inconsistent discipline (Loeber & Stouthamer-Loeber, 1987; McCord, McCord, & Zola, 1959), reliance on coercion and poor behavior management skills (Patterson, 1986), unduly harsh and/or abusive discipline (Behar & Stewart, 1982; Farrington, 1978), and low levels of monitoring and supervision (Loeber & Dishion, 1983). Recent studies also indicate that these parent management styles relate to aggression among inner-city children as well (Tolan, Gorman-Smith, Zelli, & Huesmann, 1993). However, some studies have found that, in general, African-American and Hispanic families place more emphasis on discipline and control and less emphasis on independence and expressiveness than non-Hispanic white families (Moos & Moos, 1981). In a similar manner, low levels of parental monitoring and supervision may be even more critical as risk factors for aggression in the inner-city environment, since opportunities to engage in aggression and violence are more frequent if children are left out on the streets without supervision.

In addition to parent management techniques, characteristics of the emotional atmosphere or systemic organization of the family also have been indicated as risk factors for aggression. Specifically, families of aggressive children have been found to have lower levels of emotional cohesion or closeness (Olson & Barnes, 1985; Tolan, 1988), a high frequency of negative and a low frequency of positive statements about each other (Alexander, Barton, Schiavo, & Parsons, 1976), and more defensive communications, including dominance by one family member (Hanson, Henggeler, Haefele, & Rodick, 1984). There is also some evidence to suggest that parent–infant attachments differ between aggressive and nonaggressive children, with aggressive children showing more "insecure" attachment styles as indicated by the parent's inability to soothe or comfort the child (Booth, Spieker, Barnard, & Morisset, 1992). In general, these studies imply that families of aggressive children are less likely than families of less aggressive children to provide an emotional atmosphere that is warm, caring, and supportive.

Family relationships that are abusive also increase children's risk for aggressive and antisocial and violent behavior (Earls & Barnes, this volume; Emery, 1982; Fagan & Wexler, 1987; Widom, 1989). As Widom (1989) pointed out, much recent interest has focused on the intergenerational transmission of violence, that is, the extent to which being abused or neglected as a child predicts later violent behavior. In a direct test of the cycle-of-violence hypothesis, she found a relation between being abused or neglected as a child and subsequent arrests for violent offenses, although it is important to note that the majority of abused and neglected children did not engage in subsequent violent behavior.

A third component of family functioning involves family problem-solving and coping skills. Aggressive children are more likely to come from families displaying high levels of defensiveness in family interactions (Reiss, 1981), an inefficient use of family resources when facing a problem (Tolan, Cromwell, & Braswell, 1986), and shared deviant values (Loeber & Stouthamer-Loeber, 1987). The issue of deviant shared values is particularly important when working with inner-city families who must cope with pervasive violence and concerns about safety. In our own intervention studies in inner-city communities, my colleagues and I have found that children often cite their parents' sanctioning of and support for such behavior in justifying their aggressive actions (Guerra, Huesmann, Tolan, Eron, & Van Acker, 1990). As the mother of a nine-year-old recently proclaimed, "I tell him [her son] that if someone attacks him, he should pick up a baseball bat and beat their brains out. It's not nice, but that's how it is" (*Chicago Tribune*, 1993).

CHARACTERISTICS OF PEER GROUPS. One of the prominent features of childhood peer groups is their role in shaping and organizing the behaviors of individual members. Childhood peer groups typically are defined by similarities in both values and behaviors (Cairns, Cairns, Neckerman, Gest, & Gariepy, 1988). This means that aggressive children tend to hang around with other aggressive children, and they share similar norms regarding the appropriateness of aggression. On the one hand, it is possible that "birds of a feather flock together" and that aggressive children seek out others who share both their values and behaviors. On the other hand, it may be that aggressive children simply have a more limited number of nonaggressive peers from whom to choose, since evidence suggests that aggressive children are frequently rejected by a majority of their peers (see, e.g., Coie et al., 1982) and therefore form alliances with a select group of aggressive children (with whom they may be popular, particularly during adolescence when deviant peer groups are more likely to emerge). In any case, association with aggressive peers is a risk factor for future aggression, particularly during adolescence.

It is well documented that youths who engage in delinquent acts also tend to have delinquent friends (Elliott, Huizinga, & Ageton, 1985). However, by adolescence, this association is more formalized, and serious delinquency often occurs in connection with gangs. This is particularly evident in inner-city communities where street gangs have a profound influence on the lives of children, adolescents, and adults.

Although organized street gangs can be understood as a type of adolescent social network, there are several characteristics that set them apart. First, gang members must abide by an array of stringent rules governing everything from standards of dress to conditions for revenge. Such rules exist in many adolescent peer groups, yet in gangs they are more formalized and more strictly enforced. Second, many gang affiliations are determined by cultural and territorial affinities, irrespective of particular friendship networks. Third, violence is considered both necessary and desirable in gangs as a sign of toughness and courage. Fourth, and perhaps most important in recent years, gangs have increasingly embraced a culture of materialism and have focused on economic gain (that is often related to drug-trafficking), thus leading to what can only be described as an almost distinct organizational form of criminal activity (Spergel, 1990).

CHARACTERISTICS OF SCHOOLS. Characteristics of both the school organization and specific teacher practices have been implicated as risk factors for the development of aggression. Most studies of school characteristics have been limited to surveys of effective schools rather than to experimental studies. Such surveys reveal a variety of characteristics of schools that appear to be related to positive behavior in students. These include student involvement in decision making, superordinate school goals, a focus on identity and excellence, leadership to sustain positive school values, and clear formal and informal behavior codes that were consistently enforced. Unfortunately, more systematic research on the specific effects of such organizational characteristics on student behavior is needed.

Evidence of the influence of the teacher's behavior in determining the social organization of the classroom is also emerging. Studies of teacher–student interactions suggest that coercive interaction patterns similar to those described for families by Patterson (1986) can generate and maintain children's antisocial behavior in the classroom (Hendrickson, Young, Shores, & Stowitschek, 1983; Patterson, Capaldi, & Bank, 1991). Furthermore, studies have consistently demonstrated that teachers inadvertently reinforce aggression in the classroom by attending to students when they are disruptive rather then when they are on-task and well-behaved (Rist, 1970). Moreover, teacher expectations about students they regard as potentially violent may result in self-fulfilling prophecies (Moldin, 1984). The role of the teacher has been shown to be particularly critical with urban minority youths. Students from low-income and minority groups frequently experience differential treatment in the traditional classroom. For example, Raudenbush (1983) observed classroom teachers and found that teachers of low-income students were more likely than teachers of middle-income students to minimize discussion and interaction and rely on rote learning. Teachers have also been found to provide less praise to children of ethnic, cultural, and linguistic minorities, and when praise is provided, it is given less contingently and with less enthusiasm (Fleischner & Van Acker, 1990).

Theoretical Framework. Even if it were possible to enumerate a finite set of risk factors relevant to the aggressive behavior of inner-city children, we would have only an array of risk factors suggesting a multitude of intervention foci and no understanding of the relations among these risk factors. Multiple risk factors still must be understood within the context of a broad theoretical model that organizes these descriptive data and provides guidance for the timing, context, and content of intervention programs. Theories of aggression, delinquency, and problem behavior have emerged from a range of disciplines, including psychology, psychiatry, sociology, and criminology. A detailed review of such theories is beyond the scope of this chapter. In general, these theories emphasize particular sets of risk factors and specify more precisely the mechanisms through which they operate vis-a-vis aggression.

Sociological theories generally emphasize the importance of the social group or social organization in the genesis of antisocial and delinquent behavior. Consequently, a number of related intervention efforts have emphasized group associations based on prosocial rather than deviant values and behaviors. For instance, according to social development theory (Hawkins & Weis, 1985), children are more likely to engage in aggressive or delinquent behaviors if they do not develop a commitment or a bond to conventional social life. Thus, providing opportunities, teaching skills, and promoting success in conventional (i.e., nondelinquent) activities across multiple social contexts should increase children's bonding or attachment to prosocial values and behaviors.

Psychological theories of aggression attempt to specify more clearly the individual processes implicated in the development of aggressive behavior. For example, a number of different learning theories of aggression have been proposed over the last several decades by Bandura (1973, 1991); Berkowitz (1974, 1984); Eron, Walder, & Lefkowitz (1971); Dodge (1986, 1993); Huesmann (1988); and Patterson (1976, 1986). The various learning theories differ in terms of exactly what is learned – specific behaviors, cue-behavior connections, response biases, beliefs, or scripts. In all cases, however, learning is believed to occur both as a result of directly experiencing the positive and negative consequences of one's actions (enactive learning) and as a result of viewing other's behaviors and their consequences (observational learning). Furthermore, the child's learning process is believed to be influenced by his or her interpretation of events.

The specific conditions that have been shown empirically to be most conducive to the learning and maintenance of aggression are those in which the child's behavior is reinforced for aggression and not for prosocial behaviors, or in which he or she is provided many opportunities to observe aggressive rather than prosocial behaviors. This is not to say that individuals do not vary in their susceptibility to these learning influences. Clearly, individuals with some genetic, neurological, and physical endowments living under disadvantaged circumstances will be more vulnerable than others to these learning influences. However, learning theory does provide one example of an integrative umbrella that permits organization of the risk factor research and suggests directions for primary and secondary preventive interventions.

Evaluation of Outcomes

The need for continued prevention research cannot be overstated. It is critical to ascertain whether a given intervention has had a positive impact on behavior as well as to determine the specific factors that produced such changes. In addition, it is also critical to determine whether the intervention has had any negative effects, particularly for selected groups of individuals (for example, differences in effects by gender, risk status, ethnicity, and so on). How should intervention effectiveness be determined? An examination of the types of prevention programs that have been conducted over the past several decades reveals that they essentially fall into two categories: state- and locally-funded service programs, and research programs conducted under the auspices of a university or research unit. Most service programs keep some records of number of clients seen or units of service delivered but rarely include a controlled evaluation of whether the program actually prevents or mitigates the development of aggression. In contrast, research studies, although varying in experimental rigor, provide at least some data on short-term and/or long-term effectiveness, but they are rarely generated from within the community. A growing interest in services research is developing to bridge this gap.

Unfortunately, there are still questions as to minimal standards for evaluation of behavior change. Many research studies fail to utilize well-validated outcome measures collected from multiple sources; instead, they rather frequently rely on nonstandardized measures collected from a single source. In some cases the objectivity of the rater is also of concern, as when teachers deliver an intervention program and also serve as raters of student behavior change. It is also important to examine both short-term and long-term program impact. Short-term gains that are not maintained over time fall short of achieving prevention objectives. On the other hand, the effectiveness of a preventive intervention may not be apparent immediately following the program but may emerge over time, as evidenced by differences in developmental trajectories of antisocial behavior or by delayed onset of more serious offenses.

Recent advances in assessment procedures have improved our ability to conduct prevention research. In particular, a number of standardized outcome measures, such as the Child Behavior Checklist (Achenbach, 1978), are available, and they permit comparisons of outcomes across different intervention studies as well as comparisons with normative samples (Achenbach & Edelbrock, 1981). Furthermore, multilevel assessments are being included in research protocols in order to ascertain whether and why change occurred. As Kendall & Braswell (1982) noted, two levels of assessment are critical in program evaluation: the *specifying* level that enables the researcher to determine what specific risk factors or mediators (e.g., social problem-solving skills) did and did not change as a result of the intervention, and the *general impact* level that determines whether the treatment had an effect on behavior (e.g., aggression).

Unfortunately, there are still many unresolved issues regarding the reliability and validity of many assessment measures for minority populations. For example, in a recent study (Van Acker, Huesmann, Tolan, Guerra, & Eron, 1994), my colleagues and I identified a *rater bias*; as a result of this rater bias, we found that teachers were more likely to rate African-American children as aggressive on the Child Behavior Checklist in integrated rather than in segregated schools. However, we also found that other measures of aggression (i.e., peer nominations and self-report) did not differ across these settings. Similar problems exist when measures are not sensitive to variations in cultural meaning or standards.

Program Implementation

Both service programs and research studies face difficult problems with program implementation. Service programs can be more flexible, carrying out ongoing modifications of both intervention content and procedures in order to fit the particular circumstances of implementation. Research programs lack this degree of flexibility, however, since a cornerstone of scientific research is the standardization of procedures and the implementation of the study as planned. The difficulties in conducting prevention research are exacerbated in the inner city for several reasons, including attitudes about research and prevention, the fragile organizational structure of key institutions, and levels of program participation and attrition.

While service programs often arise out of community response to or concern about specific problems, intervention research programs are often "imposed" upon the community by scholars who come and then go as soon as the research program has finished. Not only are these researchers often considered outsiders, but they are frequently not from the same ethnic and economic backgrounds as program participants. Of course, this is not always the case, and in some instances interventions that have been conducted over long periods of time (e.g., Head Start) are an integral part of the community service system. Nevertheless, scientific investigations are often met with a certain amount of suspicion, and there is often some concern about the specific goals of the research. There is also considerable apathy about prevention issues in settings where concerns about day-to-day survival are paramount and where the motivation to join "mainstream" society may be complicated by issues of ethnic identity.

Another important point is that applied research programs require a relatively organized setting with adequate resources for program implementation. This is particularly critical if the programs are extended in time and/or long-term follow-up is anticipated. However, the most impoverished inner-city areas are frequently characterized by high levels of social disorganization, in which social services are inadequate and the organizational infrastructures of key institutions (e.g., schools) are quite fragile and change regularly.

Differential participation rates can also bias research findings. One of the most difficult problems in conducting intervention studies in inner-city settings is to obtain adequate participation. Schools may be reluctant to participate because they are already overburdened with academic requirements. Contacting parents poses a significant problem, particularly when many families do not have working phones. Even when parents can be reached, they may not want to take the time to be involved or may be suspicious of outside agencies. High residential mobility also creates significant problems in terms of participant attrition, and it is not uncommon to find that more than 20% of participants drop out of a study each year.

Summary

It is evident that children growing up in the inner cities of the United States are a population at risk for the development of serious aggressive behavior in childhood and later in life. This elevated overall risk requires that primary, secondary, and tertiary prevention programs be conducted. Such programs should be driven by theoretical models of aggressive behavior that incorporate empirical data on risk factors. Although much of the risk factor research has been conducted on white, middle-class populations, recent evidence suggests that many of these factors operate in a similar manner in inner-city settings. For example, studies of inner-city children have replicated the results showing a strong relationship between aggression and rejection (Huesmann et al., 1993), and they have reported the existence of social-cognitive deficits and biases that were discovered in past studies of suburban children (Huesmann, Guerra, Miller, & Zelli, 1992; Huesmann, Guerra, Zelli, & Miller, 1992). Similarly, studies of family functioning implicate factors such as low monitoring and inconsistent discipline for both nonminority and minority families in suburban and urban settings (Darling & Steinberg, 1993; Tolan et al., 1993).

In addition to developing intervention packages based on theory and research, researchers must confront issues of program evaluation and implementation. It is critical for prevention programs to gather data on effectiveness and to develop implementation strategies that are feasible in inner-city settings. This is not to say that *all* programs should adhere to rigorous scientific standards such as random assignment, pre- and post-test assessments by unbiased raters, and rigid adherence to intervention protocols. However, a large number of such studies must be conducted, and promising new approaches must be subjected to such rigorous evaluation before being disseminated and implemented widely.

The Inner City as a Context for Intervention

Conducting preventive interventions in an inner-city setting poses challenges not encountered in more privileged environments, challenges such as inordinate levels of economic and social stress, social disorganization, the prevalence of violence, and cultural differences. Many of these concerns have been discussed in the previous section insofar as they bear on level of preventive services, exacerbation of risk factors, and program implementation and evaluation. However, before turning to a review of selected intervention programs, each of these issues should be considered in greater depth.

Economic and Social Stress

Not only are children growing up in inner-city communities likely to be poor, they are likely to be victims of chronic and persistent poverty. In this context, multiple stressors are expected, and hopelessness rather than optimism frequently prevails. Children and families are apt to experience a relentless array of negative events (e.g., substance abuse, illness, assault) in the context of uncontrollable and unchanging living conditions (e.g., substandard housing, violent neighborhoods, inadequate services). In the presence of severe economic and social stress, risk factors may be intensified, implementation of programs may be difficult, environmental conditions may not be adequate for changes to occur, and improvements may be difficult to sustain.

Consider an unemployed single mother with five children who lives in the edgy and dangerous world of a public housing development. Her neighbors are likely to be poor, her parents are likely to be poor, and her children are likely to grow up to be poor. It is probably the case that her day-to-day concerns revolve around the mundane but crucial details of feeding, clothing, caring for, and ensuring the safety of her children in buildings where elevators don't work and stairwells are pitch black. Lessons in parenting skills may be irrelevant *until* she receives job training, economic assistance, help with child care, a decent place to live, and an array of other social, educational, and support services. In fact, it is likely that her ability to function as an effective, supportive parent is diminished as a direct result of chronic poverty, as has been suggested by McLoyd (1990) and others. In this case, systemwide changes may be necessary before any individual changes can occur, although additional efforts may still be needed to affect individual change.

The same can be said for children growing up under these conditions. Lessons in the merits of prosocial behavior may be lost in an environment where prosocial deeds often go unrewarded and violence can be a route to economic gain. Gang members frequently offer food, money, and trinkets to children as young as six or seven in the hope that they will oblige with drug-related errands in the future. As a 28-year-old mother of six comments, "When they're giving your kids money and gold chains, and you know your mama ain't bought you nothing, sooner or later there's going to be trouble" (*Chicago Tribune*, 1993). How are we to teach children the long-term negative consequences of aggression and violence when it may be one of the few means available for short-term rewards?

Clearly, these are the most extreme examples, and not all inner-city children or families experience such severe distress. However, it is important to evaluate whether the effectiveness of skill-building interventions focused on academic achievement, social skills, parenting, or other competencies is moderated by variations in the levels of such stressors. It may be that competence-building interventions are simply not feasible or effective under conditions of chronic and extreme stress and that such stressors must be reduced before interventions can take hold. In addition, we must also consider the ethics of teaching people how to cope with substandard living conditions rather than acting to change such conditions.

Social Disorganization

Sampson (this volume) provides an articulate description of how community-level social disorganization in impoverished urban areas affects both child development and family functioning, a factor that, in turn, relates to increased levels of violence and crime. As he points out, children in these communities are more likely to be born with known risk factors for aggression because of inadequate health care services. As children develop, the social disorganization of the community also undermines the mechanisms of informal social control, especially the ability of residents to monitor consistently children's activities. Such disorganization also provides opportunities for illegitimate cultural organizations to emerge with their own values and norms, organizations that often include endorsement of a code of violence.

Similarly, social disorganization can undermine the ability to implement, evaluate, and sustain preventive interventions in such settings. As mentioned previously, interventions require regularities. Educational programs cannot operate if programs are shifted or schools are reorganized each year. In particular, research studies require consistent services across time. In addition to fragile institutions, communities that are disorganized are often unable to mobilize key individuals in order to gain support for the initiation or continuation of needed programs.

Prevalence of Violence

In addition to scarce economic resources and social disorganization, violence has become a fact of life in many inner-city neighborhoods. The ready availability of guns means that violence can and does have deadly consequences. Because of this fact, daily activities are often organized around avoiding and coping with violence. Children learn to take cover from stray gunfire in apartment hallways and under furniture. They see their neighbors, friends, and relatives fall victim to both intentional and random acts of violence. Alex Kotlowitz's book, *There Are No Children Here*, vividly describes the daily encounters with violence of two brothers growing up in a Chicago housing project. Research corroborates such narrative accounts. For instance, in a study of eighth-grade inner-city children Shakoor and Chalmers (1991) found that 55% of the boys and 45% of the girls reported having seen someone *shot* in the preceding year.

The high prevalence of violence in inner-city communities is likely to influence children's behavior in several ways. First, as learning theories suggest, children are more likely to develop habitual aggressive behavior if they are given many opportunities to observe aggressive rather than prosocial actions (Bandura, 1986). Not only do they learn how the behavior is performed, they are also likely to develop a set of internalized standards or normative beliefs about the acceptability of aggression (Huesmann, Guerra, Miller, & Zelli, 1992; Huesmann, Guerra, Zelli, & Miller, 1992). Anderson (this volume) describes the "code of the streets" that emphasizes the necessity, and even the desirability, of violence. Such a community-wide belief system should make it difficult to change significantly children's beliefs about its acceptability. How can children be taught that violence is not acceptable and that other people are not hostile when violence is, in fact, a part of children's daily lives and personal safety may depend on presuming that any ambiguous or unknown situation is potentially dangerous?

Second, children who grow up in violent and dangerous environments can also experience serious emotional distress. They must cope with persistent fear and concerns about safety as well as sadness, grief, and anger over the loss of loved ones and friends. As an example from our own work, my colleagues and I recently conducted interviews with second grade children living in public housing projects. We asked them what made them happy, what made them sad, and what made them afraid. Often in the same breath, children would tell us that they were afraid of "their teacher being mad at them" and "gangbangers shooting in the park." Studies of elementary school children have found that they frequently report a wide variety of symptoms after witnessing a violent event, including increased arousal, jumpiness, nervousness, sleep disturbances, memory impairment, and guilt (Pynoos & Nader, 1988). In situations of chronic danger, it is not uncommon to find more extreme accommodations, including alterations of personality, major changes in behavior patterns, and persistent posttraumatic stress disorder (Garbarino et al., 1991).

Finally, neighborhood violence significantly affects both the willingness of individuals and agencies to provide services in a community and the residents' ability to participate in such programs. In many inner-city schools, children cannot stay for after-school programs because schools are locked up due to safety concerns. Agencies may have difficulty recruiting staff to work in dangerous neighborhoods. Residents may also be reluctant to participate, especially if they must come to unfamiliar areas or stay out after dark.

Cultural Characteristics

Members of ethnic minorities, particularly African Americans and Hispanics, are overrepresented in inner-city settings. Accordingly, preventive interventions must be sensitive to the cultural characteristics of the participants. This sensitivity must cut across the entire research and/or service delivery process, including areas such as planning the intervention, generating support, collecting data, translating measures, designing and implementing the intervention, and interpreting the results. Because so much of the research on the development of childhood aggression has been conducted on white, middle-class populations – and because only recently have studies begun to examine whether these relations obtain across different ethnic groups in different settings – it is important to consider the appropriateness of a given intervention for a particular ethnic group.

It is critical to understand ethnic differences in the social norms governing daily experiences, or the *subjective culture* of a group (Triandis, 1972). Different cultures embody different social expectations regarding appropriate feelings, behaviors, perceptions, and understanding of social interaction. Rotheram-Borus and Phinney (1987) have suggested that cultural norms can be organized into four major dimensions: group affiliation versus individualism; active versus passive orientation; respect for authority versus questioning authority; and formality versus expressiveness. These differences do not imply that interventions must be culture-specific; but they do imply the incorporation of sensitivity to cultural variation on key dimensions. Multicultural interventions should examine the subjective norms of different cultures and incorporate positive values from each culture rather than attempt merely to apply dominant norms to other cultures in a "sensitive" fashion.

In addition to differences in cultural meaning, the historical experiences of different ethnic groups must also be considered. In the case of African Americans, it is important to acknowledge the potential effects of persistent oppression and racism (Dowhrenwend & Dowhrenwend, 1969). Several scholars have attempted to relate these experiences to low self-esteem, self-hatred, and frustration that, in turn, result in higher levels of violence (Pouissaint, 1972; Ramey, 1980). Given the evidence for a relation between frustration and aggression (see, e.g., Berkowitz, 1989), oppression may conceivably have a general effect on the development of aggression for certain cultural groups.

Summary

The high levels of chronic stress, social disorganization, prevalence of violence, and cultural diversity in today's inner cities present numerous challenges for preventive interventions. Not only do such conditions increase the general level of risk for all children and compound individual risk, they also make it more difficult to implement and evaluate intervention programs. Many children and families in this setting experience a multitude of stressors that can both increase the likelihood of antisocial behavior and reduce their receptivity to psychological or educational services. It is clear that minimal levels of competence and stability are required before preventive interventions can even take hold, let alone have an impact. Individuals must be able to benefit from the intervention, and the environment must be able to sustain changes. Job training is ineffective if jobs are unavailable, just as a drug-addicted mother will not benefit from parent training until she is drug-free.

Interventions must also affect both individual and contextual factors to provide support for prosocial behavior and discourage aggression and violence. This is often difficult in the inner city for several reasons. First, children must cope with both the fear and the realities of violence from a very early age and must learn to organize their lives around self-defense. For children who must navigate the dark stairwells and long hallways of public housing projects, this is particularly difficult, and concerns over personal safety often translate into a readiness to use violence as both a defensive and a retaliatory strategy. Second, variations in cultural history and cultural norms may place children at odds with prevailing ideas about educational achievement and economic success, may foster the development of a code of violence, and may make some interventions irrelevant for some cultural groups. Finally, the realities of inner-city life provide little hope for economic gain through conventional channels. It is difficult to teach children the long-term merits of staying in school when the long-term gains are less certain and the short-term merits of joining a gang are more evident.

Review of Preventive Interventions

Given the impact that violence has on the welfare of others and on society as a whole, considerable attention has focused on the development of preventive intervention programs. Many of these efforts have been carried out in economically disadvantaged areas, and some programs have specifically targeted inner-city children. Although there is no shortage of intervention programs and although the number of experimental and quasi-experimental studies has increased significantly over the last two decades, there is a shortage of well-evaluated studies. Of additional interest are studies that have not focused specifically on the prevention of aggression but that have targeted other risk factors that are related to aggression (e.g., academic achievement). In some cases, researchers have gone back to assess the relation of changes in these risk factors to aggression later in time, even though this was not the initial focus of the intervention (for example, see the review by Zigler, Taussig, & Black, 1992).

In the present review, I discuss preventive intervention studies that address at least some of the risk factors related to aggressive behavior, that focus on economically disadvantaged children, and that are applicable to inner-city settings. Rather than providing an exhaustive review or meta-analysis of all published and unpublished studies, I select examples from each of the four intervention contexts discussed previously: the individual child, the child's family, peers, and school. Although many programs target multiple contexts, I group programs according to the primary focus of the intervention effort. In some instances these distinctions may be blurred, but the categorization is maintained in order to provide clarity to the review.

Child-Centered Interventions

Child-centered programs tend to cluster around four areas of risk: physical development and health; cognitive functioning and academic performance; social/behavioral skills; and social/cognitive processes. Some interventions are quite specific to one area, such as academic enrichment, whereas other programs, those designed to influence multiple aspects of cognition and behavior, represent more broad-based approaches. In addition, some programs provide services directly to children through trained professionals, whereas others train specific caregivers, such as teachers or parents, to stimulate children's development in selected areas. These intervention programs generally fall into one of four categories related to developmental timing: prenatal/postnatal services to families; preschool enrichment programs; interventions during the elementary years; and programs for adolescents.

Prenatal/Postnatal Services to Families. To prevent problems associated with poor maternal health (e.g., low birth weight, birth trauma) and inadequate postnatal care, prenatal/postnatal programs typically provide broad-based educational and support services to mothers with known risk factors, especially poverty, single-parent status, and young age. These programs have flourished in disadvantaged areas, although research studies have been conducted most frequently in poor rural and semirural areas rather than in inner cities.

For example, the University of Rochester Nurse–Home Visitation Program (Olds, Henderson, Tatelbaum, & Chamberlin, 1986) provided prenatal/early infancy services for disadvantaged families living in a small, semirural community in New York state. The intervention consisted of home visits to expectant mothers by trained nurses during the prenatal period and a two-year postnatal follow-up for half of the women and children in the prenatal training program. The home visits focused on providing parent education about infant development, on building a social support network for the mother, and on linking the mother to other health and human service programs. The intervention program had a significant short-term impact on maternal and child health. When compared to a similar group of mothers who received only minimal services, mothers in the intervention group experienced more positive health-related outcomes, higher levels of employment, and fewer verifiable cases of child abuse and neglect. However, although these results show promise, it is important to realize that the study was not conducted in an inner-city setting, and no data on long-term outcomes are available.

A similar program for mothers raising young children in high-risk environments, the Yale Child Welfare Research Program, was carried out by Provence and Naylor (1983). This program relied on home visits by a social worker during the prenatal and early infancy period, and it was designed to help mothers with a range of medical, financial, and support services. The overall goal was to reduce the negative impact of the multiple stressors experienced by disadvantaged mothers on children's health and well-being. In a 10-year follow-up study (Seitz, Rosenbaum, & Apfel, 1985), both mothers and children in the intervention program fared better on several variables when compared to a matched nonintervention control group. Specifically, the intervention mothers were more likely to report a positive emotional atmosphere in the family and were more involved in their children's education. Looking at children's subsequent behavior, the intervention children were rated by teachers as less aggressive and disruptive than the control children.

While this study is significant in demonstrating an impact on aggressive behavior, the findings must be interpreted cautiously. Intervention subjects volunteered to participate in the program, and they were compared with a matched nonintervention control group. Since not all subjects had volunteered and since assignment to treatment and control groups was not random, it is quite likely that subjects in the intervention condition were more motivated to provide a supportive environment for their children than subjects in the matched nonintervention groups. These initial differences, rather than the intervention effects, could thus be responsible for differing outcomes.

Preschool Enrichment Programs. The preventive intervention most closely associated with poor urban children is the Head Start program. Although not restricted to the inner cities, it was one of the few programs that took hold in urban areas throughout the United States. Begun during the War on Poverty, Head Start was designed as an early academic enrichment program for economically disadvantaged and minority children. The original program was designed as a brief summer preschool experience prior to the child's entry into kindergarten. As the program evolved, it became more comprehensive in service, began earlier, and lasted longer. It also spawned a number of experimental evaluation studies, varying in quality and design, to determine its effectiveness on a variety of intellectual and social outcomes. Evaluation studies (Darlington, Royce, Snipper, Murray, & Lazar, 1980; Lee, Brooks-Gunn, Schnur, & Liaw, 1990) generally reported positive short-term intellectual and social gains, with most effects disappearing by elementary school, although more global outcome measures (e.g., high school graduation) generally favored Head Start children. One explanation for the "wash-out" of many early gains was that brief inoculation could not prevent future deprivation and disadvantage, suggesting that such programs should be continued over the course of children's development, particularly in the most disadvantaged communities (Zigler, 1987).

Two landmark preschool enrichment studies, the Perry Preschool Project and the Houston Parent–Child Development Center, have reported encouraging results using an intensive, well-articulated preschool program for the prevention of aggressive and delinquent behavior among disadvantaged minority children. Both projects randomly assigned subjects to intervention or control conditions and collected extensive data on their subjects for several years following the end of the intervention program.

The Perry Preschool Project targeted low-income African-American children in Ypsilanti, Michigan. Preschoolers determined to be at high risk for school failure were randomly assigned to treatment or control groups. Treatment children received one to two years of academically oriented preschool education between ages three and five, accompanied by frequent parent meetings and home visits. In addition to positive results immediately following the intervention, long-term benefits were also apparent. On a number of outcome measures in early adulthood, intervention children fared better than control children. Specifically, they had received better grades, scored better on standardized achievement tests, had better high school graduation rates (67% vs. 49%) and higher employment rates, were involved in fewer acts of misconduct, and had a lower arrest rate (Berreuta-Clement, Schweinhart, Barnett, Epstein, & Weikart, 1984; Schweinhart & Weikart, 1988).

The Houston Parent–Child Development Center provided both preschool enrichment and postnatal family services to low-income Mexican-American children from disadvantaged areas of Houston. The overall goals of the program were to foster academic development and prevent behavioral problems. At age one, children were randomly assigned to the intervention or control group. The two-year intervention (when children were between one and three years of age) included home visits and a one-year morning preschool program. Follow-up studies conducted when the children were in elementary school revealed that intervention children were less aggressive and more prosocial than control children (Johnson, 1988; Johnson & Walker, 1987).

Even the promising results of these projects, however, are clouded by concerns such as small sample size and high attrition rates for later follow-ups. It is clear that short-term academic gains are possible in even the most disadvantaged settings. What is less clear is whether short-term academic gains also translate into long-term reductions in aggressive behavior and whether precise timing and specific program content are important factors. Although poor academic performance is one risk factor for aggressive behavior, there are many other processes involved in the development of aggression. It may be that preschool enrichment programs also need to target directly the social/cognitive and behavioral correlates of early aggression. In fact, it has been argued that social and behavioral competence should be the primary measure of success for preschool enrichment programs (Zigler & Trickett, 1978).

Programs that emphasize social and behavioral competencies are based on the assumption that the skills they teach will generalize across situations and over time. If successfully learned, the skills should provide children with a template for mastering stressful and problematic encounters in the future. A number of preschool social enrichment programs have been developed. Although some programs have reported modest gains in social skills and reductions in aggressive behavior, the findings have been equivocal.

For example, the pioneering work of Spivack, Shure, and their colleagues (Spivack, Platt, & Shure, 1976; Spivack & Shure, 1974) emphasized primary prevention through a competence building intervention. The main thrust of their initial intervention was to promote the development of social problem-solving skills in inner-city preschool children. The Interpersonal Cognitive Problem-Solving Skills training (ICPS) was based on earlier findings that interpersonal problem-solving skills relate to behavioral adjustment in young children. Several specific skills were identified, although children's ability to generate alternative solutions to interpersonal problems was found to be the best predictor of adjustment among low-income African-American preschoolers. Hence, a major focus of the intervention program was on training children to generate multiple alternative solutions.

The specific curriculum was comprised of 46 brief "games" for small groups of children. The earlier games dealt with understanding language concepts, and as the training continued, more complex concepts were introduced. In essence, through a graduated sequence of lessons, children were taught to think of and evaluate different solutions to everyday problems. In a series of studies, improvements in cognitive skills *and* classroom behavioral adjustment (including reductions in aggression) were consistently found for intervention children and were also evident at follow-up one to two years later (Shure & Spivack, 1979). These findings seemed to indicate that early social problem-solving training was an effective primary prevention strategy for promoting social competence and preventing antisocial behavior among inner-city children.

Given this initial success, a number of replication studies were conducted. The intervention techniques commonly were similar or even identical to those in the Spivack and Shure program, and several improvements in experimental methodology were frequently made, including random assignment of children to treatment and control groups, the use of unbiased raters of children's adjustment, and continued follow-up assessments. Unfortunately, the results of these subsequent studies were less encouraging. In general, while many researchers were able to demonstrate significant improvements in children's social problem-solving skills, these gains did not appear to translate to behavioral improvements. For example, Rickel and her colleagues (Rickel & Burgio, 1982; Rickel & Lampi, 1981) attempted to replicate the ICPS training program as a secondary prevention program for identified high-risk African-American inner-city preschool children. Utilizing exactly the same training program, they found that initial differences on social problem-solving skills were reflected in the different levels of improvement for intervention versus control subjects. These improvements were not maintained at two-year follow-up, however, and no behavioral improvements were noted either immediately following or two year after the intervention.

Interventions During the Elementary Years. A diverse portfolio of prevention programs exists for elementary school-age children. Most programs for children of this age group are conducted in the school setting. Some of these programs are offered to all children in a classroom or school and are aimed at improving children's social competence and overall behavioral adjustment. Other programs target specific deficits of identified at-risk children as selective or indicated preventive interventions. A number of related prevention studies have evolved from the Spivack and Shure (1974) ICPS model. Although some programs have demonstrated modest gains in social problem solving and related improvements in adjustment, others have been less successful, and results have been discouraging for inner-city children.

For example, in an important study comparing the effects of social problem-solving training for middle-class suburban and inner-city third grade children conducted in the regular classroom, Weissberg et al. (1981) provided both groups of children with a 52-session social problem-solving training program. The classroom curriculum was composed of five major units: identifying feelings, identifying problems, generating solutions, considering consequences, and practicing behavioral strategies. In addition, six parent-training sessions were offered to help parents reinforce children's problem-solving skills. Results for the suburban middle-class children showed that children from intervention classrooms outperformed children from control classrooms on a number of key social/cognitive skills and on seven of nine teacher-rated behavioral adjustment variables, including aggressive and antisocial behavior. In contrast, the inner-city intervention children got worse on five of nine teacher-rated behavioral adjustment indices and actually increased their aggressive behavior, although in both samples initial levels of aggression were statistically controlled.

In another study with elementary school children, Hawkins and his colleagues (Hawkins, VonCleve, & Catalano, 1991) utilized the ICPS classroom curriculum with first and second grade elementary school children from low-income urban schools. They also expanded the intervention program beyond social problem-solving training to include teacher training in classroom management skills and interactive teaching and parent training in family management skills. This approach is consistent with their dynamic, multifaceted model of delinquency prevention, a strategy that emphasizes changing "units of socialization" rather than targeting individual children (Hawkins & Weis, 1985). Overall, children in the intervention classrooms were rated by teachers as less aggressive than children in the control classrooms at post-test. However, an examination of differences in outcome for black and white children separately revealed that this comprehensive intervention was effective only for white children.

Results from social problem-solving/social competence programs using a more targeted approach with children specifically identified as at-risk are also equivocal, particularly for poor minority children. Some studies have reported short-term reductions in aggression, particularly when social problem-solving programs are enhanced by the inclusion of components such as anger management (Lochman, Burch, Curry, & Lampron, 1984) and extensive rehearsal of behavioral skills (Cowen et al., 1975). In some cases, short-term effects have been maintained several years following treatment (Chandler, Weissberg, Cowen, & Guare, 1984; Durlak, 1980), although in other studies intervention effects tend to dissipate more quickly (Lochman, 1992). Many interventions conducted with lower-class minority children fail to yield even short-term effects on behavior (Coie, Underwood, & Lochman, 1991), particularly in inner-city settings (Dubow, Huesmann, & Eron, 1987; Kirschenbaum, 1979).

Because of these mixed results, it is difficult to draw any conclusions about the effectiveness of child-centered preventive interventions during the elementary school years. However, one point is worth mentioning. In several replication studies conducted with low-income minority children, interventions did appear to be more effective for subsequent cohorts of children (Coie et al., 1991; Weissberg, Caplan, & Harwood, 1991). It may be that preventive interventions are particularly difficult to adapt and implement in disorganized settings characterized by economic and social stress, and that repeated implementations are necessary before an effective matching of program and target children can be achieved. It may also be that in such settings, early inoculation cannot sustain changes and programs must be extended well into adolescence.

Programs for Adolescents. The abundance of programs for young children is offset by the relative scarcity of prevention programs that target adolescent aggression and violence. This is not to say that programs for adolescents do not exist. They do. However, most interventions that focus on adolescent antisocial behavior have been carried out as treatment programs, often involving adjudicated or incarcerated youths (for a review, see Goldstein, 1986; Guerra, Tolan, & Hammond, 1994). When prevention programs are offered, they typically are conducted in high school health or social studies classes as part of a health education/social development curriculum.

For example, Sarason and Sarason (1981) developed a 13-week social problem-solving training program for multiethnic urban high school students. The program was delivered during the students' regular health course. The intervention provided multiple opportunities for modeling and role-playing effective problem solutions. Compared to no-treatment control students, students who participated in the intervention displayed improvements in social problem-solving skills, had fewer school absences, and showed a decrease in the rate for office referrals for problem behaviors; however, no long-term follow-up was conducted.

In another study conducted in both an inner-city and a suburban middle school, Caplan et al. (1992) provided a 20-session curriculum – the Positive

Youth Development Program – to six and seventh grade children in their regular school classrooms. Classrooms were randomly assigned to intervention and attention-control conditions. The intervention program focused on improving children's competencies in six areas: stress management, self-esteem, problem solving, substances and health information, assertiveness, and social networks. Attention-control classrooms received a science curriculum that included information on the physical effects of drug use. Compared to children in control classrooms, intervention children were rated by their teachers as less impulsive and more adept at constructive conflict resolution with peers. Self-report ratings indicated gains in problem-solving skills and reductions in excessive alcohol use. In general, the program was found to be beneficial for both inner-city and suburban students, although the long-term effects are still undetermined.

Although both of these studies were conducted with inner-city minority youths, they were not specifically tailored to a particular ethnic or cultural group. In contrast, Hammond (1991) developed a 20-session training program for African-American adolescents. The program provides specific training in social skills, conflict resolution skills, and anger management. In a recent evaluation study (Hammond & Yung, 1993), 169 African-American middle school youths (ages 13 to 15) were randomly assigned to treatment or control groups. The training was provided over the course of one school semester. Three-year follow-up data indicated that 17.6% of the youths who had participated in the program had subsequent juvenile court involvement, compared with 48.7% of the control-group youths. Furthermore, control-group youths were significantly more likely to have been charged with a violent offense than intervention youths.

In a more general secondary prevention program for seventh grade urban students, Bry and George (1980) randomly assigned identified high-risk children to treatment or control conditions. Students in the treatment condition were provided with a range of services, including daily monitoring and feedback of school behavior, reinforcements for specific behaviors, meetings with research staff, biweekly teacher consultations, and periodic parent meetings. At postassessment, students in the intervention condition had improved significantly over the no-treatment control students on school grades and attendance, and they showed decreases in disruptive behavior. The intervention also had longer term effects on delinquent behavior. Self-report measures collected from students at 18-month follow-up showed significantly fewer delinquent offenses for intervention children, and examination of court records at five-year follow-up indicated that intervention students had fewer arrests than control students.

Family Interventions

Many of the child-centered programs previously described involve parents in some aspect of the intervention process. Most typically, this involvement takes the form of providing a parental support network and increasing linkages to community services (Johnson & Walker, 1987). In some cases parents are encouraged to participate in seminars or workshops to develop parenting skills, although this is often an optional component of the intervention (Hawkins et al., 1991). By contrast, family interventions have as their main goal the modification of parent–child interactions.

Two different approaches to family intervention can be identified: parent training and family therapy. Both approaches encompass a range of intervention modalities woven together by the assumption that children's behavior develops within the family context and that the focus of intervention should be at the level of the parent–child interaction rather than with the individual child alone. Parent training is usually conducted with parents alone, who then utilize newly acquired parenting skills in the home. Because it is broad-based and does not require individualized treatment, it is often the method of choice for population-based programs. Family therapy tends to focus on parent–child interactions within the context of the family system and involves an individualized treatment plan for identified children and their families.

Parent Training. Most parent training programs are derived from learning theories of behavior. Assessment studies have found that certain parent management techniques promote the learning of aggressive and antisocial behavior (Loeber & Stouthamer-Loeber, 1987; Patterson, 1986). Specifically, the positive and negative reinforcements provided by parents are assumed to contribute significantly to the development and escalation of aggressive behavior. Interventions thus focus on shifting reinforcement contingencies so that prosocial behaviors are consistently reinforced and aggressive behaviors are consistently punished or ignored (Dumas, 1989; Patterson, 1986).

There is evidence to show that parent training is effective in the prevention and treatment of children's antisocial behavior (Dumas, 1989; Kazdin, 1987; Miller & Prinz, 1990). However, as with the interventions discussed previously, the results have been equivocal. Despite studies that have shown treatment gains with children (see, e.g., Baum & Forehand, 1981; Patterson, 1986; Webster-Stratton, 1985) and adolescents (Bank, Marlowe, Reid, Patterson, & Weinrott, 1991), several studies have failed to demonstrate significant improvements following intervention or to confirm long-term maintenance of treatment effects (see, e.g., Bernal, Klinnert, & Schultz, 1980; Eyberg & Johnson, 1974; Wahler, 1980).

Low-income families living under conditions of chronic and persistent stress appear to be least likely to benefit from parent training programs. For example, Dumas and Wahler (1983) conducted two studies utilizing a standardized parent training program for families who differed both in socioeconomic status and in degree of social isolation. At follow-up assessment one year following the intervention, results indicated an increase in the probability of treatment failure for families who experienced economic disadvantage, social isolation, or both. Looking at these studies in the context of the parent training literature, it is apparent that most of the successful parent training programs have been conducted with nonminority families who were not living under conditions of extreme stress (see, e.g., Baum & Forehand, 1981; Patterson, 1982).

Why have parent training programs been less effective for inner-city minority children and their families? One possible explanation is that models developed on nonminority middle-class families are simply not relevant for all families in all settings. In some cultures respect for authority is paramount and children are not permitted, let alone encouraged, to discuss or participate in rule setting. Interventions promoting firm, clear, and understanding parenting might be readily dismissed by parents who do not subscribe to such normative beliefs about effective child-rearing practices. In addition to cultural differences, parents experiencing multiple stressors may simply be overwhelmed by day-to-day pressures. Even if interventions are able to bring about short-term changes in parenting practices, the behavior of children and their parents may ultimately respond to a myriad of powerful contextual factors that a parent training program cannot alter.

Family Therapy. Because family therapy involves the child and the child's family in an individualized treatment plan, it is limited to settings in which children have been identified for services. As such, it has not been used as extensively as parent training in prevention programs. A number of studies have examined its effectiveness as a treatment for delinquent youths and their families, although a discussion of such programs is beyond the scope of this chapter (for a review, see Tolan, Cromwell, & Braswell, 1986).

In our own preventive intervention study, my colleagues and I are currently testing a one-year family systems intervention for inner-city children and their families (Tolan & Florsheim, 1991). I present it as an example of how parent training can be combined with family therapy to provide an intervention that promotes skill development while at the same time shows a sensitivity to the circumstances of individual families. The overall aim of the intervention is to improve parent management skills, foster the development of a positive emotional atmosphere in the family, and increase family problem-solving skills. The intervention combines six sessions of parent training in small group sessions with twelve sessions of individualized family therapy. In this manner, parenting skills can be taught in the group sessions, and systemic factors that limit their utilization can be addressed in the individual sessions. Preliminary outcome data indicate that compared to nonparticipating families, families who participate in the program show increases in parenting and problem-solving skills after one year that are related to corresponding decreases in children's aggression.

Peer-Focused Interventions

Although child-centered interventions are frequently conducted in classrooms or small groups and hence involve children's peers in the intervention process, the primary focus of child-centered interventions is not on changing the nature of the peer-group interaction but rather on increasing the child's skills in managing social relations. By contrast, peer-focused interventions directly target peer influences and peer processes as a means of modifying children's behavior. Because the influence of peers increases with age (Patterson, DeBaryshe, & Ramsey, 1989), these programs are usually designed for adolescents. Three models of peer-focused interventions can be identified: (1) programs that use peers rather than adults as mentors or trainers in social development/social competence building programs; (2) peer leadership groups that bring together leaders from a variety of student cliques and groups to encourage conventional activities; and (3) programs that seek to prevent youths from affiliating with antisocial peer groups, particularly organized street gangs.

Peers as Mentors. A number of school-based programs involve peers as mentors or trainers in prosocial activities. Unfortunately, these programs rarely include any type of formal evaluation. A few treatment studies have found that children both prefer peer leaders and improve in their own behavior as a result of being a peer leader (Smith & Fowler, 1984). Research studies using adolescents have also found that peer leaders are just as successful as adults in leading training groups and that youths who expect to become leaders actually acquire skills more quickly than other youths (Goldstein, Sherman, Gershaw, Sprafkin, & Glick, 1978).

Peer Leadership Groups. A number of peer leadership programs have been derived from the Guided-Group Interaction (GGI) approach. Basically, GGI promotes conformity to conventional social rules through a series of free discussions in structured peer groups (Bixby & McCorkle, 1951). Several derivatives of GGI emerged, particularly in the 1970s and 1980s, including Positive Peer Culture, Peer Group Counseling, and Peer Culture Development. In general, these approaches all attempt to enhance the leadership skills and positive involvement of selected peers. In turn, it is also expected that these leaders will influence their own peer groups to behave in a more conventional and positive manner.

As with most programs of this type, there have been very few controlled studies. One exception was a multiple-cohort evaluation of a Peer Culture Development (PCD) program, the School Action Effectiveness Study reported in Gottfredson (1987). The program was implemented in several elementary and high schools in Chicago, Illinois. Of further interest, the most comprehensive and scientifically rigorous evaluation was conducted with the third cohort of participants after many initial programmatic difficulties had been worked out.

The overall goals of this particular PCD program were to alter peer interaction patterns to reduce negative peer influence, to increase students' sense of responsibility for their actions, to increase their belief in conventional social rules, to promote attachment to school, and to increase their self-esteem and reduce their alienation from conventional society. All eligible students were randomly assigned to either an intervention or control condition. Students in the intervention condition attended daily group meetings for a period of at least one semester. The groups included both troubled students (labeled "criterion" students) and students expected to be positive role models (labeled "noncriterion" students).

Intervention–control comparisons for elementary school students failed to show significant intervention effects on any of the multiple indicators of antisocial behavior that were assessed. Specifically, the intervention had no short-term effects on self-reports or teacher reports of problem behavior, and it showed no effect on school referrals for disruptive behavior, tardiness, or absences. In a more disturbing finding, the high-school intervention appeared to have an *adverse* effect on participants. Compared to control children, the intervention youths showed significantly more tardiness, less attachment to parents, more "waywardness," and more self-reported delinquent behavior. In most cases these differences were due to the poorer performance of criterion children, but in some instances (e.g., school tardiness), it appears that the noncriterion children were most adversely affected by the intervention. Similar discouraging effects have been noted in a study of predominantly middle-class children conducted by Feldman (1992), although in this study some reductions of antisocial behavior were found for delinquent youths when they participated in "mixed" groups containing both delinquent and nondelinquent youths.

Interventions Directed at Juvenile Gangs. Most intervention efforts with juvenile gangs have focused on redirecting gang members toward more prosocial community activities and on reducing recruitment of new members. To date, the available literature does not show much impact from gang interventions. For example, Klein (1971) reports effects from a program that provided athletic and social events and academic tutoring to 800 members of four gangs. However, following intervention, increases in criminal behavior of participants were noted. Apparently, the activities increased the time gang members spent together, thereby increasing their criminal behavior. A subsequent program was somewhat more successful when time spent together was statistically controlled. However, overall results from this type of program were not encouraging.

Other efforts have focused on preventing recruitment and initiation into gang activities. For example, a secondary prevention program for children at risk for gang involvement (not including gang members themselves) was conducted for eighth grade students in several inner-city schools in Chicago. Pairs of schools in which the same gang was conducting recruiting activities were identified, and one school from each pair was selected as an intervention site. The program, Broader Urban Involvement and Leadership Development (BUILD), was derived primarily from social development theory (Hawkins & Weis, 1985), and it stressed strategies for resisting gang involvement, understanding the consequences of gang involvement, and learning about opportunities for achieving success through conventional means. Over the course of one school year, children participated in a 12-session classroom intervention (with the rest of the children in their classes), and some target children also participated in an after-school athletics program. The target children were divided into three intervention groups: no-treatment controls, classroom intervention only, and classroom intervention plus after-school program.

At the end of the intervention, the primary outcome measure was whether or not target youths had become members of a gang. Results of the evaluation indicated that although none of the youth had been gang members at the start of the intervention, approximately 10% of the control youths, 3% of the classroom intervention youths, and none of the classroom plus after-school intervention youths became gang members during the intervention year (Thompson & Jason, 1988). However, because of the small sample size (117 children) and relatively low base rates of gang involvement across all groups, the results were not statistically significant. Although this type of program may have some promise, it is clear that more rigorous evaluation of such programs is needed.

Interventions Focused on Classroom and School Environment

Classroom-based interventions attempt to change children's academic achievement and social behavior by modifying the classroom environment. Such interventions commonly target two areas of teacher skills: teacher practices and classroom management. By contrast, school-based interventions focus on characteristics of the school organization, including size, student groupings, parental involvement, management and governance, and school climate.

Teacher Practices and Classroom Management. Most interventions with teachers have focused on modifying *teacher practices* that increase children's risk for aggression. One example of a method that concentrates on academic instruction and skills training is the Direct Instruction Model. This approach incorporates training in basic skills, systematic reinforcement for correct responses, and effective use of teaching time. Teachers who utilize this program follow a carefully sequenced curriculum, with specific methods for monitoring student progress. In a nationwide evaluation comparing this model with 12 other teaching strategies used with economically disadvantaged kindergarten through third grade children, the Direct Instruction Model produced the greatest gains in academic (particularly language and math) and social (particularly self-esteem) skills (Becker & Carnine, 1980).

Cross-age tutoring also holds promise for improving student achievement. Most tutoring programs target students who experience academic and social difficulties, although some programs have involved entire classrooms (see, e.g., Jason, Frasure, & Ferone, 1981). In general, such programs result in improved academic performance on the part of both the children tutored and their tutors as well, although their impact on children's social skills and behaviors has yet to be demonstrated (see, Cohen, Kulik, & Kulik, 1982 for a meta-analysis of tutoring studies).

In terms of *classroom management,* cooperative learning groups have been found to promote higher student motivation, more successful mastery of tasks, and higher self-esteem than individualistic classroom activities (Slavin, 1979). This strategy is also effective in promoting understanding and concern across groups of students from different racial backgrounds (Slavin, 1982). In cooperative learning groups, students of differing abilities work together as teams on selected activities. In this manner, the success of an individual student depends on the success of the other students in his or her group, and students must learn to cooperate and compromise in order to complete a task.

Cooperative learning groups can also be effective in facilitating classroom management. Other classroom management strategies that have been shown to relate to reductions in student misbehavior include establishing clear rules for behavior, giving clear directions and maintaining consistent expectations, praising students for on-task behavior and good performance, and handling student misconduct in the least disruptive manner possible (Brophy, 1979; Hawkins & Weis, 1985). Taken together, these proactive classroom management strategies enable teachers to prevent problem behavior before it occurs and thus to minimize classroom disruptions (Cummings, 1983; Emmer & Evertson, 1980). However, for those working with inner-city children, it may also be necessary to address directly issues of cultural stereotypes or self-fulfilling prophecies (Moldin, 1984), since classroom management interventions have been less successful for minority children (see, for example, Hawkins et al., 1991).

School-Based Interventions. The organization of a school can have a significant impact on student learning and behavior. A variety of interventions have been developed to impact specific organizational characteristics. However, few programs have systematically evaluated the effectiveness of school restructuring in urban and inner-city schools. Even when evaluations have been conducted, the focus has been on achievement gains, and measures of aggressive behavior are rarely included. Because achievement deficits constitute a risk factor for aggression, however, some of the more comprehensive programs are reviewed.

Felner and Adan (1988) report on the evaluation of a program designed to facilitate student transition into high school. The program was directed at low-income ninth grade minority students entering a large urban high school. In essence, the program involved only a minimal reorganization, one that both focused on keeping students together in common groups and in close proximity and expanded the role of the homeroom teacher to include a variety of counseling and administrative functions. Even with these minor changes, when compared to matched control students, intervention students showed fewer decreases in academic performance and fewer absences. These differences appeared to diminish over time, however, and few differences were evident two to three years following the intervention. Further evaluation of this program in different sites is currently underway.

In a more ambitious effort specifically tailored to predominantly African-American inner-city elementary schools, the School Development Program (Comer, 1980, 1988) represents a comprehensive effort to change the organization and management of inner-city schools to make them more child-oriented and more effective. Although the details of the Comer model are somewhat vague and unspecified, its major thrust involves the creation of three teams. The school planning and management team (SPMT) is the governance and management body of the school. Its primary task is to develop a school improvement plan with input from the entire school community. The second team, the mental health team (MHT), is charged with preventing behavior problems in the school, primarily by assuring that policies and practices promote nurturing interpersonal relationships characterized by mutual respect. The third team, the parent program (PP), uses existing parent organizations as the basis for a more comprehensive program focused on increasing parent participation in a range of school activities.

The program has other complexities, described in more detail elsewhere (see, e.g., Anson et al., 1991). A notable feature of the program in relation to inner-city schools is the prominent focus on the specific experiences of disadvantaged ethnic-minority children. Significant efforts are made to organize classroom and school activities in ways that promote both self-affirmation and validation of children's ethnic and cultural identities. Achievements of minority group members are emphasized and mainstream success is promoted. Although many evaluations of the program are still ongoing, initial data suggest gains in student achievement for children enrolled in intervention schools compared to community and national norms (Comer, 1988).

Summary

Most child-centered programs focus on a specific developmental period and target developmentally appropriate skills and competencies. Evidence from prenatal service programs suggests that such interventions can have a positive effect on infant development and that these gains may translate into long-term behavioral improvements by ameliorating certain risk factors associated with maladjustment (Provence & Naylor, 1983; Seitz et al., 1985). Preschool enrichment programs focused on academic development clearly have positive short-term effects and seem to have positive long-term effects on the behavior of disadvantaged urban youngsters (Berreuta-Clement et al., 1984; Johnson & Walker, 1987). Some researchers have also reported behavioral improvements for inner-city preschoolers following training focused on social development (Spivack & Shure, 1974), although replication efforts have been less successful (Rickel & Lampi, 1981).

Studies with elementary school children have also produced equivocal findings, particularly for minority youths, even when comprehensive programs are developed that also involve teachers and parents (Hawkins et al., 1991). Although relatively few preventive interventions have been conducted with adolescents, some programs have reported successes with respect to aggressive and delinquent behavior, particularly those that focus on the development of specific skills related to anger management and conflict resolution (see, e.g., Hammond & Yung, 1993) or provide individualized and intensive academic and behavioral monitoring (see, e.g., Bry & George, 1980). Evidence also suggests that repeated implementation of interventions in inner-city settings is necessary to maximize the match between program and participants (Coie et al., 1991).

Family interventions are most problematic under conditions of chronic and persistent social and economic stress. Although some short-term gains have been documented, treatment effectiveness has also been shown to be negatively related to economic disadvantage and social isolation (Dumas & Wahler, 1983). It is clear that family interventions in the inner-city must help families both cope with multiple stressors and promote family interaction patterns that in turn promote adaptation without promoting acceptance of the code of the streets. Simultaneously, programs must be sensitive to differences in cultural practices and cultural meaning.

Given the important role of peers in the development and maintenance of aggressive and antisocial behavior, several interventions have attempted to alter peer group networks and to redirect antisocial peer groups toward more prosocial, mainstream goals. Unfortunately, little success has been demonstrated for general group treatment approaches, such as Guided Group Interaction, and some programs have been found to have an adverse effect on participants, particularly adolescents (Gottfredson, 1987). Programs to prevent gang involvement and redirect gang activities, while critically needed in the inner city, are rarely conducted as part of a systematic research program. To date, there is little support for such programs, and there is some indication that they may have harmful effects (Klein, 1971).

Interventions that focus on the classroom and school environment can enhance student achievement, although the specific relation of such changes to aggressive behavior has received little attention. Teacher-oriented interventions that have received some support include the Direct Instruction Model (Becker & Carnine, 1980), cross-age tutoring (Cohen et al., 1982), and cooperative learning (Slavin, 1982). For programs in inner-city schools, teacher biases and expectations that may inhibit student performance must be considered, lest interventions prove less effective for minority children (see, e.g., Hawkins et al., 1991). In fact, a major school reorganization may be needed in the most distressed inner-city schools in order to empower students, teachers, and parents to work together to maximize positive student outcomes (Comer, 1988).

Conclusions

As I have pointed out throughout this chapter, conducting preventive interventions in the inner city poses challenges not encountered in more privileged environments. Factors such as chronic and persistent poverty, lack of resources, social disorganization, prevalence of violence, and specific cultural beliefs compromise intervention efforts in several ways.

First, such factors increase the general level of risk for aggression across the population. Because of inadequate health care, a child born in the inner city is more likely to suffer neuropsychological deficits related to poor prenatal care or birth trauma. Many children are born to young, single parents, who may be overwhelmed by their own economic problems and psychological distress and, hence, may be unable to provide an optimal family and home environment for their children. Schools are underfunded and understaffed, resulting in large class sizes that compromise the teacher's ability to provide quality education. The prevalence of violence promotes a code of the streets, partially as a preemptive defensive strategy to prevent being victimized.

Second, the conditions that exist in the inner city compound individual risk. Children growing up in this environment experience a type of double jeopardy. Not only is the population's risk increased, but relatively minor problems can initiate a downward spiral of person/environment interactions that serve to intensify rather than ameliorate problems and increase risk for aggressive behavior. For example, without proper diagnosis and treatment, a child with a minor learning problem may fall behind in school year after year, drop out before finishing high school, and engage in delinquent activities because few other options are available.

Third, such environmental conditions may reduce receptivity to intervention efforts. On one hand, it may be that some individuals are simply unable to benefit from psychological or educational programs until their basic problems are resolved. A drug-addicted mother will not benefit from parent training until she is drug free. On the other hand, it may be that managing the daily hassles of providing food and shelter may be overwhelming to many and thus simply preclude their interest and involvement in prevention programs. In either case, it is likely that those who *do not* volunteer for preventive interventions are those most in need of services. Because of this, evaluations of intervention effectiveness also must be interpreted cautiously when volunteer participants are compared with a nonvolunteer control group such as the one in the Yale Child Welfare Research Program conducted by Provence and Naylor (1983).

Fourth, although some programs may be potent enough at a given point in time to produce enduring effects, the conditions in the inner city make it less likely that intervention effects will be sustained. Although intensive and well-planned early intervention programs such as the Perry Preschool Project and the Houston Parent–Child Development Center have produced encouraging results in distressed communities, these findings need further replication. In some cases, even though intervention participants had better outcomes than nonparticipants, they still experienced a distressing rate of academic and behavior problems (Berreuta-Clement et al., 1984). This implies that early intervention programs, although perhaps better than no programs, might be greatly enhanced if extended in time.

What types of programs are recommended, in which social context, and at what points in time? To begin with, it is important to acknowledge that preventive interventions must do more than simply teach people how to cope with substandard conditions. Not only do such conditions increase population risk for aggression, compound individual risk, reduce receptivity to intervention, and interfere with long-term maintenance of related gains, but they also impede the healthy physical, intellectual, and social development of children growing up under such circumstances. Thus, efforts must first be directed toward ameliorating such conditions and improving the standard of living for all inner-city residents.

It is also evident that large-scale prevention research trials are needed in order adequately to assess the impact of different interventions. Although a number of studies have been reviewed in this chapter, even the best intervention studies are compromised by concerns over nonrandom assignment to conditions, small sample size, rater bias, single outcome measures, and high attrition rates during follow-up. Any conclusions drawn from this literature are tentative because further replication is needed. At best, these studies provide directions for future research and programs.

Given the evidence that habitual aggression emerges early in life, preventive intervention programs should target young children. The extant intervention literature suggests that such programs should focus on enhancing the physical, cognitive, and social development of children by providing broad-based services during the early years. Such interventions may be child-centered, such as preschool enrichment programs, or they can focus on providing families with the support and skills needed to maximize their child's development. Children and families who can be identified based on known risk factors should also receive targeted intervention programs to prevent further escalation of risk.

Because children spend a significant amount of time in schools, continued efforts should be made to provide child-centered programs in schools, those *that give* children opportunities to learn and practice effective social relations skills. Research suggests that such programs should not be directed at changing group norms or providing opportunities for prosocial activities; rather, the research suggests that they should provide specific training in skills such as impulse control, anger management, conflict resolution, and social problem solving. Classrooms and schools should also promote the learning of prosocial rather than aggressive behavior. In addition they should enhance academic development through policies such as establishing clear and consistent behavioral codes; monitoring school behavior; nurturing strong leadership, student involvement in governance, and parent involvement; and creating a visible reward structure.

As discussed earlier, habitual aggressive behavior is multiply-determined. This suggests that brief, preventive interventions that target a single risk factor during a single developmental period in a single context will most likely have only limited long-term effects on aggression and violence. For some children, early inoculation may be effective if it is potent enough to produce lasting changes in critical individual or social contextual factors. However, for children living under the more disadvantaged conditions that exist in many inner cities today, the effects of early inoculation may dissipate quickly under sustained social and environmental stress. Even if early effects are not washed out without continued intervention, they should certainly be enhanced by continued involvement and extension of efforts. It is likely that the most effective interventions will address multiple causal factors, be carried out in multiple contexts, and be extended in time over the course of development. Families, peers, schools, and communities must work in concert to provide opportunities for children to learn prosocial behavior and to create environments where prosocial behavior is both modeled and reinforced.

REFERENCES

Achenbach, T. M. (1978). The child behavior profile: I. Boys aged 6–11. *Journal of Consulting and Clinical Psychology* 46, 478–88.

Achenbach, T. M., & Edelbrock, C. S. (1981). Behavioral problems and competencies reported by parents of normal and disturbed children aged four through sixteen. *Monographs of the Society for Research in Child Development* 46, 188.

Alexander, J. F., Barton, C., Schiavo, R. S., & Parsons, B. V. (1976). Systems-behavioral intervention with families of delinquents: Therapist characteristics, family behavior, and outcome. *Journal of Consulting and Clinical Psychology* 44, 656–64.

Anderson, E. (this volume). Violence and the inner-city street code. In J. McCord (Ed.), Violence and childhood in the inner city (pp. 1–30). New York: Cambridge University Press.

Anson, A. R., Cook, T. D., Habib, F., Grady, M. K., Haynes, N., & Comer, J. P. (1991). The Comer school development program: A theoretical analysis. *Urban Education* 26, 56–82.

Bandura, A. (1973). *Aggression: A social learning analysis.* Englewood Cliffs, NJ: Prentice Hall.

(1986). *Social foundations of thought and action: A social cognitive theory.* Englewood Cliffs, NJ: Prentice Hall.

(1991). Social cognitive theory of moral thought and action. In W. M. Kurtines & J. L. Gerwirtz (Eds.), *Moral behavior and development: Advances in theory, research, and applications* (Vol. 1, pp. 45–103). Hillsdale, NJ: Erlbaum.

Bank, L., Marlowe, J. H., Reid, J. B., Patterson, G. R., & Weinrott, M. R. (1991). A comparative evaluation of parent-training interventions for families of chronic delinquents. *Journal of Abnormal Child Psychology* 19, 15–33.

Baum, C. G., & Forehand, R. (1981). Long-term follow-up assessment of parent training by use of multiple outcome measures. *Behavior Therapy* 12, 643–52.

Becker, W. C., & Carnine, D. W. (1980). Direct instruction: An effective approach to educational intervention with the disadvantaged and low performers. In B. B. Lahey & A. E. Kazdin (Eds.), *Advances in clinical child psychology* (Vol. 3, pp. 220–40). New York: Plenum Press.

Behar, D., & Stewart, M. A. (1982). Aggressive conduct disorder of children:

The clinical history and direct observations. *Acta Psychiatrica Scanadinavia* 65, 210–20.

Berkowitz, L. (1974). Some determinants of impulsive aggression: The role of mediated associations with reinforcements for aggression. *Psychological Review* 81, 165–76.

(1984). Some effects of thoughts on anti- and prosocial influences of media events: A cognitive neoassociation analysis. *Psychological Bulletin* 95, 410–27.

(1989). Frustration-aggression hypothesis: Examination and reformation. *Psychological Bulletin* 106, 59–73.

Bernal, M. E., Klinnert, M. D., & Schultz, L. A. (1980). Outcome evaluation of behavioral parent training and client-centered parent counseling for children with conduct problems. *Journal of Applied Behavior Analysis* 13, 677–91.

Berreuta-Clement, J. R., Schweinhart, L. J., Barnett, W. S., Epstein, A. S., & Weikart, D. P. (1984). *Changed lives: The effects of the Perry Preschool Program on youths through age 19* (Monographs of the High/Schope Educational Research Foundation, No. 8). Ypsilanti, MI: High/Scope Press.

Bixby, F. L., & McCorkle, L. W. (1951). Guided group interaction and correctional work. *American Sociological Review* 16, 455–9.

Blumstein, A., Farrington, D. P., & Moitra, S. (1985). Delinquency careers: Innocents, desisters, and persisters. In M. Tonry & N. Morris (Eds.), *Crime and justice* (Vol. 6, pp. 187–219). Chicago: University of Chicago Press.

Booth, C. L., Spieker, S. J., Barnard, K. E., & Morisset, C. E. (1992). Infants at risk: The role of preventive intervention in deflecting a maladaptive developmental trajectory. In J. McCord & R. E. Tremblay (Eds.), *Preventing antisocial behavior: Interventions from birth through adolescence* (pp. 21–42). New York: Guilford Press.

Brophy, J. E. (1979). Teacher behavior and its effects. *Journal of Educational Psychology* 71, 733–50.

Bry, B. H., & George, F. E. (1980). The preventative effects of early intervention on the attendance and grades of urban adolescents. *Professional Psychology* 11, 252–60.

Cairns, R. B., Cairns, B. D., Neckerman, H. J., Gest, S. D., & Gariepy, J.-L. (1988). Social networks and aggressive behavior: Peer support or peer rejection? *Developmental Psychology* 24, 815–23.

Caplan, M., Weissberg, R. P., Grober, J. S., Sivo, P. J., Grady, K., & Jacoby, C. (1992). Social competence promotion with inner-city and suburban young adolescents: Effects on social adjustment and alcohol use. *Journal of Consulting and Clinical Psychology* 60, 56–63.

Centers for Disease Control and Prevention (1991). Forum on youth violence in minority communities: Setting the agenda for prevention. *Public Health Reports* 106, 225–53.

Chandler, C. L., Weissberg, R. P., Cowen, E. L., & Guare, J. (1984). Long-term effects of a school-based secondary prevention program for young maladapting children. *Journal of Consulting and Clinical Psychology* 52, 165–70.

Chicago Tribune, September 9, 1992.

Chicago Tribune, March 7, 1993.

Cohen, P. A., Kulik, J. A., & Kulik, C. C. (1982). Educational outcomes of tutoring: A meta-analysis of findings. *American Educational Research Journal* 19, 237–48.

Coie, J. D., Dodge, K. A., & Coppotelli, H. (1982). Dimensions and type of social status: A cross-age perspective. *Developmental Psychology* 18, 557–70.

Coie, J. D., & Kupersmidt, J. B. (1983). A behavioral analysis of emerging social status in boys' groups. *Child Development* 54, 1400–16.

Coie, J. D., Underwood, M., & Lochman, J. E. (1991). Programmatic intervention with aggressive children in the school setting. In D. J. Pepler and K. H. Rubin (Eds.), *The development and treatment of childhood aggression* (pp. 387–410). Hillsdale, NJ: Erlbaum.

Comer, J. P. (1980). *School power: Implications of an intervention project.* New York: Free Press.

(1988). Educating poor minority children. *Scientific American* 256, 42–8.

(1989). Child development and education. *Journal of Negro Education* 58, 125–39.

Cowen, E. L., Trost, M. A., Dorr, D. A., Lorion, R. P., Izzo, L. D., & Isaacson, R. V. (1975). *New ways in school mental health: Early detection and prevention of school maladaptation.* New York: Human Sciences Press, 1975.

Cummings, C. (1983). *Managing to teach.* Snohomish, WA: Snohomish Publishing.

Darling, N., & Steinberg, L. (1993). Parenting style as context: An integrative model. *Psychological Bulletin* 113, 487–96.

Darlington, R. B., Royce, J. M., Snipper, A. S., Murray, H. W., & Lazar, I. (1980). Preschool programs and later school competence of children from low-income families. *Science* 208, 202–4.

Dodge, K. A. (1980). Social cognition and children's aggressive behavior. *Child Development* 51, 162–70.

(1983). Behavioral antecedents of peer social status. *Child Development* 54, 1386–99.

(1986). A social information processing model of social competence in children. In M. Perlmutter (Ed.), *Minnesota symposia on child psychology* (Vol. 18, pp. 77–125). Hillsdale, NJ: Erlbaum.

(1993). Social-cognitive mechanisms in the development of conduct disorder and depression. *Annual Review of Psychology* 44, 558–84.

Dodge, K. A., & Frame, C. L. (1982). Social cognitive biases and deficits in aggressive boys. *Child Development* 53, 620–35.

Dodge, K. A., & Somberg, D. R. (1987). Hostile attributional biases among aggressive boys are exacerbated under conditions of threats to the self. *Child Development* 58, 213–24.

Dowhrenwend, B. P., & Dowhrenwend, B. S. (1969). *Social status and psychological disorder.* New York: Wiley.

Dubow, E. F., Huesmann, L. R., & Eron, L. D. (1987). Mitigating aggression promoting pro-social behavior in aggressive elementary school boys. *Behavior Research and Therapy* 25, 557–531.

Dumas, J. E. (1989). Treating antisocial behavior in children: child and family approaches. *Clinical Psychology Review* 9, 197–222.

Dumas, J. E., & Wahler, R. G. (1983). Predictors of treatment outcome in parent training: Mother insularity and socioeconomic disadvantage. *Behavioral Assessment* 5, 301–13.

Durlak, J. A. (1980). Comparative effectiveness of behavioral and relationship group treatment in the secondary prevention of school maladjustment. *American Journal of Community Psychology* 8, 327–39.

Earls, F. E., & Barnes, J. (this volume). Understanding and preventing child abuse in urban settings. In J. McCord (Ed.), *Violence and childhood in the inner city* (pp. 207–55). New York: Cambridge University Press.

Elliott, D. S., & Huizinga, D. (1980). Reconciling race and class difference in self-reported and official estimates of delinquency. *American Sociological Review* 45, 95–110.

Elliott, D. S., Huizinga, D., & Ageton, S. (1985). *Explaining delinquency and drug use.* Beverly Hills, CA: Sage Publications.

Emery, R. E. (1982). Interparental conflict and the children of discord and divorce. *Psychological Bulletin* 92, 310–30.

Emmer, E. T., & Everston, C. M. (1980). *Effective management at the beginning of the school year in junior high classes.* Austin, TX: Research and Development Center for Teacher Education, University of Texas at Austin.

Eron, L. D. (1987). The development of aggressive behavior from the perspective of a developing behaviorism. *American Psychologist* 42, 435–42.

(1990, June 12). Understanding aggression. *Presidential Address, World Meeting of ISRA,* Banff, Alberta.

Eron, L. D., Walder, L. O., & Lefkowitz, M. M. (1971). *The learning of aggression in children.* Boston: Little, Brown.

Eyberg, S. M., & Johnson, S. M. (1974). Multiple assessment of behavior modification with families: Effects of contingency contracting and order of treated problems. *Journal of Consulting and Clinical Psychology* 42, 594–606.

Fagan, J., & Wexler, S. (1987). Crime at home and in the streets: The relationship between family and stranger violence. *Violence and Victims* 2, 5–23.

Farrington, D. P. (1978). The family background of aggressive youths. In L. A. Hersov, M. Berger, & D. Shaffer (Eds.), *Aggression and antisocial behavior in childhood and adolescence* (pp. 73–93). Oxford: Pergamon Press.

(1986). Stepping-stones to adult criminal careers. In D. Olweus, J. Block, &

M. R. Yarrow (Eds.), *Development of antisocial and prosocial behavior* (pp. 359–84). New York: Academic Press.

(1989). Early predictors of adolescent aggression and adult violence. *Violence and Victims* 4, 79–100.

Farrington, D. P., & Hawkins, J. D. (1991). Predicting participation, early onset and later persistence in officially recorded offending. *Criminal Behavior and Mental Health* 1, 1–33.

Feldman, R. A. (1992). The St. Louis experiment: Effective treatment of antisocial youths in prosocial peer groups. In J. McCord & R. E. Tremblay (Eds.), *Preventing antisocial behavior: Interventions from birth through adolescence* (pp. 233–52). New York: Guilford Press.

Felner, R. D., & Adan, A. M. (1988). The school transitional environment project: An ecological intervention and evaluation. In R. H. Price, E. L. Cowen, R. P. Lorion, & J. Ramos-McKay (Eds.), *14 ounces of prevention: A casebook for practitioners* (pp. 111–22). Washington, D.C.: American Psychological Association.

Feltham, R. F., Doyle, A. B., Schwartzman, A. E., Serbin, L. A., & Ledingham, J. E. (1985). Friendship in normal and socially deviant children. *Journal of Early Adolescence* 5, 371–82.

Fingerhut, L. A., & Kleinman, J. C. (1990). International and interstate comparisons of homicide among young males. *Journal of American Medical Association* 263, 3292–5.

Fleischner, J. E., & Van Acker, R. (1990). *Monograph on critical issues in special education: Implications for personnel preparation*. Denton, TX: University of North Texas Press.

Garbarino, J., Kostelny, K., & Dubrow, N. (1991). What children can tell us about living in danger. *American Psychologist* 46, 376–82.

Goldstein, A. P. (1986). Psychological skill training and the aggressive adolescent. In S. P. Apter & A. P. Goldstein (Eds.), *Youth violence* (pp. 89–119). New York: Pergamon Press.

Goldstein, A. P., Sherman, M., Gershaw, N. J., Sprafkin, R. P., & Glick, B. (1978). Training aggressive adolescents in prosocial behavior. *Journal of Youth and Adolescence* 7, 73–92.

Gottfredson, G. D. (1987). Peer group interventions to reduce the risk of delinquent behavior: A selective review and a new evaluation. *Criminology* 25, 671–714.

Greenberg, M. (1992). Child, peer, and family contexts for intervention. Paper presented at the Conference on Conduct Disorders, National Institute of Mental Health, Washington, D.C.

Guerra, N. G., Huesmann, L. R., & Hanish, L. (1994). The role of social norms in the learning of aggressive and antisocial behavior. In N. Eisenberg (Ed.), *Review of personality and social psychology* (pp. 140–58). Newbury Park, CA: Sage Publications.

Guerra, N. G., Huesmann, L. R., Tolan, P. H., Eron, L. D., & Van Acker, R. (1990). *Prevention of antisocial behavior in high-risk youth.* Research grant MH 48034, National Institute of Mental Health.

Guerra, N. G., Huesmann, L. R., Tolan, P. H., Van Acker, R., & Eron, L. D. (1995). Stressful events and individual beliefs as correlates of economic disadvantage and aggression: Implications for preventive interventions among inner-city children. *Journal of Consulting and Clinical Psychology* 63, 518–28.

Guerra, N. G., & Slaby, R. G. (1990). Cognitive mediators of aggression in adolescent offenders: 2. Intervention. *Developmental Psychology* 26, 269–77.

Guerra, N. G., Tolan, P. H., & Hammond, R. (1994). Prevention of adolescent violence. *Report of the American psychological association commission on violence and youth.* Washington, D.C.

Hammond, R. (1991). *Dealing with anger: Givin' it, takin' it, workin' it out.* Champaign, IL: Research Press.

Hammond, R., & Yung, B. R. (1991). Preventing violence in at-risk African-American youth. *Journal of Health Care for the Poor and Underserved* 2, 359–73.

(1993). *Evaluation and activity report: Positive adolescents' choices training grant.* Unpublished grant report, U.S. Maternal and Child Health Bureau.

Hanson, C. L., Henggeler, S. W., Haefele, W. F., & Rodick, J. D. (1984). Demographic, individual, and family relationship correlates of serious and repeated crime among adolescents and their siblings. *Journal of Consulting and Clinical Psychology* 52, 528–38.

Hawkins, J. D., & Lishner, D. M. (1987). Schooling and delinquency. In E. H. Johnson (Ed.), *Handbook on crime and delinquency prevention* (pp. 179–221). New York: Greenwood Press.

Hawkins, J. D., Von Cleve, E., & Catalano, R. F. (1991). Reducing early childhood aggression: Results of a primary prevention program. *Journal of the American Academy of Child and Adolescent Psychiatry* 30, 208–17.

Hawkins, J. D., & Weis, J. F. (1985). The social development model: An integrated approach to delinquency prevention. *Journal of Primary Prevention* 6, 73–97.

Hendrickson, J. M., Young, K. D., Shores, R. E., & Stowitsheck, C. E. (1983). The ecological perspective: Social events and behavior. *The Pointer* 31, 40–9.

Huesmann, L. R. (1988). An information-processing model for the development of aggression. *Aggressive Behavior* 14, 13–24.

Huesmann, L. R., & Eron, L. D. (1984). Cognitive processes and the persistence of aggressive behavior. *Aggressive Behavior* 10, 243–51.

(1986). *Television and the aggressive child: A cross-national comparison.* Hillsdale, NJ: Erlbaum.

Huesmann, L. R., Eron, L. D., Lefkowitz, M. M., & Walder, L. O. (1984).

Stability of aggression over time and generations. *Developmental Psychology* 20, 1120–34.

Huesmann, L. R., Guerra, N. G., & Eron, L. D. (1993). Aggression, rejection, and popularity in urban settings. Unpublished manuscript. Chicago: University of Illinois.

Huesmann, L. R., Guerra, N. G., Miller, L. S., & Zelli, A. (1992). The role of social norms in the development of aggressive behavior. In A. Fraczek & H. Zumkley (Eds.), *Socialization and aggression* (pp. 139–52). New York/ Heidelberg: Springer-Verlag.

Huesmann, L. R., Guerra, N. G., Zelli, A., Miller, L. S. (1992). Differing normative beliefs about aggression for boys and girls. In K. Bjorkqvist & P. Niemela (Eds.), *Of mice and women: Aspects of female aggression* (pp. 77–87). Orlando, FL: Academic Press.

Institute of Medicine. (1994). *Reducing risks for mental disorders.* Washington, D.C.: National Academy Press.

Jason, L. A., Frasure, S., & Ferone, L. (1981). Establishing supervising behaviors in eighth graders and peer-tutoring behaviors in first graders. *Child Study Journal* 11, 201–19.

Johnson, D. L. (1988). Primary prevention of behavior problems in young children: The Houston parent-child development center. In R. H. Price, E. L. Cowen, R. P. Lorion, & J. Ramos-McKay (Eds.), *14 ounces of prevention: A casebook for practitioners* (pp. 44–52). Washington, D.C.: American Psychological Association.

Johnson, D. L., & Walker, T. (1987). The primary prevention of behavior problems in Mexican-American children. *American Journal of Community Psychology* 15, 375–85.

Kazdin, A. E. (1987). Treatment of antisocial behavior in children: Current status and future directions. *Psychological Bulletin* 102, 187–203.

(1990). *Prevention of conduct disorder.* Paper prepared for the National Conference on Prevention Research, National Institute of Mental Health.

(1993). *Prevention and treatment of antisocial behavior in children.* Report of the American Psychological Association Commission on Violence and Youth. Washington, D.C.

Kendall, P. C., & Braswell, L. (1982). Cognitive-behavioral self-control therapy for children: A components analysis. *Journal of Consulting and Clinical Psychology* 50, 672–89.

Kirschenbaum, D. S. (1979). Social competence intervention and evaluation in the inner city: Cincinnati's social skills development program. *Journal of Consulting and Clinical Psychology* 47, 778–80.

Klein, M. W. (1971). *Street gangs and street workers.* Englewood Cliffs, NJ: Prentice Hall.

Kotlowitz, A. (1991). *There are no children here.* New York: Doubleday.

Lee, V. E., Brooks-Gunn, J., Schnur, E., & Liaw, F. (1990). Are Head Start effects sustained? A longitudinal follow-up comparison of disadvantaged children attending Head Start, no preschool, and other preschool programs. *Child Development* 61, 495–507.

Lochman, J. E. (1992). Cognitive-behavioral intervention with aggressive boys: Three-year follow-up with preventative effects. *Journal of Consulting and Clinical Psychology* 60, 426–32.

Lochman, J. E., Burch, P. R., Curry, J. F., & Lampron, L. B. (1984). Treatment and generalization effects of cognitive behavioral and goal setting interventions with aggressive boys. *Journal of Consulting and Clinical Psychology* 52, 915–16.

Loeber, R. (1982). The stability of antisocial and delinquent child behavior: A review. *Child Development* 53, 1431–46.

  (1990). Development and risk factors of juvenile antisocial behavior and delinquency. *Clinical Psychology Review* 10, 1–41.

  (1991). Antisocial behavior: More enduring than changeable? *Journal of the American Academy of Child and Adolescent Psychiatry* 30, 393–7.

Loeber, R., & Dishion, T. J. (1983). Early predictors of male delinquency: A review. *Psychological Bulletin* 94, 68–99.

Loeber, R., & LeBlanc, M. (1990). Toward a developmental criminology. In M. Tonry & N. Morris (Eds.), *Crime and justice: An annual review of research* (Vol. 12, pp. 375–473). Chicago: University of Chicago Press.

Loeber, R., & Stouthamer-Loeber, M. (1986). Family factors as correlates and predictors of juvenile conduct problems and delinquency. In M. Tonry & N. Morris (Eds.), *Crime and justice: An annual review of research* (Vol. 7, pp. 29–149). Chicago: University of Chicago Press.

  (1987). Prediction. In H. C. Quay (Ed.), *Handbook of juvenile delinquency* (pp. 325–82). New York: Wiley.

McCord, W., McCord, J., & Zola, I. K. (1959). *Origins of crime.* New York: Columbia University Press.

McLoyd, V. (1990). The impact of economic hardship on black families and children: Psychological distress, parenting, and socioemotional development. *Child Development* 61, 311–46.

Miller, G. E., & Prinz, R. J. (1990). Enhancement of social learning family interventions for child conduct disorder. *Psychological Bulletin* 108, 291–307.

Moffitt, T. E. (this volume). Neuropsychology, antisocial behavior, and neighborhood context. In J. McCord (Ed.), *Violence and childhood in the inner city* (pp. 116–70). New York: Cambridge University Press.

Moldin, S. (1984). Episodic weekend psychosis on an intensive care unit. *Hospital and Community Psychiatry* 35, 1230–2.

Moos, R. H., & Moos, B. (1981). *The family environment scale.* Stanford, CA: Consulting Psychology Press.

Olds, D. L., Henderson, C. R., Tatelbaum, R., & Chamberlin, R. (1986). Improving the delivery of prenatal care and outcomes of pregnancy: A randomized trial of nurse-home visitation. *Pediatrics* 77, 16–28.

Olson, D. H., & Barnes, H. F. (1985). Parent adolescent communication and the circumplex model. *Child Development* 56, 438–47.

Olweus, D. (1979). Stability of aggressive reaction patterns in males: A review. *Psychological Bulletin* 86, 852–75.

Patterson, G. R. (1976). The aggressive child: Victim and architect of a coercive system. In L. A. Hamerlynck, J. C. Handy, & E. J. Mash (Eds.), *Behavioral modification and families: Theory and research* (Vol. 1, pp. 267–316). New York: Bruner/Mazel, Inc.

———. (1982). *A social learning approach, Vol. 3, Coercive family process.* Eugene, OR: Castalia Press.

———. (1986). Performance models for antisocial boys. *American Psychologist* 41, 432–44.

Patterson, G. R., Capaldi, D., & Bank, L. (1991). An early starter model for predicting delinquency. In D. J. Pepler & K. H. Rubin (Eds.), *The development and treatment of childhood aggression* (pp. 139–68). Hillsdale, NJ: Erlbaum.

Patterson, G. R., DeBaryshe, B. D., & Ramsey, E. (1989). A developmental perspective on antisocial behavior. *American Psychologist* 44, 329–35.

Pouissaint, A. (1972). *Why blacks kill blacks.* New York: Emerson Hall.

Provence, S., & Naylor, A. (1983). *Working with disadvantaged parents and children: Scientific issues and practice.* New Haven, CT: Yale University Press.

Pynoos, R. S., & Nader, K. (1988). Psychological first aid and treatment approach to children exposed to community violence: Research implications. *Journal of Traumatic Stress* 4, 445–73.

Ramey, L. (1980). Homicide among black males. *Public Health Reports* 95, 549–61.

Raudenbush, S. W. (1983). Utilizing controversy as a source of hypotheses for meta-analysis: The case of teacher expectancy's effect on pupil IQ. *Urban Education* 28, 114–31.

Reiss, D. (1981). *The family's construction of reality.* Cambridge, MA: Harvard University Press.

Reitsma-Street, M., Offord, D., & Finch, T. (1985). Pairs of same-sexed siblings discordant for antisocial behavior. *British Journal of Psychiatry* 146, 415–23.

Rickel, A. U., & Burgio, J. C. (1982). Assessing social competencies in lower income preschool children. *American Journal of Community Psychology* 10, 635–45.

Rickel, A. U., & Lampi, L. (1981). A two-year follow-up study of a preventive mental health program for preschoolers. *Journal of Abnormal Child Psychology* 9, 455–64.

Rist, R. C. (1970). *The urban school: A factory for failure.* Cambridge, MA: Harvard University Press.

Roff, J. D., & Wirt, R. D. (1984). Childhood aggression and social adjustment as antecedents of delinquency. *Journal of Abnormal Child Psychology* 12, 111–16.

Rotheram-Borus, M. J., & Phinney, J. S. (1987). Ethnic behavior patterns as an aspect of identity. In J. S. Phinney & M. J. Rotheram (Eds.), *Children's ethnic socialization* (pp. 201–18). Newbury Park, CA: Sage Publications.

Rubin, K. H., Bream, L. A., & Rose-Krasnor, L. (1991). Social problem solving and aggression in childhood. In D. Pepler & K. H. Rubin (Eds.), *The development and treatment of childhood aggression* (pp. 219–248). Hillsdale, NJ: Erlbaum.

Sameroff, A. J. & Chandler, M. J. (1975). Reproductive risk and the continuum of reproductive causality. In F. D. Horowitz, M. Hetherington, S. Scarr-Salapatek, & G. Siegel (Eds.), *Review of child development research* (Vol. 4, pp. 187–244). Chicago, IL: University of Chicago Press.

Sampson, R. J. (this volume). The embeddedness of child and adolescent development. In J. McCord (Ed.), *Violence and childhood in the inner city* (pp. 31–77). New York: Cambridge University Press.

Sarason, I. G., & Sarason, B. R. (1981). Teaching cognitive and social skills to high school students. *Journal of Consulting and Clinical Psychology* 49, 908–18.

Scholte, E. M. (1992). Prevention and treatment of juvenile problem behavior: A proposal for a socioecological approach. *Journal of Abnormal Child Psychology* 20, 247–61.

Schweinhart, L. J., & Weikart, D. P. (1988). The High/Scope Perry preschool program. In R. H. Price, E. L. Cowen, R. P. Lorion, & J. Ramos-McKay (Eds.), *14 ounces of prevention: A casebook for practitioners* (pp. 53–65). Washington, D.C.: American Psychological Association.

Seidman, E. (1991). Growing up the hard way: Pathways of urban adolescents. *American Journal of Community Psychology* 19, 173–205.

Seitz, V., Rosenbaum, L. K., & Apfel, N. H. (1985). Effects of family support intervention: A ten-year follow up. *Child Development* 56, 376–91.

Shakoor, B. H., & Chalmers, D. (1991). Co-victimization of African-American children who witness violence: Effects on cognitive, emotional, and behavioral development. *Journal of the National Medical Association* 83, 233–38.

Shure, M. B., & Spivack, G. (1979). Interpersonal cognitive problem-solving and primary prevention: Programming for preschool and kindergarten children. *Journal of Clinical Child Psychology* 8, 89–94.

Slaby, R. G., & Guerra, N. G. (1988). Cognitive mediators of aggression in adolescent offenders: I. Assessment. *Developmental Psychology* 24, 580–8.

Slavin, R. E. (1979). *Using student team learning.* Baltimore, MD: Center for Social Organization of Schools, Johns Hopkins University.

(1982). *Cooperative learning groups: What the research says to the teacher.* Washington, DC: National Education Association.

Smith, L. C., & Fowler, S. A. (1984). Positive peer pressure: The effects of peer monitoring on children's disruptive behavior. *Journal of Applied Behavior Analysis* 17, 213–27.

Spergel, I. (1990). Youth gangs: Continuity and change. In N. Morris and M. Tonry (Eds.), *Crime and justice: An annual review of research* (Vol. 12, pp. 171–215). Chicago: University of Chicago Press.

Spivack, G., Platt, J. J., & Shure, M. B. (1976). *The problem-solving approach to adjustment.* San Francisco: Jossey-Bass.

Spivack, G., & Shure, M. B. (1974). *Social adjustment of young children: A cognitive approach to solving real-life problems.* San Francisco: Jossey-Bass.

Taylor, C. S. (1989). *Dangerous society.* East Lansing, MI: Michigan State University Press.

Thompson, D. W., & Jason, L. E. (1988). Street gangs and preventive interventions. *Criminal Justice and Behavior* 15, 323–33.

Tolan, P. H. (1987). Implications of age of onset for delinquency risk. *Journal of Abnormal Child Psychology* 15, 47–65.

(1988). Socioeconomic, family, and social stress correlates of adolescents' antisocial and delinquent behavior. *Journal of Abnormal Child Psychology* 17, 317–32.

Tolan, P. H., Cromwell, R. E., & Braswell, M. (1986). The application of family therapy to juvenile delinquency: A critical review of the literature. *Family Process* 25, 619–49.

Tolan, P. H., & Florsheim, P. (1991). *The metropolitan area child study family intervention manual.* Chicago: University of Illinois at Chicago.

Tolan, P. H., Gorman-Smith, D., Zelli, A., & Huesmann, L. R. (1993, October). *Family factors and delinquency in urban minority youth.* Paper presented at the annual meeting of the American Society of Criminology, Phoenix, AZ.

Triandis, H. (1972). *The analysis of subjective culture.* New York: Wiley.

Uniform Crime Reports (1992). Washington, D.C.: Federal Bureau of Investigation.

Van Acker, R., Huesmann, L. R., Tolan, P. H., Guerra, N. G., & Eron, L. D. (1994). *Teacher bias in integrated versus segregated classrooms.* Unpublished manuscript. Chicago: University of Illinois.

Wahler, R. G. (1980). The insular mother: Her problems in parent-child treatment. *Journal of Applied Behavior Analysis* 13, 207–19.

Webster-Stratton, C. (1985). Predictors of treatment outcome in parent training for conduct disordered children. *Behavior Therapy* 16, 223–43.

Weissberg, R. P., Caplan, M., & Harwood, R. L. (1991). Promoting competent young people in competence-enhancing environments: A systems-based perspective on primary prevention. *Journal of Consulting and Clinical Psychology* 59, 830–41.

Weissberg, R. P., Gesten, E. L., Rapkin, B. D., Cowen, E. L., Davidson, E., de Apodaca, R. F., & McKim, B. J. (1981). The evaluation of a social problem-solving training program for suburban and inner-city third grade children. *Journal of Consulting and Clinical Psychology* 49, 251–61.

Widom, C. S. (1989). The cycle of violence. *Science* 244, 160–6.

Wright, J. C., Giammarino, M., & Parad, H. W. (1986). Social status in small groups: Individual-group similarity and the social "misfit." *Journal of Personality and Social Psychology* 50, 523–36.

Zigler, E. F. (1987). Formal schooling for four-year-olds? No. *American Psychologist* 42, 254–60.

Zigler, E. F., Taussig, C., & Black, K. (1992). Early childhood intervention: A promising preventative for juvenile delinquency. *American Psychologist* 47, 997–1006.

Zigler, E. F., & Trickett, P. K. (1978). IQ, social competence, and evaluation of early childhood intervention programs. *American Psychologist* 33, 789–98.

Name Index

Subject Index

academic achievement, 183–4
  interventions and, 294–5
academic failure
  cumulative, 148–50, 153
  and development of aggression, 264
academic functioning, 281
  poor, as risk factor, 261, 265
academic problems
  child abuse in, 221
academic skills
  failure to learn, 152
achievement
  failures in, 143–50
acquaintanceship networks, 33, 38
adolescence
  effects of child abuse in, 229–31
  prevention programs for, xiii, 287–8, 297
adolescent development
  embeddedness of, 31–77
adult influences on violence, 182, 183–8,
    193
adult-onset crime, 152–3
affluent neighbors, 47–8
African-American children/adolescents
  prevention programs for, 288, 296
  and television violence, 189, 190
African-American families
  discipline in, 267
African-Americans, 278, 279
  crime rates among, 257
  see also blacks
aggression/aggressive behavior
  adult encouragement of, 185
  child abuse in development of, 221–2,
    227
  defined, 258
  early patterns of, 176–7
  early/persisting, 123
  late-onset, 263
  neuropsychology of, 141

prevention of, in inner city, 256–312
  theories of, 270–1
aggressive mentality
  development of, 12–14
aggressor(s), 174, 175–7, 197
aggressor effect, 189, 190, 192
agrarian violence, 89
Ainsworth Strange Situation, 223, 224
alienation, 3, 21, 28, 41–2
American Humane Association, 212n3
American Indians, 101
anger management, 196–7
anomie, 41–2, 65
anonymity, 37, 93, 94
antisocial behavior, 258, 259, 270
  becoming ensnared by consequences of,
    152
  early, 263
  neuropsychological self-control deficits
    and: hypotheses about, 137–41
  neuropsychology and, 119, 120–2
  neuropsychology/neighborhood context
    and, 116–57
  parent training and, 289–90
  problem child/problem parent
    interactions and emergence of, 128–30
  theories of, 270–1
  verbal neuropsychological deficits and:
    hypotheses about, 130–7
antisocial personality, 146–7, 153
antisocial personality disorder, 139, 147,
    153–4
Arizona, 211
Atlanta, GA, 64, 88
attachment
  child abuse and, 222–4
  and cognitive development, 228–9
  and delinquency, 51
attachment failure, 143–50
  cumulative, 145–8